FATHER OF THE TUSKEGEE AIRMEN

JOHN C. ROBINSON

FATHER OF THE TUSKEGEE AIRMEN

JOHN C. ROBINSON

PHILLIP THOMAS TUCKER

POTOMAC BOOKS
WASHINGTON, D.C.

Library of Congress Cataloging-in-Publication Data
Tucker, Phillip Thomas, 1953–
  Father of the Tuskegee airmen, John C. Robinson / Phillip Thomas Tucker.—1st ed.
    p. cm.
  Includes bibliographical references and index.
  ISBN 978-1-59797-487-5 (hardcover: alk. paper)
  ISBN 978-1-59797-606-0 (electronic edition)
  1. Robinson, John Charles, 1903–1954. 2. African American air pilots—Biography. 3. African American fighter pilots—Biography. 4. Italo-Ethiopian War, 1935–1936—Aerial operations, Ethiopian. 5. Italo-Ethiopian War, 1935–1936—Participation, American. 6. Air pilots—United States—Biography. I. Title. II. Title: John C. Robinson.
  TL540.R57T83 2011
  629.13092—dc23
  [B]
                        2011041711

Potomac Books
22841 Quicksilver Drive
Dulles, Virginia 20166

First Edition

10 9 8 7 6 5 4 3 2 1

To Sidney L. Rushing and Katie Booth, in Gulfport, Mississippi, who provided invaluable support and assistance, and to a new American president and the first black commander in chief, of whom Robinson would have been most proud. It was a distinct honor to have been enlightened by the privilege of serving with both Sidney and Katie as a fellow member of the board of directors of the John C. Robinson "Brown Condor" Historical Association.

CONTENTS

ACKNOWLEDGMENTS

I WISH TO THANK all of the hardworking people at a good many university and historical archives, academic institutions, and libraries across the United States—especially those in Chicago, Illinois; Tuskegee, Alabama; and Gulfport, Mississippi—and even in faraway Ethiopia. And I wish to give special thanks to the good people of Chicago and Gulfport who warmly embraced both myself and this groundbreaking project, and the supportive people of the Ethiopian community of Washington, D.C.

Many thanks must also go to the dedicated, visionary members of the board of directors of the John C. Robinson "Brown Condor" Historical Association in Gulfport, including Tuskegee Airman Col. Larry E. Roberts. They have provided much assistance and support for this very special project. As a member of the board, I bestowed a novel idea that they have been working hard to turn into a reality, the John C. Robinson Mississippi Aviation Heritage Museum in Gulfport. Without hesitation, these gracious men and women of Gulfport, and especially the African American community, welcomed a "Yankee" and an Air Force historian from Washington, D.C., into their homes, hearts, and the world of John C. Robinson.

Last but not least, I would like to thank Elizabeth Demers, senior editor at Potomac Books. She believed in the importance and value of this project from the beginning. Even more, she contributed her considerable knowledge and expert skills to make this a much better work in the end. Both her skillful editing and deep insights into the African American experience proved invaluable for the overall quality of this book. Likewise, Julie Gutin, production manager at Potomac Books, made many invaluable contributions of much importance. All of their efforts are greatly appreciated.

INTRODUCTION

IN EARLY 1936, a *Chicago Defender* reporter placed John Charles Robinson in a proper historical perspective: "If Race [or black] interest in aviation began in earnest with the advent of Bessie Coleman, it reached its highest point . . . with the success of John Robinson as head of the royal air force of Ethiopia. Known far and wide as the Brown Condor, Colonel Robinson has received more publicity in the press of the world than any other member of the Race ever to fly a plane. Robinson deserves all he is getting."[1] On May 9, 1936, this *Chicago Defender* journalist also noted that African Americans across the United States "do not think of Lindbergh as their idol, but of Johnny Robinson."[2]

However, Robinson's name remains little known today. Even in *Black Wings: Courageous Stories of African Americans in Aviation and Space History*, the companion volume to the recent exhibit at the Smithsonian Institute, highly respected author Von Hardesty could only admit that "Robinson's service in the Ethiopian war has remained shrouded in mystery, but there is evidence that he did make substantial contributions to the war effort as a courier pilot."[3] In fact, Robinson's contributions reached far beyond being a courier pilot, and this book was written to shed new light on what really happened.

An early aviation pioneer and war hero, Robinson was the first black commander of an independent nation's air force in both peace and in war, and only the world's second black military pilot to engage in aerial combat after Eugene Jacques Bullard during World War I. As commander of the infant Imperial Ethiopian Air Force with a full colonel's rank for nearly a year, Robinson provided an inspirational political, symbolic, and moral example for black America. To millions of African

Americans, Robinson was a courageous role model, volunteering to fight against fascism and European imperialism, and he did so for longer than any other American, black or white.

Robinson also embodied the popular spirit of Pan-Africanism, which galvanized black America's support for Ethiopia's struggle for independence against Fascist Italy's imperial designs and colonial ambitions. Perhaps most important, Robinson served as a powerful anti-fascist, pro-democracy, anti-colonialist symbol to black and white Americans alike. Robinson flew for Emperor Haile Selassie against Benito Mussolini's invading Italians at a time when an isolationist America remained apathetic toward Ethiopia's tragic fate. For the Ethiopian people during the Second Italo-Ethiopian War from 1935 to 1936 and afterward, Robinson loomed large as a "national hero." And at home, he fulfilled that inspirational role not only for black Americans of his generation but also for the next generation, the famed World War II Tuskegee Airmen.[4]

During World War II, African Americans across the United States warmly embraced the ideological and moral concept of the Double V campaign: victory against fascism overseas and victory against racism at home. Robinson was the first and only African American to voluntarily engage in his own personal Double V campaign throughout the course of the Second Italo-Ethiopian War, while struggling against the odds to transform Emperor Selassie's collection of antiquated aircraft into a viable air force. Significantly, Robinson was the first American aviator to fight against fascism abroad, before the Tuskegee Airmen embarked upon a similar crusade during World War II more than five years later.

Ironically, Robinson's wartime activities in Ethiopia overshadowed his equally significant contributions in the United States. Long before the Second Italo-Ethiopian War began in October 1935, Robinson gained recognition as a black aviation pioneer, especially in Chicago, which he transformed into a leading center for black aviation. Throughout his life, Robinson defied racism at home and overseas at a time when relatively few Americans, black or white, openly challenged institutionalized racism and segregation. As early as September 1935, the *Campus Digest*, the student newspaper at Tuskegee Institute in Tuskegee, Alabama (Robinson's alma mater), proclaimed Robinson as an important "race pioneer in the field of aviation." Indeed, Robinson earned the distinction of becoming an inspiring example for blacks mired in the oppression of Jim Crow America. From beginning to end, this young African American from the Deep South consistently persevered to overcome seemingly insurmountable personal and racial obstacles to create a unique and distinctive legacy.[5]

By the summer of 1936, Robinson was acclaimed from coast to coast as "the No. 1 Flyer of His Race."[6] Even by late 1941, Robinson was yet widely heralded as "black America's best-known aviator."[7]

As significant, the Brown Condor of Ethiopia who "covered himself with glory [in] trying to preserve the independence of the last African empire," as described by a *Chicago Defender* journalist, was also the father of the Tuskegee Airmen.[8] Whereas the Tuskegee Airmen story enjoys widespread recognition today, Robinson's contributions as the person most responsible for initially laying the foundation for the emergence of aviation at Tuskegee Institute has been forgotten. As early as May 1934, Robinson presented Tuskegee with a clear vision for its destiny, offering significant social and economic possibilities for aviation's promise as a challenge to a racist Jim Crow society.

Indeed, without Robinson's early initiatives and his inspirational example during the formative period between the wars, Tuskegee Institute might have never developed its famed aviation curriculum under the auspices of the federal government's Civilian Pilot Training Program in 1939, which eventually trained hundreds of black pilots at Tuskegee Army Air Field during World War II. In order for the program to succeed, aviation had to have been firmly in place at Tuskegee Institute before America's entry into the war. As the primary proponent of Tuskegee's aviation program in the 1930s, and because of what he accomplished in Ethiopia, Robinson was the inspirational founding father of the Tuskegee Airmen.

To this day, Robinson remains little known or appreciated even by Tuskegee Institute, from which he graduated. Additionally, most surviving Tuskegee Airmen are unaware that Robinson was the aviation visionary who convinced the school and its conservative officials of the possibilities for blacks in aviation, nearly a decade before Tuskegee's pilots began their wartime missions.

Robinson first gained widespread recognition as an early leader of Chicago's black aviation community. Robinson entered aviation at a time when it was virtually impossible for African Americans to do so. Despite the odds stacked against him, Robinson became the first African American to break the color barrier at the prestigious Curtiss-Wright Aeronautical School in Chicago, the leading institution of its type in the Midwest. Although Robinson started out as the school's janitor, he eventually became not only a student, but also its first black instructor, after successfully recruiting the first black class in the school's history.

Additionally, Robinson was also the first instructor to teach black women in aviation mechanics and flight training. Robinson founded not one but three aero clubs for black adults in the Chicago area: the Aero Study Club, the Brown Eagle Aero Club, and the Challenger Air Pilots' Association. In the late 1930s, Robinson and the nucleus of his aero clubs, his former students at Curtiss-Wright, played a key political role in championing the inclusion of black military aviators in the all-white U.S. Army Air Corps, which eventually included the future Tuskegee Airmen.

Just south of Chicago, Robinson also established the first Department of Commerce–accredited black airfield, located at Robbins, Illinois. It was the first airfield in America owned and operated solely by blacks. In short, Robinson accomplished more in black civilian and military aviation both inside and outside the United States than any other African American in the period between the wars.

Unfortunately, Robinson did not write a memoir or autobiography. Nor does any extensive collection of his private correspondence exist. Moreover, he spent nearly a decade of his relatively short life living outside the United States. Robinson died in 1954 in an airplane crash during a rescue mission in Ethiopia. He was buried in Addis Ababa, where he lies today in obscurity, forgotten by both of the countries he called home.

In a striking paradox in regard to the historical record, other less accomplished aviators garnered more recognition than Robinson did in his short life. Robinson's leading role in rebuilding the Imperial Ethiopian Air Force after the Italian occupation has been overshadowed by the better-publicized later Swedish aviation effort, especially that of Count Carl Gustaf von Rosen, who has become a Swedish hero. And perhaps nowhere else in the American nation have the many important contributions of African Americans been more ignored than in Mississippi, where Robinson was born. This tragic burden of Mississippi's racial past has obscured the notable achievements of many remarkable black men and women, none more so than Robinson. He has become another historical casualty of the Deep South's casual dismissal of African American achievement.

Despite the oppressive Jim Crow environment of south Mississippi or perhaps because of it, Robinson never lost sight of his own dreams, including that of an aviation program at Tuskegee Institute and inspiring an entire generation of African Americans, both male and female, to imagine that anything was possible, including the great dream of taking flight in the skies of limitless possibilities.

1

A Rare Beacon of Hope, Gulfport

SURROUNDED BY A RICH CARPET of green pine forests, the low-lying farm-lands of the Mississippi Gulf Coast were sandy and deficient in comparison to the dark rich soils of upland Mississippi. Yet this poor soil worked in the gulf coast's favor; unlike so much of Mississippi, dominated by rural and agricultural back-wardness, the coastal region had a unique history of commercial and economic de-velopment. New railways, replacing those destroyed by Union armies in the Civil War, brought sudden prosperity along the Mississippi Gulf Coast. Spanning from east to west along the coast, the first railroad connecting New Orleans, Louisiana, and Mobile, Alabama, was completed after the war. Then, along the flat coastal plain of south Mississippi, the construction of the Gulf & Ship Island Railroad, stretching from Jackson, Mississippi, south to the gulf, brought new vitality to the Mississippi Gulf Coast by the turn of the century. Captain Joseph T. Jones, a Penn-sylvanian, laid out a small community named Gulfport in 1895, at the crossroads of these intersecting rail lines. Located at the southernmost end of the Gulf & Ship Island Railroad along the Mississippi Gulf Coast, Gulfport grew quickly. Linking the people of the Mississippi Gulf Coast to the North and its lucrative commercial markets, Gulfport provided a new start for the people of south Mississippi, both black and white.[1]

In 1896 Jones erected a lengthy pier that stretched some forty-five hundred feet into the placid saltwater, protected by the thin barrier islands of the Mississippi Sound. Because of the sound's shallow depth compared to the gulf's rougher waters beyond, Jones dredged out a deep trench. He carved this channel sufficiently wide and deep at twenty-four feet to allow the ambitious little port to open for ocean-

1

going traffic in January 1902. Gulfport had been successfully transformed into a deep-water port, thanks to the sixteen-mile-long shipping channel that stretched to Ship Island's southern end and the Gulf of Mexico.[2]

African Americans migrated to the town from Mobile, Alabama, and Pascagoula, Mississippi to the east, from Bay St. Louis to the west, and from Mississippi's interior.[3] Robinson grew up in Gulfport, but he was born in Franklin County, Florida, on November 26, 1905, in the small town of Carrabelle. This tiny community was located slightly northeast of St. James Island, at the mouth of the Apalachicola River, and the sprawling Apalachicola Bay. Carrabelle was situated amid the pine forests, salt marshes, and wetlands of the northwest section of the Florida panhandle.[4]

Robinson's family had been living in the Carrabelle area since slavery's dark days of misery. Celeste Robinson née Huff, John's mother, longed for a life beyond Carrabelle's confines, and Gulfport beckoned. In 1906, she journeyed west with one-year-old John Robinson Jr. in her arms. She also brought a young daughter, Bertha, who was born on July 26, 1902.

Celeste possessed ample good reason to depart Florida, where life had not been particularly kind to her. She had been forced to start over after the death of her husband, John Robinson, in a tragic accident on Carrabelle's docks, where he worked as a longshoreman.

In Gulfport, Celeste eventually married "a fine man," Charles C. Cobb. Both Gulfport and Cobb were the best things that could have happened to Celeste and her children. Hard-working and pious, Cobb was ten years Celeste's senior, and a good match for a young woman with two small children.

Cobb was talented and smart, and he made a good living as one of the Pullman porters of Chicago's George M. Pullman Company, which manufactured elegant "palace" (sleeping) railroad cars. In this occupation, he was fortunate compared to most African American males in Jim Crow Mississippi. Employment as a Pullman porter was one of the few well-paying occupations available to Southern blacks. Most significant for Cobb, the steam-driven locomotives passing out of the segregated Deep South led to more progressive parts of the country, where he faced less discrimination.[5]

The African American porters, originally all ex-slaves, were simply called "George" by white passengers. Porters from the North met with strict segregation at the railroad stations of Mississippi. The Magnolia state was only one of three states where such harsh racial segregation at stations still existed at the turn of the century. Unfortunately, employment for Charles as a Pullman porter lasted only for a relatively short time. He wanted to spend more time with his family at Gulfport.[6]

Cobb became a respected pillar of Gulfport's black community, which was segregated from white Gulfport in Jim Crow Mississippi. He provided a lasting spiritual example and inspirational influence on young John. Charles was one of four trustees of the African Methodist Episcopal Church in town.[7]

Robinson grew up in a conservative, religious-minded, and hard-working household. His "family was close, and Robinson considered Charles Cobb his father."[8]

In the year 1910, by the time John Robinson was age five, aviation was yet in its infancy. The Wright brothers' low-level flight over the sand dunes of windy Kitty Hawk, North Carolina in mid-December 1903 made history less than two years before Robinson was born. Ironically, at that time, few Americans or Europeans realized the significance of this revolutionary invention, which was to play such an important part of Robinson's—and the nation's—life.[9]

But John's life would never be the same after an unforgettable event in late 1910, thanks to the exploits of a flamboyant aviation pioneer named John Moisant.[10] Of French heritage and from a wealthy Canadian family, this slight-built, scholarly looking aviator had been a bold adventurer, including time spent as a soldier of fortune in Central America.[11] Eager to participate in the aviation revolution, Moisant went to France, which was then the aviation center of the world. There, he built an airplane mostly from scratch. Completed in February 1910 and weighing under two hundred pounds, Moisant's light airplane was made of thin aluminum rather than the usual wood and fabric, an Aluminoplane.[12]

John and his brother formed Moisant International Aviators, Inc., to promote aviation around the world. The first two events, air shows, were planned for Richmond, Virginia; and Chattanooga, Tennessee, respectively.[13]

After successful air shows at Richmond and Chattanooga, John Moisant and the Moisant International Aviators flew west to Memphis, Tennessee, for a sixteen-day performance, which began on December 1, 1910. From Memphis, on the east bank of the Mississippi River, the Moisant flyers then flew southeast to northeast Mississippi.

Here, during the first air show in Mississippi, Moisant flew on December 20 over the small agricultural community of Tupelo, despite a harsh winter storm blowing in from the northeast, with freezing temperature and flurries of snow. Called a "blue norther" in Texas, this sudden storm descended south from Canada and abruptly ended the air show. Moisant and his flyers then headed due south. At top speed, they flew near the Mississippi towns of Starkville, Philadelphia, and Meridian, which were farther south and east of the state capital of Jackson, to reach the warmer weather and fair winds along the Mississippi Gulf Coast.[14]

Moisant and his aviators reached both the Mississippi Gulf Coast and better weather conditions far south of Tupelo without incident. With the big New Orleans air show scheduled soon to begin, the Moisant flyers turned west upon sighting the gulf's blue waters at the southern end of the lengthy coastal plain covered in dense pine forests—an air route later used by Charles A. Lindbergh during a barnstorming flight, before his solo trans-Atlantic flight in May 1927. Reinvigorated by the warm, fair skies along the gulf coast, the Moisant flyers then flew west from the Mississippi Gulf Coast toward New Orleans.

Because Moisant had cut the Tupelo air show short due to the storm, the aviator now had some spare time. He decided to land in the largest community that he spied along the Mississippi coast, Gulfport. He also needed to refuel and rest. While Moisant circled Gulfport, the other flyers continued on toward New Orleans.[15]

Moisant began to descend toward the north side of the chain of barrier islands and the placid waters of the Mississippi Sound, just north of the gulf, near the Mississippi shore. His airplane, a Pusher bi-plane with a large float attached to the bottom, came down with a smooth ease on the calm waters of the Mississippi Sound.[16] Here, along a stretch of sandy shoreline known as East Beach at the foot of 23rd Street, a large crowd of Gulfport's citizens, both black and white, gathered in awe. It was the first time they had seen an airplane. Everyone, from Gulfport's leading white citizens, to the black shoeshine boys, watched in amazement while Moisant descended from the blue skies.[17] Among the crowd of spectators were John and his mother, Celeste.[18]

The sight of Moisant's aircraft landing in the waters just off East Beach made an unforgettable impression on five-year-old Robinson. In the words of Katie Booth, who was born in Gulfport in 1907 and knew Robinson in both Gulfport and later in Chicago, "When he was a kid . . . he stood on the beach and watched the first 'aeroplane' land in Gulfport. Right then he was thrilled with the idea of flying." John and Celeste could hardly believe their eyes: a real flying machine descending from the skies over Gulfport to land in the Mississippi Sound, thanks to the early winter storm that blew suddenly into Tupelo.[19] John would never forget that aircraft and its dashing aviator.[20] The date was December 21, 1910. Robinson made up his mind that one day he would fly like the daring Moisant. Thereafter, his aviation obsession would never desert him.[21]

Robinson had seen Moisant during one of his last flights. The aviator flew from Gulfport to New Orleans late on December 21. On December 31, 1910, during the New Orleans air show, Moisant was killed in a failed landing attempt, after a day of flying in the wintry skies above the Mississippi River and the broad expanse of Lake Pontchartrain.[22]

After leaving his Pullman job, Robinson's stepfather, Charles C. Cobb, worked for the Gulf & Ship Island Railroad in Gulfport, near the family home. The small railroad machine shop was situated near Gulfport's train station, almost within sight of the Mississippi Sound. Such a position with the leading business on the Mississippi Gulf Coast promised a bright future for his family. Charles became a mechanic in the railroad machine shop at the railroad yard. But in time he would reach the highest position possible for an African American, working as a railroad engineer in the steam engine shop at Gulfport's railroad yard, making good pay and earning a measure of prestige.[23]

For an African American in south Mississippi, this elevation in position was no small accomplishment. Compared to his peers, Cobb had already risen far in life, both socially and economically, due to his own hard work, skill, and determination: invaluable lessons not lost on young Robinson. Most important, John learned the value of perseverance and patience from his stepfather's long struggle to achieve success in life: by starting at the bottom and then working his way up, after proving his worth and abilities to both blacks and whites alike. Robinson gradually began to learn how to deal successfully with local whites, both lower class and those in power, upon whom a Southern black man's future in life often depended, especially in Mississippi.

The family likewise benefited from the enterprising nature of John's mother. A proud, intelligent woman who was blessed with a savvy business sense, Celeste rented out rooms in the family's large two-story wood-frame house at 1905 31st Street in northwest Gulfport.

The Cobb-Robinson family house (Celeste retained her first husband's last name, despite her subsequent marriage) was a large structure, consisting of more than four thousand square feet. Situated on a dusty street, this home was a sprawling mansion compared to the little, wooden shanty houses, shacks, and Civil War–era log cabins that most Mississippi blacks, especially those of the impoverished Mississippi delta, called home. Even in Gulfport many African Americans lived in much smaller wooden "shotgun" houses that some owned with pride, while others rented. Like their slave ancestors on the Deep South's plantations, Gulfport's African Americans grew small vegetable gardens in their backyards to supplement their diets or to provide extra income. The wood-frame houses of many Gulfport's blacks were mostly painted green with unwanted paint bought from the white community. These plain, simple structures that dominated the African American community were less than one-fourth the size of the stately house owned by the Cobb family.

An ideal location for a boarding house, the Cobb family home was situated in the heart of Gulfport's thriving African American community known as the Big Quarter, a name that indicated the relative prosperity of the town's bustling black section. Here, African Americans lived far better than the majority of blacks in upstate Mississippi. With New Orleans less than ninety miles away to the west, the Quarter (as it was known to its residents) revealed an ethnic and cultural distinctiveness not unlike that of the French Quarter of New Orleans.[24]

The Big Quarter, then situated on Gulfport's northwest side (today it is in the town's central and historic district), was vibrant and full of life both day and night. Located on the north side of the railroad tracks that paralleled the Mississippi Gulf Coast and to the west side of the railroad line that cut Gulfport in half from the north, this community was a world unto itself, though ironically not totally isolated from white Gulfport.

For the most part, such a development was inevitable because of the harsh segregation of Jim Crow Mississippi. As in so many other Deep South towns, the proverbial railroad tracks served as Gulfport's color line, separating black from white. Whites enjoyed panoramic views of the Mississippi Sound from the best property and largest houses, surrounded by ancient oaks with Spanish moss hanging from thick limbs that touched the ground— dating back to the antebellum period. Two separate but unequal worlds existed on each side of the tracks. As did their ancestors in slave days, African Americans had once again successfully created their own distinctive and sheltering world within the larger community of Gulfport—a safe haven that offered a measure of security in a hostile Jim Crow environment.[25]

Even though in Gulfport the lives of many blacks were relatively good, racial restrictions were rigidly imposed. So powerful were these time-honored distinctions that the clear dividing line that separated the black from the white world was an unwritten law. This artificial racial boundary rested on an imaginary foundation of an assumed black inferiority. Every black and white person of Gulfport knew exactly why and where this racial border existed. To one and all, this invisible boundary was known locally as "the Mason-Dixon Line."[26]

As a young man John benefited from a boomtown environment and its relative prosperity. Gulfport's population had swelled to around ten thousand people by 1910, when John was five years old. Overall, the Mississippi Gulf Coast was relatively cosmopolitan in contrast to the backwardness of the rural Mississippi interior. The Big Quarter was filled with new, enterprising citizens from across the South, like Celeste and her children. In relative terms, a freer flow of new ideas and more open attitudes, all except in matters of race, made Gulfport a somewhat more enlightened environment along the Mississippi Gulf Coast. The African American part of town prospered along with the white community, though not to the same extent.

During these formative years, John drew strength from a stable home life and a nurturing family environment where money, unlike in most African American families of Mississippi, was not the most pressing concern. The family fulfilled the American dream by gaining middle-class status both through Cobb's hard work and his technical expertise, as well as through Celeste's business savvy. Year after year, she continued to make a steady income from room rentals. An astute businesswoman, Celeste took full advantage of their house's size and the large numbers of Gulfport's black workers who needed rooms to rent. She cooked meals for the boarders as part of the rent. The family's large house, which had been purchased by Cobb, was the most obvious sign of Charles's and Celeste's dual success.[27]

As a onetime Pullman porter, Cobb had already seen much of America. He had ascertained that a good many opportunities existed outside Mississippi's borders and its racially restrictive environment: a lesson he passed down to John. Cobb had repeatedly viewed the prosperity of Americans beyond the Deep South's confines, offering a vision of future possibilities.

Consequently, Charles and Celeste possessed high aspirations. They dreamed of a brighter future not only for themselves, but especially for John and Bertha. They fully understood how the good life they had made for themselves could bestow upon their children advantages that they had never experienced.[28]

Even though they enjoyed middle class status, or perhaps because of it, both parents were determined that their son would aspire yet higher. They consequently taught John that there were no limitations to what he could accomplish. Extra income gained from Celeste's boarding room enterprise and from Cobb's job at the railroad machine shop was saved to fulfill one of the greatest ambitions of African American parents in Jim Crow America: a college education for their son. Year after year, both parents worked hard to save money in order to send John to Tuskegee Institute, the premier black institution in the Deep South.[29]

Robinson eagerly embraced his parents' educational ambitions and conservative values. A college degree from Tuskegee Institute was a ticket to the good life for an African American man, especially in Jim Crow America, where educational and employment opportunities were scarce.

Robinson was intelligent and committed to making his dream of a Tuskegee degree come true. In addition, he was healthy, active, and full of life. Growing up muscular, tall, and strong, Robinson relished the outdoors and physical activity. His schoolboy friend Harry Charles Tartt recalled that at their segregated Gulfport high school, Robinson could outrun and out-jump everyone in his class.[30]

Indeed, "Johnny, as he likes to be called, . . . played the games of the normal boy of his age [and] built wagons [and] shot marbles. . . . But greatest of all his hobbies was flying kites" in the windy, sunny skies of Gulfport.[31]

Flying kites fueled Robinson's love of all things related to flight. Blessed with natural curiosity, John was eager to learn about all aspects of life, leading to a wide variety of interests. Though a fine student, he was anything but a stereotypical studious, intellectual type. Indeed, "he was very enthusiastic about sports," excelling in the challenge of competition. Robinson combined both an intellectual curiosity and passion for learning with a love of outdoor activities.[32]

Like most young men across the United States, both black and white, the sport that he loved most passionately was America's great national pastime, baseball. Like other young men of Gulfport, John liked to watch the black baseball teams, such as the Mobile Dodgers, the Mobile Black Shippers, or the Black Pelicans of New Orleans, play high-spirited games at the Gulfport ballpark on 29th Street, just a few blocks east of his home. The home of two future baseball greats, Leroy Robert "Satchel" Paige, the most famous hard-throwing pitcher of the Negro Leagues; and Hank Aaron, the most prodigious African American home run hitter, Mobile was represented by numerous teams. Other teams included the Mobile Tigers, the Mobile Brooklyns, and the Mobile Black Bears. These talented African American ballplayers traveled along the dusty roads of the gulf coast from Pensacola, Florida, to New Orleans while raising interest in baseball across the South, especially among the black communities. At the Gulfport ballpark Robinson and his friends viewed the athletic feats of rising black baseballs stars. One such gifted ballplayer was Hank Aaron's father, who played for the Mobile Dodgers.[33]

Even America's national pastime was separated by race. But here at the Gulfport black ballpark on 29th Street, not far from Robinson's home, African Americans socialized at sporting events in their own community. The Negro Leagues' athletes gave African American fans some of the few black heroes to admire in the dark age of Jim Crow.

After baseball games dominated by speed on the base paths, Robinson walked home, passing through the Big Quarter. Like the antebellum slave communities that gave blacks in bondage the necessary support system to survive slavery's horrors, so did Gulfport's African American community serve as an emotional and psychological refuge for young Robinson in his segregated world. Isolated from white Gulfport by the invisible "Mason-Dixon Line" to the south, the Big Quarter was prosperous, thanks to the railroads and the timber, seafood, and shipping industries. Unlike the vast majority of Mississippi's African Americans, most of Gulfport's blacks possessed disposable income. They spent freely on what were considered luxuries to other African Americans in the Magnolia state. Most important, this community was dynamic in overall cultural terms, where past traditions and memories of ancestors—in the tradition of West Africa—were held close to residents' hearts.[34]

This conservative and stable black community provided Robinson with considerable social and cultural support during his formative years. Such a nurturing environment firmly grounded John, and provided a sturdy foundation of core values embraced by hard-working, industrious black citizens who, even though mired in second-class status, were committed to getting ahead in life and in fulfilling the American Dream.

A host of successful black business establishments, including small restaurants, funeral homes, groceries, hairdressers, etc., were located within a few blocks of the Cobb family home. For young John, these businesses provided ample evidence of the value of hard work and future possibilities. Such commercial successes also bestowed a sense of ethnic pride, illustrating a host of positive lessons for John even within the strict racial limitations. Other aspects of life in the African American community—although they did not provide a positive example except for their enterprising nature—were the nests of gambling dens and houses of prostitution. After all, many black and white longshoremen and seamen spent a good deal of time in Gulfport, far from home, family, and social rules. Here, beyond the boundaries of artificial racial and social restrictions, blacks and whites came together to mingle as one.[35]

Nevertheless, a stable home life and his parents' inspirational example were a more lasting influence in John's life. They felt that education, especially for African Americans, was the key to advancement. Located barely one block from the Cobb home stood the all-black elementary school John attended. He absorbed new information and ideas like a sponge. After completing the sixth grade at age ten in 1915, John attended the Gulfport High School for the Colored for seventh and eighth grades, only one block farther than the elementary (his older sister had also attended this school). John continued to develop an active interest in all things mechanical. From an early date, he delighted in learning how mechanical things worked and how they could be fixed: an early, informal preparation for Tuskegee Institute in the future.[36]

Besides education, religion created a strong spiritual foundation for the young man. Religious services and observances were a time-honored tradition of spiritual regeneration among African Americans since slavery. Located at the corner of 31st and 21st Streets, only one block from the Cobb home, stood the modest St. Paul African Methodist Episcopal Church. This AME church continued a religious legacy first begun by Richard Allen, born in Philadelphia, Pennsylvania, in 1787. John worshiped on Sunday at this church, which would hold civil rights meetings in the 1960s. Here, he gained invaluable moral lessons that ridiculed the injustice and hypocrisy of Jim Crow America. Long before he had read Thomas Jefferson's immortal words that "all men are created equal" in the Declaration of Independence, Robinson learned in Gulfport that all men were equal in God's eyes.[37]

The rise of the AME church began after the Civil War, when restrictions on black preachers and African American worship practices since antebellum days were eased. Independent black churches thrived across Mississippi and the South, after African Americans departed the established white churches.[38] For instance, the African Methodist Episcopal Church, one of the oldest black churches in America, possessed only 20,000 members in the mid-1850s. But by 1876, more than 200,000 African Americans worshiped at AME churches. Perhaps Robinson learned about the history of these early black churches from religious leaders or even ex-slaves.

The importance of the spiritual and moral influence of the black church can hardly be overestimated in the development of African American political and community leaders. During John's formative years, the vibrancy of the local black church had a significant positive impact on his outlook on life and faith in the future.[39]

Most important, the African American church provided positive role models for young black males like John. The leadership role of black preachers in African American society extended back to the days of slavery. Powerful traditions of worship, gospel music, and preaching had deep roots in the vibrant tribal cultures of West Africa, the ancestral homeland of most African Americans. At the Gulfport church, members of the black community not only worshiped together but also socialized in various community functions that further strengthened their bonds. Such religious social activities provided a bright spot for a black community yet coping with injustices and ugly realities.

In attending church every Sunday morning, John also found an opportunity to get closer to his pretty friend, Miomi Godine. Miomi long remembered how he used to walk her to Sunday school.[40] Already at a relatively early age, young girls were attracted to John's outgoing personality, and the handsome young man returned their interest in full.

By the time he reached high school, the basic elements of John Robinson's strong personality had evolved, and maturity dominated. Gifted with intelligence and ambition, he had become a natural leader among his classmates. He developed a willful personality even at a relatively early age. But John was not a leader in an overly aggressive or obnoxious way. He resisted the temptation to bully, identifying with his peers rather than taking advantage of them. Therefore, he was popular with boys and girls alike.

One classmate, Reverend Harry Charles Tartt, a future black chaplain during World War II, was Robinson's close childhood friend. He described John as having been "dynamic" even at a relatively early age. His fellow classmates looked up to Robinson and were not disappointed. Tartt recalled how Robinson "was my role model" as early as high school. According to Reverend Tartt, Robinson possessed a very "outgoing" personality. Tartt recalled how John displayed a high degree of intelligence and possessed an inquisitive nature from an early age. If he embarked upon a specific task, Robinson was sure to see to it through to its completion. "He would never take no for an answer," Tartt remembered.[41]

Meanwhile, Robinson's early fascination with aviation was re-energized by newspaper accounts of the daring aviators of World War I. He learned how these "Knights" of the air battled in the skies over the Western Front. John was only eight when the Great War erupted in Europe in August 1914, and that conflict continued until he reached the age of twelve. From newspaper accounts of the air war over France, Robinson grew fascinated with military aviation. These thrilling stories of young American, French, German, and British airmen during the Great War continued to fuel "this dream to fly."[42]

Ironically, living on the Mississippi Gulf Coast from June to November could be almost as dangerous as a distant battlefield in Western Europe. Mother Nature's full fury struck Gulfport in the summer of 1916 when John was eleven. In July, even before the peak of the season, a hurricane demolished Gulfport. Driven by 104 mile-an-hour winds, this fierce storm lingered several days on the coast, inflicting considerable damage. While Gulfport's populace, which had no advance warning system, prayed for deliverance, the Cobb house survived the high winds and falling trees.[43]

Robinson continued to focus on academics. His intelligence made him stand out among his peers. Tartt, who was a fellow student with Robinson until the tenth grade, recalled how Johnny Robinson "was smarter than anyone else in that school."[44]

But perhaps Robinson's most notable trait besides his mechanical aptitude, even at an early date, was his eagerness to accept almost any new challenge, including those that were seemingly impossible. He was highly competitive by nature. For instance, an amazed Reverend Tartt never forgot how "he would accept any challenge," with a willingness that surprised those around him. The teenage Robinson "in high school would try everything," recalled Tartt.[45] Georgia-born Janet Harmon Bragg, a future black pilot who knew John well as an adult, said, "He never grew tired of trying, but finally wearied the other fellow of refusing."[46]

His natural competitiveness rose to the forefront in academics and sports. "In high school he could outrun" everyone. And he could easily "outdo everyone," recalled Tartt of the young man with the most dominant, but likeable, personality in his class.[47]

Robinson's positive outlook on life and his abilities made him extremely confident. But, unlike many other young men, Robinson was not arrogant, despite outshining his peers in intellect and athletics. Nevertheless, he developed some cockiness that was inevitable because of his youth and inexperience. Such cockiness and confidence, however, were prerequisites for aviation. Most of all, Robinson was determined to get ahead in life.[48]

The mere prospect of a teenage African American making money in Gulfport was slim at best. But the ever-ambitious Robinson jumped at the first opportunity to make a few dollars, when he was first old enough to do so.

At the busy Gulfport train station, near the railroad yard, where his stepfather worked each day except weekends, Robinson became a shoeshine boy. But this enterprise was a potentially risky undertaking for the young man. Older, more experienced shoeshine boys controlled the market in the lucrative area around the train station. This was the best arena for business in Gulfport, because of the stream of white travelers coming in and out of town. Suddenly sharing profits by allowing an interloper into their most profitable territory was not a popular proposition for the older boys.

Consequently, his career was short-lived. He fought repeatedly with a host of larger and older shoeshine boys in a futile struggle to obtain the busy corner to ply his trade. He was beaten, and rather badly, not once but three times, before he decided to give it up. But, of course, Robinson wanted far more in life than to shine shoes, especially for haughty white Southern visitors to Gulfport.[49]

Robinson already looked well beyond his narrow racial limitations. He wanted a good job with regular wages like his stepfather, and with more prestige than that of a lowly shoeshine boy. After much effort, John, at age thirteen and only in the ninth grade, finally obtained a coveted position at the Bee Hive Department Store on Fourteenth Street in Gulfport in 1918. America's entry into World War I had caused a manpower shortage at the store, creating more opportunities for black workers.

John performed menial labor, and he was a kid, but at least it was a start, and had far better prospects than shining shoes. He gained invaluable experience. For the first time, he learned how to work for "the man." Robinson cleaned stockrooms, delivered packages to Gulfport residents and white businesses in town, and swept floors after school and on Sunday, after faithfully attending church with his family.[50]

Far too many of Gulfport's mature and grown black men, however, swept floors and cleaned up after white people who ran businesses and made more money in a year than the average African American in Mississippi could make in a lifetime. John was eager to do more and move ahead with his life, including life beyond Gulfport.

In 1919, when he was fourteen, he applied for a job with the Chandler Supply Company in Gulfport. This small company supplied equipment to ocean-going vessels and transported ship parts across the nation. Historically, the Mississippi Gulf Coast had long-time connections with both the shipping industry and the U.S. Navy. President Andrew Jackson established the Naval Reserve Tract of land in 1832 along the Back Bay of Biloxi, Mississippi, to ensure suitable large sections of high quality lumber—ancient oaks—to build American naval vessels.

Tall for his age, John began driving a large truck for the company around Gulfport, while still attending high school, at age fourteen. Acquiring this part-time job was in itself a noteworthy accomplishment, one that astounded his high school peers. Along with his fellow students, Tartt remembered how "we didn't know how in the world he could drive a truck." As Tartt noted, Robinson "was the kind of a man who stayed with the job." All the while, John continued to learn more about people of different backgrounds and social positions.[51]

Throughout this period, the overall high quality of his high school education continued to keep Robinson moving in a positive direction. Here, at the Gulfport High School for the Colored, Annie Mae Gaston recalled how, "we had some of the best teachers, who really taught you."[52]

African American teachers bestowed knowledge about the lives of famous black leaders, such as Booker T. Washington and W. E. B. Du Bois, and other African Americans "who reached the top," recalled Tartt. Tuskegee Institute was also discussed, providing more inspiration for Robinson to attend the famous school one day. These mostly female instructors taught students about the complexities of world events. Most important, Gulfport's teachers also gave Robinson and his fellow students a healthy self-image. They believed that their pupils could accomplish anything they set their sights on. This was especially significant, because most of "our parents didn't read or write," recalled Katie Booth, who was a well-rounded product of Gulfport's segregated school system. She became a professional medical chemist, after earning a degree in industrial chemistry, which was rare for women, black or white, in her day, and later became a civil rights activist. Clearly, Gulfport's superior education for young African Americans was a key in molding the character of young men and women bound for future success.[53]

Even though he engaged in blue-collar work and thanks in part to the well-grounded education he received in high school, John kept his sights focused upon what he really wanted in life, an aviation career. He would not be seduced by the relatively good wages—even though it was the most he ever made in his life—or the relative comfort of a non-challenging, mundane existence in Gulfport. Complacency was not part of John's personality. At fifteen he graduated from the tenth grade in 1919 with high grades, excelling in his studies. This was his last year of schooling, because Gulfport's blacks were unable to attend school past the tenth grade.

Higher education was only possible for Robinson and other African Americans, if they traveled far beyond their community. For Gulfport's young men and women this meant attending the all-black Tougaloo College in Jackson, Mississippi, 150 miles north of the Mississippi Gulf Coast. If John wanted to continue his education, he would have to leave his family and friends, and the security of the Big Quarter, behind.

Life in the Big Quarter was seductive in many ways. All around Robinson were examples of black successes in a variety of businesses and private enterprises. And all of Robinson's friends and relatives lived on the Mississippi Gulf Coast, providing another reason to remain in the comfortable security of his hometown. In addition, Gulfport was the only home he had ever known.[54]

Nevertheless, John immediately made preparations for realizing his dream of attending Tuskegee Institute. He continued to develop his mechanical and technical abilities. Robinson demonstrated a "natural propensity for work on and about machines" of all kinds early on, which only grew as he got older.[55] While his fellow graduates wasted their summer enjoying themselves by chasing women, fist-fighting, and drinking hard liquor, Robinson took a technical training course at Gulfport. He now gained more mechanical skills, enhancing his chances of succeeding in mechanical training at Tuskegee Institute.[56]

Despite concentrating on his studies and his workaholic ways, John still found ample time to have fun during his first summer after graduation. A good dancer, Robinson was becoming "a ladies man," and acquiring a reputation that was well-deserved. After all, he was handsome, tall, and "good-looking."[57]

The first known photograph of Robinson reveals one of his typical summertime recreational activities along the Mississippi gulf coast at Gulfport's docks, swimming. This rare photograph was taken of Robinson and a group of his friends after they had just completed "a daring swim across the channel at the Gulfport harbor" (according to the caption written on the back of the photo) on a hot summer day in 1920.

At the docks, the Collins brothers—John and Toddy—and four other young men from Gulfport accompanied Robinson. Older brother Lee Collins played in the jazz band of Louis "Satchmo" Armstrong, the trumpet-playing great from New Orleans. Also along with them were three pretty young women. This trio of women—identified as sisters Bernice and Beatrice Hurd, and Lucile Trollen—provided ample motivation for Robinson and his friends to impress the pretty ladies by swimming across the deep channel of the Mississippi Sound.[58]

As revealed in the 1920 Census records, when Robinson reached the age of fifteen, he was known in the Cobb family, his friends, and especially his girlfriends as "Johnnie." He would be called "Johnnie" throughout his life. Despite his many future accomplishments in life, Robinson would very much remain the same old "Johnnie," without a swollen ego or pretensions that have marked so many successful men.[59]

Life continued to be stable for the Robinson family. John's sister, Bertha, was severals years older than her brother, age eighteen in 1920. Like John, she was intelligent, hard working, and studious. Bertha was also consumed by a desire to get ahead in life, and this, too, meant a career beyond Gulfport one day.

Bertha graduated from Straight College, now Dillard University, which had been founded in 1869, in New Orleans. After her marriage in 1928, Bertha became a popular teacher for Gulfport's black youth, continuing a tradition of teaching excellence.[60]

In 1920 when John was sixteen, a new business opened up directly across the street from his house, the Hall Funeral Home. Other businesses—not exclusively African American even though located in the heart of the Big Quarter—flourished as well. For instance, at the end of Robinson's home block to the north on the corner of 20th Street stood a large brick grocery store operated by a family of Greek immigrants. As in most port cities, especially New Orleans to the west, more multiculturalism and differing ethnicities existed in booming Gulfport, unlike other sections of Mississippi, such as the upstate, rural areas.[61]

As John grew older, however, he saw the prevalence of bigotry more clearly. The ugly specter of racism was ever-present, especially when he ventured into the town's white section. John occasionally visited his stepfather at the railroad yard in white Gulfport, where railroad station facilities were segregated. But in fact everything—in both life and death—was segregated, including eating establishments, trains, and toilet facilities.

Therefore, John began to increasingly see how white Mississippians viewed him as a lowly, second-class citizen of little worth. He resolved that not only would he not be crushed by the oppressive weight of this unjust Jim Crow environment but also would have to fight—sometimes covertly, other times openly—against the institutionalized system of racism that he would encounter throughout his life in the United States. In contrast to how he was treated because of his race, John carefully evaluated each person he knew or met, black or white, based upon their individual personality, their most redeeming qualities, and overall character. He could readily recognize those relatively few whites who could be befriended, as well as those he must avoid at all costs. But for the most part, "he liked the people [of Gulfport], both black and white."[62]

In learning these invaluable life lessons, John gained much experience about the intricacies of human nature, both good and bad. He was a people person, liking both whites and blacks, especially if they treated him fairly. Robinson gained well honed, highly developed interpersonal skills to cope with a wide range of individuals. This special talent made him highly effective in dealing with people regardless of race, class, or background.

In this way, Robinson was able to take negative racial experiences and utilize them to fuel his personal motivation, transforming negatives into positives. This unique quality was yet another invaluable asset learned in part from his parents. Additionally, a certain amount of psychological escapism existed in John's fascination, if not obsession, with flight. After all, he was a young black male mired in a repressive Deep South environment, where prejudice and racism flourished. Therefore, the seductive lure and the vivid imagery of the majesty of flight in John's mind might have represented a certain amount of freedom from the bigotry and discrimination that made life difficult for so many African Americans in Mississippi.

Most of all, the idea of flight was not only an all-consuming passion, but also a liberating experience of the mind. John's fascination with flight had fueled his imagination and spirit ever since first viewing Moisant's flight to Gulfport in December 1910.

For Robinson, aviation became a symbolic means of personal liberation by which he could rise high and soar above a negative racist environment and the world's problems. While Robinson's segregated life was centered around only a few square blocks of the Quarter that included the home and church, Robinson continued to closely embrace the ambitious dream of an aviation career. After all, he had learned from an early age that nothing was impossible. The twin goals of attending the Tuskegee Institute and soaring high in the skies continued to burn brightly within the heart and mind of young John Charles Robinson.[63]

2

TURNING POINT: TUSKEGEE INSTITUTE AND GOING NORTH

THE YEAR 1920 was a major turning point in Robinson's life. He was only fifteen, had graduated from high school, and completed his technical training course, but was unable to continue his education in Gulfport because of Jim Crow laws.[1] Tuskegee Institute did not offer aviation courses, but the school, located in east-central Alabama, was known for its excellent automobile mechanics program. At this point, John's best opportunity was to focus on a technical career. After all, he must have realized, an automobile engine and an airplane engine were similar.

The period immediately after the Great War's end saw the advent of an automobile age that revolutionized American society. Becoming a mechanic would not only help John pursue his ultimate dream of flying, but also provide him with a lucrative career. With his natural aptitude for all things mechanical, Robinson was confident that he could successfully meet any technical challenge at Tuskegee Institute.[2]

Tuskegee was located nearly three hundred miles northeast of Gulfport. After an emotional farewell with his family, relatives, and friends at the Gulfport railroad station, Robinson departed for Tuskegee Institute in the late summer of 1920. His mother, Celeste, gave him a small Bible and some of her hard-earned savings.

Jim Crow dogged Robinson's steps: he was forced to ride in the black section of the segregated railroad car. The rail journey across rural Mississippi and Alabama to Tuskegee cost more than his meager funds allowed, and so Robinson had to ride the rest of the way over dusty roads by wagon. He journeyed through the gently rolling hills of the Creek Indian country of southcentral Alabama, south of the state capital of Montgomery.[3]

19

Those Gulfport friends who knew Robinson, like Katie Booth, were not surprised by his departure, and she remembered, "He wanted to do more than work at the docks or railroad. He had his dreams."[4]

Then known as the Tuskegee Normal and Industrial Institute, the school was established when Governor Rufus Willis Cobb signed into law a bill to create a school for blacks in Macon County. The school's first principal and leader was Booker Taliaferro Washington, who succeeded Frederick Douglass as the primary spokesman of African Americans during the post-Civil War period. Like Douglass, who had been enslaved on the eastern shore of Maryland, Washington was also the son of a white father and a slave mother. The Virginia-born Washington had survived slavery, recalling how he had "to go to the 'big house' at meal-times to fan the flies from the table" as a small boy.[5]

Determined to overcome his slave past, Washington received an education at Hampton College (then known as Hampton Normal and Agricultural Institute) on the Virginia peninsula. Located on the brown waters of the Hampton River on the lower Chesapeake Bay, Hampton Institute had been founded in 1868 only three years after the Civil War. After graduation, Washington dedicated himself to teaching.[6]

In May 1881, Washington received the opportunity "to begin my life work," by taking charge of "a normal school for the coloured people" at Tuskegee. The idea of creating a school was inspired by the success of Hampton Institute.[7]

Upon his arrival at Tuskegee in June 1881, Washington was shocked to find that no school buildings existed there. The school, more of an idea than a reality, had to be built almost from scratch. Tuskegee's first classes, for both men and women, began on July 4, 1881 in a "dilapidated shanty" and an old black Methodist Church. Both structures had been given to Washington on loan.[8]

In regard to African Americans recently out of bondage, Washington was convinced "that, in order to lift them up, something must be done more than merely to imitate New England education as it existed."[9]

Washington understood that it would take more than the standard white education to improve the lives of former slaves. He knew of blacks who were "learned in Greek, but [there were] few carpenters [or experts in] mechanical drawing [or] engineers, bridge-builders and machinists . . . or [experts] in agriculture."[10]

First and foremost, Washington believed that the former slaves must become proficient in the useful occupations. He described this educational philosophy as "an integrated training of the head, heart, and mind."[11]

Washington summarized the important developments that transpired at Tuskegee during the institute's formative period: "I knew that, in a large degree, we were trying an experiment—that of testing whether or not it was possible for Negroes to build up and control the affairs of a large educational institution, I knew that if we failed it would injure the whole race."[12]

Education was the key for African Americans to lift themselves out of poverty. But exactly what kind of education was necessary for blacks to advance in American society at a time when the United States was evolving more into an industrial giant, while leaving an agricultural way-of-life farther behind?[13]

Combined with an "industrial education," or vocational approach, Washington embraced the concepts of racial solidarity to create self-sufficient black communities that could prosper outside the discriminatory white world: a seemingly rational response to the increasing segregation of Jim Crow America. Washington's Tuskegee Normal and Industrial Institute focused on promoting thirty-six industries "that are those of the South, the occupations in which our men and women find most ready employment."[14] Tuskegee Institute thrived not only as an educational institution but also as an enduring symbol of hope for blacks across America. Consequently, Washington was widely acclaimed, as early as 1897, as "the Moses of his people."[15]

The school sought to educate the whole person, in character as well as profession. In Washington's words, "we do not neglect or overlook in any degree the religious and spiritual side." He emphasized, "Tuskegee and its people possesses ideals in thought, morals, and action."[16] Indeed, the Tuskegee experience bestowed a balanced mixture of religion, industriousness, and discipline to build character. As explained by Emmett J. Scott, Booker T. Washington's chief aide and the highest-ranking African American in Woodrow Wilson's administration, "character-building is the Alpha and Omega of all that Tuskegee stands for."[17]

Scott elaborated: "From the moment the new student comes on the grounds until he leaves, he is appealed to in ways innumerable to regard life as more than bread and meat, as more than mere mental equipment. Cleanliness, decorum, promptness, truthfulness—these are old-fashioned virtues, and are more properly taught in the home, but in Tuskegee they mean everything. Tuskegee not only acts as a teacher, but assumes the role of parent, and lays emphasis on the importance of these virtues every moment of the time from the entrance of the student until Commencement Day."[18]

One of the industries promoted at Tuskegee was designated as machinery. This specialized mechanical field was tailor-made for Robinson's special talents, and he arrived with high hopes and ambitions.[19] Robinson embraced the Tuskegee Institute experience with a passion, not only entering the field of automotive science in the Department of Mechanical Industries, but also worshiping on Sunday at the institute's small chapel.

Robinson was determined to succeed at Tuskegee. He worked harder than ever, resulting in the development of one of his principal values: "I am a believer in discipline."[20] He also gained additional pride in the past achievements of African Americans, including Washington, Douglass, and Harriet Tubman. Indeed, "Pride of race, though not so written in the courses of study, is as much a part of Tuskegee's work as agriculture, brick-making, millinery, or any other trade, and quite as important. This may be called sentiment, but it makes for race development quite as much as any of the material things taught in the classroom or shop. Self-respect demands race pride."[21]

Meanwhile, the confident young man from Gulfport soon became one of the "best mechanics" at Tuskegee. Not surprisingly, Robinson excelled more at mechanical science than any other subject, scoring his highest grades, while earning only average grades in English and mathematics. One noteworthy achievement was a groundbreaking class project in which he led a group of his fellow students in building a working automobile.[22]

But Robinson was not complacent about his success as a top student. To acquire additional technical expertise, he studied on his own at the school's library, which had been funded by steel baron Andrew Carnegie. Here, in his spare time while other students frolicked, he read textbooks about automobiles and aviation.

Like other students, he lived in a dormitory, and probably seldom ventured forth into Tuskegee's white community. During this period, he made a lifelong friend in his roommate, Anselm J. Finch. At age eighteen and after the most studious period of his life, Robinson became a proud graduate of Tuskegee Institute at the spring commencement ceremony of 1923.[23]

With a degree in mechanics, Robinson was now one step closer to his aviation dreams. His ambitions were higher than being a mere automotive mechanic, however. Many white Southerners appreciated Tuskegee Institute because they believed that vocational training would keep African Americans permanently in inferior social and economic positions across the South. Robinson was about to turn that racist theory upside down. His Tuskegee education would serve as a springboard to bigger and better things. In addition, Robinson also contradicted Washington's philosophy that African Americans should remain in the rural South after graduation. Despite being from a small town, Robinson embraced the more progressive view that the major northern cities of the United States offered the best opportunities for African Americans, especially those with a degree from the most prestigious black college in America.[24]

Robinson knew that his mechanical expertise would be the best way to break through the limitations of segregation to create a career in aviation. He felt confident that if he could fix an automobile engine, then he could also repair an airplane engine. Indeed, young Robinson had now "hitch[ed] his wagon to the stars."[25]

But Robinson faced a host of rigid racial barriers, which, in Albert Einstein's words, were part of the "worst disease" in American society. The future commander of the famed Tuskegee Airmen, Benjamin O. Davis Jr., described the dilemma for African Americans who, like Robinson, wanted to be pilots: "As for me, now seventeen [in 1929], I still wanted to fly airplanes, but the harsh reality was that there was no way for a black man to become a professional pilot. The United States then offered few career opportunities of any kind to black people. I could not think of any realistic way to get into flying."[26]

Consequently, Robinson was forced to defer his dream. First and foremost, he had to make a living. However, he did not want to return to his hometown. An unfortunate black man named Alex Smith had been lynched by a white mob in Gulfport on March 21, 1922, while Robinson was studying at Tuskegee Institute. It was an ugly reminder of the South's deep racial divisions.[27]

The North offered greater opportunity, social mobility, and racial tolerance. And no place in the North beckoned more to Robinson than the thriving city of Detroit, Michigan. It was the automobile capital of the world, the home of black America's heavyweight boxing champ Joe Louis, and had a sizeable African American population. Detroit, therefore, seemed the perfect place for a young black automobile mechanic to make a new start. Most important for Robinson's long-term aviation strategic game plan, Detroit was also the home of Lockheed Aviation's parent company, Detroit Aircraft.[28]

Black newspapers, especially the *Chicago Defender*, had long beckoned Southern blacks to head north to escape the South's oppression. Inspiring words of hope spilled forth from the pages of the most influential black newspaper in the United

States: "Every black man for the sake of his wife and daughter should leave . . . every spot in the south where his worth is not appreciated enough to give him the standing of a man and a citizen in the community."[29]

In fact, no African American newspaper in America exposed racial injustices more than the *Chicago Defender*. It served as a defiant voice that relentlessly condemned racism. Georgia-born Robert S. Abbott, who had learned his journalistic trade at Hampton Institute, founded the *Chicago Defender* in 1905. After yet another brutal lynching of a black man in Memphis, Tennessee, the *Chicago Defender* emphasized the wisdom of African Americans departing the South for the more racially tolerant North: "Do you wonder at the thousands leaving the land where every foot of ground marks a tragedy, leaving the graves of their fathers and all that is dear, to seek their fortunes in the North?"[30]

The *Chicago Defender* was widely read by blacks across Mississippi, including Gulfport, throughout the 1920s. Like no other newspaper, the *Chicago Defender* had played a key role in sparking the great migration of African Americans to the North during the Great War. From 1916 to 1919 more blacks departed Mississippi than from any other Southern state. To one African American from Mississippi, the height of this black exodus to the North seemed "like the Judgment day." Consequently, in an attempt to silence the truth, white Southerners sought to keep this influential newspaper out of the Deep South, considering it the "greatest disturbing element," to infiltrate the oppressive land of Dixie.[31]

Six weeks after he arrived in Detroit, the young Mississippian found an assistant automobile mechanic position at a large automobile garage in the bustling city. Robinson stayed in a boarding house, which was probably located in Detroit's black section. Likeable, diplomatic, and nonthreatening, Robinson became the only black mechanic working with a half dozen other white mechanics.[32]

Robinson performed so competently in his new job that he soon advanced to the position of head mechanic. His new salary allowed him to rent a small flat that offered more privacy and better living conditions than the crowded boarding house. Meanwhile, Robinson also conducted his own mechanical experiments in his spare time and eventually transformed miscellaneous parts into a working automobile. With considerable pride in what he had achieved, he drove along Detroit's busy streets and through the largest urban center he had ever seen.[33]

If he could build a car on his own, Robinson knew that he could perhaps construct an airplane, if he purchased a kit from the aircraft manufacturer. In Detroit, he bought and read detailed technical manuals about aircraft mechanics and engines, studying intently just as he had in his spare time at Tuskegee Institute.

The considerable risks involved in flying were apparent to John, who harbored no illusions in this regard. In early May 1926 during a June 30 practice flight the day before an air show at Jacksonville, Florida, black pilot Bessie Coleman, at the young age of thirty-three, met a tragic fate. Coleman was not wearing a safety belt and was not at the controls when her plane's gears jammed. The JN-4 Curtiss Jenny biplane suddenly spun out of control, nose-dived, and then turned over. Before the pilot could regain control, Coleman, the former Chicago manicurist turned aviation pioneer, tumbled out of the open cockpit at an altitude of five hundred feet without a parachute.[34] Clearly, flying was nothing to be taken lightly. A pilot, or passenger for that matter, could neither afford to be complacent nor overconfident in regard to either their aircraft or their own flying skills, regardless of their level of experience. Both the art of flight and aircraft itself had to be respected at all times.

On one balmy Sunday autumn day in 1926 after working nearly two years in Detroit, twenty-year-old Johnnie Robinson drove to Willow Run, a small airfield located immediately east of Ypsilanti, Michigan, a rural area near Detroit. As expected, Robinson was immediately rebuffed by the first white barnstormer he approached. But after learning that one aircraft, a JN-4D Curtiss Jenny, needed some engine work, Robinson offered to fix the problem in exchange for a free flight, which normally cost $5.00. Now an expert mechanic, Robinson was easily able to repair the engine trouble. Robert J. Williamson III, a friend of the barnstormer, was busy flying Sunday school class members. He agreed to take Robinson up at no cost in return for detailed instruction from the barnstormer about a complicated stunt maneuver.

As a wide-eyed passenger, Robinson flew for the first time in his life, enjoying the ride in the Waco Nine aircraft, which seemed to float through the blue skies. He was awed by the sweeping views of the countryside from the open cockpit. After landing on the grassy air strip, Robinson asked Williamson if he would teach him to fly for payment. Robinson's bold proposal was simply not possible due to the racist taboos of the times.

The sympathetic Williamson, however, then gave John some invaluable advice. He asked Robinson if he believed he could obtain an automobile mechanic's job in Chicago. If so, then Williamson advised him that he should then learn about aircraft mechanics and flight at the best aeronautical institution in the North, the prestigious Curtiss-Wright Aeronautical (or Flying) School in Chicago. Williamson's advice kindled a new ambition in Robinson.[35]

A year after his first flight just outside Detroit, the twenty-one-year-old Robinson also drew inspiration from the dramatic flight of another young, mechanically minded man who possessed an obsessive love for flying—Charles A. Lindbergh. In May 1927, the first trans-Atlantic solo flight of the "Lone Eagle" excited the world, and "inspired more [black] youths to seek instructions to fly."[36]

Lindbergh's solo flight from the East Coast to Paris made Robinson even more determined to learn to fly. Chicago beckoned as never before.[37] In the words of his friend Janet Harmon Bragg: "Equipped with a determination to succeed, an inspired Robinson turned his eyes toward Chicago, that bustling ambitious city by the lake, where [black] men, good and true, have a chance to win" their place in life.[38]

With his few belongings, Robinson moved to Chicago sometime in the summer or fall of 1927. He was twenty-one. Chicago was the Midwest's most prosperous city. Here, a large number of blacks owned and operated businesses, benefiting from an economic and social upsurge of the vibrant African American community on Chicago's south side. Chicago was also the home of a popular African American movement, part of a larger cultural and economic renaissance that emphasized the importance of black solidarity. Thousands of African Americans had migrated north for the well-paying jobs generated by America's involvement in World War I and the large number of vacancies left by white soldiers.[39] The *Chicago Defender* had long advised blacks to "leave that benighted land [of the South because] you are free men. To die from the bite of the frost is far more glorious than that of the [white lynch] mob."[40]

Barely ten years before, another young hopeful African American, who also had excelled in school like Robinson, had departed the South's oppressive cotton fields, poverty, and racial intolerance and headed for Chicago—Bessie Coleman. After a successful new start in Chicago where she had learned to speak French and became interested in aviation from *Chicago Defender* articles, this determined young woman who had been raised in Waxahachie, Texas, obtained her pilot's license in France in June 1921. Of mixed black and American Indian (Choctaw) heritage, she became the first African American ever to receive a pilot's license. She had to go to France because she was barred from entering flight school in the United States because of her color. At the time, the fifteen-year-old Robinson had been attending school in Gulfport.[41]

Robinson found employment with the Yellow Cab Company. Here, he worked in the machinery department, putting his technical skills to good use repairing a fleet of taxicabs. John continued to possess yet another means—a key advantage—by which to get ahead in the white world: a friendly, open, and good-natured personality free of bitterness and racial resentment. With a combination of mechanical skill and a good sense of humor, he made a highly favorable impression on his coworkers. Robinson was able to make whites like and even admire him not only for his professional expertise, but also for his outgoing personality.

Most of all, he impressed his white supervisors at the cab company. His boss soon promoted him "to a position of either sub-foreman or foreman" at Yellow Cab. Demonstrating leadership ability, he supervised an entire crew of hard-working mechanics. Like so many other black migrants from the Deep South, Robinson was now making more money than ever before in his life. For him, Chicago was indeed the promised land of "Canaan."[42]

Robinson thrived on the South Side, the heart of the vibrant black community. This culturally distinct section of Chicago was known as the "Black Belt." The racial boundary—ironically not unlike Gulfport's racial dividing line—was clearly defined for both blacks and whites: 22nd and 55th Streets, and Wentworth and Cottage Grove Avenues. During the booming World War I years, the "Black Belt" had grown into a bustling city in itself. Now, in the mid-1920s, the African American community was in full bloom. Once again, Robinson was at the right place, and at the right time. By the time that Robinson arrived, Chicago had swelled to nearly 3 million people to become one of America's largest cities. Between 1920 and 1930 Chicago's black population more than doubled, growing from nearly 110,000 in 1920 to almost 235,000 only ten years later in 1930.[43]

When he arrived in Chicago, Robinson very likely initially stayed with his uncle Benjamin Herndon, and then obtained a room at a YMCA. Here, Robinson met a young man who shared a passion for mechanics and aviation, Arkansas-born Cornelius Robinson Coffey. Robinson soon moved out of the YMCA to rent an apartment with the money he had earned as a foreman at Yellow Cab.

Rents were relatively high on the South Side, using up much of Robinson's savings and later, his income. Overall, housing was scarce for African Americans, not only because of white hostility that forced black families into a relatively small area, but also because the city was swollen with so many hopeful black migrants from the Deep South. Across the South Side, African Americans rented apartments and houses at relatively high cost, though they were inferior to comparable white dwellings.

Chicago's South Side was also known as Bronzeville. Ironically, Robinson might have been initially somewhat disillusioned to once again ascertain, as in Detroit, that even in the big Northern cities, blacks were segregated in their own communities, much like Gulfport's Big Quarter.

In Chicago, this distinctive African American community was dominated by a black elite who possessed leading social and political positions and enjoyed a measure of power. A strong black political machine represented the South Side's residents, wielding considerable influence. African American entrepreneurs owned their own restaurants, barbershops, beauty shops, automobile garages, and other small businesses on their versions of Wall Street and Broadway, and especially along a busy main thoroughfare known as the Stroll.

Robinson's social life reached new heights, and he began dating his future wife, Earnize, who he met in Chicago. Earnize's background reflected more of an urban upbringing, but not much else is known about her. In addition, African American political and social organizations, such as the Appomattox Club—named in honor of Gen. Robert E. Lee's surrender at the central Virginia village of Appomattox on Palm Sunday, April 9, 1865—and the Frederick Douglass Center, reflected a strong respect for black pride and a rich cultural heritage. Forsaking the unrealistic vision of an integrated community in Jim Crow America, both African American leaders and the proud citizens of the "Black Belt" had created a largely self-sufficient "black metropolis."[44]

Chicago's lure also drew John's older sister, Bertha. After graduating from Straight College in New Orleans (known today as Dillard University), she headed for Chicago and initially also stayed with Uncle Benjamin Herndon, after which she moved in with her brother. Bertha eventually returned to Gulfport, where she married Herbert L. Stokes in 1928 and embarked upon a distinguished career as an educator—not only in Mississippi but also in Arkansas and finally in New York City—and as a civil rights activist.

After saving a large portion of his income along with money made by his new wife, Earnize, Robinson took another step toward fulfilling his dream. With opportunities for higher advancement closed to him at the white-owned Yellow Cab Company because of Jim Crow realities, he took the bold move and struck out on his own.[45]

With Earnize, he opened up his own automobile repair garage at 47 East 47th Street on the South Side. After paying the rent and gaining the owner's permission, he transformed a former hardware and blacksmith shop into a full-service garage. Robinson now entered the ever-growing small black business class of Bronzeville. This was no small accomplishment for a young man so recently from the Deep South, and was a Horatio Alger–like story in many respects. Most of all, Robinson's upward climb resulted from not only ambition and vision, but also hard work.[46] As his friend Janet Harmon Bragg wrote, Robinson wanted "to widen his knowledge of his trade, and to learn the business side of it, [so] he launched a little shop of his own."[47]

Robinson's aviation ambitions yet burned brightly, and his garage would eventually serve as a stepping-stone to his greater goal.[48] In time, Robinson' automotive repair business succeeded to the point where he was able to hire a number of assistants. Now with enough free time to experiment, he was determined to convert an automotive engine into an aircraft engine.[49]

He and good friend Cornelius R. Coffey first tinkered with a motorcycle engine in their spare time in Robinson's garage. His hard work and success allowed him an opportunity to take a new position that was too good to pass up. He became an automobile mechanic at a white Chevrolet dealership owned by Emil Mack, an enlightened man of German descent, in Elmwood Park, Illinois. Coffey, a full-time mechanic at Mack's business, helped to open the door for Robinson. This may have been a part-time position, as Robinson still managed his own garage. Here, at the Elmwood location, Robinson and Coffey collected as many spare automobile and airplane parts as possible. By pooling their meager resources, they then purchased a used motorcycle engine and an airplane kit. By utilizing the motorcycle engine and with their combined technical expertise, the two close friends made plans to recondition their first airplane, a Waco 9, on their own.[50]

When the Waco neared completion, Robinson and Coffey moved their experimental aeronautical activities from Robinson's garage to an available room at the Acres Airport in Melrose Park, Illinois. To pay for it, Robinson struck a deal with white airport officials. Robinson and Coffey now repaired the automobiles and motorcycles of the airport's white owners and patrons in exchange for coveted working space at the white airport facility. Here, in this new, more favorable environment, Robinson planned to acquire the necessary flying hours from a certified flight instructor in order to qualify for his pilot's license. A suitable flight instructor needed not only to be fully accredited, but also had to be free of prejudice.[51]

Robinson eventually found his ideal flight instructor, open-minded and receptive at the Acres Airport, Warren Melvicke, who hailed from Chicago's large Polish community. No one would be more responsible for teaching Robinson about the intricacies and dynamics of flight than Melvicke. With Melvicke as his copilot, Robinson would take the controls and "solo" for relatively short distances.[52]

At age twenty-five, Robinson had waited his entire life for this moment. February 1, 1930, was colder than any he had experienced during all his years on the Mississippi Gulf Coast. But not even the freezing weather or the gusty winter winds were sufficient to deter Robinson from finally gaining the opportunity to embark on his "first solo, which is a crucial point in a pilot's flying career."[53]

Twenty years before, Robinson had stood as a young boy in the noisy crowd along the Mississippi Sound to see his first aircraft in flight. And now, nine hundred miles from his hometown, he was finally about to embark upon his first solo flight. If Robinson could learn to fly in this unforgiving and challenging environment, then he would be well prepared for flight almost anywhere. Under the dull, wintry skies, Robinson's aircraft gained speed and it lifted off the runway. He took "to the air like a duck to water," and quickly mastered his first solo flight, fulfilling his childhood ambition.[54]

During this period, Robinson also became more interested in motorcycles. The steady business from owning the automobile repair garage afforded him with extra money to purchase a motorcycle. By all indications, Robinson was passionate about not only mechanics but also speed. To earn more money and to satisfy his new passion, Robinson performed—mostly on weekends—at a local circus. Known as "Death Valley," John's death-defying one-man motorcycle act was quite popular. He was gaining a widespread reputation throughout Bronzeville.[55]

As Janet Harmon Bragg described in the *Chicago Defender*, "Chicagoans remember the many exploits of Robinson on the motorcycle as he performed numerous stunts on the 'wheel' up and down Indiana Avenue, riding forty and fifty miles an hour, [and no one] was more colorful in a motor vehicle than Robinson."[56]

But despite his reckless streak and love of speed, Robinson was a stable and hard-working citizen. As a husband and an enterprising, prudent businessman, he was also responsible. Carrying with him Deep South's conservative values and his strict Baptist upbringing, Robinson was still traditional in fundamental ways, including marriage. While he lived in Bronzeville, he continued to find additional personal and spiritual strength in worship at the South Park Baptist Church.[57]

Most important, Robinson also continued to see aviation as the key to tearing down long-existing racial barriers for future generations. Robinson envisioned how African Americans could elevate themselves both economically and socially by means of flight.

Robinson met other young aviation-minded African Americans, including fellow Tuskegee graduates, in Chicago. In 1927 he formed the Aero Study Club, which was later renamed the Brown Eagle Aero Club. The first meetings of Robinson's aviation organization were held in the 3800 block of Indiana Avenue, and attended by "a handful of girls and boys interested in aviation."[58]

One member of the Brown Eagle Aero Club recalled Robinson's efforts to complete the mechanical work on his Waco. Robinson built the craft primarily from an airplane kit that had been purchased from the Heath Parasol Airplane Company and an "old" motorcycle engine. In the words of a member of the aero club, after "wrecking an old motorcycle, Robinson used the four cylinder motor from it and other parts he purchased piece by piece and built his first plane. Even members of the Brown Eagle club considered it a joke, but Johnny took it seriously; he knew what he was doing, and to the surprise of his associates on the test flight, the plane [the Waco 9] flew perfectly. Thus, he established himself firmly with the other members of the club, and created in them, not only implicit faith in his ability and skill, but in aviation as well."[59]

Robinson wisely took the precaution of having the night school instructor at Curtiss-Wright Aeronautical School make sure that the aircraft was airworthy before any flight attempt.[60]

Robinson now understood that he needed additional funds to create a greater awareness of aviation throughout Chicago's black community. One member of the aero club explained the extent of the challenge: "Realizing it takes money to carry forward any venture, Robinson sought help from his friends and local businessmen, but all his pleas fell on deaf ears. This method failing, he tried giving pay parties in the hope of raising money. The first of these was a dance at the Cafe de Paris, on 31st Street."[61]

Robinson now became more enterprising in his efforts to secure funds. He went to the Department of Commerce and obtained permission to drop from the air a large number of printed flyers that advertised the dance, sponsored by his Brown Eagle Aero Club. Robinson also secured influential support from the *Chicago Defender*, especially publisher Robert S. Abbott, who strongly endorsed his vision for promoting aviation in the black community.

On the established day, high above the large building that housed the offices of the *Chicago Defender*, Robinson "performed several stunts for the benefit of thousands of persons who gathered near the office to watch the air maneuvers of the young pilot," according to Janet Harmon Bragg. "Despite the bitter cold weather, Robinson carried out his plans. He not only flew over the great South side but [also] circled the fashionable Gold Coast. Robinson's hands were frozen during this flight, causing a bad landing at the field which resulted in some minor damages to his plane."[62]

To additionally promote aviation to black youth, Robinson organized fundraising picnics, social events, and dances on both Christmas and New Year's Eve 1929, which were held by the Brown Eagle Aero Club for, "The Afro-American Youth in Aviation." Staged at Warwick Hall on 47th Street, not far from Robinson's automobile repair garage, the dance was also part of his plan "to unveil a plane he had designed and built, going to the trouble and expense of dismantling it and reassembling it in the hall." The center of attention, of course, was Robinson's shiny, new Waco airplane, which stood at one end of the dance floor for all to see, sit in, and admire.[63]

These popular aviation-related social activities coincided with the more serious focus on aviation lectures and discussions headed by Robinson, and drew greater attention to aviation. Perhaps because he and his wife, Earnize, had no children of their own, he was even more determined to work with and uplift black youth. Robinson continued to view aviation as the ticket to greater opportunity and equality for the next generation of African Americans. Additionally, these social events served as fundraisers to support the aviation activities of the Brown Eagle Aero Club, now based at Acres Airport in Melrose Park.[64]

Most of all, the visionary Robinson wanted to spread a greater awareness of aviation not only in Chicago, but also eventually throughout the North and the South. He hoped that demonstrations of excellence by black aviators would break down racial barriers, opening the door to social and economic advancement for African Americans. In this sense, Robinson was formulating his own strategy for waging his own personal war against racism.

Robinson was attempting to accomplish in peacetime in the late 1920s what the Tuskegee Airmen would eventually achieve in the 1940s: proving black competency, expertise, and proficiency—or equality to whites—in the most technically advanced arena, aviation.

Robinson desired to become a certified pilot, which meant acquiring additional flying time. His well-conceived plan for locating the Waco aircraft at Acres Airport had been for the purpose of befriending white instructors to gain flying lessons. With extra time and money, the twenty-five-year-old succeeded in his ambition. He secured additional pilot training, racking up more flying time to quality for a private pilot's license. He also attempted to enroll in available master mechanic's courses at a number of aeronautical schools. He mailed in applications and hoped for the best.[65]

In Janet Harmon Bragg's words, Robinson "was stung by the 'flying bug' [and] from this assault, never recovered! He sent numerous applications to aviation schools, but was turned down each time after he appeared in person and the officials saw the color of his skin. But, undaunted by the frequent rebuffs, Robinson kept trying. He never grew tired of trying."[66]

Even though Robinson repeatedly applied for admission to a number of aviation schools by mail, his sights were set primarily on gaining entry into the premier school—the all-white Curtiss-Wright Aeronautical School—in the Chicago area. Robinson sent in his application by mail with the required application fee. With an impressive resume and extensive experience, Robinson was finally accepted, but was immediately refused entry when he showed up in person. Fearing the exodus of white students and the loss of revenue as well as possible white hostility directed toward the first black student in the school's history, officials curtly informed Robinson that a mistake had been made. They then offered to return the registration fee, but Robinson smartly refused to take the money. He knew he had his foot already in the door, and would not remove it.

This humiliating experience was especially frustrating because he knew full well that his mechanical and technical expertise had been discredited and dismissed only because of his race. Robinson realized that he was more qualified than most applicants, a fact that only made him more determined to succeed in gaining entry.[67]

Meanwhile, popular interest in aviation among all Americans, both black and white, had grown throughout the United States during the late 1920s. After Robinson first formed the Aero Study Club in Chicago 1927, he organized the Brown Eagle Aero Club only two years later, after the great stock market crash in 1929. These were the first black flying clubs in Chicago's history. Most significant in historical terms, though not generally acknowledged, Robinson's aero clubs predated "a small group of [African American] aviation enthusiasts, led by William Powell— one of the first black pilots [who] organized the Bessie Coleman Aero Club in Los Angeles, California to promote aviation in the black community. On Labor Day in 1931 it sponsored the first all-black air show in the United States."[68]

Despite being rejected by the all-white Curtiss-Wright Aeronautical School, Robinson was determined not to be denied and went on the offensive. Boldly, he requested to see the president in person. He met with the school's head, Director L. M. Churbuck, catching him by surprise in his office. Robinson would have to win over Churbuck if he ever wanted to realize his dream. Despite no positive result emerging from the initial meeting, Robinson was not discouraged. He continued to see Director Churbuck, a native Canadian, at every opportunity, appealing his case with an arsenal of subtle charm, undeniable reason, and skilled diplomacy that would eventually prove irresistible. At last Churbuck buckled. He allowed Robinson entry into the school as a janitor to work on the weekends, when the aviation ground school courses for white students were conducted.

Churbuck wanted no trouble at his school. He cautioned the young man that he would encounter resistance from Southern students. Robinson ignored the warning, sensing more positive developments than negative. After all, he already knew a good deal about Southern whites. His childhood in Mississippi helped to prepare him for encountering racism at Curtiss-Wright.[69]

Determined to make the most of this once-in-a-lifetime opportunity, Robinson reasoned that he could continue to operate his automobile repair garage through the week, while working as a janitor at Curtiss-Wright at night on the weekends, and continuing to gain additional flying hours to qualify for his private pilot's license at Acres Airport. If he could not officially beat the Jim Crow system to gain entry as a student, he was determined to be at least initially connected with the school regardless of how lowly the position. This minor moral victory—no small accomplishment in itself—was significant. With one foot in the door, he was taking the first steps of his larger plan to eventually fulfill his aviation ambitions.[70]

Robinson's plan for entry was similar to that employed by Tuskegee's founder, Booker T. Washington, to enter Hampton Institute. When the head teacher declined him entry into the school as a student, he persisted until she finally relented. She then gave Washington the menial task of cleaning a classroom. Washington "had the feeling that in a large measure my future depended upon the impression I made upon the teacher in the cleaning of that room."[71] Both Washington and Robinson had found an enterprising way to ensure a better future for themselves by first accepting janitorial positions—humiliating work for two men of promise, but only additional fuel for their desire to succeed.[72]

3

BREAKING DOWN MORE
RACIAL BARRIERS

ROBINSON WAS DETERMINED to make the most of his new position as a nighttime janitor on weekends at the all-white Curtiss-Wright Aeronautical School. Attending this school had been Robinson's goal since leaving Detroit.

During the early summer of 1929, the two most legendary aviation business names in the United States, Curtiss Aeroplane and Motor Corporation and the Wright Aeronautical Corporation, had come together in one of the largest corporate mergers at that point in American History.[1] Robinson was determined to spend as much time as possible around the faculty members and instructors, whose aeronautical expertise had made Curtiss-Wright the premier aviation educational institution in the land.

Inside the stately halls and quiet classrooms, Robinson acted like a sponge. He was on a personal mission to learn everything that he could as a passive, but extremely observant onlooker. Carefully calculated as part of his overall strategy, his quiet, unassuming presence was initially overlooked. Robinson was thus able to make ugly racial stereotypes work in his favor, transforming them into positives.[2]

No one questioned or suspected anything out of the ordinary while Robinson was busily cleaning the classrooms and washing the windows at the school on weekend evenings when classes with white students were in session. He maintained a low profile and quietly swept the floor at the back of the class while soaking up every word, thought, and argument bantered around the classroom. Robinson closed his automobile repair garage in the late afternoon, and then raced to the Curtiss-Wright Aeronautical School to clean all the classrooms except the one where the class was to be held. Then, he worked ever so slowly, listening to all that was said.

Robinson's close attention to detail was especially focused when teachers lectured on the complexities of aeronautical science and the most technical aspects of flight. School friend Harry Charles Tartt described how Robinson "was always cleaning classroom floors at lecture time."[3] When the class took a break, Robinson remained behind to copy the lecture notes, especially drawings and equations, from the blackboard. Fortunately, no one paid much attention to this young, good-natured black janitor from faraway Mississippi. Thanks to his color, Robinson became invisible.

Month after month, Robinson continued to soak up knowledge. The unobservant white instructors unwittingly allowed him a greater opportunity to listen and observe. And, whenever possible, Robinson reinforced his clever ruse by being excessively polite in the Southern tradition, to ensure that his presence would cause no irritation or draw the spotlight.

After carefully targeting those he deemed as the most open-minded, Robinson began to casually talk to the most approachable students about various aspects of mechanics and aviation. The fact that this young janitor could talk with intelligence and at length about some of the most complex technical intricacies of mechanics, aeronautical science, and airplane engines must have surprised these white students. Robinson impressed a chosen few white students with the extent of his knowledge. In doing so, he gradually gained their admiration. As Robinson had hoped, a common love of aviation began to overcome racial differences, forging a bond between the young white students and the older black janitor. Robinson shortly even began to "assist them with certain mechanical problems."[4]

Robinson made such steady progress that "the students asked him why he didn't join the classes. Bashfully, he explained the color problem."[5]

With interpersonal skill and careful diplomacy, Robinson thus broke the rigid color barrier with these Curtiss-Wright students in a friendly, informal manner. Even though these white students hailed from upper class backgrounds and large, all-white urban areas in the North, Robinson, a small town product from the Deep South, established a common bond that transcended color and class based upon a mutual passion for aviation.

But Robinson wanted to achieve much more. After learning to what extent he could impress the white students, he began to reason that if he could cause white students to admire, if not respect, the breath of his technical expertise, then perhaps he also could similarly impress the esteemed instructors at Curtiss-Wright. And if he could win the respect of the white faculty instructors, then might this achievement eventually open the door for his official entry into the school as a student?

When the school closed at night, Robinson had the classrooms all to himself. He learned from the aeronautical science equations the instructors had left on the blackboards. The knowledge-hungry Robinson also scrutinized lecture notes left on faculty desks. And the classrooms contained seemingly countless aviation books, which he hungrily devoured.

Ironically, even though no one realized it, Robinson might well have been the most dedicated student at the Curtiss-Wright Aeronautical School. Even his lowly status and janitorial position fueled Robinson's desire to study harder. Whenever possible, John laid down his broom or mop to derive as much information from textbooks, lecture notes, and other papers as possible, gaining more detailed knowledge of aeronautical science that provided him with the education that Jim Crow society had so unfairly denied him.[6]

Because of what he had learned, only within "a few weeks, Robinson had won the confidence of the instructors and the students with his skills."[7] Not long thereafter, as recalled by friend Janet Harmon Bragg, Robinson's "penchant for working with machines frequently found him [tinkering] with motors and doing other things about the place usually done by the mechanics" of the aeronautical school.[8]

Various accounts exist as to exactly how Robinson finally gained official entry to the school as a student. According to Reverend Tartt, Robinson was eventually allowed to enroll, to appease students and instructors who had befriended him, because top school officials never really expected this young African American to succeed. One skeptical senior faculty member even had made a bargain with Robinson that the instructor never expected to be fulfilled: if Robinson first passed the examination for the aviation ground course, then he could gain entry into the school as a student. Indeed, "Believing this black would fail, the school good-naturedly allowed him to take the test. Robinson passed with flying colors."[9]

With "Robinson's exhibition of mechanical skills, Mr. Churbuck relented," allowing the young black man from Mississippi the unprecedented opportunity to become a student. Additionally, some evidence suggests that Robinson's employer, Emil Mack, was behind the threat of a lawsuit for his employee to gain entry into the school. Regardless, Robinson now planned to enroll in the flight instruction and the aircraft mechanics courses.[10]

Bragg theorized on the dilemma faced by the school at this time: "In the field of aviation, officials of aeronautical schools were faced with the questions: Shall we permit the Negro to enter the new and promising field? If we do, how far will he go? It would be unfair to say that they concluded a Negro wouldn't go far, and that they might as well accept his money for the efforts, which they felt sure would be futile. Perhaps that is true! Perhaps they thought a Negro would find the task too difficult, become disgusted and quit cold. If this was the impression [then when] Curtiss officials got to Robinson, they were badly mistaken. Future events proved this to be unlikely, because Robinson eventually became one of the best-liked individuals connected with the school."[11]

At long last and after so much effort, Robinson walked confidently into his first class after having been officially admitted as a full time student. And because he had already won over so many teachers and students, including the director, he did not face a thoroughly hostile environment. Nevertheless, Robinson's "acceptance at the time was not [met completely] with 'open arms.'"[12]

Without connections of any kind, Robinson was able to directly influence Director Churbuck, the head of the Curtiss-Wright Aeronautical School, who eventually became a believer in the possibilities for blacks in aviation. Initially having been set against the entry of African Americans in his school, Churbuck's views were changed forever by Robinson's determination and arguments.[13]

Many challenges yet remained for the school's first black student, however. Robinson already knew he would have to work twice as hard as anyone else precisely because of his color. Robinson proved so exceptional in all technical aviation aspects, however, that he literally forced the school not only to accept him as a student but also to embrace him as an equal, because his aeronautical expertise already had demonstrated his equality.[14]

Nevertheless, Robinson yet faced a good many personal slights from some of the Southern students. They attempted to deliberately provoke Robinson, who smartly refused to take the bait that might have caused him to get kicked out of school. One sympathetic instructor, Jack Snydor, intervened to keep the most racist white students in check. He angrily "lectured the white students on Robinson's achievements. . . . Attitudes changed, and [Robinson soon graduated] with high honors."[15]

But fortunately, Robinson faced only relatively minor racial provocations. Though no doubt infuriating, such incidents were relatively insignificant compared to what he had seen or experienced in the Deep South and his own hometown. As a mature adult, Robinson easily overlooked these racial slights. He refused to allow his lofty aviation vision to be dampened by thoughtless words, overt prejudice, and ignorance that he had seen his entire life.[16]

Robinson could also easily overlook the racial slights because he was putting his newly acquired aviation knowledge to good use in the black community. He shared his aeronautical expertise with the students of his aero club, which met on Sundays.[17]

After his successful first flight on February 1, 1930, Robinson continued to acquire additional flying hours at Acres Airport in order to qualify for his private pilot's license. He also continued to repair the motorcycles and automobiles of white owners and patrons of the airport for free in exchange for additional flying hours.[18]

Therefore, in a relatively short time, Robinson became a highly proficient and experienced flyer and mechanic. In the words of a member of Robinson's Brown Eagle Aero Club, "By th[is] time Johnny had grown daring [as] he would fly anything that would turn a propeller."[19]

But Robinson was determined to become so proficient in aeronautical science and aviation that he hoped to eventually qualify as a mechanical instructor at the Curtiss-Wright Aeronautical School.[20]

In May 1931 Robinson graduated at the top of his class, after two years of intense study. As the first black student and graduate at Curtiss-Wright Aeronautical School, Robinson now became the proud owner of a certificate as a master mechanic of aviation.[21]

His own success was not enough, however. Robinson wanted to open the doors for other African Americans to study aviation. He, therefore, went repeatedly to Director Churbuck's office in relentless attempts to convince him "to give other members of his Race an opportunity to study aviation." This was no small undertaking. Robinson had to convince the school's head "that the Negro is capable of learning anything and can make good at it." Robinson's audacious proposal shocked Churbuck, who was once again "taken by surprise" by Robinson's nerve and unprecedented vision. Director Churbuck informed Robinson that he needed "time to think over the matter." Knowing that this was Churbuck's way of saying no, Robinson then diplomatically "pleaded with Mr. Churbuck not to delay his answer very long." Robinson persisted in his efforts and once again steadily wore down Churbuck's resistance. The director now allowed Robinson to teach aviation and "instruct other black students if they recruited enough of them for a class."[22] If Robinson "could get twenty-five Negro students, he would start a class."[23]

Robinson eagerly accepted Churbuck's challenge. Indeed, "this seemed like pie to Johnny. Just twenty-five students. Why, he could get 125," or so he believed.[24] Bragg never forgot how he tirelessly "canvassed the neighborhoods of the South Side to urge blacks to get into aviation, whether as airplane mechanics or pilots."[25]

However, Robinson discovered that finding young black men and women with a burning passion for aviation equal to his own was not as easy as he had thought. It was not that an interest in aviation did not exist in the black community. It was that few people of color believed such a bold proposition was even possible. After all, the citizens of Bronzeville knew the Curtiss-Wright Aeronautical School was reserved for whites only. Therefore, many cynical, streetwise African Americans on the South Side felt that Robinson's seemingly outlandish proposition to teach black students aviation at Curtiss-Wright was a scam of some kind, and remained wary.

As Bragg explained, "The Negro was skeptical; I was myself until I went down to the school and saw for myself. He toiled day and night trying to get the twenty-five students. He showed an aviation [motion] picture and gave lectures to various clubs and churches, canvassed from house to house, contacting anybody who looked as if he might be the least bit interested in aviation."[26]

Robinson was forced to become more innovative in his recruitment strategies. He developed the idea of advertising his future aviation class in the *Chicago Defender*. Before she visited the school in person, Bragg had "read in the *Chicago Defender* about aviation ground-school classes that were to be held for blacks at the Aeronautical University, formerly a Curtiss Wright [Aeronautical] school."[27]

Robinson was also able to draw prospective students from the social group of aviation friends and associates, especially members of his Brown Eagle Aero Club. They had begun meeting informally at either Robinson's home or automobile garage, or both, for some time by now, after he had cleaned the classrooms at Curtiss-Wright at night on the weekends. Robinson had shared invaluable technical aviation knowledge month after month to aero club members. In fact, he had already become an inspirational teacher of aviation for African Americans.[28]

Finally, in Bragg's words, "It took him exactly six months to get about twenty students [and] after a couple of months more had passed, he finally got the agreed number of students."[29]

Most important, Robinson finally demonstrated to Director Churbuck and officials of the school that a previously untapped resource of potential students existed right under their noses—ambitious black youths, both men and women, from the South Side who, like Robinson, were fascinated by aviation. Robinson's efforts thus appealed not only to a sense of fairness, but also to the school's future growth and enhanced economic possibilities.

Significantly, Robinson also simultaneously proved to the school's officials there was a definite need for a black aviation instructor at the school. By this means, Robinson took advantage of Jim Crow's societal divisions, proving that a black instructor was necessary both to attract and teach African American students to ensure additional funds for the school's coffers. And who could possibly be more qualified to instruct these black students of Chicago's South Side than the school's first black graduate, the bright, articulate Robinson?[30]

As Bragg explained, Robinson's personal success in acquiring the required number of students and in breaking down yet another racial barrier loomed large: "He was made a member of the aeronautical faculty [and now would] not go back to the university as a janitor [or student]—the only member of his Race who ever held the position on any of the universities of the Curtiss-Wright schools."[31]

As promised, Director Churbuck appointed Robinson as assistant instructor for night classes for the school's first African American students. It was now Robinson's task to transform these eager young men and women into competent aircraft mechanics and future pilots. Robinson was now paid—another first for an African American—to teach aviation mechanics and the principles of flight at the most prestigious aeronautical school in the United States. Once again he accomplished what was seemingly impossible in the dark age of Jim Crow.[32]

Almost single-handedly, Robinson ensured that Curtiss-Wright Aeronautical School, which later changed its name to the Aeronautical University of Chicago, would have not only its first black graduate and instructor, but also the school's first all-black class for the fall of 1931. This was the first black aviation class in United States history. What was equally astounding about this development was the fact that it occurred so soon after Robinson's spring graduation in the same year.

Indeed, this historic milestone was a tribute to John's determination to promote aviation in the black community. Robinson was convinced there was a permanent place for black youth in aviation. Thanks to John's efforts, his black students would also benefit from the same facilities, tools, and technical textbooks and aviation training manuals used by white students.[33]

The first black class of 1931–1932 at the Curtiss-Wright Aeronautical School consisted of thirty-five African Americans, including six black women. Only eight students graduated from this intense ground school training after one year of instruction, thanks in no small part to Robinson's high expectations. A most demanding instructor and a perfectionist, Robinson fully expected his students to work as hard as himself. Meeting every Tuesday and Thursday evening after his own work day managing his automobile garage with Earnize, Robinson, who wore a business suit, taught aviation to students in white work coveralls.

Two remarkable women were among the graduating class, Janet Harmon Bragg and Willa Beatrice Brown. Attractive, vivacious, and blessed with high cheekbones befitting a model, the ravishing Brown had been a teacher at Roosevelt High School in Gary, Indiana, before moving to the bright lights of Chicago and then quite by accident meeting Robinson, who was smitten at first sight like most men. Following in the footsteps of her idol Bessie Coleman, the intelligent, personable Brown became, in 1937, the first African American woman to earn her pilot's license in the United States, and was later the first black woman to earn a commercial pilot's license.

From the beginning, Robinson was open-minded toward women aviators at a time when the majority of males, both black and white, were not. Therefore, he had opened the door at the school for aviation enthusiasts of both sexes and ensured that it would stay wide open. Robinson was the first African American instructor to train black women in aviation mechanics at an established aeronautical school in the United States.[34]

Like Brown and another woman in the class, Amber Porter, Bragg had also been inspired by the barnstorming Bessie Coleman. Bragg was the first woman among the twenty-five African Americans students Robinson recruited, and she later emerged as an aviation leader in her own right.[35]

A registered nurse and a proud graduate of Spelman Seminary (later Spelman College), in Atlanta, Georgia, Bragg, like Robinson, had departed the Deep South for the better opportunities available in Chicago. She described her entry into the mysterious world of aviation when she became a student of Robinson's: "Classes were held two evenings a week. I drove to the first class at 14th Street and Michigan Avenue."[36]

Another promising member of Robinson's first class at Curtiss-Wright was an enthusiastic teenager named Harold Hurd. He and three friends had been attempting to build an airplane on their own since 1929, "planning to teach ourselves to fly it," explained Hurd. When Robinson heard of this grass roots aviation experiment, he recruited Hurd and his friend William Jackson to his class. Thanks to what he learned about aviation in the prewar period and especially from Robinson, whom he long viewed as a "Big Brother," Hurd became a fine aviator and served with the Tuskegee Airmen as a sergeant major during World War II.[37]

Clearly, this period was a heady time for both Robinson and his new class of enthusiastic young students, who were making racial history in Chicago.[38]

Like their charismatic instructor from faraway Gulfport, the students relished the fact that they were breaking new ground and shattering old racial stereotypes and barriers. In Bragg's words, "Our class was well educated and eager, anxious to learn all we could during the winter months [of 1931–1932] so that when warmer weather [spring of 1932] came we actually could learn to fly" from Robinson.[39] Bragg was impressed by their young instructor because "Robinson was tall and muscular, ebullient, adventurous, and seemingly carefree, but nevertheless also dedicated to safety."[40]

Another promising student of Robinson's 1931–1932 class was his old friend Cornelius Robinson Coffey, who later established his own flight training school, the Coffey School of Aeronautics at Harlem Airport, on Chicago's South Side. Coffey would eventually marry one of Robinson's students in this first class at the Wright School, the enchanting Willa B. Brown.[41]

When Robinson began his service in Ethiopia in 1935–1936, Coffey became the primary leader of black aviation in Chicago. His aviation school—like Tuskegee Institute, Hampton Institute, and other black institutions, such as Howard University in Washington, D.C.—would become part of the Civilian Pilot Training Program, later the War Training Service Program, which trained African Americans as pilots for combat, the future Tuskegee Airmen.[42]

Coffey's eventual crowning aviation achievement would not have been possible without Robinson's initial aviation efforts in the 1930s. The latter successfully "converted [Coffey] from an auto mechanic to an airplane and engine mechanic and interested him in becoming a flyer."[43]

From beginning to end, Robinson's aviation ground course remained most demanding. Relying upon traditional values of hard work learned from his family and at the Tuskegee Institute, Robinson was strong on discipline in both his personal life and his work, especially when it came to aviation. He was an exacting taskmaster who demanded the most diligent efforts from his students, both male and female.

Bragg recalled how, "Robinson excelled as an instructor in aviation because of his keen insistence on real discipline." Robinson taught courses such as meteorology, aerodynamics, navigation, and civil air regulations. Even though the attrition rate of the first black class was high, at nearly 70 percent, only the best and brightest survived Robinson's uncompromising high standards to graduate. Clearly, these graduates were the cream of the crop who enjoyed impressive aviation careers in later life.[44]

Bragg also described what she and the other students learned from Robinson: "After meteorology, in which we learned that clouds were not slushy snow but a real danger to pilots, especially when towering cumulus clouds could be followed by a violent summer storm, we studied navigation. With no road signs in the skies, we had to learn how to get from one place to another and back to where we started, using both road maps and aeronautical charts. Then there were the rules and regulations to learn, and aerodynamics. Parts of the airplane, and how each work with the other to keep us in the air, brought new terms which, I think, we all learned easily because already we had become dedicated [and] we learned. The training has remained invaluable to me."[45]

After passing Robinson's grueling aviation requirements, which were far more rigorous than any student had initially expected, the first black class at the Curtiss-Wright Aeronautical School graduated in the spring of 1932, only one year after Robinson's own graduation. For ample good reason, Robinson was proud of these dedicated black men and women who attained certifications as aircraft mechanics.[46]

But Robinson was destined to break yet another color barrier: by the beginning of the 1931—1932 school year , Robinson taught not only other African Americans but also white and Asian students.[47]

The presence of these Chinese students indicated how war clouds were beginning to descend upon the world. After the Japanese invasion of Manchuria in 1931, Chinese students came to Curtiss-Wright Aeronautical School for aviation training. Thanks in part to Robinson's efforts, these Chinese students later evolved into "the nucleus of the Chinese Royal Air Force in China's defense against Japanese aggression."[48]

One student remembered Robinson taught "classes two or three times a week, with attendance good for a time. He taught master mechanics, aeroplane theory, private pilot ground course, limited commercial ground course, meteorology, parachute, navigation, and aeroplane instruments. He was classed as one of the best instructors on the staff. He taught white and yellow races, as well as the black."[49]

Meanwhile, Robinson continued to promote aviation in the black community at large. From the initial Aero Study Club and then the Brown Eagle Aero Club,

he then organized the first official black flying organization in Chicago, the Challenger Aero Club in 1931.

This latter organization included Robinson's Curtiss-Wright students, both
men and women, such as Bragg, Bill Jackson, and Hurd. Bragg wrote: "Our whole
Aeronautical University class was so enthusiastic about the prospect of flying that
we formed the Challenger Aero Club." Brown and another woman, Doris Murphy,
were also enthusiastic members of Robinson's aviation club, as was Dale L. White.
Grover C. Nash was yet another gifted member of Robinson's aviation organization. Later, Nash became a respected instructor at Dunbar Vocational School in
Chicago, named for famed black poet Paul Laurence Dunbar. The versatile Nash
would become the first African American to fly the U.S. airmail over the expansive
prairies of Illinois in 1938.[50]

The Challenger Aero Club had grown out of the Brown Eagle Aero Club and
those first early informal gatherings—the Aero Study Club—between Robinson
and his eager students at his automobile repair garage on East 47th Street, after the
Tuesday and Thursday evening classes at Curtiss-Wright ended. Here, Robinson's
aviation classes at the school had continued informally, with students possessing
more time to ask detailed questions than the relatively short class-time periods in
the evenings usually allowed. Young male and female students discussed all aspects
of aviation until the late night hours. The Challenger Aero Club continued this
educational aviation tradition. Bragg described how: "Johnny Robinson was elected
as the association's first president."[51]

All the while, Robinson became more proficient as a flyer himself. He learned
to fly a wide variety of aircraft, gaining additional expertise. Before long Robinson
"could fly them all" at Curtiss-Wright Aeronautical School and the Acres Airport.
To gain additional flying hours to qualify for a pilot's license, Robinson had maneuvered to secure "a job at a South Side flying field [Acres Airport]. Instead of receiving his pay in money, Robinson took flying time as compensation in order to build
up flying hours with the view of qualifying to comply with the Federal regulations
governing flying." After first gaining his private pilot's license—no. 26,042—in
1930, Robinson later earned his transport pilot's license.[52]

With these hard-earned flying licenses in hand and with the Curtiss-Wright
officials so "impressed with Robinson's flying skills," he found "a job taking planes
from one state to another for the Curtiss Flying Service."[53]

By this time, Robinson had become the leading black aviator in Chicago. His
flying skills far exceeded those of the average aviator because he never ceased learn-

ing and accepting new challenges. Bragg explained how Robinson "went up on the 'slightest provocation.' He was a daredevil from the start, principally due to his experience as a performer on the motorcycle in a circus, where he performed the 'Death Valley' act."[54]

The Challenger Aero Club, which later would become known as the Challenger Air Pilots' Association, was only one part of his larger aviation vision. Robinson was on a personal mission to transform Chicago into the leading center of black aviation. Additionally, he viewed his Brown Eagle Aero Club and then his Challenger Aero Club as part of an overall strategic plan to lay a solid "foundation for the ultimate creation of [the first] black airline company" in the history of the United States. An ideal location, Acres Airport provided the necessary facilities for the pilot training and aviation mechanical training of Robinson's club members.

Without warning, however, Acres Airport was sold to a land developer, ending the cozy relationship that Robinson had established with the airport's white owners. A separate airport for black aviators was now absolutely necessary. As one of his students explained, "This young man, knowing what a hard time he had at the airport, and knowing that some of the fellows would not be as careful with things around the field as he was, wanted them to have an airport of their own [and therefore] searched around to find one, and finally located one at the little all-Race town of Robbins, Illinois, [but] the field was not very large."[55]

Robinson met with the mayor of the small black community of Robbins, Illinois, just south of Chicago. An adroit negotiator, he struck a deal to use an old airfield located on vacant city property that he had scouted out and deemed suitable. He would have to pay rent money to the city of Robbins. This presented yet another obstacle, because Robinson was low on funds. Quite simply, notes Janet Harmon Bragg, he "did not have the money to pay the rent of the field, nor money to buy materials to build a hangar." Consequently, Bragg went into a partnership with him to get the field and she, Coffey, and Albert Crosby, a Challenger Aero Club member, collected materials to build the hangar after Robinson drew the hangar's blueprint. Unfortunately, only he could read the blueprint, so when Robinson was not on the field, the work on the hangar had to cease.[56]

He and his Challenger Aero Club members, in Bragg's words, constructed an airport almost from scratch: "We had to supply all the time, labor, and materials. The land had to be leveled, trees cut down, rocks moved, and ditches filled for a northeast-southwest runway."[57]

Located in Cook County, Illinois, about fifteen miles southwest of the heart of Chicago, Robbins had been first developed as a suburban community for working–class African Americans. The first inhabitants had taken up residence in the area in 1892. But most blacks had moved to Robbins during the period between 1911 and 1917, thanks in part to the jobs created by the World War I. The first black suburb of Chicago, Robbins officially became a village in December 1917, with more than three hundred residents. Here, the bottomlands and prairie made for an ideal landing site for aircraft.

Under Robinson's leadership, his group of black men and women aviators embarked upon the project of carving out a primitive, but suitable, airstrip on the flat terrain of a wide field. In addition, from new materials recently purchased, Robinson and the others constructed a wooden hangar that he had designed. Robbins's black mayor assisted with some timely support to justify the rental fee, sending out lawn mowers to cut down the high grass and weeds, while also providing some gravel for the lengthy runway.

Bragg described the bonding experience that forged greater solidarity among Robinson and his aviation enthusiasts with the united effort, describing how "every Saturday, Sunday, and holiday we met in Robbins to work. I often took lunch for everyone: hot dogs, which we cooked over a fire, potato salad, lemonade or pop. Sometimes our Robbins neighbors helped with the work; at times it seemed like we had help from the whole little village. Albert Crosby, one of our club members, used his truck to haul cinders from a railroad yard. We used the cinders, the residue from coal burned by steam locomotives of the period, for the runway; these had to be spread, leveled, and tamped down. As I remember, Crosby's truck often would go only in reverse! It was back-breaking work, but we all loved it."[58]

Robinson's new airport, now the headquarters of his Challenger Aero Club, was finally completed in January 1933. The airfield, however, had to be approved by the Department of Commerce before it could be used. Fortunately, the new airfield was okayed "as an approved air field, the only accredited flying field owned and operated by Negroes in the United States."[59]

While continuing to operate his automobile repair shop with his wife, Earnize, Robinson now also "managed" the Robbins Airport. In the years ahead, he would continue to train "scores of pilots, mechanics, navigators, and parachute jumpers who became the nucleus of [the] Chicago-based national association of black aviation enthusiasts" of the future Challenger Air Pilots' Association.

Naturally, the first priority of Robinson and his aero club were to secure a number of aircraft, but money was tight with the American nation caught in the grips of the Great Depression. Fortunately, the irrepressible Bragg rose to the fore. In her own words, "Toward the end of summer, it occurred to us that we didn't have an airplane for our new airport so, with the advice of Coffey and Robinson, I bought a used airplane, an International [Model F-17] with a XV-OX-5 90-horsepower [water-cooled and eight-cylinder] engine, from a man named Freitag. I didn't even see the plane first, for which I think I paid $500, because I trusted Coffey and Robinson. It was a biplane, painted red, with two open cockpits and the barest of instrumentation, only a compass, an altimeter, and tachometer, [and] the fuselage framework was wood, covered with fabric."[60]

Bragg and other members of Robinson's aero club viewed the first flight of the little red biplane with considerable pride. She described how, "It was a glorious day when Coffey and Robinson flew my plane to our new airport, but it also was getting cold, the end of the summer flying season. We would have to wait through the winter [of 1932–1933] before we actually could learn to fly."[61]

Bragg, along with other Challenger Aero Club members, learned to fly during the spring of 1933, after the runway and airport at Robbins were completed. The serious-minded young man from south Mississippi bestowed sage advice as well as his own life philosophies that served him well: "Now that we have an approved flying field of our own, we have a hard task before us. We have got to work on a very strict basis because if any kind of accident happens, it will kill everything I have tried to do. I am the operator of this field. Don't take anything for granted. Working on the planes here will not be any guesswork. When in doubt, ask me. There will be no acrobatic flying over the field. You have decided to go into aviation. It is nothing easy. You must make up your mind to put the necessary time and effort into it. You have to follow my instructions or you don't need me, and you must learn to fly not passably, but well. If a man has veritable genius for flying, if he is cool, confident, fearless, and if he performs feats of unexampled brilliance, still, if he lacks common sense, he will not make a good flyer. The law of gravity makes no provision for first offenders. When you get into the air, you either fly or you do not fly, and if you don't fly you will be embarrassed. So, I am warning you to be careful of everything and watch your step."[62]

No one benefited more from Robinson's diligent aviation instruction than Bragg. As she recalled, "As an instructor, I think he excelled any pilot. He was always anxious about his students. When you did anything wrong pertaining to flying, there was no exception to the rules. I never forgot the bawling out he gave me . . . I being the only woman flyer in the class at this time, had had my way about everything. One day Johnny and I were flying directly west and the sun was in my eyes. I could not see the horizon and I started turning around. He said, 'Keep to the West.' I kept flying in another direction. He said again, 'Keep to the West.' I still ignored his command. Finally, he said, 'I'll take the controls now' [and] flew back to the field and landed. I knew what was coming, so I tried to put in a winsome smile, but it did not do any good. He said, 'You will fly as I tell you or you will get another instructor. Here's your plane log book and your pilot's log book. I know several good white pilots you can get to teach you. You think I am not competent enough. When you think you can fly my way I will be too glad to teach you.'

"I told him the sun was in my eyes. He said, 'Yes, I know the sun was in your eyes, and incidentally we were flying the same direction and in the same plane. I knew just how long I wanted you to fly in the sun, which is part of flying and experience you need, and if you are going to do the instructing, I will sit in the back cockpit from now on until you think I am able to fly alone.' He walked off the field and left me out there with the plane to get back to the hangar as best I could. From then on he didn't have any more trouble with me. . . . He was the best aviator [that I or any of his students] have ever met."[63]

After gaining more than thirty hours of flight time, Bragg embarked upon her own determined quest to earn her private pilot's license. Robinson was the man who had recruited her as a novice aviation student and served as her expert flight instructor. He was by her side to bestow guidance, advice, and encouragement. In this way, Robinson relived his own thrill of first flight through the progress of his young students.[64]

As Bragg explained, "When I was ready to take the test for a private pilot's license, in a rented plane, Johnny Robinson accompanied me to Pal-Waukee Airport, north of the city [of Chicago], where I took the test and passed with no problems."[65]

Thereafter, Bragg, who had been an RN, became known as "The Flying Nurse." She also wrote a number of informative columns about African Americans in aviation for the *Chicago Defender*.[66]

With the onset of warmer weather in 1933 Robinson's "airport at Robbins was becoming quite popular. Sundays, when the weather permitted, friends, relatives, and strangers wound their way through the crooked roads to reach the Robbins airport. Some wanted to take a ride with Johnny [Robinson] after they watched him make a perfect take-off and then later land gracefully. The field operated fine all the summer and fall."[67]

Even though the African American community of Robbins and the all-black airport were separated from whites, racism occasionally raised its ugly head. The residents of nearby white townships simply "did not like the idea of Negroes flying directly over their houses." When forced down prematurely with mechanical problems before reaching Robinson's airport, some black flyers were promptly arrested by white authorities. Robinson was almost arrested by white policemen on trumped up charges of "flying too low, or anything for an excuse to arrest him, but it never made him angry, and he always smiled about it," according to Bragg. Fortunately, the mayor or the chief of police at Robbins "always came to Johnny's rescue." Therefore, the support of the Robbins community "gave the Aero club a sense of security at Robbins Airport. Members of the club could focus on sharpening their skills, instead of worrying about racial obstacles."[68]

Robinson also flew as a barnstormer to promote black aviation, his aero club, and the airport at Robbins. Robinson honored historic breakthroughs in black aviation—unknown to disinterested whites—in formal ceremonies to generate interest. Only two years after Robinson began flying, for instance, two young pilots dreamed they could become the first African Americans to successfully complete a transcontinental flight. Known affectionately as the Two Flying Hobos, James Herman Banning, the barnstorming pilot who was the first African American to earn a pilot's license from the Department of Commerce, and Thomas C. Allen, the capable mechanic who, like Banning, also hailed from Los Angeles, completed the first transcontinental flight by black pilots in 1932.[69]

Banning's life paralleled Robinson's own life in many ways. From Oklahoma, he had journeyed to Chicago in the early 1920s to fulfill his aviation ambitions. Banning, however, failed to gain entry into a Chicago aviation school. Not to be denied, he moved to Des Moines, Iowa, to learn how to fly from an open-minded white army officer. As a cruel fate would have it, Banning was killed in an airplane crash only one year after his historic transcontinental flight.[70]

Meanwhile, the Challenger Aero Club continued to thrive under Robinson's tutelage, leadership, and inspiration. The popular club soon possessed three aircraft, with two owned by Robinson and Coffey, and the other by Bragg. Then, member Earl Renfroe purchased his own airplane. But another setback occurred when the

Chinese Curtiss-Wright student pilots wrecked Robinson's plane either in taking-off or attempting to land. According to Bragg, when Robinson "returned to the flying field one day [he] found his plane had burned to ashes, there being left only the framework and that was beyond repair. . . . [Robinson] had rented the plane to some Chinese boys to fly."[71]

More bad luck befell Robinson's Challenger Aero Club when the high winds of a spring thunderstorm swirled over the airfield in early May 1933. The storm wrecked the hangar at the Robbins airport. Bragg remembered that, "the small hangar we had built at Robbins, which was difficult to get my plane in and out of because of the supports we put in, was blown down during a storm. Fortunately, Robinson had made arrangements with the white-run Harlem Airport in Oak Lawn [Illinois], another southern suburb, to use a small area on the south side of the field, [and] we erected a small building as our club's headquarters. It was a new beginning—an airport with much better runway lengths. . . . At Harlem we changed the name of the club to the Challenger Air Pilots' Association, but most of us continued to use the old name [Challenger Aero Club] for some time."[72]

Once again, Robinson came to the rescue. Indeed, after "the freak [May] storm came and blew the hanger down and destroyed the planes, [then] this was the end of the Robbins airport. No one was able to raise enough capital to have the field rebuilt [but] Johnny [Robinson], having a host of white aviator friends, contracted one of them and acquired the use of an airport. . . . It was located on 87th Street near Harlem. Johnny carried the whole gang with him."[73] At this time, Robinson benefited from his relationship with an influential white aviation friend of German heritage, Fred Schumaker. Identifying with the young, enthusiastic black flyers, Schumaker now allowed Robinson and his aviators to fly their aircraft in and out of his new Harlem airport at 87th Street and Harlem Avenue in Oak Lawn, Illinois.[74]

In May 1934 Robinson decided to fly down to his alma mater, Tuskegee Institute, on a special mission. Robinson's flight was to be no idle recreational excursion. He planned to fly into the heart of the Deep South in the attempt to convince the conservative Tuskegee Institute officials to embrace the new age of aviation, by offering aviation courses to black students.[75]

During this period, Robinson "was stationed at this field [Harlem] when he [planned to make] the trip to Tuskegee. It had always been his ambition to fly back to his alma mater during commencement," wrote Bragg.[76]

After doing what he could for African Americans in Chicago, Robinson was now determined that black youths across the United States should gain equal opportunities in the field of aviation. Quality aviation educational facilities for African American youth outside of Chicago were non-existent. Indeed, Robinson sought to "recreate the Curtiss-Wright experience at a Negro College that owned huge acres of land and a vocational program featuring automobile engine mechanics and welding. With Chicago as the hub, [Robinson] believed a Negro flight service company could prosper in the Midwest and the South. Since Tuskegee Institute had a strong program in auto mechanics and welding and owned enough acreage for an airport, Tuskegee was selected as the first Negro College to approach with the idea of initiating a flying school [because] Robinson also felt that his student affiliation with Tuskegee would be an advantage."[77]

With a publicist's and dreamer's intuition, Robinson's mission to Tuskegee Institute and lengthy "trip was timed with the graduation of the senior class of 1934, and was therefore a homecoming for Robinson, [who] felt that the flying demonstration and his status as an alumnus would be enough to convince Tuskegee President Robert Russa Moton to start an aviation school at Tuskegee Institute," as summarized in one modern work.[78]

Most of all, Robinson targeted Tuskegee Institute because an aviation program there would provide boundless opportunities to the next generation of African Americans. To plead his case as he had done to Director Churbuck to open the door to black aviation at the Curtiss-Wright Aeronautical School, he planned to meet with the school's leading officials, including President Moton, who headed the institute from 1915 to 1935. Tuskegee Institute was prepared for Robinson's arrival by air, after Captain Alvin J. Neely had already set up this important meeting with the school's leaders.[79]

Bragg explained that Robinson "and the boys worked hard on the plane [a two-seater International that Robinson had equipped with an extra fuel tank for the lengthy flight], getting it ready for inspection so that he would be able to fly down safely."[80]

But the flight southeast from Chicago to Tuskegee Institute was beset with risks from the beginning. The long distance flight to the Deep South was a daunting challenge for the Chicago aviators. In fact, Robinson now prepared for the third-longest cross-country flight ever embarked upon by African Americans.[81]

Bragg, who was present at the Robbins Airport with Robinson in the early morning of May 22, 1934, described the flight as it was about to take to the skies:

"Johnny was getting tired and disgusted [because] the plane was on the line and had been warmed up. Suddenly he hopped into it and gave it the guns. It was the take-off for Tuskegee."[82]

But "when he got to the end of the runaway and was ready to take-off, the motor stopped. Every aviator ran to see what was the trouble, [but] before they arrived . . . Johnny was out of the plane and turning the propeller." One of Robinson's students, Grover Nash, was to accompany him on the Tuskegee trip in another plane, a Buhl "Pup." Besides the mechanical problems, Robinson now suddenly encountered a personnel problem as well. Ironically, his good friend, the normally mild-mannered Coffey, was the source of the difficulties. Quite unexpectedly, "Coffey, who was to be the copilot and navigator for Johnny, became suddenly upset when he discovered that there was no parachute. He said he was afraid of falling down in the mountains of Alabama. Nash had taken off and circled the field several times while Johnny and Coffey were still arguing about the parachute." Nevertheless, in the end, Coffey "decided to go along with him, parachute or no parachute."[83] This is the first recorded incident that indicated a growing fissure between Robinson and Coffey's friendship.

Later, Bragg described the flight to Tuskegee and the obstacles encountered along the way: "Coffey and Robinson decided to fly to Tuskegee Institute in Alabama for Robinson's tenth class reunion. They hoped to persuade the faculty to start a flying school, with students learning to fly but also taking regular Tuskegee courses. They crashed their OX-6 powered International en route in Decatur, Alabama [in northcentral Alabama northwest of Tuskegee] but [Grover C.] Nash [whom Robinson had taught to fly] had been flying along with them in his new single-seat Buhl Pup and lent it to Robinson, who continued on to Tuskegee" on his own.[84]

Indeed, the take-off from Decatur proved more risky than the landing. While "the landing was well done . . . the take-off was made with great difficulty [because] the air was light and there was very little lift, [and] just as he was about to take off something happened and the plane crashed into a chimney of a nearby farm house and floundered down into a cotton field. The damage was considerable and this ended the flight to Tuskegee in the big plane [but then] Johnny flew Nash's plane the rest of the journey, while Coffey and Nash finished the trip to Tuskegee in a bus."[85] In the sparkling May sunshine, Robinson flew at full speed south to Gestow, a bright new aviation dream and vision.

4

Twin Dreams—Tuskegee and Ethiopia

On the hot afternoon of May 22, 1934, twenty-nine-year-old Robinson returned to his alma mater, Tuskegee Institute, in dramatic fashion.[1] He carried with him the bold vision for an all-black aviation school that would include an annual air show to promote aviation among black youth across the South. Robinson wanted to transform Tuskegee from a traditional school that provided mostly vocational training to one that offered the most advanced technical training possible.

In less than a decade, Tuskegee would serve as the center of black flight training during World War II. Hundreds of young African Americans would fly as military pilots in fighter aircraft, or as crewmen of the first black bomber unit in history, the 477th Bombardment Group (Medium), of the 332nd Fighter Group.[2]

At this time, even though Tuskegee Institute was the most highly respected school of higher learning for black Southerners, it was still trapped in a restrictive Jim Crow world. Here, the outdated dream of Tuskegee's founder, Booker T. Washington, only lifted up blacks within the narrow, confining framework of an oppressive racial system, ensuring their subordinate status in American society. Tuskegee's curriculum thus appealed to the white ruling class in the South because it prepared African Americans for inferior positions and places in society. Consequently, younger and more progressive black leaders, with whom Robinson agreed, increasingly criticized Tuskegee Institute.

After viewing his alma mater from the blue skies above, Robinson descended in his Buhl "Pup." He brought the one-seat monoplane down with the easy skill of an experienced flyer. An assembled crowd of spectators, students, teachers, and officials looked on in excitement and aticipation.[3]

The seemingly effortless grace with which Robinson landed his light sports airplane in a broad oat field made the landing look much easier than was the case. Charles A. Lindbergh described one such impromptu landing also in Mississippi in 1923, four years before his epic solo flight across the Atlantic: "An experienced pilot can see at a glance nearly everything necessary to know about a landing field. He can tell its size, the condition of the ground, height of grass or weeds, whether there are any rocks, holes, posts or ditches in the way, if the land is rough and rolling or flat and smooth; in short whether the field is suitable to land. The success of a barnstorming pilot of the old days was measured to a large extent by his artfulness in the choice of fields from which to operate."[4]

This was the first time that these young African American students, mostly from the rural South, had ever seen an aircraft flown by a black pilot.[5] To many black Southerners, the sight of a black flyer must have seemed miraculous.

According to historian Robert J. Jakeman, Robinson's landing in the field of oats at Tuskegee that May afternoon was historically significant, because it "marked the beginning of Tuskegee's first attempt to enter the air age."[6]

Indeed, Robinson sought to convince the provincial officials at Tuskegee Institute, especially President Robert Russa Moton, the school's second president, to become part of the aviation revolution.[7]

President Moton viewed aviation as a potential threat to a safe and comfortable status quo, however, to Tuskegee's traditional educational priorities, and perhaps even to his elevated position. Indeed, he was "too cautious in their adoption of modern vocational training that were considered highly technical, nonagricultural, and within the domain of white men."[8]

Colleague Cornelius Robinson Coffey felt that Tuskegee officials were reluctant about embracing aviation because they were concerned that white Alabamians would not tolerate blacks flying over their communities, "possibly angering the whites."[9]

Robinson was more successful in convincing future Tuskegee president Dr. Frederick Douglass Patterson, then the School of Agriculture's director, and other Tuskegee officials, that aviation could have a real role at Tuskegee. Robinson suggested the school build an airport to showcase black aviation talent, in addition to promoting the idea of an African American air show. Robinson knew that exhibitions of black flying skills would promote aviation to large numbers of African Americans across not only the South but also across America.[10]

In the end, Robinson's aviation initiative would upend the traditional and philosophical mindset of Tuskegee officials. The seed he planted eventually germinated to full flower during World War II. He convinced some of Tuskegee's top officials to see the future of black aviation by emphasizing that the institute could benefit from this vast untapped potential of African American students, the same argument he successfully employed at Curtiss-Wright.

Robinson pro-aviation arguments were reinforced by the fact that he was from the Deep South and was part of the Tuskegee family. Robinson exemplified the essence of Tuskegee's original purpose: an inspiring, positive model for how African Americans of determination could accomplish anything, with a good education. Robinson's own successful transformation from a small town Mississippian to the leading black pilot and teacher in Chicago was living proof for how blacks could succeed in aviation.[11]

By introducing the exciting new possibilities of aviation, he laid the initial foundation for the emergence of the Tuskegee Airmen in the early 1940s. In this sense, Robinson was in fact very much the father of the Tuskegee Airmen. Without Robinson's early and timely initiatives and example the Tuskegee Airmen might never have taken flight during World War II to fly into the pages of history.[12]

In the words of a local historian in Gulfport, Mississippi, "It was purely because of Robinson's accomplishments that Tuskegee was included in the Army's program to train pilots for World War II—black pilots [and most important Robinson] knocked down that barrier."[13]

Less than six months after Robinson's visit, the Tuskegee Institute took its first steps forward in directly supporting black aviation by promoting the September 1934 Pan-American Goodwill air tour of two gifted black pilots, Charles Alfred Anderson and Dr. Albert E. Forsythe. This was an initial, but important, step forward.[14]

In the words of Tuskegee Airmen historian Jakeman, "Robinson's flight highlighted dramatically for the Tuskegee community the growing black presence in aeronautics. This recognition of black interest and participation in aviation was perhaps crucial to Tuskegee's support of a proposal that came shortly after Robinson's flight."[15]

While Robinson was back in Chicago, Anderson and Forsythe reaped the benefits of his May trip to Tuskegee. These two flyers had already made history by becoming the first African American aviators to successfully complete a round-trip, transcontinental flight, from Atlantic City, New Jersey, to Los Angeles, California, in 1933. Born in Nassau, Bahamas, and raised in Jamaica, Forsythe, who possessed a medical degree from a Canadian university, and had a successful medical practice, was a Tuskegee graduate like Robinson. Pennsylvania-born Anderson, who was from the Shenandoah Valley, earned his private pilot license in 1929.[16]

On Tuskegee Institute's grounds, Anderson's and Forsythe's fine-looking aircraft, a Lambert Monocoupe, was officially christened the *The Spirit of Booker T. Washington* on September 15, 1934, less than four months after Robinson's arrival. Tuskegee now enthusiastically supported and raised funds for the popular aviation event. As Robinson had envisioned in May, Tuskegee's overall image was improved with its prestige linked to these aviation efforts.[17]

In addition to President Moton's address, the highlight of the ceremonies was a speech presented by Booker T. Washington's granddaughter, Nettie H. Washington. She tied the historic past of former slaves to the future for aviation-minded African Americans, and emphasized the importance of those members of the "Tuskegee Family" who were now daring aviators in America's skies. Washington especially paid tribute to Robinson, whom she described as a "licensed aviator connected with the Curtis[s] Flying School in Chicago."[18]

Also in attendance was Benjamin Oliver Davis Sr., the head of the military department at Tuskegee Institute. Seasoned by decades of service in the U.S. Army, he was an old buffalo soldier and a veteran of the Spanish-American War and the Philippine War.[19]

Davis would become America's first black general in the history of the United States Army. And, most important, his son, Benjamin Oliver Davis Jr., would serve as the leader of the famed Tuskegee Airmen during World War II.[20]

In the end, Tuskegee Institute embraced aviation with a passion and depth that would have been impossible without Robinson's May 1934 flight. Many African Americans now realized that "no investment of time and money [would be] so pregnant with such magnificent possible results to both Tuskegee and the Negro race in America" than aviation.[21] However, Tuskegee was initially frustrated by the failure of the Pan-American Goodwill flight, which ended with a crash in the West Indies, delaying "Tuskegee's entrance into the air age."[22]

Robinson's vigorous promotion of aviation to Tuskegee Institute's officials was destined to far outweigh the short-term negative impact of the Pan-African flight's failure. Tuskegee officials now viewed Robinson as the one African American aviator who could keep alive the future promise of aviation at the school.[23]

After his May 1934 flight to Tuskegee, Robinson continued his activities to promote aviation to black youth in the Chicago area, especially through the Challenger Aero Club. This association's popular activities included air show demonstrations, dances, dinners, and even parachute jumps by members. Friend Janet Harmon Bragg wrote how Robinson was somewhat discouraged immediately after flying from Tuskegee: "Returning to Chicago disgusted and disappointed over the crack-up [of his plane on the way to Tuskegee], he never forgot to keep his broad smile, which always seemed to make difficulties disappear. Before long Johnny had another plane and was flying again."[24]

When he first went to inspect the biplane for sale, Robinson deliberately took his time, viewing other aircraft with greater interest to mask his top priority. After inspecting each aircraft and asking a good many questions, Robinson then selected the Commandaire, seemingly out of consolation.

The white owner of the biplane then brought out the paperwork to formalize the transaction. A price was established, after Robinson drove down the cost by emphasizing the aircraft's defects. When the deal was complete, Robinson then shocked the owner by suddenly blurting out, "I have no money!" Instead of becoming angry at wasting so much time with a penniless, overly talkative young black man, the white owner was amazed by Robinson's sheer audacity. As if not understanding what Robinson had said, the owner asked, "you mean you come in here and want a plane but have no money?" Without hesitation or batting an eye, Robinson simply retorted, "That's Right!"

Robinson then convinced the owner that if he could purchase the aircraft now, he would pay for it later. The nation was mired in the Great Depression, and the owner needed money. Incredibly, Robinson left the airfield with not only pride in striking the deal but also a new airplane, the Commandaire, without paying a cent. As promised, he later paid the entire balance to the owner.[25]

In the end, the fierce May 1933 storm that had destroyed Robinson's airplane hanger at the Robbins Airport proved to be a blessing in disguise. Thanks to his connections with white aviators, he and his Challenger Air Pilots' Association found a better setting that was no longer situated in an isolated location like Robbins. As he had done at Curtiss-Wright and Acres Airport, Robinson had also broken the color barrier at Harlem Airport on the southwest side of Chicago.

Here, on the modern airfield with well-groomed, sod runways managed by experienced whites whom Robinson had befriended, he and his aviation organization benefited immensely from this new arrangement. During this period, the Challenger Air Pilots' Association became "[well] known to all air ports in and out of Chicago. It is also known in Ethiopia, France, and England. . . . The organization has its own hangar [at the southwest corner of] the Harlem air port. There are five planes that are owned by different members of the club" by the spring of 1936.[26]

Early on, Robinson fully understood the psychological, moral, and symbolic importance of memorializing black aviation history and African American aviators, male and female. No single event was more honored by Robinson than the annual flight over Bessie Coleman's grave at Lincoln Cemetery on Chicago's South Side. He had been the first to drop flowers from the skies on Coleman's grave in 1931—the year that Powell formed the Bessie Coleman Aero Club in Los Angeles—on the anniversary of her tragic April 30, 1926, death. Every April 30 thereafter, Robinson performed the same solemn memorial service over Coleman's grave, while the members of his Challenger Air Pilots' Association held an honorary ceremony and observance. The flyover became a revered tradition for Robinson and other black aviators of Chicago. The church of Reverend J. C. Austin, the South Park Baptist Church in Bronzeville, where Robinson and devout members of the Challenger Air Pilots' Association worshiped, also sponsored other association aviation activities.[27]

By early 1935, Robinson's Challenger Air Pilots' Association boasted more than thirty members. More than anyone else, Robinson had played a key role in making Chicago an influential center of black aviation that not only rivaled, but also surpassed Los Angeles. Robinson had become the most widely recognized and respected leader of black aviation in Chicago. With more than 30 percent of America's black licensed pilots in the United States, and thanks to Robinson's efforts, Chicago had evolved into what was recognized at the time as the vibrant "center of Negro aviation" in the United States by 1935. Robinson's noteworthy achievements in Chicago, however, lacked the publicity reaped by the West Coast flyers of Los Angeles, who benefited from promotion by being in the movie capital of the United States. Therefore, relatively "little attention [was given] to [Robinson's] Chicago group, which acquired considerable momentum in the 1930s," concluded aviation historian Von Hardesty, who has long underestimated Robinson's overall accomplishments in both war and peace.[28]

But the most formidable challenge—black aviators serving in a military role and especially as pilots—was yet far out of reach, because African Americans were officially excluded from the United States Air Corps. Now with news of a looming war between Italy and Ethiopia in faraway East Africa, Robinson's thoughts turned increasingly toward the possibilities for black pilots in U.S. military service.

A more immediate solution was soon forthcoming. One Challenger, a young, daredevil parachutist named George Fisher, proposed that the members of Robinson's Challenger Air Pilots' Association should attempt to gain entry into the Illinois National Guard as an Air Reserve Squadron.[29]

By this time, a sufficient number of capable pilots and aviation mechanics—both air and ground contingents, as well as a few aircraft—existed in the Challenger Air Pilots' Association to make up a fully functioning aviation squadron. Blacks, however, were not allowed to serve in the Illinois National Guard. Robinson persisted in his appeals for the establishment of a military unit of black aviators.

Finally, his efforts paid off. In early 1935, Robinson and his organization gained a historic concession from Illinois, winning a state charter as a Military Order of Guard, Aviation Squadron.[30]

In turn, this state charter then gained official approval from the War Department, even though the Military Order of Guard, Aviation Squadron, was an independent organization that existed outside of the Illinois National Guard. For the first time in history, Illinois bestowed an organizational status to a black aviation unit, comparable to that of a state militia. As the Military Order of Guard, Aviation Squadron, the male aviators of the Challenger Air Pilots' Association served proudly as members of the first all-black military aviation unit in 1935. Robinson's unit was the "first Negro aviation squadron designated" by the government, both state and national, in United States history.[31]

More than half a decade before the formation of the Tuskegee Airmen of World War II fame, Robinson's vision of black military aviators became a reality. Robinson then designated—as required—one Challenger Air Pilots' Association aircraft as the property of the Military Order of Guard, Aviation Squadron. Evidently designed by Robinson, a distinctive unit emblem was painted on the side of the squadron's designated military aircraft, and might have been worn on uniforms by unit members.

In essence, the Military Order of Guard, Aviation Squadron, was a volunteer para-military aviation organization that consisted of all-black aviators. Robinson shared command of the aviation squadron with Coffey. Both men served as the unit's highest-ranking members, with the rank of lieutenant colonel. Fisher was appointed major. Other Chicago pilots and former Robinson students, like Harold Hurd, served as trusty lieutenants.

Once again, Robinson had accomplished what was seemingly impossible for African Americans to achieve in Jim Crow society. He successfully organized, formed, and gained recognition for what was America's first military aviation unit consisting entirely of blacks.[32]

But, as usual and as could be expected, Robinson had a much larger purpose and strategic goal in mind by this time, as his vision of a black military air corps was tied to the twin concepts of black political consciousness in the United States, and the global spirit of Pan-Africanism.

Indeed, Robinson and his aviators were particularly sympathetic to Ethiopia. Located in the Horn of Africa, the ancient, independent nation of Ethiopia was now threatened by imperialist Fascist Italy. Some of the young men serving in Robinson's aviation unit were also members of the National Association for the Advancement of Colored People (NAACP), the Urban League, and other progressive black political organizations in the United States. These black aviators, especially Robinson, were focused on developments in regard to the fate of people of color far beyond America's shores. As members of Chicago's middle class, who possessed both the time and resources to be activists, Robinson and his fellow airmen were deeply committed to social change and progress.

By this time, therefore, Robinson envisioned a volunteer military unit of experienced, well-trained black pilots and mechanics to defend Africa's oldest Christian nation, if and when the Italians invaded it.

Commanded by Lieutenant Colonel Robinson, seven airmen of the Military Order of Guard, Aviation Squadron, were eager to assist in Ethiopia's defense. If proper arrangements could be made with the Ethiopian government, Robinson planned to lead the way for these aviation squadron members to serve as military aviators in Ethiopia. Because of America's neutrality laws, however, the eight black American volunteers would not be allowed to go to Ethiopia together or as anything even remotely resembling a paramilitary unit. Consequently, they planned to travel to Ethiopia one by one. As the unit's acting commander, Robinson concluded that he would have to go to Ethiopia first. Once there, he planned to lay the foundation for relocating the all-black Military Order of Guard, Aviation Squadron of Chicago, which would be resurrected as a military aviation unit to defend the threatened East African nation.[33]

In 1915, not long after World War I had erupted in Europe, Captain Raynal C. Bolling had organized the first volunteer aviation unit—all white—in American history. Twenty years later, Robinson created the first all-black volunteer military

aviation unit. While Bolling had prepared his aviation unit for United States service on the Western Front in France during the World War I, Robinson planned
to lead his aviation unit to a faraway war on the African continent.[34]

Robinson also faced the central dilemma of all blacks in America who sought
advanced careers. Benjamin O. Davis Jr. explained the quandry: "If education-
ally qualified, [African Americans] could become doctors, lawyers, ministers, businessmen, and teachers, but only where there was little or no mixing with whites.
I thought that perhaps I could become an engineer and move to South America,
as some blacks were doing, seeking careers not available to them in the United
States."[35]

Even as an experienced pilot with considerable technical skill, Robinson faced
a comparably disadvantageous situation in the United States, only made worse by
the Great Depression. Much like Davis, Robinson began to realize that a brighter
future in aviation lay not in the United States, but well beyond its borders.[36]

In addition, America's infant aircraft industry, which was crippled by the
world economic collapse, afforded no viable avenue for employment of African
Americans in highly skilled and technical positions. The lack of aviation opportunities for blacks even included the Curtiss-Wright Corporation, which only barely
survived the most severe economic downturn in American history.[37]

And despite the recent gains reaped by African Americans, the U.S. air mail
service, commercial aviation, and especially military aviation were still all closed to
blacks, no matter how qualified. Robinson, therefore, longed for a new place beyond America where he could reach his full potential.

Like Robinson, Davis also understood the dark side of the American experience for blacks. He described how the real land of freedom and true equality was
actually located far away from America's shores: "In Europe, [African Americans]
moved about without restriction and encountered no discrimination of any kind.
It seemed ridiculous and totally unnecessary that, for non-whites, life outside the
United States could be equal and free for all, while at home it was so frequently
painful."[38]

Racism in America continued to demonstrate a dangerous, violent side. In
1935 in Florida, where he had been born, and especially in Robinson's home state
of Mississippi, the lynching of African Americans by white mobs continued unabated while only winked at by law enforcement and white politicians.[39]

The spirit of Pan-Africanism, the desire for a better life, and the moral cause
of defending a threatened African homeland thus beckoned Robinson to Ethiopia.

By the time George L. Washington, the head of the Department of Mechanical Industries at Tuskegee Institute, finally decided to present Robinson with an offer to teach Tuskegee's first aviation course, the latter was already thinking in larger moral and geopolitical terms. While Robinson was well known by Chicago's black community, he was not yet widely recognized throughout the United States. His upcoming role in Ethiopia would change that, however, vaulting him on to a world stage and into the headlines of leading newspapers, both black and white, across the United States.[40]

A BLACK AIR FORCE IN ETHIOPIA

Having been named the Negus Negusti, or the King of Kings, in early April 1930, Ethiopian Emperor elect Ras Tafari Makonnen, or Haile Selassie, meaning Power of the Trinity, was a man of vision. The former Regent and the symbolic Lion of Judah, Selassie was attempting to force his ancient East African nation, a Christian medieval feudal land, into the modern age. Not restricted by conservatism or bound too tightly by ancient traditions, Selassie was open-minded and freethinking. He embraced new ideas and initiatives to promote his country's progress in a modernizing effort to push his nation into the twentieth century.

Ethiopia cherished a past that was deeply rooted in ancient and Biblical history, defying Egyptians, Greeks, Romans, Persians, and Muslims who sought to occupy what was known then as Abyssinia. But more recently, no nation in all Africa had been more successful at thwarting European conquest and exploitation since the Sixteenth Century. Built upon a rich religious, philosophical, and cultural heritage, the ancient Solomonic state of Ethiopia had survived as an independent Christian nation in part by beating the Europeans at their own game: buying weaponry and building military strength in the tradition of the European Powers to protect its independence from the imperialism that had subjugated the African continent.[41]

Ethiopia even possessed a fledgling Imperial Air Force, but in reality, this infant air force was more of a dream. Like Robinson, Selassie viewed aviation as the key to his nation's future. Selassie's "lifelong love affair with the airplane" began in November 1922, with an impressive British aircraft demonstration. Upon viewing the Royal Air Force's performance, Selassie "instantly understood how important air power could be in Ethiopia."[42]

Selassie's idea to create a modern, independent air force for Ethiopia was ambitious. After all, at this time, the United States possessed its own Air Corps, but it was still a part of the United States Army. The Imperial Ethiopian Air Force was not formidable by Western standards, but nevertheless represented the first and only air arm of an independent black nation in Africa. Long before the Tuskegee Airmen story began, the novel concept of black military aviators was alive and well in faraway Ethiopia.

In fact, modern air power had played a role in Selassie's rise to power. Aircraft had allowed him to crush Ethiopian rebel opposition, bombing them into submission. Flown by European pilots, "the airplane would confirm his kingship" by destroying opposition forces in early 1930. Thereafter, rebellious Ethiopian chieftains viewed resistance against Selassie as "futile" because of his "invincible" warplanes that could rain destruction from the air.[43]

But Selassie's plan to create an air force was opposed by an expansionist Italy. Italy possessed its own imperialistic and Machiavellian plans for Ethiopia's future, considering increases in the number of Ethiopian aircraft as a potential threat to its grand designs of conquest. Emperor Selassie never forgot "the objection of the Italian envoy arguing that the Ethiopian Government should not be allowed war planes [and felt] this proves that . . . the Italians have been planning and preparing for a long time to make war on Ethiopia."[44]

With open conflict between Ethiopia and Italy fast approaching, Selassie began to question why his air force, the most modernized branch of his nation's military, should consist solely of well-trained French pilots and not black aviators. After all, white aviators serving a proud black nation seemed contradictory to this fiercely nationalist leader, who cherished Ethiopia's distinguished, centuries-long military heritage. And, most important, Ethiopia's manpower needed to be tapped for the upcoming conflict.

Selassie, therefore, wanted to establish the first all-black air force in history. But first he would have "to break the French monopoly in the country's aviation program." During the early 1930s, the emperor had been influenced by a dynamic group of intellectuals of the Young Ethiopian Movement. Nationalistic and xenophobic, these educated men from some of Ethiopia's leading families were strongly opposed to any Western, white, and foreign influence in Ethiopia, including the emperor's European advisors and aviators.

Thanks to pressure exerted by the leaders of the Young Ethiopian Movement, including Ethiopians who had studied in America, Emperor Selassie began to seek out black technicians and experts in the United States in 1932. Simultaneously,

Selassie had learned more about the well-publicized African American pilots in the United States, breaking aviation records and performing flying feats of distinction.[45]

African Americans filling military aviation roles in Ethiopia would fit into a larger program, conceived by African American Professor Earnest Work, who served as the Ethiopian Minister of Education. He encouraged educated black Americans to migrate to Ethiopia to start a new life. An all-black Imperial Ethiopian Air Force would be the pride of not only Ethiopia but also of all of black Africa. In addition, an air force of black pilots would symbolize intellectual, mechanical, and technical equality in the most advanced technical arena—aeronautics—of the white and Western world.[46]

By 1930, the most well known African American pilot, thanks largely to his unmatched skill in self-promotion, was Hubert Fauntleroy Julian. Unlike Robinson, Julian was not an American. He had been born on the Caribbean island of Trinidad as a British subject. Julian had learned to fly in Canada, before moving to the United States in 1921. At best, this outspoken West Indian possessed "a controversial career as a showman" during the Golden Age of Aviation.[47]

The flamboyant Julian first gained recognition as the World's Champion Daredevil Parachutist, after a jump at Harlem, New York, in 1922. Julian also attempted a 1924 trans-Atlantic flight from Harlem, New York, to Ethiopia, but this fund-raising exploit, promoted as a return to the "Land of Our Fathers," proved to be a disaster. Julian's controversial flight—investigated by postal authorities and the Federal Bureau of Investigation—lasted less than five minutes, when his Boeing hydroplane crashed into Flushing Bay, New York. Julian nearly drowned before being pulled from the wreckage just in time.[48]

Julian's humiliating fiasco was a serious setback to the overall image of black aviation. To gloating whites, Julian's crash seemingly provided more evidence of alleged African American inferiority. The *New York Herald Tribune* and the *New York Times* printed lengthy stories with large headlines deriding Julian's failure, including "Harlem's Ace Flops into Flushing Bay at Start of Globe Circling Trip."[49]

But Julian was not finished in attempting to make a name for himself. He promoted trans-Atlantic flights to Africa in both 1926 and 1928, but nothing materialized due to his own ineptitude, in addition to the lack of funds and support.[50]

Julian's publicity stunts and especially his proposed flight to Ethiopia, however, came to Selassie's attention by the early 1930s. Selassie, therefore, had invited Julian to serve Ethiopia, including flying during his coronation ceremony at the nation's capital of Addis Ababa. Julian became the first black aviator to serve Ethiopia, including as the emperor's private pilot.[51]

Before Robinson's arrival in Ethiopia, Selassie contemplated handing Julian the job of managing the cadet aviation-training program, which was operated by French airmen as part of the emperor's plan of replacing blacks with whites. Julian however, failed to measure up to the emperor's high expectations. [52]

Ironically, the fact that Julian was the first black aviator to serve Selassie, and because he was a master at self-promotion, played a large part in guaranteeing Robinson's general obscurity in regard to his role in Ethiopia to this day. Julian had run afoul of the emperor elect shortly before his November 2, 1930, coronation as Ethiopia's new emperor. A well-publicized incident leading to Julian's disgrace centered around Selassie's white deHavilland Gypsy Moth biplane. Julian was forbidden to fly the cherished new aircraft, a gift to the emperor-elect from a leading aviation firm in London. But Julian openly defied the orders. While preparing to participate in the coronation ceremony, he took off on his own, only to crash the sleek biplane into the top of a large eucalyptus tree.[53]

The next day, an enraged Selassie expelled Julian from Ethiopia. Some evidence also indicates that he may also have been paying too much personal attention to a female member of the royal family. This incident had far-reaching negative repercussions for the image of black aviators in general. Adding insult to injury, this obvious example of black aviation ineptitude was widely covered by the international and American press.

The *New York Times* carried a headline—which embarrassed black America as well as Robinson—on October 31, 1930 that read: "Ethiopia Banishes Harlem 'Colonel.'" But in fact, Julian was never a colonel—a self-imposed rank when he was in the United States—of the Imperial Ethiopian Air Force. White editors and journalists mocked and publicized Julian's poor performance to support their own personal racial prejudices about alleged black inferiority, especially in regard to the art of flying. The *New York Herald Tribune* carried the story of Julian's debacle under the heading of "An Abyssinian Tragedy." This incident also reflected badly upon both the emperor elect and Ethiopia in general.[54] These setbacks were not lost to Robinson, who felt a sense of obligation to repair the widespread damage.[55]

But the failure of an African American serving an African nation also tarnished both the overall image and spirit of Pan-Africanism in America. Julian's personal difficulties with Selassie fueled the negative stereotype of the inability for blacks to cooperate together for a greater good.[56]

From beginning to end, Julian's antics only "reinforced white America's pre-conceived notion that blacks were at best inept pilots, seriously undermining the credibility of legitimate black aviators striving to prove that whites did not have a monopoly on flying aptitude. By the mid-1930s he had become an embarrassment to serious-minded blacks and he was soundly condemned by black editors."[57]

By this time in the eyes of white America, Julian symbolized one of the ugliest white stereotypes of African Americans: "the swaggering, boastful black who claimed to be an expert pilot but was actually quite incompetent, the aeronautical equivalent of Kingfish," of the popular *Amos 'n Andy* radio show.[58] In planning for aviation possibilities in Ethiopia, Robinson wanted to prove that a civilian black pilot could not only demonstrate aviation expertise and technical competency in the air, but also that African Americans could fulfill a military aviation role, including that of a combat pilot.[59]

By early 1935, much of black America was focused on the brewing crisis in Ethiopia, after the initial bloody clashes between Ethiopian and Italian troops near the Somaliland border in the east in early December 1934. Fearing these "border" clashes held the potential to spark a much larger conflict, Europe now seemed to hold its collective breath. All the while, the prospect of war became an ever-increasing possibility as Italy mustered for an invasion of Ethiopia.

Indeed, the war's approach was hastened by a relatively minor incident at Walwal, situated in the windswept deserts of the Ogaden, which lay between Selassie's nation and Italian Somaliland, in southeast Ethiopia. In this remote arid lowland of camel caravans, relentless sandstorms, ancient trade routes, and nomadic tribes, the Italians were actually positioned sixty miles inside Ethiopia, far outside the Somaliland border. The Italians coveted Walwal because of its more than one thousand wells. The Italians had attempted to exclude the Ethiopian military from securing precious water supplies on Ethiopian soil on the false premise that these wells were located inside Italian Somaliland.

The Italians and their black Somali allies, who were fierce Muslim warriors, had attacked the Christian Ethiopian troops without warning on December 5, 1934. Then, the Italians unleashed the overpowering might of bombers, light tanks, and armored cars on the virtually defenseless Ethiopians. The onslaught left more than one hundred Ethiopian dead.[60]

Emperor Selassie was stunned by this blatant display of aggression. Now with a pretense for war, Italian prime minister Benito Mussolini presented a humiliating ultimatum to the Ethiopians on December 11. The Italians demanded Ethiopia's immediate recognition of the Walwal area, and its precious wells, as part of Italian Somaliland—despite the proper border, sixty miles east, which had been established in the 1897 Treaty between Italy and Ethiopia—and to acknowledge Ethiopia as aggressor.

In addition, Mussolini requested a formal apology, monetary reparations, the punishment of Ethiopian commanders at Walwal, and other unreasonable demands, including Ethiopian troops' "render[ing] honors to the Italian flag" on Ethiopian soil. Emperor Selassie could not acknowledge what was untrue, especially when it meant the "surrender of sovereignty." Of course, Selassie's inevitable refusal provided Mussolini with another flimsy excuse for the eventual invasion.[61]

Emperor Selassie appealed to the League of Nations to settle the dispute, expose the blatant Italian expansionism, and prove his nation's innocence. In Selassie's mind, the Ogaden incident provided an opportunity for the League of Nations to live up to its moral obligations. After all, the League's primary mission was to deter unjust aggression that might escalate into world war. Mussolini, however, would never allow the League of Nations, or anyone else to halt his imperialistic ambitions.[62]

Unfortunately, the Ethiopians placed far too much faith in the West and white leadership. In Selassie's words, "We thought that the Covenant of the League would protect us from [the Italians'] attack."[63] Italy, which had been preparing for war for years, now had its excuse. Only Ethiopia stood in the way of Italy's imperialist ambitions to exploit the entire Horn of Africa. Consequently, Mussolini declared Ethiopia a "threat . . . to our East Africa colonies."[64]

With war on the horizon, Ethiopia desperately needed Western assistance, including military advisors and educated technicians and aviators. Selassie sought to gain as many African American experts, assistants, and advisors as possible.[65]

Robinson expressed his sentiments about the tense situation in Ethiopia during an early January 1935 meeting with black community and business leaders sponsored by the Associated Negro Press in Chicago. Here, he made the promise that he would volunteer to serve to defend Ethiopia's independence in the face of Italian aggression. With prophetic insight, Robinson viewed Ethiopia as the most visible stage and positive means to promote black aviation to the world, while defending Africa's oldest independent black nation once war erupted.[66]

The most respected businessman at this meeting was Claude A. Barnett, director of the Associated Negro Press (ANP), which he had organized in Chicago in 1919. He was a friend of Dr. Malaku E. Bayen, a member of the Ethiopian royal family who was attending medical school at Howard University in Washington, D.C., and who was a leader of the transplanted Ethiopian community in the nation's capital. At this time, the handsome, young man was the "most influential United States-educated Ethiopian" in America. Most important, Bayen was one of Emperor Selassie's cousins, and was determined to create a close, permanent bond between African Americans and Ethiopians. As he wrote in a carefully worded letter to Barnett in 1935, Bayen was on a mission "to have our government convinced that their cooperation with western Negroes would be a quick solution to our need[s]" in Ethiopia. Bayen eventually served as the emperor's personal physician during the upcoming Second Italo-Ethiopian War.[67]

As Selassie explained, "My private doctor, Malaku Bayen who studied medicine at Howard University in Washington, D.C., was the only qualified medical man in the front line of the Abyssinian army [by the war's end], and was attached closely to my staff throughout the war."[68]

This chance meeting in Chicago between Robinson and Bayen was a fateful one for the ambitious aviator. In Robinson's words: "I had through Mr. Barnett of the Associated Negro Press, contacted a nephew of the Emperor studying medicine at Howard University [in Washington, D.C.], and told him of my desire to enlist in the [nucleus of the] air forces of Ethiopia."

Bayen was now the key Ethiopian connection between the emperor and African Americans and the State Department. Convinced that Italy planned to conquer his ancient nation to increase its overseas empire, Bayen attempted to secure African American volunteers for Ethiopia. Employing the moral high ground and a sense of obligation to the African Motherland, he had long emphasized that the "American Negro, through racial kinship, is duty-bound to support Abyssinia." Bayen even obtained a list of African American pilots from the Department of Commerce. He then sent letters requesting active support for Ethiopia from these talented U.S. citizens, including students enrolled in courses on commercial aviation.[69]

Most of all, Bayen was impressed by Robinson's sense of dedication and willingness to sacrifice his life's work in America to assist Ethiopia. He also admired Robinson's long list of aviation accomplishments and high level of experience, including his six hundred hours of flying time. Such aviation expertise would make Robinson an invaluable asset for the fledgling Imperial Ethiopian Air Force.[70]

But Julian's erratic behavior in Ethiopia had tarnished the reputations of all African Americans who desired to serve Ethiopia. While the Chicago chapters of the United Aid to Ethiopia and the Friends of Ethiopia embraced Robinson, ironically, the Ethiopian government, especially the emperor, remained more cautious. Selassie wanted no further public relations disasters, especially when his militarily weak nation stood on the verge of war with a major European power. Yet, Bayen met again with Robinson, and was completely won over. He sent a highly favorable report to Selassie in Addis Ababa, Ethiopia's capital, along with a list of personal references and professional credentials.

Emperor Selassie wired an April 1935 cable and an official invitation for Robinson to join Ethiopia's defense. He offered Robinson an officer's commission in the armed forces, but this offer was made on the condition that Robinson would have to serve in Ethiopia for a period of at least one year. Making a commitment of one year was fully acceptable to Robinson. He made his final decision without reservation or hesitation. Wrote Robinson, "Through him [Dr. Bayen], I was given further directions," including details about journeying to Ethiopia.[71]

Bragg described some of Emperor Selassie's initial reasoning in regard to utilizing Robinson's abilities and potential: "If this young American can construct an aeroplane from the ground up, he would be considered. Ethiopia has everything to make planes, from the ore to the most expensive woods. I have flyers. What I want is someone to teach mechanics and everything that goes with it."[72]

Robinson was indeed this special "someone," and Selassie desperately needed a viable air force with war seemingly inevitable. Therefore, Robinson was also secretly appointed by the emperor "as a consultant in the development of the Royal Air Force."[73]

Selassie was especially eager to secure Robinson and his extensive aviation expertise for both military and civilian roles. Someone with Robinson's qualifications fulfilled a variety of key requirements. First, Selassie had been preparing his military for conflict with Italy nearly a year before the Walwal incident. Moreover, Robinson was a black aviator with considerable experience as an aviation trainer and a proven leader, requirements necessary to raise the overall standards and quality of the infant Imperial Ethiopian Air Force while increasing its morale and strength.

But yet another political consideration for Selassie was the fact that Robinson was an American. With war imminent, Selassie continued to gain foreign assistance and material aid, but primarily from small countries such as Sweden and Belgium, which seemed to pose no design to gain influence or power in Ethiopia, as the emperor desired. At this time, an isolationist, anti-colonial America—unlike France and Great Britain—fit the emperor's special requirements for Ethiopia's need to distance itself from European nations with colonial empires, especially those with imperial ambitions in Africa.[74]

Later in May 1936, Robinson would be forced to make the politically astute claim to Associated Press reporter Charles Norman that he had traveled to Ethiopia, only after he "got word to Haile Selassie proposing development of commercial flying in Ethiopia. The result was a bid."[75]

Of course, Robinson's cautious statement was made to veil the emperor's role and to disguise his own future military involvement in Ethiopia. After all, the fact that Ethiopian officials, including the head of state, had violated U.S. neutrality laws that legally forbid American citizens from serving as volunteers in foreign armies in wartime was something that Robinson weighed carefully. Meanwhile, war between Ethiopia and Italy was growing ever closer. Mussolini had planned for conflict with Ethiopia as early as 1932. And now the lack of a unified Western response in support of Ethiopia continued to favor future aggression without the risk of serious cost or penalty, as shown by the Walwal incident.

Selassie was only too well aware that Italy possessed the industrial capabilities to unleash a mighty offensive effort against his homeland. In the fall of 1933, Mussolini had dispatched Marshall Pietro Badoglio, the chief of the Italian General Staff, to Italian Eritrea on Ethiopia's northern border, during a so-called inspection tour—the first step in preparing for the invasion of Ethiopia from the south. Adding muscle, Italian forces in Italian Somaliland, east and southeast of Ethiopia, had been reinforced with ample amounts of armored cars, troops, and aircraft. Clearly, Italy had been building up its forces in the Horn of Africa for some time.

During the autumn of 1933, an Italian émigré newspaper carried an exuberant story of Italy's much-anticipated invasion of Ethiopia. This article emphasized that the Italian invasion would be launched with a large number of infantry units bolstered by a fleet of modern aircraft. Italy's popular press declared that a special national destiny promised that "Ethiopia was Rome's place in the sun." Emperor Selassie needed a viable air force, and Robinson, before the Italians struck to fulfill historical and imperial ambitions.[76]

In the early spring of 1935, Robinson faced a decisive turning point in his young life. He chose to serve in Ethiopia instead of going back to Tuskegee Institute to become an aviation instructor, forsaking his most cherished dream. This decision was not made any easier for Robinson by the attempts of his Gulfport family and wife, Earnize, to discourage him.[77] Despite the distinct possibility of never seeing his wife, family, or country again, Robinson's final decision was primarily a moral one. When war finally erupted, the international stage could serve as a showcase for black aviation military achievements, if Robinson rose to his supreme challenge.

With larger goals in mind, Robinson now looked far beyond Chicago, his family, a successful aviation career, and his coveted role as a respected leader in the black community in order to stand up to the march of fascism and to show the world that African Americans belonged in the skies as military aviators.

THE SPIRIT OF PAN-AFRICANISM

By this time, Robinson was a firm believer in the spirit of Pan-Africanism, which was part of the "Back to Africa" movement that was popular in black America. Emotional, spiritual, and psychological bonds of transplanted Africans with their mother country was a constant theme throughout African American history. To survive, slaves had maintained many central elements of their rich West African culture. Awareness of this distinct heritage was a source of pride for people in bondage. During the colonial period, even free blacks often proudly referred to themselves as Africans—especially Mandingos or Congos—rather than the slave masters' designation, "negro."[78]

Like no other African nation, Ethiopia possessed a "long held special place in the hearts and minds of many Afro-Americans," because of its ancient heritage and success in remaining free of European and Muslim conquest over the centuries. Blacks around the world viewed Ethiopia as an enduring symbol of black liberation and independence.[79]

Biblical references to Ethiopians and Abyssinians had inspired African Americans since slavery's days. One verse in Psalms was especially inspirational: "Ethiopia shall soon stretch out her hands to God," a metaphor that now inspired hope for a successful resistance against European colonialism and imperialism. In her 1846 memoirs, Zilpha Elaw, a free African American woman from Pennsylvania, who preached fiery sermons to both blacks and whites, wrote how, "my soul was set at glorious liberty; and, like the Ethiopic eunuch, I went on my way rejoicing in the blooming prospects of a better inheritance with the saints in light."[80] She also proclaimed proudly that African Americans were "from the Ethiopean [sic] family," and saw them as her "Abyssinian brethren."[81]

For more than two centuries, the symbolically named Abyssinian Baptist Church had been a regular feature of religious life in Harlem, New York. To generations of African Americans, Ethiopia and Africa were viewed symbolically as one and the same. In 1881, African Americans dreamed of fleeing America's racial nightmare and again returning to Africa "to rehabilitate Africa and found an Ethiopian Empire as the world has never seen."[82]

Such deep-seated idealistic longings of African Americans for the ancient Ethiopian homeland were early expressions of the spirit of Pan-Africanism, which became more politicized in the 1930s. Pan-African writers, like Edward Wilmot Blyden, described how the Ethiopians were in fact "the most creditable of ancient peoples" in the world. And Africans and African Americans of the Ethiopian Research Council, formed in 1934 in Washington D.C., proudly proclaimed how Ethiopia was "one of the oldest living civilizations in the world. In the Classical Age it was universally regarded as one of the greatest and most powerful nations."[83]

The lopsided Ethiopian victory at Adowa over the Italians in the First Italo-Ethiopian War on March 1, 1896, that thwarted the advance of European colonialism and imperialism in 1896 had also generated a resurgence of Pan-African feeling across the United States. To African Americans, "victorious Ethiopia became a beacon of independence and dignity. The biblical Ethiopia, which had already inspired a widespread movement of religious separatism known as Ethiopianism, now assumed a more cogent and palpable reality."[84]

Ethiopia's romantic image became intertwined with black political life and progressivism in the Twentieth Century, including at the Pan African Conference, in London in 1900. Jamaican civil rights activist Marcus Garvey employed Africa and Ethiopia in synonymous terms. Appealing to racial pride, he spread the gospel of Pan-African sentiment after World War I. Garvey, a fiery black nationalist, emphasized the richness of a distinctive cultural and racial heritage rooted in a distinguished African past. Garvey advocated the "Back to Africa" movement, believing Liberia, America's only successful ex-slave colonization effort in West Africa, was an ideal place for African Americans to migrate.

Garvey emphasized that "Negroes had no choice but to remove themselves completely from American society [and] not only rebel against their economically and socially subservient position in white America, but must overcome the feelings of inferiority with which whites had indoctrinated them." Hence, young black men and women, across the United States, including Robinson, eagerly embraced Ethiopia's broad appeal. Symbolically, the official anthem of Garvey's Universal Negro Improvement Association was entitled, "Ethiopia, Thou Land of Our Fathers." Pan-Africanism flourished during the heady years of the Harlem Renaissance from World War I's conclusion to the 1930s. Leading black writers of the Harlem Literary Renaissance also promoted the Pan-African faith and spirit. One such writer, Lucian B. Watkins, penned a poem entitled "Star of Ethiopia." Another respected writer, Claude McKay, implored, "Lift your heavy-lidded eyes, Ethiopia! awake!"[85] Ethiopia's romantic appeal even emerged into popular American sports culture, with one Negro Baseball League team known as the Ethiopian Clowns.

But Ethiopia's symbolism was more spiritual than anything else. African American religion helped to spread Pan-African thought across the United States. Ancient Ethiopian civilization was idealistically viewed as utopian because it was free of white domination and racism. Consequently, during Robinson's lifetime, many African Americans claimed Ethiopia as the ancient Motherland. Most of all, Ethiopia represented the glory of an independent black nation and a vibrant religious tradition with ancient Solomonic roots untarnished by ruling white Europeans, who were now masters of all of Africa, except Ethiopia and Liberia.[86]

Most important in regard to its direct impact upon the evolution of Robinson's maturing political thinking and consciousness, "Black nationalism had prewar roots in Chicago."[87] In 1913 and only a year before World War I, two "Abyssinian Jews" launched the International Peace and Brotherly Love Movement in Chicago. This black pride organization was based upon the principle that "the Negro is the right Jew." Black leaders emphasized that African Americans should "confess his [true] identity," accept his real destiny, and then migrate back to Ethiopia.[88]

Indeed, it was not Harlem, the vibrant center of black culture during the 1930s, that witnessed the deepest fusing of a spiritual renaissance and reverence for the ancient Ethiopian past, Pan-African thought, and black nationalism. Chicago, instead, evolved into the leading center of the popular movement known as Abyssinianism after the Great War.[89]

Abyssinian Movement members proudly called themselves Ethiopians and Abyssinians. Known as the Star Order of Ethiopia and the Ethiopian Missionaries to Abyssinia, this popular movement, more nationalistic than Garvey's, was most active in Chicago. The Abyssinians believed that all black men should return to the true African Motherland and live in peace in the independent, free black nation of Ethiopia. In 1920, when Robinson was age fifteen, one of Chicago's Abyssinian leaders, dressed in African garb, burned the United States flag to demonstrate his pro-Ethiopia and Pan-African spirit, resulting in a violent clash.[90]

In 1927, when Robinson was living in Chicago, Ethiopian officials visited the city to offer good wages and free land to black professionals—engineers, physicians, dentists, and mechanics—if they would migrate to Ethiopia, the "Last of Free Africa."[91]

Such well-publicized Chicago initiatives caught Robinson's imagination and appealed to his sense of romantic idealism, empowerment, and black nationalism. Like other African Americans, the development of a spirit of Pan-Africanism and Abyssinianism within Robinson's heart and mind represented a significant elevation of political and cultural thought for the rapidly maturing young man from the Deep South. He took great pride in a glorious history of the ancient independent black nation and the African Motherland.[92]

Robinson's solid education in Gulfport had taught him and other blacks, like his boyhood friend Reverend Tartt, about W. E. B. Du Bois, and other inspirational leaders in black history. Du Bois was the editor of the NAACP's magazine, *The Crisis*.[93]

Du Bois was also the leader of the Niagara Movement, which rejected Booker T. Washington's philosophy of accommodation. Robinson's own personal views were more like those espoused by fiery Niagara Movement leaders. Ahead of his time, Robinson possessed an activist, almost crusading, spirit. Fortunately for Robinson, what had developed in Chicago since the Great Migration to the North was a great enhancement of a distinctive black cultural and political consciousness and the rise of cultural pride and black nationalism. African American newspapers like the influential *Chicago Defender* played a leading role in popularizing a Pan-African consciousness. For Robinson, this enhanced racial consciousness and pride in a distant African past laid a sturdy foundation for his firm commitment to Pan-Africanism and Ethiopia's defense by 1935.[94]

At this time when Italy was about to invade Ethiopia, black America, including Robinson, identified with the plight of their underdog "Ethiopian brothers." By the mid-1930s, a "strong racial identification" was made by Robinson to this threatened ancient land once known as Abyssinia.[95]

Clearly, by the mid-1930s, Robinson's perspective had been transformed by his cumulative experiences at Tuskegee, Detroit, and especially Chicago, broadening his mind, perspectives, and horizons. In Chicago, he was now making more money and enjoying more personal prestige and success than ever before. After all and as early as the 1920s, African Americans in Chicago had gained political and economic power almost unmatched anywhere else in the United States. Robinson benefited immensely from this enlightened and intellectually progressive environment.

Robinson could not deny the fact, however, that Chicago's South Side was yet an institutionalized ghetto, despite its relative prosperity. Bronzeville was closed off from the world by an ugly, invisible wall of white hostility, discrimination, and racial hatred. Far too much poverty, crime, corruption, and misery for people of color still existed. The widespread discrimination and racism that Robinson saw around him in both the North and South had caused the native Mississippian to embrace more of a proactive, almost militant, philosophy and broad Pan-African outlook as a solution to America's central dilemma throughout its history.[96]

Quite simply, Robinson had outgrown not only his native South, but also the North. As in flight, he now soared high above the narrow-minded attitudes, regional prejudices and perspectives, and localized provincialism that dominated the lives of those who viewed the world from a more narrow perspective.

In part because he had found a Gulfport-like closed environment, Robinson's experiences in the North also paved the way for his internationalism and activism. In the North he had first seen, heard, and met other blacks from large metropolitan areas across America, including New York, Philadelphia, and Los Angeles. From these associations and friendships, Robinson began to see not only a commonality but also a closer identification with African Americans from across the United States. He had also encountered blacks from the West Indies, British territories like Jamaica, Bermuda, and the Bahamas, and perhaps even from Africa. By the mid-1930s, this feeling of brotherhood and black solidarity for Robinson extended far beyond the country's borders, and all the way to Ethiopia's distant shores.

Robinson now identified with blacks around the world and their plights, regardless of what state, region, or nation, developing an abiding concern for people of color around the world. He also identified not only with these different cultures in faraway lands but also their struggles for dignity and human rights. He believed that Africans were his own people and that Ethiopia was his real spiritual and maternal homeland.

In the words of Professor William R. Scott, "Although many Afro-Americans felt and displayed profound compassion for the Ethiopian people during the Italian invasion of 1935/1936 and wished to volunteer for combat duty in the nation's armed forces, it remained for John C. Robinson, a thirty-year-old resident of Chicago's black South Side, to translate these militant sentiments of Pan-Africanism into concrete and positive action."[97]

Yet, Robinson contradicted the stereotypical image of an angry black militant who was bitter toward the white world. He continued to enjoy friends and close associations with both races in Mississippi and in Chicago. Robinson knew that people had to be valued not for their color, but based on their positive personal qualities and character. Therefore, even though preparing to risk his life in defending a black nation that he had never seen before against white aggression, Robinson possessed white friends and associates in the aviation community of Chicago, including the officials and instructors at the Curtiss-Wright Aeronautical School, as well as in his everyday life.[98]

A complex individual in a contradictory world where simplistic racial stereotypes dominated, the enigmatic Robinson was destined to become the most notable symbolic and representative example of the spirit and true meaning of the essence of Pan-Africanism, black nationalism, and internationalism during the mid-1930s and in the upcoming Italo-Ethiopian War.

HISTORIC BLACK MILITARY AVIATION ROLE

Known as the "Black Swallow," native Georgian Eugene Jacques Bullard flew with the famed Lafayette Escadrille. He fought for France during World War I, becoming the first black military aviator and fighter pilot in May 1917, when Robinson was only age twelve. He engaged in aerial combat, shooting down German aircraft on the Western Front. Bullard received his flight training in France, like Bessie Coleman, because he could not do so in the United States.[99]

Racial prejudice against blacks in uniform persisted in the United States, despite the heroism of thousands of black troops in the Civil War and the Spanish-American War. One especially racist evaluation was an official 1925 army study, based upon biased views of black military performance in World War I. Produced by the faculty and students of the Army War College, this then-respected study was titled, "The Use of Negro Manpower in War." It denounced African Americans as inferior in intelligence, initiative, and even physical courage.[100]

Unfortunately, this distorted study was destined to have a "decisive" impact upon the already considerably prejudiced thinking of high-ranking white civilian and military officials of the War Department in regard to black military capabilities, especially in aviation.[101]

Himself the victim of racial discrimination at West Point and during his sub-sequent distinguished army career, Benjamin O. Davis Jr. lamented how "the Army had approved this 'study' and used it as the basis for its discrimination against blacks."[102]

Of course, the impressive roles and many sacrifices of African Americans in all of America's wars since the American Revolution indicated that the exact opposite was true. Nearly forty Medals of Honor won by black troops from the Civil War to the Spanish-American War spoke eloquently of African American courage on the battlefield.[103]

By the mid-1930s, only around 6,000 blacks served in the U.S. Army out of about a total of 350,000 troops, and not a single African American served in mili-tary aviation across America.[104] Historically, African Americans had found more freedom on the high seas, where men were treated with greater equality than on American soil.[105]

Besides Robinson, other African Americans, such as Benjamin O. Davis Sr., were motivated by the splendid battlefield performances of black troops on Ameri-can soil and overseas. As Benjamin O. Davis Jr. wrote, "My father believed in Amer-ica despite all its deficiencies [and as] a serious student of American history, he was proud of the performance of blacks in America's wars from the Revolution on."[106]

While Davis Jr. attempted in vain to enter military aviation by way of the Army Air Corps in 1935, Robinson tried a more unconventional approach: serving as a volunteer in Ethiopia's fledgling air arm with war imminent in faraway Africa.

ABYSSINIA

After fighting erupted at Walwal in December 1934, the world's attention, espe-cially black America's, was riveted on events in Ethiopia. While Western Europe and the world only debated or remained apathetic toward Ethiopia's plight, Robin-son prepared to take action. He would become the only African American to serve Emperor Selassie and the Ethiopian Army during the war's entirety.

Without African Americans having an opportunity to strike an organized blow against racism in the United States, the upcoming Italo-Ethiopian War pro-vided a means by which a young black man could fight racism, institutionalized as fascism, on the battlefield. By this time, racism and fascism were one and the same for people of color. Reflecting a common black perception, novelist Langs-ton Hughes correctly labeled fascists as the primary enemy of "Jim Crow peoples" around the world.[107]

But what was significant about Robinson's upcoming role in Ethiopia's defense was that it was a solo effort. In this way, Robinson continued his tradition of breaking new ground primarily on his own, leading the way and going where few African Americans dared tread. In psychological terms, it almost seemed as if the more formidable the obstacle, the more Robinson jumped at the chance and rose to the challenge. In addition, he was about to become a military aviator in an active interventionist role even though he was without any combat experience or military experience, except for brief service in the Illinois aviation squadron.

Previously, Robinson's accomplishments were largely focused not only on self-improvement and personal success, but also in shattering the racial barriers that stood in his way to open the door for other African Americans, especially youth. But the Ethiopian chapter of Robinson's life would be altogether something different. For the first time, his efforts would be played out on the other side of the Atlantic and on an international stage. To fully understand the timely significance and symbolic importance of his interventionist role, Robinson's contributions must be analyzed in its proper historical context and perspective.

A popular myth exists today that the first time that Americans, both black and white, volunteered to stand up against the rising tide of fascism occurred in Spain. Hundreds of Americans served in the Abraham Lincoln and George Washington battalions during the Spanish Civil War in 1936–1939. Nearly ninety African Americans served the Republican cause in Spain, including at least two black aviators, who flew with a group of American pilots of the Spanish Republican Air Force.[108]

Before the outbreak of the Spanish Civil War, therefore, Robinson was the first American and first African American to personally engage in the struggle, and for the war's duration, against fascism on the first battlefields of what would soon become a world war that pitted democracy against totalitarianism. American volunteers, both black and white, would only rise up en masse to serve in Spain after they had seen Italy's ruthless conquest of Ethiopia. Ironically, scores of African Americans served in Spain precisely because they had not fought in Ethiopia—seen as a missed opportunity—and were inspired by Robinson's earlier example of active participation.

Robinson was about to fulfill an interventionist military aviation role, like the American volunteers of the Lafayette Escadrille during World War I who returned the favor for French support during America's own struggle for independence.

Robinson possessed another symbolic military link to the past. Escaped slaves primarily from Virginia flocked to Virginia's Royal Governor Lord Dunmore's proclamation promising freedom to slaves if they fought for the British during the revolution's early days. Hundreds of African Americans warred against their former masters, battling Virginians on their home soil. Symbolically, these African Americans served in an all-black unit known as the Ethiopian Regiment.[109] And now more than a century and a half later, Robinson was about to return the compliment by serving in behalf of the ancient East African nation of Ethiopia against the imperialist ambitions of another European colonizing power.

This threat to Ethiopia's life stemmed from a potent combination of fascism and the time-tested formula of overseas colonial expansion, which had made Europe powerful and wealthy for centuries. The bitter political, social, and economic legacies of World War I's aftermath had set the stage for fascism's rise in Europe, first as a cultural phenomenon, and then as an ultra-nationalist political movement that swept aside the existing political order. Fascism, founded in Milan in 1919, occupied an ideological position between Marxism and Western liberalism, developing into Italy's dominant political, social, and intellectual force now galvanized by the charismatic Mussolini.[110]

A totalitarian state regime that dominated virtually all aspects of Italian life, fascism became "the major phenomenon of our century," lamented historian Zeev Sternhell.[111]

Italy's prime minister, Mussolini, who was one of the original founders of Italian Fascism, inspired the Italian people by proclaiming the dawn of a glorious new era.[112] A blacksmith's son, Mussolini hailed from humble origins, generations of peasant farmers. Named in honor of the Mexican revolutionary Benito Juárez, who battled for his nation's independence against the French invaders of Mexico in the mid-Nineteenth Century, Mussolini became a Socialist, political agitator, journalist, and prolific writer, including works of both fiction and biography.[113]

An Italian Army veteran who earned a corporal's rank like Adolf Hitler during the Great War, Mussolini was fascism's greatest promoter and embodiment. In Italian, the word *fascism* meant "bundle," which symbolized the legendary "Fasces"—the bundle of rods bound around a long-handled Roman axe to represent strength through unity—of the Imperial Roman Empire. Mussolini worshiped Imperial Rome's glories, when the ancient empire had ruled much of the known world, including North Africa. He also idolized Napoleon Bonaparte, the Corsican "little corporal," in part because Mussolini rightly considered him an Italian. Like the National Socialists, or Nazis, of Germany, discontented Italians and disillusioned Great War veterans rallied around Mussolini and the promises of fascism.[114]

Mussolini sought to transform a backward Italy into a world power. Believing himself a chosen man of destiny, Mussolini wanted "to make Romans out of Italians."[115] Most of all, Mussolini was obsessed by the vision that Italy must take its rightful place among Europe's great nations. Il Duce (as Mussolini was also known) rationalized his expansionism, or taking the lands of others, by following the example of other Western powers, because "they all have fruitful colonies [and] surely Italy must have fruitful colonies too." Indeed, Mussolini envisioned a modern Italian empire like that of ancient Rome, stretching throughout the Mediterranean region to include North and East Africa. Ethiopia was the "linchpin" of Mussolini's ambitious dream of a Greater Italy that included the Horn of Africa.

Mirroring Hitler's rapid rise to power during the 1930s, Mussolini harbored grievances stemming from World War I, even though Italy was among the victorious nations: Italy had not been allowed by the Great Powers to acquire overseas colonies. Only one-third of Italy was arable, causing Mussolini to declare, "We are hungry for land." Another factor fueling Italy's desire for expansion was the relatively small Italian population, only a paltry 42 million. Knowing that fascism's future success rested on its aggressive expansion overseas to obtain riches and resources, Mussolini coveted Ethiopia so that Italy would no longer remain a second rate power.[116]

Italy's imperial destiny, Mussolini believed, was to create the new Rome, reaping new glories for the Italian people. He envisioned himself as the new Julius Caesar. In October 1932, he aroused national pride by proclaiming to the Italian people: "The twentieth century will be the century in which Italy will return for the third time to be the leader of human civilization."[117]

According to the racist thinking of the day, Italy's greatness also called for spreading Italian "civilization." Mussolini declared that it was Italy's right and duty to "civilize Africa, and [Italy's strategic] position in the Mediterranean gave her this right and imposed this duty on her." Italy already possessed a key strategic advantage to easily invade Ethiopia, controlling the land on two sides of Ethiopia: Eritrea to the north, and Italian Somaliland to the east and southeast. Therefore, Italy viewed Ethiopia as a natural geographic extension of its colonial empire, fueling Italy's righteous sense of a special destiny. By 1935, therefore, Mussolini felt he possessed a natural right to conquer, own, and exploit Ethiopia and its people.

Ironically, these same catalysts—the idealistic "civilizing mission" and to gain living space for the nation that would propel Hitler's armies into Russia's vastness in June 1941 also sparked Mussolini's invasion of Ethiopia. And, like Hitler's invasion of Russia, Italy's war in Ethiopia would also be a savage racial conflict without pity or mercy. Much more than a typical imperialistic grab for land, Mussolini transformed his aggression toward Ethiopia "in the shape of a contest between the black and white races."[118]

Adhering to the popular racist beliefs of European superiority, Mussolini based his military and strategic thinking largely "in racial terms." And like Hitler, he seriously underestimated the United States' potential to oppose Italy from a jaundiced racial perspective, because Mussolini considered America a degenerate "land of Negroes and Jews."[119]

Given these ambitions and perspectives, combined with the need to turn Italians' attention away from internal governmental failures in strengthening the national economy, Mussolini's most popular recourse was to embark upon a conquest to resurrect a new Roman Empire and unleash "spiritual, political, and economic expansion" by waging total war upon a non-industrialized, economically backward feudal nation: "It was not a question of whether [Mussolini] could afford to fight, but whether he could afford not to."[120]

Yet another pressing motivation for Mussolini to attack Ethiopia was to salvage Italy's tarnished national honor. An inspired army of Ethiopian warriors humiliated his nation's military when Mussolini was only thirteen, a crushing defeat the Italians never forgot. On Mussolini's rosewood desk at his sprawling Palazzo Venezia office, within sight of the Roman Coliseum, he had placed a book about that disastrous 1896 Italian campaign in the First Italo-Ethiopian War and the bitter Italian defeat at Adowa, the reminder of a humiliating past that must now be exorcized at all costs.

Defeat at Adowa, or Adwa, was a stunning reversal on an unprecedented scale for a Western power at the hands of a black nation. The beginning of this fiasco grew out of a typical European game of Great Power politics. As part of its cold war against France, and aided by the united front of its German and Austria allies under the Triple Alliance after Italy had secured Eritrea in 1889, Italy's invasion was a brazen attempt to secure more territory situated near the strategically important Suez Canal and to gain greater access to the Mediterranean.

The British had allowed Italian expansion into the Horn of Africa and around the Red Sea to keep French influence to a minimum in the strategic area on the

Red Sea, the Blue Nile and its headwaters in western Ethiopia, and the British-controlled Suez Canal, which had opened in 1869. Suddenly Ethiopia had gained new strategic, economic, and commercial importance to cynical Western leaders and politicians eager to exploit weaknesses.

English-Italian cooperation focusing on the exclusion of imperialist France from this strategic area meant that Ethiopia had become a mere pawn of the Great Powers. As part of Mussolini's imperialist dream, the Italian people and government confidently expected Ethiopia to be transformed into an Italian colony by way of expansion southward from Eritrea, but the Ethiopian people were determined to defend their nation at all costs.[121]

On March 1, 1896, in the eerie mountainous landscape of black volcanic rock and buttes located directly north of Addis Ababa, around the small northeast town of Adowa just south of the Eritrea border, the Italians had suffered their greatest overseas defeat in their history. In September 1895, a modern Italian army of twenty thousand, under Lieutenant General Oreste Baratieri, had pushed south from the Italian province of Eritrea. Confident of an easy victory over black warriors, the mighty Italian army had surged into northern Ethiopia and planned to march straight into the capital city of Addis Ababa. The strategic plan called for pushing south along the old historic road leading from the capital to southern Eritrea: an invasion route that would be utilized by Mussolini's forces almost exactly forty years to the day later in the autumn of 1935. Eager to launch a surprise attack to quickly wipe out an Ethiopian resistance that was expected to be meager at best, General Baratieri had made the fatal mistake of dividing his advance into three separate columns, emulating Napoleon's proven tactics on Europe's central plains.

Meanwhile, Emperor Menilek II and his Ras—feudal warlords—had rallied ninety thousand of Ethiopia's best warriors to meet the invaders. Menilek had united almost the entire Ethiopian nation with such inspiring words as, "Enemies have come who would ruin our country and change our religion. With God's help I will get rid of them." At the end of February 1896, the Italians had also made the classic mistake of advancing into Ethiopia without cavalry, or without an effective reconnaissance force or intelligence-gathering capabilities, especially when already handicapped with inadequate maps. Nevertheless, the over-confident Italians had pushed into the rough terrain just east of Adowa. Here, the Ethiopian warriors awaited the Italian advance, lying in ambush among the rugged, arid hills and deep ravines east of Adowa.

With the advantages of years of experience in fighting the Mahdists, Islamic warriors of the Sudan, the Ethiopians were well prepared for the interlopers. Unlike the Italians, they were situated on familiar ground amid the rocky, lunar-like terrain of Tigre Province. Also, the Ethiopians possessed ample amounts of modern firearms, gained from trading, ironically, with Italy and from past victories over equally overconfident enemies. They also had the added advantage of large numbers of red-cloaked Galla, a combative nomadic people with a large cavalry force.

Catching their opponent by surprise, the Ethiopians struck first and hard. The separated Italian columns were out of mutual supporting distance, and the rough terrain and deep gorges were a recipe for disaster. Moreover, the Italians felt they were only facing an undisciplined horde of savages. Carrying reminders of their spiritualism with them, the Ethiopians wore colorful traditional war costumes with copper and gold crucifixes around their necks. These black Christian warriors charged into battle to defend their faith on a feast day dedicated to Ethiopia's patron saint, St. George, who allegedly slew a dragon.

In short order, more than six thousand Italians and their allies were killed, and nearly fifteen hundred wounded. In addition, the Ethiopians captured nearly three thousand men, including both Italians and black Eritrean allies, and some disloyal Ethiopians as well. Italy's crushing defeat at Adowa was "the greatest single disaster in European colonial history," leading to the fall of the reigning Italian government in Rome. Ethiopia's independence was preserved for future generations to come. The world was shocked by the one-sided military victory won by the Ethiopians, who had been underestimated once again by the West.[122]

The Italians' disastrous repulse in the mountains of northeast Ethiopia became not only a source of pride for Ethiopians, but also for African Americans. While, internationally, whites were stunned by the Adowa fiasco, a new admiration for Ethiopia and her people developed among people of color around the world.

For African Americans of Robinson's generation, Adowa was a rare symbolic and psychological "victory of blacks over whites." One British historian observed how the 1896 campaign "was the first revolt of the Dark Continent against domineering Europe." Consequently, an upsurge in racial pride swept across the United States, Africa, and the Caribbean. Thereafter, black leaders from around the world made honorary pilgrimages to Ethiopia. Like no other event in Africa's history, the victory at Adowa "profoundly affected black Americans."[123] Ethiopian military success seemed to portend that Africa's greatness could be resurrected in the future, because Adowa was "the first time since Hannibal [that] an African people had successfully repulsed a major European army [and the] significance of this battle was not lost upon Afro-Americans."[124]

The unexpected Ethiopian victory at Adowa also left a lasting political and psychological impact across Italy, which experienced a national disgrace that Mussolini exploited to the fullest. By 1935, "Italians, despite Mussolini, still smarted under the humiliation of Adowa where the Abyssinians had massacred them in 1896, [therefore] Mussolini, like Hitler, was [bent upon] avenging an earlier degradation, returning to Italy, as on a bloody salver, its self-respect." Like the Italian nation, Mussolini was consumed with an obsessive "Adowa complex." The past, both ancient and modern, was about to dictate Ethiopia's future.[125]

By this time, Mussolini had become a "'prisoner of prestige' [and] he had to keep on doing something [as] Hitler was stealing far too much space from him in world headlines."[126] Therefore, Il Duce massed a powerful army on the Ethiopia–Eritrea border just north of the ancient land of the Solomonic Lion of Judah, after the first clashes at Walwal in December 1934. Based on an earlier plan to conquer and occupy Ethiopia and quickly transform it into an Italian protectorate, Mussolini planned to overwhelm Ethiopia and smash all resistance in record time.[127]

Italy was now attempting to play catch-up, rushing headlong into the old imperialist game—relatively new for modern Italy—of the Western European powers gaining control of weaker nations for crass exploitation. And Ethiopia was now "the only territory left" in Africa open for European conquest.[128]

But Ethiopia, unlike the United States, had been a member—ironically sponsored by Italy—of the League of Nations since 1923. However, Western powers desired to maintain the status quo to preserve their own colonial empires. This selfish imperialist priority of the major European powers allowed Mussolini a free hand in Ethiopia to grab his own colonies. Both "the British and French government [played the leading roles in] selling the Abyssinians down the river."[129]

Indeed, Ethiopia had been sold out by the cynical realpolitik of the Western powers long before the mid-1930s. An October 1896 peace convention had been signed between Ethiopia and Italy, ensuring that Italy would keep a firm grip on Eritrea and the port of Massawa on the Red Sea. And in the Anglo-Italian Protocols of 1891 and 1894, Great Britain recognized that Ethiopia was still part of Italy's sphere of influence, in order to limit France's expansion into Africa, and in recognition of British Nile basin interests. Therefore, Italy's colonial ambitions in Ethiopia would not be challenged.[130]

Even though the Treaty of Friendship between Britain and Ethiopia was signed in 1897, Ethiopia was thereafter laid on the table to be carved up like a pie by greedy, hungry hosts. In a treaty signed between Italy and Eritrea in 1900, Eritrea had been permanently severed from Ethiopia. To counter increasing German influence, a secret Tripartite Treaty had been concluded in 1906, which divided Ethiopia into three spheres of influence. Therefore, despite its mountainous perch and defiance, Ethiopia was now strategically vulnerable, without an industrial base, allies, or access to the sea.[131]

The Great Powers were concerned that another Italian defeat by black Ethiopians might lead to unrest among people of color in their own colonial possessions around the world, and thus would allow the sacrifice of Ethiopia, which they viewed as expendable for world stability, in 1935.

Thanks in part to the Great Depression and the world war's legacies, the League of Nations existed in name only by the mid-1930s. The international organization possessed neither the moral nor armed might to stop naked aggression against a member. Hoping to save his nation from Rome's "civilizing mission," Emperor Selassie naively placed his faith in the collective security and false promises of the League, especially in Great Britain and France. Tragically, the emperor, like the Ethiopian people, was about to learn some hard lessons about realpolitik and the moral decay of the Western powers.[132]

Emperor Selassie described how "We had not thought that Italy would violate the obligations upon which she had entered within the League of Nations and . . . when she attacked Walwal and killed our soldiers, we notified the League of Nations because it seemed to the United States that the League might restrain Italy from waging a major war [while Italy] was piling up war material in the vicinity of our borders."[133]

Cynical, but realistic in regard to race relations, Robinson later wrote in a 1935 letter that revealed his disillusionment over the world's lack of concern for Ethiopia's tragic plight: "the League of Nation[s] is just another White man's bluff. White people will all ways [sic] stick together in the end when it comes to the color question."[134]

Robinson was not guilty of exaggeration. Even as part of the secret agreement in which Italy had joined the Allies' side during World War I, Italy's right to Ethiopia had already been recognized by the Western powers for her support against Germany. And now, to the Great Powers, Ethiopia was not an independent Christian nation deserving of protection; rather, it was "Italy's prize."[135] Mussolini and his golden dream of a new Roman Empire was about to lead Italy "to his, and the world's, apocalypse in distant Ethiopia."[136]

With Ethiopia about to be invaded, Robinson deferred all of his ambitious plans in the United States, including teaching aviation at Tuskegee Institute. Robinson evidently asked G. L. Washington, the head of the Department of Mechanical Industries at Tuskegee, to hold the faculty position open for him, after his one-year commitment to Ethiopia.[137]

Long before he departed for Ethiopia, tens of thousands of Italian soldiers had been boarding troop ships that had steadily departed the port of Naples, Italy, almost on a daily basis, by the summer of 1935. Like Robinson, these young men, mostly of the Catholic faith, were bound for a new adventure in faraway East Africa that would prove far from romantic. Quite unknowing, Robinson was soon heading straight into the eye of the storm.[138]

5

COMMANDING EMPEROR SELASSIE'S
IMPERIAL ETHIOPIAN AIR FORCE

EAGER FOR A NEW CHALLENGE, Robinson made final preparations to leave the United States. Dr. Bayen helped him secure a passport and book passage for the end of May 1935 journey to Ethiopia. He was about to become a leading player in a "classical tragedy."[1]

Robinson knew that he needed a cadre of well-trained black flyers, aviation technicians, and mechanics to assist him, and Chicago, the center of aviation in the North, was the best place to secure such experienced aviation volunteers.

Most of these airmen were not only members of the Challengers Air Pilots' Association but also had served in the Military Order of Guard Aviation unit in Chicago. Robinson was convinced that the well-trained "Challengers, most of whom were accomplished pilots and mechanics [with] their designation and experience as a Military Order of Guard Aviation unit, provided the expertise needed to assist Ethiopia in the development of an Air Force." These volunteers planned to eventually join him in Ethiopia, after he arrived in Addis Ababa.[2] As Robinson explained, "I told my fellow pilots [in Chicago] that I would do everything I could to get them in the [Imperial Ethiopian] air force here [in Ethiopia]."[3]

Robinson held no reservations about resigning from the Curtiss-Wright Aeronautical School after six years of doing work he loved. Ernest Hemingway gave ample warning to newspaper correspondents bound for Ethiopia that "if they were wounded the vultures would first peck out their eyes and then tear out their livers."[4] Robinson ignored the warning.

At this time, Robinson perhaps made out his will with a Chicago lawyer just in case he met his demise overseas. He took some comfort in the fact that he could depend upon his wife, Earnize. Evidently trained in mechanics by her husband, she would manage his South Side automobile repair garage side in his absence. The Robinsons had no children, and Earnize was a capable, smart businesswoman in her own right. She was not unlike John's mother, Celeste, who combined business sense with common sense.[5]

An accident, evidently an automobile or motorcycle mishap, occurred only three days before Robinson's scheduled departure from Chicago. As friend and former student Janet Harmon Bragg explained, "Several days before he left his arm was broken in three places but he was ready to go."[6]

Clearly, nothing could stop Robinson at this point. Bragg had been thunderstruck by the news of his decision to go to Ethiopia, especially after sustaining a serious injury. As she wrote: "I never forgot the expression on his face when he told me about [leaving for Ethiopia]. On that day he had purchased books on ores and studied everything that Ethiopia had to offer."[7]

Without fanfare or any notice on May 2, 1935, except the emotional goodbyes with his wife and friends in Bronzeville, Robinson left Chicago by rail. After reaching the East Coast, he boarded a steam liner in New York Harbor for the lengthy trip across the Atlantic. He planned first to travel to France and then on to Ethiopia.[8]

Significantly, "when Robinson boarded a steamer bound for the horn of Africa, he [not only] reflected the concerns of many black Americans for Ethiopia," but also was one of only a handful of activists who backed upon those "concerns" with action.[9]

As if pulled onward by some unseen force of nature, perhaps destiny or fate, Robinson was on his own during his trip to Ethiopia. He described the lengthy journey across the Atlantic, past the Rock of Gibraltar, and then into the Mediterranean Sea's blue waters during May:

> I proceeded to Cherburg [*sic*], France and then to Paris where at the Ethiopian consulate I was given my orders. It was Port Said [Egypt and at the head of the Suez Canal] that I had my first contact with what I was up against. As I was told the ship had a stay of several hours in the port, I went ashore to look the town over. As I walked thru the streets, it dawned on me that I was being followed. Across the street from me were a man and a lad of about nine years. Everywhere I went, they followed until I stopped suddenly at a corner.

Then the lad came over and addressed me in Amharic, the language used in Ethiopia. I couldn't answer and just threw up my hands. He then asked me something in French. I was still at sea and couldn't answer. Finally he came through in English. I was amazed and didn't know how much to say since he could talk English. He took me across the street to his father and I learned that he was the Ethiopian consul in Port Said. But it puzzled them as to my identity. They thought at first I was an Ethiopian, later they said if I were not an Ethiopian and could speak English, I must be a Chinese [some Chinese students were aboard Robinson's ship returning home after studying in Paris]. They wanted information concerning one Robinson, coming down from Paris en route to Ethiopia. I had a hard time convincing them I was an American and was Robinson.[10]

From Port Said the steamship pushed down the narrow confines of the Suez Canal and into the Red Sea. Traveling southeast down the Red Sea to Ethiopia, it then passed through the straits of Bab al Mandab and the Gulf of Aden. At last, Robinson reached the busy port of Djibouti, the capital of French Somaliland.

After a journey of more than seven thousand miles, Robinson wrote:

Continuing my trip, I arrived in Djibouti. Knowing I couldn't speak the language, I cabled a message asking the [Ethiopian] consul there to have someone meet me. My arm, then broken, was giving me trouble because of the excessive heat. I found my way to a hotel where the proprietor spoke English and made my wants known. I hadn't been there long before the consul came over looking for me. And when he asked if Robinson was there, I was pointed out. That night, after moving to the [Ethiopian] consulate, a huge banquet was given in my honor and the next day I started on the railroad to Addis Ababa, some 480 miles to the southwest.[11]

After boarding a wooden train car of the only railroad in this part of Horn of Africa, Robinson rode the rails of the Franco-Ethiopian Railroad, or the Djibouti-Addis Ababa Railroad, southwestward. Not long after leaving Djibouti, the rickety train crossed the Ethiopian border. From slatted windows, to keep out the stifling heat, Robinson marveled at the sight of the low-lying lands of the bleak Danakil Desert, which was so unlike the lush greenery of his native Mississippi. This harsh land of eastcentral Ethiopia was arid, colorless, and did not look at all how Robinson had imagined Africa to be. And the intense heat of this desert, with little vegetation, distinguished only by endless rocks and sand, was far hotter than the Gulf of Mexico coast, since Ethiopia was much closer to the equator.

After traveling by rail southwest to a point around two hundred miles east of Addis Ababa, as the land gradually rose higher in elevation, Robinson met Emperor Haile Selassie for the first time at Dire Dawa—the halfway station on the railroad—in eastcentral Ethiopia. The meeting was an unforgettable experience for the twenty-nine-year-old Robinson. As he described the journey through a wild uninhabited country, a desert wasteland, and the hot plain of the suffocating lowlands, "This trip takes three days. And it was on my first stop after boarding the train I met the Emperor. It was an unofficial visit. I was taken into his presence, bowed in and bowed out. Not a word was spoken."[12]

Such deference was in keeping with the strict traditions of a tightly structured hierarchical Ethiopian society, and "according to the custom of Ethiopian kings which has survived since antiquity," wrote Emperor Selassie. Robinson had answered Selassie's appeal for African Americans to come back "to the homeland" and "their fatherland," and the emperor was most appreciative.[13] It was an unforgettable experience for a young man brought up in the world of Jim Crow.

Born Ras Tafari Makonnen in 1892, Selassie had prevailed in a ruthless power struggle—against other Ethiopian leaders, including the empress and a cousin—for the throne's possession. A modern man with a European education, Selassie hailed from the province of Harar in the country's southeast corner, where he had been governor, like his father before him. Selassie had successfully defended Ethiopia against numerous Muslim threats. He was, however, more of an intellectual and diplomat than a warrior in the traditional Ethiopian sense.[14]

Devout and studious by nature, Selassie was determined to maintain Ethiopia's distinct Orthodox and Solomonic heritage, because, as he wrote, the "Christian faith, which our fathers had hitherto carefully retained by fighting for their faith with the Muslims and by shedding their blood." He was most proud of the fact that displayed across the Ethiopian flag, decorated with a Christian Cross, was written, "The Lion of the Tribe of Judah has prevailed."[15]

In fact, few nations could claim a longer legacy of independence, or a more distinguished heritage, especially its Solomonic tradition. Ethiopia had existed as an independent empire since 1100 BC. In 480 BC, the powerful Persian army of King

Xerxes who invaded Greece and wiped out King Leonidas's three hundred Spartans at Thermopylae, included Ethiopian warriors. Around 323 BC, ambassadors from Ethiopia offered homage to Alexander the Great. Ancient Greeks bestowed the name, from "ethiopes" and "Aethiops," upon these dark-skinned people. Only in the Middle Ages had Ethiopia, which was its classical name, become known as Abyssinia. While Mussolini boasted about Roman greatness because of its imperial past, Ethiopia possessed a historical legacy older than ancient Rome's. Emperor Selassie explained how "Ethiopia has been the bastion of Christianity for more than a millennium among the savages and pagans in the arid desert." Maintaining its ancient culture, religion, traditions, and legacy of freedom from foreign control for centuries, Ethiopia was truly the unconquerable "land of the lion." The Solomonic legend of Ethiopia laid an ancient claim to the ancestry of King Solomon and the King of Judea, or Israel, by way of Queen Sheba, Makeda.[16]

At the arid northern end of the East African Rift Plateau, or Great Rift Valley, the Queen's royal palace was located in the ancient holy city in the Tigre Province, Axum. Founded around 1000 BC, Axum was the center of government and Ethiopia's first capital. Invading Muslim warriors had once burned down this religious center, but the Ethiopian Christians eventually prevailed and rebuilt the church on the same site.

Moreover, the Ethiopian people were proud of their heroic past in successfully defending a distinctive Christian heritage—the Christian Orthodox Church—against Islamic threat from the lowlands and deserts of both Muslim nations Sudan, to the west, and Saudi Arabia, to the north. Ethiopians boasted of a revered recorded history, written in the ancient language of Geez, an Afro-Asiatic language, dating back nearly two thousand years.[17]

Located just north of the equator, Ethiopia was larger than any nation in Europe except Russia. Known as the Woina-Dega, or the highland of the grape, the central Ethiopian heartland was the most temperate region, containing most of the nation's population. Here, mountains and highland plateaus towered some five thousand to eight thousand feet, providing a cool climate to a rugged land located so near the equator. With some jagged peaks reaching fifteen thousand feet, this region was known as the Dega in the north and northwest. Carved out by centuries of erosion, steep valleys ran north–south through the Ethiopian highlands, the largest of which is the Great Rift Valley, the cradle of humanity. Formed of volcanic rock, Ethiopia's arid highlands served as the headwaters of Africa. The three months of rainy seasons in the rugged highlands gave birth to the Blue Nile, the largest river in Ethiopia. The Blue Nile fed the mighty Nile, the world's longest river, after it emptied from Lake Tzana to join the White Nile, near Khartoum. Then the Nile continued north to Cairo just before entering the eastern Mediterranean.

Robinson reached the railroad's terminus at the capital of Addis Ababa, nestled in the lush central highlands, on May 29, after nearly a month of travel from New York City. He entered the stately Addis Ababa Railroad Station, built in 1929. Also arriving in May were scores of newspaper correspondents from around the world, but mostly from the United States and Western Europe, drawn by the looming conflict.

Spread out over a high plateau at an elevation of eight thousand feet, Addis Ababa stood at the foot of towering Mount Entoto, which rose up to the north, and the lengthy range of the Entoto Mountains. Groves of palm trees, as well as fast-growing eucalyptus trees imported from Australia by Emperor Menelik II, made the capital's setting atop the high plateau especially picturesque. Temperatures in Addis Ababa, meaning "New Flower," were much cooler than in the sweltering lowlands through which Robinson had journeyed.

Consisting of both modern buildings and sun-hardened mud and stone houses of traditional design, circular tukuls with thatched roofs, and all spread out in haphazard, but traditional fashion, Addis Ababa was a sprawling city full of dogs, children, and a people of a vibrant culture. Addis Ababa was dustier, more confusing, and dirtier than any city Robinson had seen in America.

Inhabited since Biblical days, Addis Ababa was created in large part by Emperor Menilik II, after his great victory over the Italians at Adowa in 1896. Like Peter the Great and St. Petersburg, Emperor Selassie planned to transform Addis Ababa into a modern city. Here, Robinson viewed stately St. George's Cathedral, with its beautiful interior artwork, the principal house of worship in the city's heart. Italian prisoners captured at Adowa in 1896 had constructed this cathedral for the Orthodox religion.

Robinson was impressed by the ancient sights of the capital. These included the church-like stone mausoleum of Emperor Menelik II atop a high hill. Symbolically, two large and stately marble Lions of Judah guarded each side of the main entryway to the imposing memorial. Ethiopia's royal symbol was a male lion with a crown topped with a crucifix. Nothing Robinson had experienced either in the North or South had prepared him for Addis Ababa. And in the western part of town, he must have enjoyed the busy Mercato, the largest and perhaps nosiest out-door market in all Africa.

Some weeks would pass before an opportunity came for Robinson to meet again with Emperor Selassie. At this time, Robinson was not prepared to assume official duties. His broken arm had yet to fully heal, therefore, he continued to tour the capital and the surrounding area like a curious tourist. Ancient buildings, ritu-als, and customs many times older than America's founding presented a haunting sensation. After all, the "splendor and sophistication" of ancient Ethiopian civili-zation had once "rivaled ancient Rome's." But this was a nonindustrialized land, which was dominated by grazing and subsistence agriculture, a feudal society. As in ancient times, the donkey was still the primary mode of transportation. Ethio-pian daily life was distinguished by lengthy caravans of camels, and tall black men and graceful women dressed in the glowing white shammas and other colors that denoted various tribes. Stoic herdsmen watched their herds of cattle, humpbacked Brahman types, spread out across the flowing grasslands and in the fertile river val-leys, while herds of goats grazed along green hillsides.[18]

Coffee trees grew wild in the central highlands of Ethiopia. This cool, high-altitude, and wet climate was ideal for coffee cultivation, and the coffee belt ran through Ethiopia's heart. From these cool highlands, the cultivation of coffee had spread throughout the world. Robinson must have basked in the rich-tasting Ethio-pian coffee, or high-quality arabica, perhaps the world's finest.[19]

He continued to keep his plans for a military aviation role a secret to those he met at Addis Ababa, as war had not yet erupted. As Robinson penned in a June 3, 1935, letter: "I told every body here I was a tailor and was born here, but had been in America for 25 years. All the people believe it because I look just like an Abys-sinian. Mr. Bayen told me to say this to the people so they wouldent [sic] know my purpose here."[20]

Robinson's arrival in Addis Ababa had coincided with Italy's preparations for the upcoming invasion. By the end of May, an estimated nearly 1 million Italians were mobilized for military service. These included crack military units such as the Gavinana Division, which was composed mostly of young men from the beautiful Italian city of Florence; Tuscany; the Peloritana Division in Sicily; and the Alpini Division. Proud Italian units included the Aosta Lancers, which was one of the elite commands of the Italian Army. Less elite Italian units consisted of divisions of Mussolini's "Black Shirts," or the Fascist militia. Organized on the lines of the ancient Roman army, the "Black Shirts" had been formed in 1922. Robinson knew little, if anything, of the extent of either these massive war preparations, or the over-all might of Italy's military machine that was about to descend upon Ethiopia's me-diaeval society of nomads, warriors, sheep and cattle herders, and farmers, who were ill-prepared for the ugly realities of modern warfare.[21]

Here, at the bustling capital in the central highlands, Robinson took a room at the Hotel de France, where many foreigners stayed and socialized. Meanwhile, most newspaper correspondents were lodged at the Hotel Imperial. To his surprise, Robinson discovered a good many foreign, white European, military advisors, who had attempted to modernize Ethiopia's feudal military, which was one of Emperor Selassie's major initiatives. A half dozen foreign embassies were located in Addis Ababa, which also ensured that the capital was full of Europeans, including doz-ens of newspaper correspondents. As revealed in a June 3, 1935, letter, Robinson was surprised to find that unlike in the black community of Gulfport, "all the com-merical [sic] businesses in this Country is run by White people, Indians from India, Turks, and Egyptians. They have more Greeks here than any other White race."[22]

Belgian advisers, who were mostly officers paid by the Ethiopian government (like Robinson), continued to train the emperor's Ethiopian Imperial Guard, which protected Selassie from harm. Swedish advisors, who were as anti-fascist as the Belgians, also attempted to modernize the Ethiopian military. These advisors hoped to create a modern, regular, army—as opposed to the unreliable, untrained, and often rebellious feudal militias and levies of the Ethiopian warlords—with the Ethiopian Imperial Guard serving as its nucleus. Despite their Islamic faith, even a handful of Turkish officers assisted the emperor in his efforts.

Ironically, even though this outside expertise was a key to his nation's and military's modernization effort, Emperor Selassie's employment of so many white European advisors and technicians had inspired criticism not only in Ethiopia but also in black America. With war about to erupt, however, the emperor sought "not to limit foreign influence" in his country, because of xenophobic feeling based on prejudice, which Robinson could understand. However, one vocal critic was none other than Pan-African leader Marcus Garvey, who derided the emperor as "play-ing white."

Besides Selassie's Imperial Bodyguard (yet undergoing training by the Belgian military mission), the Swedish military mission to Ethiopia consisted of high-ranking officers, including a general who operated an officer training school, a three-year cadet program, located not far from Addis Ababa at one of the emperor's summer palaces. The officer training school was opened by the emperor in April 1935, just before Robinson's arrival in Addis Ababa. Clearly, Emperor Selassie had embarked on an accelerated attempt to modernize his military at the last minute before the Italians struck.[23]

Not long after his arrival, Robinson began to train Ethiopian pilots, which was no small challenge with Ethiopians speaking only Amharic and lacking both education and technical backgrounds. Through an interpreter, Robinson attempted to teach the aspiring pilots to bolster the capabilities of the Imperial Ethiopian Air Force. Three weeks after he had first met him at Dire Dawa, Emperor Selassie summoned Robinson to his English-style Imperial Palace in Addis Ababa. Robinson stated: "It was not until three weeks later that I had my first interview with the Emperor. He asked me if I liked the work I had been assigned to [training young Ethiopian pilots] and I told him any work I did to help Ethiopia was to my liking. He asked that I say something else, but I had nothing else to say and went out."[24]

Knowing that he had made the correct decision in coming to Ethiopia and casting his fate with the threatened ancient nation, Robinson later described the emperor "as a devout Christian and an ardent patriot, who bound his war-like chiefs together . . . by exercising an iron will."[25]

From the beginning, Robinson employed his aeronautical expertise in the capacity of an expert "consultant in the development of the Royal Air Force," or the training of pilots and advising on aviation matters. Meanwhile, Hubert F. Julian, despite reaching Ethiopia a few weeks before Robinson had, was not assigned to the Imperial Ethiopian Air Force in any capacity.[26]

Unlike the troublesome Julian, Robinson's interpersonal and diplomacy skills, and aviation expertise ensured that he would remain on good terms with Emperor Selassie and the Imperial Ethiopian Air Force. Besides impressing Emperor Selassie and gaining "the emperor's confidence," which was no small accomplishment after the disastrous Julian affair, Robinson also quickly won over high-ranking members of the royal family. In time, "Makonnen, the Duke of Harar, the emperor's second son [and] John Robinson [became] very good friends."[27]

Indeed, Robinson transcended cultural barriers, even though xenophobic feelings were quite strong in Ethiopia, thanks in part to Julian's antics. Nevertheless,

Robinson easily overcame wide cultural differences and negative stereotypes about African Americans held by Americans, Europeans, and even Ethiopians. From beginning to end, he "was popular among both Ethiopians and Americans."[28]

Using one of the few operable aircraft of the Imperial Ethiopian Air Force, Robinson initially employed an old French plane, a Potez 25 A2, which had been delivered to the emperor in 1929. More important, he immediately earned a captain's commission in the Imperial Ethiopian Army. In the days ahead, Robinson gained more confidence among the Ethiopians with his leadership qualities and aviation expertise, even though his broken arm had not yet fully healed.

Robinson then acquired an American-made Beechcraft. This aircraft was far superior to the emperor's small fleet of a dozen antiquated French planes that made up the fledgling Imperial Ethiopian Air Force. Robinson now possessed the newest, fastest, and best aircraft in the Imperial Ethiopian Air Force.

Meanwhile, Julian continued to fulfill some of the worst stereotypes about African Americans, which would continue to negatively affect Robinson. As Robinson penned in a letter condemning Julian's indiscretions, "American Negroes that have come here have made the white people word [ring] true." More specifically, Julian had not paid his bills, including hotel, and "beats the [Ethiopian] servants," wrote a disgusted Robinson.[29]

Robinson viewed Julian as a cancer, who steadily eroded the Ethiopians' desire to secure African American assistance for the war effort. As Robinson wrote, "I realy [sic] believe the higher Abyssinian [Emperor Selassie] wants the American Negro, but Julian [and others] have made some bad examples."[30]

On August 8, 1935, a now healthy Robinson at last encountered Julian in person. By this time, bad blood existed between the two, and tension was high. This lingering antagonism actually went back to Chicago in 1934, when Julian sought out Robinson and the Challenger Air Pilots' Association to solicit support for his planned trans-Atlantic flight by renting one of the association's planes. When Julian's proposed rental amount was rejected by Robinson and Coffey as much too low, an incensed Julian angrily ordered the two out of his Chicago hotel room. And now another hotel reunion—some seven thousand miles away from Chicago—between Robinson and Julian was about to make international headlines.

At the Hotel de France in Addis Ababa where Robinson stayed, Julian was informed by white newspapermen, who had baited him, that Robinson had spoken ill of Julian's aviation skills.

When Robinson came down the stairs from his room, an infuriated Julian was ready and waiting. Julian struck first. Desiring to remain in the good graces of Emperor Selassie, Robinson did not strike back. The confrontation was broken up by white journalists who were looking for a juicy story about the two black flyers. Later in a letter, Robinson described the unfortunate incident: "In Addis Ababa he came over to the hotel where I was staying and slapped my face. He was angry because he thought I had had something to do with an article making fun of him which appeared in the United States." Leading white newspapers such as the *New York Sun* eagerly picked up this widely publicized incident between the two black aviators in Ethiopia. Knowing the importance of gaining outside support and maintaining the image of black solidarity, Emperor Selassie and top Ethiopian officials were naturally upset by the Julian–Robinson incident. They feared the bad press would ensure that no additional black volunteers would be forthcoming from America, at a time when the emperor was intent on obtaining black volunteers that he had even begun to turn down white volunteers, including aviators, from the United States.

Because of his unprovoked assault, Julian was banished from the capital, then appointed the commander of a small infantry command at Ambo, far to the north. A humiliated Julian departed from Addis Ababa in mid-September, heading north "in a huff [which ensured that he would forever be] out of the limelight he loved."[31]

Despite the fact that he was not the instigator, the fight's widespread publicity caused Robinson some embarrassment. In a lengthy letter, Robinson apologized to Claude A. Barnett, the man who was partly "responsible for Robinson's venture to the African Empire," for this incident caused some criticism at home and against Robinson's friends and supporters back in Chicago, including Barnett: "I am sorry I caused you all to be razzed, and will try to redeem my self if I can."[32]

With the disgraced Julian and his legacy no longer a problem for him, Robinson soon emerged as Emperor Selassie's top aviator, while Julian shortly departed the country for good. Unlike Robinson, Julian would never see military action against the Italians. He would eventually return to Addis Ababa from the north in the fall of 1935, however, not long after the Italians invaded. Then, Julian, "the stormiest petrel in the Ethiopian Army," would be suspected of planning to assassinate the emperor, while in the Italians' pay. He would be cleared of the charges, but would be forced to leave Ethiopia by mid-November.

With his arm healed and in good health, Robinson now accepted the coveted offer from Emperor Selassie to head the Imperial Ethiopian Air Force. He was promoted to the rank of full colonel around mid-August 1935. This advancement was the highest rank ever bestowed upon an African American in American or Ethiopian history. Colonel Robinson also became Emperor Selassie's personal pilot.

Surprisingly, Robinson's advancement even made headlines in the *New York Times*—on August 23, 1935, it ran a story headlined, "Ethiopia Gets New Flier." A skeptical white journalist for the *Times* wrote: "An [and the first] American Negro aviator, known as 'the brown Condor of Ethiopia,' has replaced Hubert Julian. He is John C. Robinson of Chicago, the first American volunteer for services in Emperor Haile Selassie's army. . . . Robinson has been up every day in a single seated plane and his flying ability has electrified the populace" of Addis Ababa and Ethiopia.[33]

This was the first American journalist to use the "brown condor of Ethiopia" nickname for Robinson. At this time, the word "brown" referred to the fact that African Americans had emerged as a "new people," who were neither African nor European, "but both—and something more," or brown.[34]

Even Robinson was amazed, in his own words, by his sudden and "rapid advancement." By this time, Emperor Selassie's Imperial Ethiopian Air Force "existed essentially on paper and in the minds of the deluded." Robinson's formidable task was now to transform a relatively small number of nondescript, older aircraft into a viable air force on the eve of Italy's invasion of Ethiopia; unfortunately, the chronic shortage of revenues that made the modern rearmament, especially in regard to modern aircraft, a virtual impossibility.[35]

CREATING THE IMPERIAL ETHIOPIAN AIR FORCE

Robinson was now thrust to center stage as the only African American serving in a leading military role. Indeed, "Robinson [would be] the only black American in the Ethiopian armed forces; he held high commissioned rank and served in a new and elite branch, the air force."[36]

As recognized and fully appreciated by Emperor Selassie and other leading Ethiopians in Addis Ababa, Colonel Robinson was the exact opposite of Julian: a mature and reliable personality of high character possessing an impressive list of past aviation accomplishments, including overcoming adversity and racial barriers. Historian Joseph E. Harris wrote how, "John Robinson was a man of a different cast. Although he had been denied entrance to several pilot classes in the United States because he was black, he persisted, eventually becoming the first black graduate of the Curtiss-Wright Aeronautical School, in Chicago. Later he was one of the school's instructors. Though the first American to serve Ethiopia in a military capacity, Robinson was not a vocal, publicity-minded headliner. He did not perform in exhibitions but taught others and flew private planes. He was less widely known than Julian, but he gained considerably more experience as a pilot."[37]

By August 1935, Robinson's headquarters were located near the Akaki Airport on the southwestern outskirts of Addis Ababa, where his small air force of around a dozen aircraft was stationed. A separate base for the Imperial Ethiopian Air Force was located next to the Akaki Airport, and was known as Janhoy Meda Akaki. Robinson would later move his headquarters here.

Emperor Selassie realized that his tiny cadre of flyers, essentially a handful of French citizens, could cause an ill-timed diplomatic incident and the loss of Western support if it was ascertained that they were serving Ethiopia against Italy, especially if this happened by capture or death in combat. Therefore, Selassie decided these Frenchmen would not fly for Ethiopia whenever open warfare erupted, causing the first French aviators to begin to depart Ethiopia not long after Robinson's arrival in late May 1935. To fill this void, Robinson's dual solution called for not only training large numbers of Ethiopian pilots but also securing African American volunteers from the United States. He realized that an elite cadre of well-trained African American flyers could form a solid nucleus upon which a viable Imperial Ethiopian Air Force could be eventually created.

A small cadre of Ethiopian pilots who had received some initial flight training in Europe were available, but these zealous volunteers were still in the process of gaining additional aviation training at Janhoy Meda Akaki from Robinson and French aviators. Emperor Selassie, nevertheless, continued to turn down white volunteer pilots who had traveled to Ethiopia on their own expense, and even white Americans offering to come to Ethiopia's aid. Emperor Selassie wanted an all-black air force, and Robinson worked tirelessly to achieve this goal.[38]

While the Ethiopian pilots continued to receive some flight training from the few French flyers who remained, Robinson worked overtime to give additional aviation instruction to the young Ethiopian airmen at the training facilities at his air base, Janhoy Meda Akaki. Indeed, he "instructed many natives in aviation technology (including flying)," recalled Bragg. But Robinson's greatest challenge was to increase the number of aircraft of the Imperial Ethiopian Air Force. In an interview by a Baltimore, Maryland, journalist of the *Afro-American*, Robinson stated with regret that only a handful of operable aircraft were initially available to him in Ethiopia, and they "were from seven to eight years old and in bad condition."[39]

Some of these antiquated aircraft, including four biplane French Potez 25 aircraft, had assisted Selassie, then known as Ras Tafari Makonnen, in the decisive battle against a rival warlord, Ras Gugsa of Gondar, in early 1930. Selassie's March 1930 success at Anchim, north of Addis Ababa, was a decisive military and political victory. For the first time in Ethiopian history, he employed two aircraft flown by French pilots, who strafed the Ethiopian opposition with impunity. Achieved by the demonstration of air power capabilities, Ras Gugsa's defeat and death paved the way for Selassie's rise as emperor.[40]

Thanks to this victory only five years before, the emperor became an enthusiastic proponent of air power's importance. After all, the key to Selassie's early success had been because of his own farsighted vision of using aircraft and foreign pilots. Indeed, this all-important victory at Anchim resulted because "Tafari had created this fledgling air force only a few months earlier, and its personnel consisted of two French pilots [even though] the air force was a token, but it was also a strategic fact."[41]

Indeed, these French biplanes also had played an offensive role. French airmen dropped small bombs and grenades by hand on the thirty-five thousand-man army of Beghemder with effective results. This battle of the Plains of Anchim broke the back of rebel resistance from the Beghemder Province, which had been threatening Tafari's authority since 1928.[42]

Nevertheless, the so-called air force that Robinson inherited was in name only. Even though nearly a dozen aircraft existed in the Imperial Ethiopian Air Force, only three aircraft were fully operational, before the Beechcraft's arrival from the United States. Besides three French aircraft that could be repaired, another three planes were of "limited value," while three others were entirely "useless." With good reason, Robinson regretted how these aircraft "are of ancient vintage." Besides the four small French Potez 25 biplanes, two-seaters which looked like leftovers from World War I, two other aircraft of the Imperial Ethiopian Air Force had been gifts to the emperor at his November 1930 coronation: a large Farman monoplane from France, and a light Breda sport plane from Italy.

Meanwhile, besides training Ethiopian pilots, Robinson continued to make the older aircraft operational at the Janhoy Meda Akaki. The Ethiopian government had ordered the construction of several new airfields, evidently based on Robinson's personal recommendations, to accommodate what Emperor Selassie optimistically envisioned as a large air force. The Janhoy Meda Akaki base served as both Robinson's and the Imperial Ethiopian Air Force's headquarters throughout the Italo-Ethiopian War. From the beginning of his appointment as the Imperial Ethiopian Air Force's commander to the time that war erupted, Colonel Robinson made a number of additional aircraft fully operational, adding to the few fully operational aircraft that he had inherited. By the late summer of 1935, thanks in large part to Robinson's efforts, "Ethiopia had a fleet of eleven aeroplanes, of which only eight were serviceable, and they were used mainly for transport."[43]

Robinson's task was immense in regard to creating combat-ready aircraft, "none of which was equipped for combat or bombing."[44] Included in this fledgling air force were the four French Potez 25 aircraft, and a light attack and tactical reconnaissance aircraft, which the emperor had purchased in 1927. Known for its quality and resilience and powered by Lorraine-Dietrich piston engines, this plane was one of the most esteemed French aircraft in the 1920s and 1930s. The reliable Potez saw service in more than twenty nations around the world. Some Potez 25 aircraft of Robinson's air force were equipped with fixed forward-firing machine guns synchronized to fire through the propeller. Robinson also was in charge of two Fokker monoplanes, which were in "good condition, but lacked spares," one single-engine French Farman monoplane, and one small Italian Breda sport airplane.[45] In addition, a single German tri-motor Fokker airplane, a rebuilt Moth from England, and a little monoplane—a modified De Havilland Moth—christened the *Ethiopia I*—were also part of Robinson's air force. The lone American aircraft was not only part of the Imperial Ethiopian Air Force, but also Robinson's pride and joy. This was the prized Beechcraft, which carried twelve passengers.[46]

To Robinson's delight, this was the fastest plane in the miniscule Ethiopian air corps. Because of the arms embargo that barred Ethiopia from acquiring military aircraft, only civilian aircraft could be obtained from the outside world. The swift, sleek Beechcraft, therefore, had been covertly smuggled into the country, most likely by train.[47]

Founded by former World War I Army Air Service pilot and postwar barnstormer Walter H. Beech in 1932, the Beechcraft Aircraft Corporation produced superior aircraft that were well respected around the world. Some were even owned by Hollywood celebrities. First established in Wichita, Kansas, this aviation company begun operation as the Travel Air Manufacturing Company in 1924. By 1929,

Beech's Air Travel became the largest producer of commercial aircraft, both mono-plane and biplane, until it was purchased by the Curtiss-Wright Corporation in 1931. Beech's aircraft were world famous for their record-setting performances in competitions and races across America.

Built at the Beechcraft Aircraft Corporation plant in St. Louis, Missouri—af-ter the hard times of the Great Depression forced the company to relocate from Wichita, Kansas—the Beech 17L, first produced in 1934, had been created by Beech's determination to build the world's finest aircraft. Beech manufactured the "five-place biplane, having the interior luxury and passenger comfort of a fine se-dan, a top speed of 200 miles per hour (mph) or better, a landing speed no higher than 60 mph, a nonstop range close to 1,000 miles." Drawing upon his experience as an Army Air Service flyer, Beech's futuristic aviation vision became a reality with the Beech 17L, a negative stagger plane. Capable of cruising at 152 mph and with a top speed of 166 mph thanks to the power generated from the 225 horsepower Jacobs engine, the Beech 17L, was known as the "Staggerwing." A flying machine that Robinson literally fell in love with from the beginning, this splendid Beech-craft would soon prove faster than any Italian fighter in Ethiopia's skies.[48]

Despite the aircraft's "classic design," its overall appearance as a biplane be-guiled its superior power, easy controllability at all speeds, sound aerodynamic characteristics, high visibility for pilot, favorable stall and recovery characteristics, speed, and overall easy grace in flight. Beech's aeronautical masterpiece was shipped throughout the world. But only one of the thirty-six manufactured planes made by Beech in 1935 ever reached Robinson in Ethiopia. Robinson's efforts to secure the fastest aircraft in Ethiopia would save not only his life but also perhaps Emperor Selassie's in the days ahead. Clearly, this was a "great airplane," indicating that Rob-inson's choice had been well thought out. Before evidently having ordered the air-craft, he might have learned of this aircraft's superior performance capabilities from M. Thaning, the Danish counsel-general at Johannesburg, South Africa, who shat-tered "every existing cross-country flight record in that part of the world."[49]

By far, the Beechcraft was the most advanced aircraft in Robinson's Imperial Ethiopian Air Force. This was the only airplane in Emperor Selassie's meager fleet that could outperform—or outrun—even the swiftest Italian combat fighter in case of pursuit. Robinson, therefore, flew Haile Selassie across Ethiopia mostly in this aircraft, as well as most of his personal missions. Consequently, the Beechcraft became known simply as "the Emperor's aircraft."[50]

Colonel Robinson's two Fokker monoplanes were in relatively good condition for service, after the necessary mechanical improvements were made. The Fokker aircraft were designed by the brilliant Dutch aeronautical engineer Anthony Fokker, who had created the finest single-seat aircraft of World War I, and designed the means—an interrupter gear mechanism—for a machine gun to fire through a rotating propeller.

Meanwhile, Robinson worked on all other existing aircraft. All four French Potez aircraft, for instance, needed serious overhauling—especially the small His-pano-Suiza engines—in order to become fully serviceable. At least two of these air-craft had been in Ethiopia for the past six years.[51]

Among the oldest aircraft of the Imperial Ethiopian Air Force was the Potez 25 A2 Serial no. 3. This airplane was named *Nesre Makonnen*, or the Prince Ma-konnen, which was written in large white Amharic script across the dark green fu-selage.[52]

To gain additional firepower, Robinson had some of his light aircraft mounted with machine guns for protection.[53]

Therefore, since taking command of the Imperial Ethiopian Air Force, Colo-nel Robinson continued to work into the fall of 1935 to achieve his twin objectives: not only repair and overhaul the majority of the air force's aircraft, but also to se-cure additional airplanes to increase its strength. And the only means of obtaining modern aircraft was by direct purchase from other nations or directly from private aircraft industries. But this goal was becoming increasingly more difficult, because the neutrality bill that forbid the sale of weapons, armament, and aircraft to Ethiopia.

Already well armed and with a recently strengthened military might, "Ita-ly needed [only] secondary war materials [and] the effect of the [arms] embargo would be to give Italy everything she needed while withholding from Ethiopia the things she needed most," especially aircraft.[54]

Robinson, therefore, had to rely more upon his own resourcefulness to secure additional aircraft. But how could aircraft be accomplished after the arms embargo was imposed on Ethiopia in the summer of 1935? Robinson always found a way, however. With Ethiopia and Italy on the verge of war and "despite embargoes and difficulties, arms and munitions poured" into Ethiopia.[55]

Ironically, Robinson was able to secure three additional aircraft from another fascist power, Hitler's Germany. Germany was now Italy's European rival because of Germany's designs on Austria, the Fuhrer's native homeland. Wishing Italy would get tied down in a lengthy war of attrition, Germany sold other weaponry, besides aircraft, to Ethiopia, including anti-tank weapons. Therefore, the Ethiopians, including Robinson's Imperial Ethiopian Air Force, "obtained financial assistance and armaments from Hitler's Third Reich in order to fight its fellow-fascists."[56] Later, Emperor Selassie declared that Germany had in fact provided more war munitions to Ethiopia than any other nation. So much war matériel flowed into Ethiopia from Germany that the German Embassy was forced to officially deny persistent rumors of "having offered Haile Selassie army and air force instructors, plus three hundred armoured cars on credit."[57]

While most of Robinson's planes were light aircraft, some were heavier transports. The largest planes were three German Junkers 52 aircraft. Flown by volunteer German crews, these Junkers were sent by Hitler to deliver supplies and weapons to the Ethiopians. One Junkers aircraft was flown by a German pilot named Ludwig Weber, who reached Ethiopia via Sudan. He would become the agent of Junkers in Addis Ababa, but also served faithfully in Robinson's air force, sometimes as the emperor's personal pilot. Weber would be killed, however, in the upcoming war. Powered by three engines, these transport aircraft were slow and ponderous, but they were also durable and tough. Ideal for demanding service in Ethiopia, the JU 52 was destined to become perhaps the best transport aircraft of World War II, and certainly the finest transport planes in Robinson's Imperial Ethiopian Air Force. After already having inherited one tri-motor German Fokker aircraft when he first took command, Robinson would fully utilize these three tri-motor transport aircraft. They would prove invaluable in transporting tons of supplies sent by Robinson to the front in the months ahead.[58]

The all-metal Junkers aircraft represented the cutting edge of aviation development. Professor Hugo Junkers was one of the leading aircraft experts not only in Germany but also in the world. Constructed of corrugated metal, these dependable Junkers 52 tri-motor transport aircraft were "a significant aviation success." The sturdy, tri-motor Junkers transports were capable of carrying heavy loads and flying long distances—ideal requirements for service across a sprawling, mountainous country like Ethiopia, especially when Selassie's nation would have to face Italian military threats on multiple fronts.[59] Besides the tough-minded Weber, who possessed solid leadership ability, and the additional German volunteers, Robinson's Imperial Ethiopian Air Force would contain other Europeans, including at one time or another Gaston Vedel, Baron von Engel, Comte Schatzberg, Andre Maillet, and Thierry Maignal, during wartime, because of the belated beginning of the Ethiopian pilot training program. Another volunteer of the Imperial Ethiopian Air Force was a Russian pilot, Lt. Mischa Babitchev. He was the son of an Ethiopian mother and a Russian father. Robinson had initially counted on French pilots, but most of these airmen departed in the late summer and early fall of 1935, except Count Hilaire du Berrier. Robinson gained invaluable technical assistance, however, from a French aircraft mechanic named Demeaux (first name unknown). Another Russian volunteer pilot was a former colonel of the Russian Imperial Air Force, Theodore Konovaloff, also flew with courage for Ethiopia. Both Weber and Demeaux played roles in assisting Robinson in modifying aircraft to make them serviceable to meet urgent wartime requirements.

Robinson also could count on at least six Ethiopian pilots, including Bahru Kaba and Asfaw Ali, who flew the French Potez aircraft throughout the war. They completed their pilot training under Robinson's supervision before the war's beginning. Robinson rated one fine Ethiopian pilot as "excellent", but only one Ethiopian pilot, Mulu Asha, could speak English. Eager to defend his nation, this young man became a trusted "lieutenant" under Colonel Robinson.

In addition, another of Robinson's right hand aviators was a capable French pilot and aviation mechanic, the English-speaking Charles Chaudiere. Robinson could relay effective orders by relying on Chaudiere to instruct the other Frenchmen of the Imperial Ethiopian Air Force, before the final departure of the relatively few remaining French airmen not long after the war's beginning. Asha, who later would be killed on the southern front during an Italian air attack, translated Robinson's instructions in Amharic to his Ethiopian airmen.[60]

With war drawing ever closer, Colonel Robinson continued to create greater offensive capabilities in his air force. Along with technical and aviation experts like Ludwig, Demeaux, and Chaudiere, Robinson either personally made or directed modifications to enhance his small fleet of civilian aircraft by bestowing bombing capabilities. Therefore, at Janhoy Meda Akaki, Robinson eventually "had 12 aircraft with around a hundred ten kg bombs."[61]

Nevertheless, Robinson's air force continued to be hampered by limited offensive capabilities by the end of summer 1935, especially in regard to bombing. Of course, this situation was not historically unusual for nations developing air power. During the early days of World War I, the military air arm of the major European powers employed aircraft, initially unarmed, in the primary roles of reconnaissance and observation. Only later were aircraft armed on both sides to meet wartime conditions, mostly in regard to defensive protection. Bombing came later.

The story of the U.S. Army air arm was no different. Initially, the primary mission aircraft of the U.S. Army Air Service was employed solely in observation roles during World War I. At the time, the main mission requirement of the Corps Observation "was primarily to keep the friendly command informed of the general situation within the enemy lines by means of visual and photographic reconnaissances."[62]

From beginning to end, Robinson fulfilled these important duties on multiple fronts, relying on visual observation and careful surveillance of Italian positions to gather vital intelligence from the air instead of from photographs. Because the Imperial Ethiopian Air Force lacked significant offensive capabilities, Robinson's initial mission assignment was to relay military intelligence directly to Emperor Selassie at Addis Ababa from the front. This mission was of critical importance and risky because of the long distances and mountainous terrain. Robinson's reconnaissance flights became the most effective sources of intelligence gathering for the emperor to ascertain Italian intentions, concentrations, and to relay orders to Ethiopian commanders on the front lines. This key role for Robinson, which began long before the Italo-Ethiopian War's start, was the same as American observation aviation units during the Great War, because "their main purpose [was] a thorough reconnaissance and surveillance of the [front] in order to keep [commanders] informed constantly as to the situation and developments in the enemy territory."[63]

But unlike the American aircraft in 1918, Robinson flew his long-range reconnaissance missions without fighter protection—a dangerous undertaking. After all, during World War I, "the long-range reconnaissance [of Air Service aircraft] for the purpose of added security, the airplane undertaking the mission was accompanied by two or more protecting airplanes."[64]

Naturally, flying without protection made Robinson a tempting target for Italian fighter aircraft, whose pilots must have been dismayed, if not shocked, upon first sight of a black aviator soaring through Ethiopian skies.

Meanwhile, Robinson continued to modify and tailor his air force out of what little he had at hand, because the nucleus of the air arm that he inherited was much like those during the early days of the Great War. He, therefore, employed his aircraft not only for reconnaissance, but also for supply and communications. Robinson described how these older aircraft of the Imperial Ethiopian Air Force were "useful in scouting, conveying messages to the front and supplies to the Red Cross."[65]

Fortunately, Robinson was a highly skilled and experienced flyer. Thanks to his barnstorming days, he possessed the skills to dart in and out of deep valleys, and then out-distance his more numerous Italian opponents. But more protection was needed. Robinson and his aviation technicians and mechanics continued to arm as many aircraft as possible. After much effort and technical innovation, all four French Potez aircraft were mounted with machine guns.

Meanwhile, Robinson continued to scour Ethiopia for additional aircraft, because some of the emperor's airplanes were still "unaccounted for." One aircraft, an air ambulance, appeared unexpectedly through the efforts of Count Carl Gustav von Rosen, an aristocratic Swedish nobleman who was related to two other Von Rosens, both counts, from Sweden. These two politically connected noblemen had attended Emperor Selassie's coronation in early November 1930. But Count Carl Gustav von Rosen possessed an unconventional streak, including a well-deserved reputation as the "black sheep" of the family. Von Rosen flew to Ethiopia in his own two-seat aircraft to offer Selassie his services. Later, the count's small Swedish plane, the first to be marked with Red Cross designations, crashed during a take-off from Addis Ababa. Robinson would assign Count von Rosen, in one of the tri-motor German Fokkers, to the job of transporting medical supplies to the front, just as he himself did.[66]

Another aircraft Robinson obtained came from the emperor's personal physician, Dr. Adrien Zervos. He was a member of the capital's large Greek community. A talented physician, he already had flown across Ethiopia on emergency medical missions.[67]

Eventually Robinson more than doubled the number of available aircraft. Some were obtained covertly until additional airplanes were secured along more legitimate channels, when the League of Nations eventually lifted the embargo in October 1935. A reporter from the *Enterprise* of Riverside, California, who described Robinson as "Haile Selassie's Ace Airman," wrote, "The colonel [Robinson] said the Ethiopian air force numbered 24 planes in all, of which only three" would remain by the war's end. This total of twenty-four aircraft of the Imperial Ethiopian Air Force, reached at some point in late 1935 or early 1936, was also confirmed by Professor Negussay Ayele.[68]

Robinson somehow eventually acquired thirteen aircraft—from the initial eleven both serviceable and non-operable—by any means possible, and from unknown sources in both 1935 and 1936. Evidently, Robinson acquired most new aircraft covertly, like the German Junkers he received from the largest European supplier of war matériel to Ethiopia, Germany. In addition, Robinson obtained other aircraft from the Red Cross and other Ethiopian aid organizations, or from volunteers, like Count von Rosen, who flew to Addis Ababa.

Robinson also gained aircraft by clandestine means from other American companies, like Lockheed or Douglas Aircraft Corporation, which had "onerous export programs" that played a role in rearming Germany, despite restrictions imposed by the Treaty of Versailles. American companies continued to violate the rules of post–World War I disarmament to reap handsome profits, because "disarmament was a farce." By way of a commercial agent in Berlin, Germany, Lockheed attempted to sell fighters, XP-900s, to Ethiopia. If so, then this arrangement would in part explain how Robinson was able to build up the Imperial Ethiopian Air Force's strength.[69]

Robinson also enhanced the overall manpower strength of the Imperial Ethiopian Air Force by either training or securing seventy Ethiopians. These airmen included some expatriates, who had returned to defend their endangered native homeland. The Martin brothers, the London-based sons of the Ethiopian minister to England, received aviation training from instructors in England in preparation for service in Robinson's air force. As Robinson related in an interview published in a Baltimore newspaper: "There were seventy native pilots and one from Sweden. A number of the native pilots were trained in France and Germany years before."[70]

Selassie needed Robinson to serve in a prominent military role not only for his aviation expertise, but also because he hoped that his young African American commander might generate support from the United States. Selassie now desired "all black men" to rush to Ethiopia's defense, before it was too late. Therefore, Colonel Robinson occasionally played a diplomatic role, talking to the American ambassador in Addis Ababa and requesting U.S. sympathy and support for the Ethiopians.[71]

Meanwhile, at Addis Ababa, Emperor Selassie continued to encourage his people to defend the sacred homeland. The emperor stated that "Ethiopia desires only [to ensure] safeguards of her integrity and independence for all time. The Italians, trying 'to civilize' the Ethiopian people by aggression, will find us a united people [and it is far] better [to] die free than live as slaves."[72]

While hoping for the League of Nations to intervene, the emperor galvanized Ethiopia's defense against the Italians, who were determined "to destroy your religion and mine, confiscate our goods, and place us under harsh discipline"—or slavery.[73]

In fact, Selassie had previously underestimated the extent of the Italian threat. For years, nationalistic Italian journalists had been imploring in no uncertain terms that the Ethiopian nation "must be destroyed." To accomplish Mussolini's goal, more than 200,000 Italian troops were positioned in the Horn of Africa, preparing to pounce on their victim.[74]

Robinson continued to cope with an overall disadvantageous environment and situation that produced a seemingly endless number of obstacles. Ironically, the least expected obstacle proved to be the Ethiopians themselves. To his dismay, Robinson initially encountered a good deal of culture shock in Ethiopia, because cultural differences were heightened under the stress of war preparations. Making observations on his new environment, a philosophical Robinson wrote how "things [were] much different than I expected [but] in some cases much better and in other cases 100 percent worst [sic]. I can readily see for an American Negro to succeed here he must possess the following qualifications—First A strong Stomach—A Silent tongue—A king Heart—An Iron hand—The Patience of Job, and above all things know his line of work."[75]

As he usually did in difficult situations, Robinson focused upon the most positive aspects of the Ethiopian people, their ancient culture, and heritage. As an enlightened Robinson explained, the American "People can't understand that there is a vast difference between these two civilizations. They cannot be compared. When once this is understood, we will not be willing to call Ethiopia uncivilized."[76]

In Ethiopia, Robinson encountered a people who were strangers to him. They were deeply religious and devout, immersed in their ancient Christian religious customs, traditions, and practices. Most Ethiopians were pious members of the Coptic Christian Church, or the Ethiopian Orthodox Church. Ethiopians of the central highlands dressed unlike any people Robinson had ever seen before, wearing traditional clothes of white—long and flowing shammas, a rectangular shawl—and went barefoot in a country without paved roads. Women wore brightly colored garments, especially red, to the marketplace. Robinson was surprised that many Ethiopians "were unable to understand how he, a black man, could be an American citizen."[77]

ETHIOPIA'S MULTICULTURAL DIVERSITY

Ethiopia was a multicultural nation, consisting of a mixture of races and many tribes of different ethnic and cultural backgrounds. Though considered black by Americans, the Ethiopian people were a mixture of Arab, Caucasian, and African. Ethiopians often carried Biblical names, like many African Americans. Three distinct racial groups dominated Ethiopia. The Amharas lived in the central plateau and highland region, along with the Tigreans, who were located farther north. Many Ethiopians, especially the Amharas and Tigreans, possessed light complexions, slight builds, and Caucasian features, such as thin lips and sharp noses. The term Abyssinian was in fact the European name for the Amharas, who were a mixed race Hamitic people of northern and eastern Africa. Many centuries before, they had mixed with Semitic peoples who had migrated south across the Red Sea from Persia and southern Arabia before the birth of Christ.[78]

The second distinct group of Ethiopians were the Galla, another Hamitic people. Also a mixed race people, they occupied the highlands of west and southwest of Ethiopia. In general, even though they mixed with Semitic peoples from southern Arabia and were related to the Somali peoples, the Galla were darker in color than the Amharas. And most Galla were Muslim. Living near Kenya, the Sudan, and the Nile, the darkest-colored people or last group, the Shankillas, were the lowland dwellers of the heavily forested border regions of south and southwest Ethiopia. In general, they had an overall larger bone structure and stouter builds, with more pronounced Negroid features, such as those of the Anuak and Nuer tribes of the Nile.[79]

Muslim tribes—the Somalis, Issa, Danakils—and other tribes occupied the Ogaden Desert of eastern and southeast Ethiopia. In appearance and in general, these peoples looked more like the Amharas and Gallas.[80]

In addition, Ethiopia was the land of black Jews. These were the Falasha people of Begemder Province in the area north of Lake Tana. A mixture of both Hamitic and Semitic people and true Old Testament believers unfamiliar with the New Testament, they proudly claimed descent from one of the lost tribes of Israel. According to their legend, when driven out of Egypt and led into Palestine by Moses, who took an Ethiopian wife, they split off and then migrated south to Ethiopia. Distinctive Falasha synagogues, topped with the Star of David, dotted the landscape of Ethiopia.[81]

Unlike in the United States, status in Ethiopian society was not determined by skin color, but by class. Robinson felt much like his former Curtiss-Wright student Bragg, who revered Ethiopia and her people, in part because "it was inspirational to see that a country could be governed by blacks, and that blacks were those who made the country successful."[82]

And quite unlike African Americans, most Ethiopians with whom Robinson associated had never been slaves, nor had their ancestors. Due in part to a lengthy history of successful resistance against foreign interlopers and the inaccessibility of their mountainous land, the Ethiopian people had never been completely conquered. In part, this legacy of successful resistance had, moreover, allowed Orthodox Christianity to thrive.

Pride in a distinguished heritage, a distinctive culture founded upon the royal lineage to King Solomon, and Orthodox religious traditions were intense among Ethiopians. Every March 2, for instance, Adowa Day was celebrated in honor of the great Ethiopian victory. The upcoming struggle of the Ethiopian people was destined to be a moral and holy crusade against multiple threats: white European domination or colonialism, Catholicism, imperialism, and fascism. For such reasons, Robinson greatly admired the Ethiopian people, even while bewildered by certain aspects of their culture and mentality. He eventually learned to speak Amharic.[83]

By September 1935, General Emilio De Bono, commander in chief of Italian forces in Eritrea, had amassed five regular divisions, five Black Shirt divisions, and the considerable air might of the Regia Aeronautica in preparation for a most "formidable military effort" possible.[84]

In front of the neat formations of his divisions of Black Shirts, Mussolini had lectured his troops on their duty: "Abyssinia, which you are about to conquer, we shall have totally. If she dares resist our formidable strength we shall put her to pillage and fire [as] you will have powerful armaments that nobody in the world suspects. You will be strong and invincible, and soon you will see the five continents of the world bow down and tremble before Fascist power."[85]

The amassing of so much Italian strength of a modernized army ensured that the upcoming conflict would be yet another "colonial war of European proportions." Mussolini was determined to achieve an overwhelming victory as quickly as possible. In Mussolini's own words: "For the lack of a few thousand men we lost the day at Adowa! We shall never make that mistake [again because now] I am willing to commit a sin of excess but never of deficiency."[86]

Like their dynamic leader, the Italian soldiers were likewise consumed with avenging the Adowa disaster. Some Italian tanks aligned in neat rows on the border bore the name of the infamous battle written on their steel war machines, a "call for vengeance."[87]

On October 2, 1935, just before ordering the invasion, Mussolini spoke in Rome before a large crowd enthusiastic about the prospects for Ethiopia's conquest: "A solemn hour is about to strike in the history of the Fatherland. Not only is an army marching toward its objective, but forty million Italians are marching in unison with the army, all united because there is an attempt to commit against them the blackest of all injustices, to rob them of a place in the sun. . . . With Ethiopia we have been patient for forty years. Now enough!"[88]

After months of careful preparation, all was ready for the mammoth Italian invasion. Earlier, Mussolini had written Gen. De Bono that when "we [are] obliged to take the initiative of operations at the end of October or September, you ought to have a combined force of 300,000 men (including about 100,000 black troops in the two colonies) plus 300–500 airplanes and 300 rapid vehicles—for without these forces to feed the offensive penetration the operations will not have the vigorous rhythm which we desire" to achieve decisive victory.[89]

Even by European standards, Italy's invasion force was overwhelming in strength and modern weaponry. Mussolini felt that everything, especially Italy's future and his own political power base, now depended upon Ethiopia's swift conquest. Therefore, Italy's massive concentration of forces were "commanded by the best Italian generals, and served by the largest and most perfected armament that has ever been assembled on African soil."[90]

Meanwhile, ignorant of the horrors of modern warfare, Ethiopia's warriors were supremely overconfident of victory. In their minds, Adowa's success was only the beginning of the crushing of any Italian army that foolishly entered the sacred lands of Ethiopia. The new Belgian plenipotentiary minister, M. Janssens, reported how Addis Ababa was full of talk of "throwing the Italians in Somalia back in the sea."[91]

Webb Miller, a sympathetic white correspondent of the United Press, wrote with a growing sense of despair, "I was disgusted by the hypocrisy, two-faced maneuvering, and double-dealing of the British, French, and Italian statesmen and by the prospect of watching the aggression of a nation with all the modern resources for slaughter upon an ignorant, backward, comparatively defenceless people."[92]

OUTRAGE ON THE HOME FRONT

But Mussolini's invasion was much more than naked aggression. In fact, the seeds for the outbreak of the World War II were sown with Italy's invasion of Ethiopia. One analytical Ethiopian was correct in emphasizing, "It is 1914 [all] over again, and we are Serbia": the catalyst that had ignited World War I was when the archduke of Austria was assassinated by a Serb nationalist in Sarajevo.[93]

Even though Ethiopia was a member of the League of Nations, in Winston Churchill's words, "The League of Nations [only] proceeded to the rescue of Abyssinia on the basis that nothing must be done to hamper the invading Italian armies."

Except for minor sanctions imposed upon Italy, an impotent League of Nations and the rest of the world would stand idly by to watch the rape of Ethiopia. The league and Western leaders turned away from the concept of collective security and their responsibilities of ensuring a peaceful world. The strategic Suez Canal, the main artery by which Italy sent troops and supplies to Ethiopia borders, was not closed, nor was an embargo placed on oil, which Italy needed to fuel its modern war machine. In the end, the failure of Western leadership to stop Italian aggression in Ethiopia would thoroughly discredit the League of Nations. Consequently, the League would be doomed in part for not attempting to save Ethiopia in 1935, while emboldening the march of fascism, especially in Nazi Germany.

Not only the Western European powers, but also the United States was guilty of lacking the will to halt Italian aggression. An isolationist United States possessed no realistic policy for Africa. And America's large Italian population, which translated into millions of Democrat votes for President Franklin D. Roosevelt, also ensured that America would take no forceful action to save Ethiopia. At this time, white Americans had no interest in supporting a faraway war in behalf of an African nation about to be invaded by whites, even if they were fascists bent on conquest.[94]

As indicated in a speech on October 2, 1935, Mussolini was correctly convinced that "the real British people" (like Americans) were not "disposed to take the risk of plunging Europe into a disaster in order to defend an African country, universally branded as a country without a trace of civilization."[95]

Therefore, one angry *Chicago Defender* editor denounced "another 'holy alliance' [that now] exists between Great Britain, France, and Italy. That there will be no war between them [which] is to the detriment of Ethiopia. At last the cloak has been removed and the three nations who have for countless centuries lived by international plundering and territorial aggrandizement are now showing their true colors. Ethiopia must contend alone, against these fearful odds, for the common privilege of existence. She has been politely abandoned by the Christian nations, whose standards of civilization she has been urged to emulate."[96]

Born and raised on Jamaica, a Caribbean colony and former sugar island exploited for centuries by Great Britain's commercial and economical interests, Marcus Garvey now denounced that the "white world is gone mad . . . behaving in the 20th Century in no better manner than when their ancestors lived in the caves and were primitive barbarians and savages [because to] the south of Europe, Mussolini [now] is preparing to devour a set of people in far off Ethiopia, simply because they will not allow him to penetrate their country and take it away for his own savage use, [yet] he calls these people savages and says he wants to civilize them."[97]

Only belatedly would white Americans see the upcoming struggle in Ethiopia in clear moral terms and fascism as evil, but by then it would be too late. Such views were now commonplace across black America, however, which saw the encroaching conflict as a moral struggle of extreme importance for the future: Africa's oldest independent black nation, little more than a sacrificial lamb, stood alone against not only fascism, but also against white domination, colonial exploitation, and racism. Even before the Italian troops swarmed into Ethiopia like a locust plague, black America enthusiastically rallied as one. Black America responded with "an outpouring of cold fury." One African American writer condemned Italy's "wanton aggression" and shortly described how: "I know of no event in recent times that stirred the rank and file of Negroes more than the Italo-Ethiopian War."

As early as August 1935, when Robinson took command of the Imperial Ethiopian Air Force in Addis Ababa, an estimated crowd of twenty thousand African Americans participated in a mass meeting in Harlem to protest Italy's imperialist aspirations toward Ethiopia. They carried Ethiopian flags and signs of protest that warned Mussolini to keep his "HANDS OFF ETHIOPIA." Later, huge rallies were held at Madison Square Garden in New York City. Black newspapers across America deplored the shameful "conspiracy" of white nations, especially the League of Nations, which would allow the "rape of Ethiopia" for their own selfish interests. Black committees of solidarity were organized, including the American Committee for Ethiopia. Special religious services were held at hundreds of black churches and prayers said in African American communities across America for Ethiopia's salvation. Inspired by the Bible's many references to ancient Ethiopia, thousands of African American worshipers prayed, reflecting the solemn mood of black America by the tense summer of 1935: "Great God, grant [that] no Ethiopian soldier misses when he fires and that every Italian bullet go astray. Amen." Other heartfelt prayers for Ethiopia's salvation implored: "Grant that [the Italians] may fear Thee and flee from Thy wrath."

Such moral support was in vain, because the "American black community, however, enjoyed almost no political influence over Administration foreign policy at the time." In time and across the world, Emperor Selassie would symbolize morality, courage, and righteousness in the face of oppression and impossible odds. Robinson also would serve as an enduring symbol of active physical and moral resistance against fascist aggression. While white America and the Western democracies lacked the moral fortitude to stand up against fascist aggression, indignant black Americans lacked the power and resources to follow Robinson's solitary example.[98]

From the beginning to the end of the conflict, Robinson would become the only American, and only African American, to serve Ethiopia in a military capacity. Robinson's role was without precedent in a number of groundbreaking ways. First and foremost, no African American had ever commanded the entire air force of any nation in history before Colonel Robinson. And he led the first racially integrated air force in history. In the cause of freedom, American aviation volunteers rushed to the assistance of allies during both world wars. Unlike Robinson, however, these flyers became world famous. Films, books, and documentaries have glorified those Americans, who volunteered to fight before America's entry into both World Wars.

Before the United States' entry into the Great War, the Lafayette Escadrille and the largest organization of all-American volunteers—the Lafayette Flying Corps—was composed of more 250 American flyers and airmen. These volunteers were the first American flyers in combat, just as Robinson was the first and only American aviator destined to fight in Africa and for Ethiopia during the Second Italo-Ethiopian War from beginning to end. Later, the Lafayette Escadrille flyers were incorporated in the U.S. Army Air Service during World War I. And before the Japanese attack on Pearl Harbor, Hawaii, on the morning of Sunday, December 7, 1941, the famed Flying Tigers, or the American Volunteer Group, under Claire Lee Chennault, became legendary fighting on behalf of the Chinese people against Japanese aggression.[99]

Then, after Great Britain's miracle in evacuating Allied forces from Dunkirk, France, in May 1940 and before the United States' entry into World War II, other American volunteers formed the Eagle Squadron, "a modern Lafayette Escadrille." Like its forebear, the Eagle Squadron compiled a distinguished war record in its fight to stop the march of fascism.[100]

Historians have overlooked the fact that between World War I, 1918, and America's entry into World War II, 1941—a span of twenty-three years, or nearly a quarter of a century—the most prominent American military aviator in a high-level leadership position and in command of an independent air force in a wartime environment was John Charles Robinson, who was relatively unknown in white America. Far from home, Robinson was also about to fight in the name of Pan-Africanism, morality, and anti-fascism. He had always been an underdog throughout his life, especially in struggling against racial barriers in the United States. The Italo-Ethiopian War of 1935–1936 would be little different for the young man, except that this dramatic confrontation now would be played out on an international stage, and was as much of a moral struggle against racism as a military one.

6

The Fascist Invasion of Ethiopia

REALIZING FAR TOO LATE that no assistance would be forthcoming, Selassie mobilized his countrymen in late September with a stirring appeal: the "Emperor has lost all faith in the ability of the League of Nations to save his country."[1]

Revealing his growing desperation, Selassie emphasized: "Everyone will now be mobilized and all boys old enough to carry a spear will be sent to Addis Ababa. Married men will take their wives to carry food and cook [and] those without wives will take any woman without a husband. Women with small babies need not go. The blind, those who cannot walk, or for any reason cannot carry a spear are exempted. Anyone found at home after receipt of this order will be hanged."[2]

On this same day, September 28, Langston Hughes's "Ballad of Ethiopia" was printed in the *Afro-American*:

> Where the mighty Nile's
> Great headwaters rise
> And the black man's flag
> In bright freedom flies
> All you colored peoples
> No matter where you be
> Take for your slogan
> Africa Be Free
> All you colored peoples
> Be a man at last
> Say to Mussolini
> No! You shall not pass.[3]

119

Robinson, Emperor Selassie, and the Ethiopians now realized that a cynical realpolitik on both sides of the Atlantic had left Ethiopia abandoned and completely on its own. In the words of Italian undersecretary of state Fulvio Suvich, "the Ethiopian war was made by a gentlemen's agreement with England" and France.[4]

Leaving Emperor Selassie and his people to the mercy of the formidable Italian war machine, the European Powers and the League of Nations had turned their backs on "the very existence of Ethiopia."[5]

The tragic prophecy of Tecle Hawariate's words to the League of Nations were about to be fulfilled, because Ethiopia was so "weak and [has been] deprived of the means of organizing the defence of its territory and of its very existence, both of which are threatened. Will the Council assume responsibility, in the eyes of the world, for allowing [Italy's invasion] preparations to continue unchecked for the massacre of a people which constitutes a menace to none?"[6]

In the pages of the *Chicago Defender*, A. N. Fields lamented the premeditated "intent to dismember Abyssinia [which] was wrapt in the delicate morsel of a desire to spread civilization and Christianity undertaken [by Italy] with at least a preliminary understanding with both Great Britain and France. The rich resources of Abyssinia long have been coveted by the imperialist robbers and land vultures, [and] social and political considerations of England disturb her with the thought [that] should Abyssinia win a decisive victory over Italy it would mean the awakening of the darker people of Africa to the fact that the European white man is not invincible in war."[7] An emboldened Mussolini reemphasized to Gen. De Bono in mid-May: "I have made it understood that we shall not turn back at any price. It is absolutely indispensable not to alter the date—October [1935]—which we have fixed for the beginning of the eventual operations."[8]

Mussolini had concentrated 300,000 soldiers on Ethiopia's ill-defended borders by summer's end. Selassie and the Ethiopian people were anything but ready to meet an overpowering Italian onslaught. As the emperor explained: "There are no factories to produce war materials in our country, in order to make preparations on our part. We did not have enough money to make purchases abroad. We asked for loans [but] we did not find anyone who would lend to Us. We did not suspect that Italy would start a war without notifying [Ethiopia] of her decision to engage in hostilities [and therefore] we had not proclaimed mobilization from the moment of the Walwal attack"[9]

In contrast to the massive Italian troop concentrations, including Eritrean allies, relatively few Ethiopian soldiers held only scattered frontier posts along both fronts, including the Ethiopian-Eritrean border marked by the Mareb River. The northernmost Ethiopian defensive position was located at Adowa. Colonel Robinson undertook numerous missions on the northern front in the Tigre region. Here, at the northern end of the Ethiopian Rift, the Italians had concentrated for a mighty push south on Addis Ababa.

As directed by Selassie, Robinson's mission was also to carry sensitive and "classified government documents," and orders, to the front. Robinson flew an old French Potez biplane because it was smaller, and hence less detectable to Italian eyes, than the Beechcraft, which was reserved for flying the emperor. Also, unlike the Beechcraft, the French Potez was now armed with machine guns for protection.

From its open cockpit, Robinson surveyed thousands of Italian troops, along with the concentration of tanks, armored cars, and supply trucks, and their extensive invasion preparations. His reconnaissance was risky, especially with Italian aircraft swarming in the skies.

Robinson's intelligence revealed that the Italians were about to launch their invasion south toward the capital. As soon as possible, he appraised Emperor Selassie of the massive Italian troop concentrations on the border between Eritrea and Ethiopia. Robinson then flew back to the weakly held Adowa front, where he was now headquartered. Even though this frontier position had no airfield, he continued to survey the border situation along the Mareb River Valley, where he was forced to make careful landings on the flat, desert terrain.

The rainy season in the northern Ethiopian highlands in the interior ended in September. The Italians would not open their great offensive campaign until the weather improved. It seemed somewhat incongruous that this dirty collection of mud tukul huts in the middle of nowhere possessed so much historical significance and meaning for both Ethiopia and Italy. Adowa was a small provincial market center of only around six to seven thousand people.

The overconfident warriors of Ras Seyoum, one of Selassie's top lieutenants, were stationed there. The Adowa sector was also the first defensive line protecting the capital. Seyoum's warriors also protected the strategic Imperial Road that led south into the interior and the dusty towns of Makalle and Dessie, about halfway between the northern front and the capital, and then went straight into Addis Ababa.

One of Robinson's most dependable "foreign" experts was Colonel Theodore Eugenovitch Konovaloff. A former engineer and recent arrival, he had seen military service in Egypt and Turkey as a Russian Imperial Air Force colonel. A non-Communist, or White Russian, Konovaloff was with Robinson at Adowa. He had inspected the Ethiopian defenses along the arid northern frontier. As Ras Seyoum's advisor, the Russian colonel's military expertise resulted in the erection of a thin line of trenches situated along the rugged mountainsides overlooking Adowa.

While Robinson's aerial reconnaissances continued to be flown along the northern border, he also reconnoitered the other front to the east and southeast along Italian Somaliland, where another heavy concentration of Italian troops, around 60,000 men, were spied from the air. It was obvious, however, that the main attack would erupt from the north.

In his off hours, Colonel Robinson walked through Adowa, which was distinguished by the historic Church of Giorgis, or St. George, Ethiopia's patron saint. His brightly painted image covered church interiors across the land. Even the battle flags of the Ethiopian warriors were decorated with brightly colored images of the knightly St. George, appearing as a black man, slaying the fabled dragon. It was at the Church of Giorgis that Emperor Menelik II had prayed just before his warrior army achieved its stunning success over the Italian invaders on the first day of March 1896.[10]

On a hot September 30, Ras Seyoum held a festive dinner at his *ghebbi* at Adowa. In attendance was every person of rank and status at Adowa, including Colonel Konovaloff, and almost certainly Colonel Robinson. Traditionally, Europeans and Americans were not allowed to attend such sacred Ethiopian feasts, but this pressing wartime environment and Adowa's advanced defensive had altered this ancient custom.[11]

Now the dry season was beginning in Ethiopia, stretching from October to February. If the Italians were going to attack, it would come during this period. Still, in Robinson's curt analysis, he explained the emperor's misplaced optimism even at a relatively late date: "His Majesty did not believe war would come. He believed the League of Nations would prevent war."[12]

Ironically, most Ethiopians believed that Mussolini's Italians were fearful of actually launching an invasion because of Adowa's haunting legacy. Consequently, across Ethiopia, and especially in "Addis Ababa, life continued for most people as if there were no Italian armies growing on Ethiopia's borders."[13]

In early October, Robinson believed that Mussolini was only bluffing and made a prediction that would come back to haunt him: "Personally, I don't think [the war] will start at all, [but] there might be a little fighting on the frontier. . . . No one here agrees with me, but time will tell."[14]

In part indicating his own lack of military experience, Robinson's assessment could not have been more misplaced. Ironically, Colonel Robinson's and the Ethiopians' rude wake-up call would soon come shortly at Adowa, the exact place where the Italians had been surprised in 1896. Now it would be the Ethiopians' turn. Robinson had just arrived from Addis Ababa, as he explained, "I arrived in Aduwa on Wednesday [October 2] with dispatches in my airplane. I stayed overnight."[15] Indeed, throughout this period, "Col. Robinson ha[d] the dangerous mission of carrying military dispatches between Emperor Haile Selassie and the various Ethiopian commanders at the front."[16]

In the early morning hours of October 3, Mussolini ordered his Ethiopian invasion to begin. To achieve complete surprise, he had not declared war, providing a successful formula not unnoticed by Hitler, who would embrace it in the years ahead. Around 100,000 Italian front-line troops massed in multiple lengthy columns, of three powerful corps, rolled south from Eritrea, crossing the Mareb River on a shaky pontoon bridge. Among this massive invasion force were Italy's finest soldiers, such as the elite Valpusteria Alpini, or Alpine mountain troops. The Italian juggernaut crossed the border without meeting Ethiopian opposition of any kind. Marching under banners of bright colors, beardless young Italian soldiers sang songs, while dreaming of reaping glory in East Africa. Italian forces were finally on the move to secure, in Mussolini's words, their nation's "place in the sun."

Meanwhile, a noisy fleet of Italian Caproni bombers, manned by skilled pilots, bombardiers, and crews, of the La Disperata Bombardment Squadron, lifted off from their Asmara air base in the predawn darkness. Flying in a disciplined formation toward their objective of Adowa, Mussolini's bombers streamed south across the Eritrean border and deeper into Ethiopia.

The La Disperata Bombardment Squadron was named in honor of an aggressive band of Fascists in Florence, Italy, where the Renaissance had once flourished with such magnificence so long ago. With the big Caproni bombers of La Disperata unleashed, all hell was about to break loose in Adowa. After first catching a glimpse of the fast-approaching Italian bombers in the pale sunrise, the Ethiopian servant of the White Russian military advisor to Ras Seyoum ran through the shabby, mudhut town screaming, "They're coming! They're coming!" When Colonel Konovaloff asked who was coming, the Ethiopian yelled, "The whites! They're already almost here!"[17]

Selassie later wrote of the ruthlessness of the Italian surprise attack: "After completing all their preparations, they crossed the border by aeroplane . . . without informing either us or the League of Nations of their decision to begin the war; they flew to Adwa. In the civilized world . . . when one state intends to wage war against another it will not do so without notification. But Italy, without regard to her honour and good name . . . began the war without any declaration whatever."[18]

In one war journalist's satirical words, with the inspirational war cry of, "On to Aduwa! The greatest modern army Africa has ever seen was about to show its might against an unfortified cow village."[19]

Mussolini's oldest son, Vittorio, was part of the Caproni's sweeping aerial assault. Proud of this elite bombardment squadron, the twenty-two-year-old was eager for the opportunity to finally reap "revenge . . . for the heroic death of our soldiers, who forty years ago fell victim to overwhelming odds."[20]

These well-trained Italian airmen of the 15th Bomber Squadron were now commanded by the aristocratic Count Galeazzo Ciano, an aggressive tactical leader. Ciano had ordered his bombers to fly in low over Adowa to ensure pinpoint bombing strikes and strafing runs with the dawn's first light. Determined to cover himself with glory, Count Ciano signaled for Alessandro Pavolini to drop the first load of bombs on a virtually defenseless Adowa, with just sufficient sunlight available for the Italian bombardiers to select targets.

The other Italian bombers of the 15th Bomber Squadron followed suit. Thirteen Caproni Ca 90s, the world's largest, most powerful bombers when first built in 1929, dropped their bomb loads on Adowa. Powered by six engines, the giant bombers now unloaded what was described as "hell from the skies."

By this time, Adowa was all swirling chaos, with horrified citizens racing for cover. The bombardment demolished the mud and wattle huts and started fires on surviving structures. The first Ethiopians killed in this new imperialistic war were civilians. Later, with heartless glee, Vittorio Mussolini described how it was "very amusing" to watch the bombs explode and tear to pieces defenseless Ethiopians.[21]

Robinson described the surprise bombing raid, writing how, "four large bombing planes arrived over the city on Thursday at break of day and began bombing. They caught the city asleep and unaware. The majority of the inhabitants grabbed whatever belongings they could and ran to the outskirts of the city."[22]

Robinson was fortunate to survive the first explosions that ripped through Adowa with a vengeance: "I tumbled out of bed when I first heard the sound of the bombs."[23]

The best account of what Robinson endured came from the words of a war correspondent, whose article appeared in the October 14, 1935, issue of *Time*: "One of those [civilian] huts [targeted by Count Galeazzo Ciano] was being used as a hospital by Swedish missionaries, and in it at the time of the raid was a U.S. Negro aviator from Chicago, John Robinson, known to correspondents as 'The Brown Condor of Ethiopia.' Condor Robinson's task was to ferry dispatches from Addis Ababa to provincial Ethiopian commanders in an ancient monoplane. Back in Addis Ababa last week he was able to give foreign correspondents an accurate description of the first casualties of the war, said he: 'I was sitting in the Swedish hospital chatting with some of the doctors when we heard a sudden whistling around. I said, 'That's a bomb.' I was only joking at first but for some reason we all ran outside. I immediately ran toward the airdrome and I saw terrified women and children flocking to the hospital where they thought they could be safe. That's why they were killed. The bombing was indiscriminate and it also was inaccurate. I saw a squad of [Ethiopian] soldiers standing in the streets, dumbfounded, looking at the explosions. They had their swords raised in their hands" in impotent defiance.[24]

At this time, however, Robinson neither sought immediate shelter, nor sprinted for refuge in the caves in the nearby mountains to join many of Ras Seyoum's warriors in hiding. As he wrote in a letter on November 21, 1935, only five days before his thirtieth birthday, with his usual flair for downplaying the event: "I was in Aduwa the day it was bombarded [not once but] twice."[25]

Like a true airman, Robinson's first immediate concern was for the safety of his airplane. In a desperate, if not foolhardy, rescue mission, he made a dash for the small Potez. After the first series of explosions, Robinson explained how he "ran to the place where [he had left] his plane."[26] With assistance, Robinson and a handful of Ethiopian soldiers reached his vulnerable airplane, before it was hit by either bombs or machine gun fire. They then quickly moved the aircraft to a "secure and camouflaged area."[27]

Colonel Robinson, "for the rest of the day and night . . . remained there" beside the aircraft.[28] La Disperata's airmen unleashed two hard-hitting air strikes that dropped bombs on a small town devoid of military targets. An ugly omen of events to come, the Italians bombed a civilian population with little concern for consequences—early indications that Italy's war would be a genocidal and racial conflict waged as much against Ethiopia's civilians as its soldiers.

Throughout the bombardment, Adowa mustered no resistance except for a few of Ras Seyoum's defiant soldiers, who fired rifles up in the air at the roaring Caproni bombers. Robinson was shocked by the carnage. This was his first glimpse of not only modern warfare, but also war waged without mercy.[29]

In the bombardment's midst, Colonel Robinson described the soldiers standing in the streets dumbfounded, looking at the planes soaring above. There was "great confusion [and] houses were going up in smoke."[30]

But throughout Robinson paid more attention to his aircraft than anything else. He wrote, "I was not able to see what havoc the second bombing attack wrought because I was trying to find a more secure hiding place for my plane. I did, however, see two planes droning ominously, circling the apparently doomed city."[31]

This was the first time that Robinson witnessed the effectiveness of strategic bombardment as a weapon of destruction and terror. As Vittorio Mussolini later wrote: "I saw with sorrow, as will happen to me every time I miss a target, that I obtained only meager results, perhaps because I expected huge explosions like the ones you see in American films. These little houses of the Abyssinians gave no satisfaction to a bombardier."[32]

Robinson described the horror: "Many people sought refuge at the Red Cross hospital [but the] bombs dropped in the neighborhood of the hospital and most of the people killed and wounded fell near there."[33]

The foremost Italian airman of this bombing raid was Count Ciano, who possessed diplomatic experience in Brazil, China, and the Vatican. He was the son of a distinguished Italian admiral and hero of World War I. Ciano enjoyed his lofty station in Mussolini's inner family circle, as Il Duce's son-in-law. Mussolini had even played the role of matchmaker between the count and his daughter, Edda. Ciano had long been Mussolini's right-hand man. Before the war and as the youngest minister in Europe, he had served as Mussolini's foreign minister and his leading emissary to Nazi Germany, although he would eventually become critical of Hitler. Ciano also served as the minister of press and propaganda. Even more, "after Mussolini himself, no one in Italy played a more important role in the history of fascism" than Ciano.[34]

As fate would have it, the ambitious Count Ciano, at age thirty-two, only went to war because he felt it was a good political career move and because Mussolini's two sons had enlisted. To sarcastic Italians with a wry sense of humor, the ever-stylish count was simply known as "the son-in-lawissimo."[35] Glory would be short-lived, however, as he would be executed by Il Duce in 1944. But in 1935, he was the proud, ambitious leader of the La Disperata squadron, which began at Adowa to earn infamy throughout Ethiopia as "baby-killers."[36]

An Italian pilot even more ruthless in war than the sophisticated, articulate Count Ciano was Ettore Muti from Ravenna, Italy. The colorful, scarf-wearing Muti looked like a dashing Hollywood idol in the swashbuckling Errol Flynn mold, but he was a ruthless killer in the air. Muti lived hard and fast, socializing with grace and a distinct flair in Rome with the Fascist elite. Muti even served as one of the official bodyguards for Mussolini's sons. This former secretary of the Fascist Party held Western intellectualism, liberalism, and enlightened thought in utter contempt.[37]

In the dark shelter of a secure cave in the hills overlooking Adowa, the Ethiopian warlord, Ray Seyoum, initially responded to the devastation brought by the Italian planes by crying, "Great God of Ethiopia, what is happening?" What was in fact happening at Adowa was "the beginning of Ethiopia's defeat by the [modern military] machine."[38] Like Robinson, Ras Seyoum barely survived the air attack on Adowa. His distinctive red tent headquarters had been targeted by the Caproni pilots. "Ras Seyoum's red tent was . . . bombed by an air squadron commanded by Count Galeazzo Ciano," wrote a *Chicago Defender* reporter.[39]

Robinson wrote, when "I left the city, it wasn't possible to [count the] number the dead." Based in part on its success in this war, "Italy's Regia Aeronautica [was destined to become] one of the best-tested and proudest air forces in the world."[40]

Much of Italian air power's might rested upon the foundation of the revolutionary air power doctrines of theorist Giulio Douhet. He had led the Italian Central Aeronautical Bureau in World War I, and then served as Mussolini's first minister of aeronautics and head of aviation. A believer in the importance of a large, independent air force as early as World War I, Douhet espoused the novel concept that modern air power was destined to forever alter the dynamics and nature of warfare. He promised decisive victory with strategic bombardment, destroying an opposing nation's industrial base, resources, and will to resist.

By 1933, Mussolini, who embraced Douhet's theories on the importance of an independent air force, was in charge of the Air Ministry. But it was Italo Balbo who was most responsible for creating the modern Italian Air Force. An Italian national hero, he was well known for his aviation achievements before the war, serving as minister of aviation and as Italy's first air marshal. Balbo became Mussolini's dependable "right-hand man."

Douhet described how Fascism's rise in Italy resulted in a "revolution which really provoked thought" about air power's strategic importance. When not in bed with his mistress—Claretta Petacci—who was an Italian air force's lieutenant's wife, Mussolini had pushed for new advances in military aviation, including mass production of aircraft. In fact, only "in the air did Mussolini make concessions to the new age."[41]

By 1935, therefore, the modernized Regia Aeronautica was a strong, independent air force: a futuristic vision not to become a reality in the United States for more than a decade. Fueled by a toxic mix of racism and nationalism, combined with the doctrine of air superiority, Italian air power would fully demonstrate that the concept of strategic bombing against the Ethiopians would be as highly effective as it was unmerciful.

Despite his considerable aviation knowledge, Robinson underestimated the Italian Air Force, its well-trained pilots, and air power's offensive capabilities. In part, this widespread underestimation might have stemmed in part from Ethiopian propaganda, which minimized Italian war-waging capabilities to bolster a national false sense of security and confidence.[42] Robinson's relatively naive views about Italian air power also revealed his background as a civilian aviator. He further lacked knowledge of the recent rapid technological advances in military aviation, especially in Europe. He had believed in early October and shortly before the bombing of Adowa: "Frankly, I do not believe that the modern equipment that Italy is planning to use against Ethiopia will be of any value."[43]

He also incorrectly believed that the bombers of the Italian Air Force would experience difficulty in conducting bombing raids over Ethiopia's towering mountain ranges. Such high altitudes affected small aircraft like Robinson's Potez, but not the Caproni bombers powered by half a dozen engines. Robinson thought that Ethiopia's mountains would force Mussolini's bombers to fly at high altitudes beyond their endurance capabilities. He was badly mistaken in this regard.

Colonel Robinson even speculated that the Italian bombers could not perform at altitudes of more than six thousand feet. Therefore, Robinson felt secure for the capital's safety because the imposing Dega mountains, to the north and northwest of Addis Ababa, towered to a height from eight thousand to ten thousand feet. Snow-covered despite being located so close to the equator, the highest mountain peak in Ethiopia, at more than fifteen thousand feet, was Mount Ras Dashen in the Semien Mountain Range of northern Ethiopia—the "Roof of Africa." Even the sprawling plateaus of the central highlands stood at commanding heights of between five thousand to eight thousand feet. Robinson was convinced these peaks and jagged pinnacles of solid rock would serve as effective barriers to Italian bomber raids.[44]

Ethiopia's mountain ranges were not high enough, however, to impede the Caproni big bombers, despite their heavy payloads.[45]

By this time in 1935, as one aviation expert correctly summarized, "Modern course-setting sight and super-efficient [bomb] release gear have made possible quite icredible accuracy in high-altitude bombing."[46]

And in the United States during July of 1935, the XB-17 successfully underwent its first test flight. A new era in strategic bombardment was dawning with the successful test flight of America's five-thousand-mile–range heavy strategic bomber. Eventually, this strategic bomber became the Flying Fortress, or B-17, of World War II fame.[47]

In Ethiopia, Italian aviators embraced the most lethal offensive aspects of Douhet's air power theory: "the objective must be destroyed completely in one attack, making further attack on the same target unnecessary. . . . The complete destruction of the objective has moral and material effects. To have command of the air means to be in a position to wield offensive power so great it defies human imagination."[48]

In addition, the Italians adapted specialized aerial tactics to conform to the realities of the specialized nature of warfare in Ethiopia. Italian aircraft of the Regia Aeronautica would continue to launch attacks by flying at low altitudes and out of the clouds to repeatedly catch enemy military forces by surprise. Such lethal air strikes were designed to shatter the morale of the Ethiopians, whose outdated warrior concepts of bravery in battle equated to those traditional beliefs of ancient times.[49]

General Frank Andrews, an American air power advocate of the 1930s, placed the importance of Italian air power in an overall geopolitical perspective in regard to the conflict raging in Ethiopia: "It is quite possible that Italian Air Power—bombardment aviation—prevented England from openly assisting Ethiopia against Italy."[50]

The Italian air war waged against Ethiopia was to demonstrate the validity of Douhet's theoretical premise and bold claim that, "In view of the carrying capacity and range of modern airplanes and the efficiency of present destructive materials, these advantages are such that a country in possession of adequate air forces can crush the material and moral resistance of the enemy . . . that the country can win regardless of any other circumstances whatsoever."[51]

America's most outspoken air power enthusiast was General Billy Mitchell, who advocated Douhet's "air power first" philosophy. He wrote prophetically in 1925: "It is probably that future wars again will be conducted by a special class, the air force, as it was by the armored knights in the Middle Ages."[52]

The war in Ethiopia verified air power theories. In the words of Major Ralph Stearley, of the U.S. Army, "The Italian Air Force played a vital role in the entire invasion, [air] attack operations had proved the most important, [and] air power had shown itself indispensable to victory" in Ethiopia.[53]

Indeed, the decisive, "fatal advantage was in the air, where an Italian air force, numbering over three hundred aircraft on the northern front and about one hundred aircraft on the southern front, had the sky to itself." The Italian Air Force possessed almost total air superiority, except for what Colonel Robinson and the fledgling Imperial Ethiopian Air Force could offer in the form of only limited, but spirited, resistance.[54]

Robinson was not the only one who misjudged the strategic situation, overestimating the strength of Ethiopian resistance and the alleged vulnerabilities of Italian air power. One European general believed that to "subdue a country like Ethiopia it would take an army of 250,000 or 500,000 men at least 15 years."[55]

On October 4, the day after the bombing of Adowa, Colonel Robinson made preparations to fly away from the village's smoldering ruins, the dying, and the busy makeshift hospitals, including those hit by bombs. He would never forget the surreal nightmarish experience at Adowa. The sight of so many dead and wounded Ethiopians sickened the young native Mississippian. Robinson now understood the horror and ruthlessness of modern warfare.

From the level terrain just outside of Adowa, Robinson took off alone in his French Potez biplane with "some important papers" for the Emperor. With his Potez only able to reach a maximum speed of 129 mph, Robinson now flew as fast as possible over the rugged terrain of the Ethiopian highlands, south to Addis Ababa.[56]

Robinson now encountered aerial combat for the first time in his life: "The day after [the bombing of Adowa] I started back to Addis Abeba with some important papers and was attacked by two Italian airplanes [and now] I really had the closest call I have ever had in my life."[57]

Despite being outnumbered by the swarming Italian aircraft, Robinson gamely fired back at his combat-trained opponents and "got off several rounds" that hit his target when they were close, even while he continued to maneuver to evade his pursuers. In a letter written shortly thereafter, Robinson boasted that the Italian pilots of the two fighter aircraft will certainly "remember what I did for quite a while."[58]

Robinson, however, regretted the fact that he did not possess a fighter aircraft as modern and combat-ready as those of the Italians. As Robinson wrote: "I dident [sic] mind being attacked, but I wish my airplane had been of a later type, I think I would have given them a wondreful [sic] lesson." But "any way I think they will remember."[59]

Robinson's ammunition was soon exhausted in quick bursts of fire from the machine gun mounted on the Potez. He was forced to break off the engagement and attempt to escape. Most of the way from Adowa to the capital, he "was pursued . . . by six Italian pursuit planes while carrying important documents for the Ethiopian king. The Italian planes were almost on his ship's tail before he escaped, by resorting to desperate measure of 'hedge-hopping' over and between the rocky crags that form that part of the country's terrain."[60]

During this vigorous pursuit, Robinson's barnstorming skills saved his life. With the Potez only able to reach an altitude of just more than nineteen thousand feet, the Italian fighters could easily shoot down Robinson from above, if they had gained the advantage of a higher altitude. Therefore, he flew low, and closely hugged the deeply gorged terrain of the Simien Mountains to elude the Italian fighter pilots, who flew faster, more maneuverable modern aircraft.

This little-known aerial combat in the skies over northern Ethiopia was significant because this was "the first time an African American pilot, serving an African nation, was engaged in air combat."[61]

When Robinson finally landed safely at Addis Ababa, he surveyed the damage to his aircraft that had carried him to safety. Numerous bullet holes in his plane revealed just how closely he had come to getting shot down. As he later wrote: "One part of the wing on the airplane I was flying had ten [bullet] holes in it."[62]

Robinson now began to realize that the two bombing raids that struck Adowa so suddenly and his narrow escape from the Italian fighters were nerve-racking experiences that appealed to his adventurous side. As he wrote in a letter on November 21: "Well I will never forget that day [October 3], and the day after."[63]

Now a veteran of aerial combat, Robinson was only now beginning to learn how the Italian "bombing planes did [the] most damage" in this war.[64] Waves of bombers and fighters of the Italian Air Force developed a lethal efficiency in "the modern technique of massacre."[65]

Count Ciano, commanding the 15th Bombardment Squadron, agreed. In one guilt-ridden letter after an especially devastating bombardment of defenseless Ethiopians, Ciano described the ugly realities of this war: "We have carried out a slaughter."[66]

Ironically, before the war's beginning, most Ethiopian warriors, and perhaps even Robinson himself, had openly mocked the Italian Air Force's capabilities. The common sentiment among these tough fighting men, whose warrior fathers and grandfathers won the great victory at Adowa, had been, "Oh, planes don't frighten us. Our priests know certain words; they say them, and the planes will crash."[67] But thousands of dead and maimed Ethiopian soldiers would shortly provide a grim testament to the fallacy of this misplaced bravado and faith.

After the Regia Aeronuatica wreaked havoc on whatever feeble Ethiopian resistance could be found, Italian ground forces continued to roll forward in a three-pronged invasion from the north, virtually unopposed during October's first week.

Emperor Selassie had earlier pulled troops away from his nation's borders to demonstrate to the world that Italy would have to begin its aggression against Ethiopia without provocation. Selassie now placed his faith in a Fabian strategy of withdrawal before overwhelming might: to make the invaders more vulnerable by stretching their logistical and communications lines to the limit as they advanced farther south and deeper into northern Ethiopia's mountains before initiating a major engagement.

As time went on, Robinson was shaken by the systematic crushing of Ethiopian resistance, and his mood grew increasingly pessimistic about Ethiopia's chances for success. With so many foreign correspondents and diplomats stationed in Addis Ababa to cover the war, Robinson received discouraging international news for these sources: "I talked to an Indian newspaper man who works for a German paper. He said his paper just instructed him to write anti-Ethiopian articles from now on, as the German government is turning toward Italy in a friendly way. And expects to sell them a large amount of war equipment."[68] This was an early indication of a united fascist front, the Axis Powers, that paved the way to World War II.

Ethiopia was now engaged in a life-and-death struggle. Robinson had been the first eyewitness to bring Emperor Selassie the grim news of the devastating attack on Adowa, warning that far worse was to come. Selassie ordered a general mobilization on October 4. Rallying the Ethiopians, he spoke brave words to unite his people in "this holy struggle" against the invaders. He implored those who could not fight now "must aid us with their prayers out into the field. For the Emperor [and] for the Fatherland."[69]

By this time, Selassie was convinced that Italy now "wanted to acquire our people as slaves after destroying Ethiopia's independence [because Italy] coveted Our venerable country—meaning to deprive her of her liberty and to destroy it—which was well known for her antiquity and which has lived in freedom for more than 2,000 years."[70]

Especially after the devastating air strikes on Adowa, Selassie had "lost all faith in the ability of the League of Nations to save his country." He, therefore, ordered his armed populace to concentrate at Addis Ababa in preparation for a march north to Dessie, around 175 miles north of the capital and soon to be the imperial headquarters in the field. An estimated quarter of a million Ethiopian warriors, after the emperor "bestowed his imperial blessing" on the troops, pushed north from the capital with visions of easy victory.[71]

As equally confident of success as their Italian and Eritrean counterparts, the Ethiopians were highly motivated to defend their sacred homeland. After all, patriotic appeals called for Ethiopians to march to the northern front, because "an enemy has invaded our sacred territory. He brings with him death-dealing war machines, cannon, air ships, poison gas, to kill us and civilize us after. Our country is poor financially, but we are rich in valor and courage. We will die free rather than become slaves."[72]

Meanwhile, black America was outraged by the Italian invasion and the devastation it brought, especially because it had been unleashed without a declaration of war. Like no other event in modern times, the attack on Ethiopia created a sense of moral outrage in black communities across the United States.[73]

Influential black newspapers like the *Afro-American* on October 19, 1935, condemned the invasion and urged: "every colored person throughout the world should do his utmost to maintain the independence of the fatherland."[74]

But active support for Ethiopia was not without risk for African Americans, especially in the Deep South. The *Chicago Defender* reported of the dangers faced by especially brave black citizens of Mobile, Alabama, because of their pro-Ethiopia activities: "Defying those lynch forces which seek to prevent Negroes and poor whites from organizing to improve their conditions, a group of citizens have set up a Friends of Ethiopia committee to collect funds and medical supplies for the Ethiopian people."[75]

This intolerance and organized backlash, however, explained in part why relatively little support for Ethiopia would be forthcoming from black America. Consequently, the most widespread support from African Americans for Ethiopia was primarily moral and spiritual, and came from "Christian blacks pray[ing] day after day, asking God if He has forsaken His children down below the Red Sea."[76]

But Ethiopia now needed much more than prayers from black America to survive this life-or-death struggle. Selassie had early realized as much, imploring how: "If the Italians are proud of their weapons against us, we on our part are proud that our greatest weapon against them is the help of God. Our flag, red, yellow, and green, and our seal with the legend 'the lion has prevailed' are the symbol of our independence; lest this symbol of our freedom should prevail, it is a great honour for our good name and our history if we die shedding our blood to the very last drop."[77]

After having informed Emperor Selassie of Adowa's destruction by the crack Regina Aeronautica, Colonel Robinson resumed his role at Addis Ababa as the Imperial Ethiopian Air Force's commander. Watching death and destruction raining down from the skies now gave Robinson new unsettling insights into man's inhumanity to his fellow man, modern warfare's horrors, and the fact that the airplane could be so successfully employed as a terrible vehicle of death—this shattered Robinson's innocence and his naive illusions about life and war, including the fact that aviation was on its way to becoming the most destructive tool ever invented in human history. Yet, even though discouraged, Robinson wrote with grim resolution: "I shall stay here and deliver everything there is in me, [even though I might] go down in death."[78]

In Addis Ababa, meanwhile, Robinson's tireless efforts to transform an inadequate air force into a viable one now reached a frantic pace. He no longer possessed the luxury of time, and he knew it. Robinson realized most of all that he now needed an experienced cadre of well-trained and dedicated African American pilots. Robinson was the lone African American serving in Ethiopia.

By this time, Cornelius Coffey was to have been on his way from Chicago to join Robinson in Ethiopia. However, the war's sudden outbreak caused him to come down with a case of cold feet. Not fulfilling his promise, Coffey wrote, "I came within six months of a trip to Ethiopia myself, but Italy invaded Ethiopia and the trip had to be canceled. I often think about how close I came to making the trip. But God had other plans for me." Robinson, however, still believed that Coffey was planning to join him in Ethiopia.[79]

Robinson was now on his own in regard to receiving any assistance from any of the experienced members of the Challenger Air Pilots' Association.[80] He attempted to secure as many African American aviators as possible, but without success.[81]

Even though he possessed a dozen foreign pilots in his air force, Robinson still wanted to fulfill the emperor's ambition of creating an all-black air force. In addition, gaining African American flyers would allow more time for Robinson's Ethiopian pilots to secure additional flight training and experience. If everything worked according to Robinson's plan, the young Ethiopian pilots could perhaps be molded into a comprehensive fighting unit, after having first solidified around a nucleus of experienced African Americans. Robinson, Emperor Selassie, and others hoped that a reinvigorated Imperial Ethiopian Air Force might buy time needed to prolong Ethiopia's subjugation, or to produce a stalemate. General Frank Andrews, of the U.S. Army Air Corps, "could not refrain from noting that the outcome of the war would have been very different if Ethiopia had possessed an effective air force."[82]

Ironically, Robinson continued to be hampered in his efforts because of the traditional values of the Ethiopian warrior, who served as yet another obstacle to the creation of an air force. In an article written by an Associated Press reporter that appeared in the *New York Times*, the emperor himself explained "that even if Ethiopia had sufficient money to purchase bombing planes, it would not [because] the use of bombing [was] contrary to all Ethiopian ideas of gallantry in battle [and] called attacks from the sky cowardly. At the present time [October 20, 1935] Ethiopia has virtually no air fleet beyond a dozen mediocre observation planes. . . . The Emperor also has about twenty aviators, of whom a half dozen, including John C. Robinson of Chicago, are foreigners, but there are not even sufficient airplanes for this number."[83]

As so often in the past, however, Robinson still attempted to accomplish the impossible. He also continued to be responsible for keeping Emperor Selassie appraised of the latest military developments on the northern front. Week after week and in flying his fastest monoplane, he continued to provide timely intelligence of the Italians' movements and dispositions. In Robinson's words, he was responsible for "scouting [or reconnaissance, and in] conveying messages to the front" in harm's way. Robinson acted not only as the Imperial Ethiopian Air Force's commander, but also coordinated the Ethiopian activities of various Western organizations, including the Red Cross, and volunteer physicians from different countries. He faced seemingly insurmountable logistical problems of supplying the front lines by air: "With the war on, I worked out a systematized system to carry doctors and Red Cross and other medical supplies to the front."[84]

Most Western aid to Ethiopia was medical, because the Ethiopian army possessed only a rudimentary medical service of its own. Therefore, the various "volunteer units of the Red Cross [continued] coming from Europe [and] stepped in to fill the gap."[85]

On both the northern and southern fronts, Robinson organized and supervised the distribution of Red Cross supplies from volunteer organizations from Sweden, Finland, Great Britain, Holland, and Egypt.[86] He also "campaigned for American Negroes to mobilize Ethiopian Red Cross units" for service in Ethiopia.[87]

In addition, other war-related missions, including unorthodox ones, for the Imperial Ethiopian Air Force beckoned with seemingly endless regularity. For instance, when Dr. Robert W. Hockman was killed by an exploding Italian bomb, the physician's body was flown from the front, evidently by Robinson, for a dignified burial with military honors in Addis Ababa.[88]

Most important, Robinson served as "the principal means of communication between the government [and the emperor at Addis Ababa] and the front lines [both the northern and southern fronts] of battle" throughout the war. Since he was the most experienced flyer, Robinson flew most of these risky missions.[89]

Robinson was able to utilize a relative handful of aircraft to their full capacity, but even this achievement was only possible after he and his aviation mechanics and technicians had made the necessary modifications and repairs, including the complete overhauling of planes and engines, on the wide variety of Imperial Ethiopian Air Force aircraft.

As if once again teaching aviation back at Curtiss-Wright in Chicago and despite a number of European aviation mechanics at his disposal, Robinson also played a leading role in repairing, servicing, and improving his aircraft for active service.

Because "the smaller monoplanes [had] no spare parts," Robinson was forced to cannibalize these aircraft to make them more serviceable. When not focused on logistical priorities, repairing aircraft, and training Ethiopian recruits, Robinson continued to provide vital intelligence to Emperor Selassie from the front.[90]

Because "the Emperor had never really intended to launch [Robinson and his Imperial Ethiopian Air Force] against the four hundred Italian bombers [these aircraft] were used for carrying messages and personages from place to place, and though there were various accidents, not one of them was shot down in the air by the enemy."[91] Indeed, "with such limited resources [and capabilities] the Ethiopians made little, if any, attempt to pit their antiquated flying machines against the Italians in combat."[92]

As if not saddled already with enough tasks, Robinson played yet another key role for Ethiopia during the conflict: fortifying Ethiopian morale by providing an inspirational example of outside support, especially from America. From an early date, Robinson "was, according to numerous reports, immensely popular [and his wartime] fame in Addis Ababa seems to have been widespread."[93] This lone African American from so far away was increasingly becoming "something of a national hero to the Ethiopian people," lifting the morale of not only Selassie but also Addis Ababa.[94]

Reconnaissance missions flown by Robinson to the front were both physically and mentally demanding. As if barnstorming, he flew missions back and forth to the front without modern navigation equipment or maps. These disadvantages forced Robinson to memorize as much of Ethiopia's landscape as possible, following rivers and mountain ranges. Besides the position of the blazing Ethiopian sun in the sky, a pocket compass, which ominously always pointed toward the northern front and the main Italian invasion force, was Robinson's only means of most accurately ascertaining directions when in flight.[95]

Typically, Robinson's reconnaissance missions were often hair-raising. Fast-flying Italian fighters could suddenly dart out of the thick layers of clouds at practically any moment. Robinson described the extent of the danger that he and his other flyers faced: "We have planes capable of flying well . . . but they are of ancient vintage and are as slow as snails in comparison with modern Italian planes."[96]

Out of necessity, Robinson had to be extremely alert and vigilant at all times during his repeated lengthy flights to the front lines. From the vantage point of his aircraft's open cockpit during long-range missions, he constantly scanned the distant horizons and higher elevations. Most of all, Robinson carefully searched for the distant specks in the sky that were approaching Italian aircraft at long range.

To maneuver safely out of danger, Robinson often dove headlong, darting in and out of deep canyons of the uncharted Great Rift Valley, and turning in wide detours to avoid approaching or pursuing Italian aircraft. Timely evasive maneuvers were necessary to escape the much faster and more maneuverable Italian fighter aircraft, unless, of course, Robinson flew the swift Beechcraft. Whenever he was surprised by Italian planes, his superior flying skills and maneuverability repeatedly saved Robinson from a fiery death. By far, the most dreaded tactical scenario for Robinson was if an Italian fighter maneuvered to gain an advantageous position on his tail. Such a dilemma was almost a sure guarantee of getting shot down. Making his missions—both before and during the conflict—even more precarious was the fact that Robinson flew them without a parachute, risking Bessie Coleman's unkind fate.

Fortunately Robinson was young and in good health, possessing quick reflexes and excellent eyesight. And most of all, he was a highly skilled pilot who could more than match the flying abilities of the Italian pilots. These qualities would often mean the difference between life and death. Robinson thus continued to serve as Emperor Selassie's personal pilot during the war: "I flew His Majesty [to the front] three times. The emperor is not the big warrior type of Ethiopian, but he is fearless. His friends finally prevailed on him to give up flying. Once the Italians were only two hours behind us in the air."[97]

Robinson described this close call for Selassie when flying the emperor far from the safety of Addis Ababa: "Once we were in a certain spot just two hours ahead of Italian pursuit planes, which evidently had information [from spies in Addis Ababa] the emperor was coming."[98]

When meeting the emperor or during inspections and parades, Robinson proudly wore a resplendent uniform that displayed his military rank. Later, he was described by a journalist in his uniform: "Thirty-one years old, a handsome Negro with a swooping mustache and a diminutive goatee. He wore his imperial uniform of whipcord pants, khaki shirt, khaki tie, and brown leather jacket with the embroidered gold order of the conquering lion of Judah on his left breast."[99]

While a busy Robinson labored long and hard to build-up the strength of the emperor's fledgling air force, the Italian Air Force continued to unleash its vengeance. Italian flyers, without fearing opposition either in the air or from anti-aircraft fire on the ground, flew assignments for little more than their own personal amusement. Count Ciano enjoyed the slaughter to an extent that even unsettled some of his closest friends: "When you see a concentration of Ethiopian troops, you give them a few rounds with a machine gun and they scatter and hide in the long grass. Then, when you fire a few more rounds at random, each of them thinks the bullets are falling near him, and they promptly emerge and run in all directions, when you can pop them off in real earnest."[100]

Such ruthlessness, rooted in a toxic blend of national pride, arrogance, and racism, shocked not only other Italians but also people around the world. Count Ciano's vivid account was published in the *Evening News* of London, in mid-October 1935, less than two weeks after Robinson survived the two bombings of Adowa and his escape from the Italian fighters.[101]

Adowa's fall represented a vengeful victory savored by the entire Italian nation, fueling confidence for a triumphant push all the way to Addis Ababa. The Italians had celebrated their success, with soldiers of the 84th Infantry, Gaviana Division, having even "carried a stone piece of equipment, a fragment of a Roman column, brought all the way from Italy to be propped up in the market square of Adowa in memory of the dead of 1896." With much fanfare, the Italian flag had been raised before the Church of the Savior of All the World. Ecstatic Italian soldiers, now more convinced of Rome's historic destiny, rejoiced at having at long last "avenged the humiliation of Italy, of Europe, and the white race." The holy city of Axum, just slightly southwest of Adowa, soon fell to the western flank column of the Italian army. Meanwhile, to escape the Italian avalanche of blitzkrieg, Ras Seyoum's forces retired south to the safety of the Simien Mountains, moving closer to Addis Ababa.

After surging around eighty miles south below the Eritrean-Ethiopian border, however, General Bono suddenly halted his advance after capturing Makalle, the capital of eastern Tigre, without a fight. Here, on the dusty Imperial Road leading south to Addis Ababa, the confident Italian commander planned to reorganize his forces in order to solve a host of pressing logistical problems stemming from the rapid advance. In addition, the experienced general wrestled with the ghosts of Adowa's legacy. This haunting lesson from the past warned him of the folly of advancing too swiftly and in piecemeal fashion, which had paved the way to the 1896 disaster. At nearly age seventy, General Bono was both prudent and cautious. He had carefully staged his advance south through the imposing mountains and toward Addis Ababa.[102]

On November 7, a day before Makalle was captured by the Italians, Emperor Selassie addressed Americans in a New York City radio broadcast that was translated from Amharic to English. The desperate emperor made a final urgent appeal for assistance, before it was too late: "The mails of Ethiopia have been laden for months with American letters of sympathy and offers of help or services, a most heartening sort of communication from a distant people. . . . You people of the United States can help [but] I ask no one to take the sword against Italy."[103]

Essentially, the emperor was appealing to President Franklin D. Roosevelt and the United States, which was not a League of Nations member, to impose sanctions against Italy. Only a week after the Italian invasion, the League of Nations had branded Italy as the aggressor and voted to support sanctions, but these were relatively minor and of no consequence in halting Italian invasion plans. No serious thought was given to closing down the Suez Canal to stop the steady flow of Italian troops and war materiel to Ethiopia.

Sanctions were officially imposed on November 18, a month and a half after the attack on Adowa. But these economic sanctions were "little more than a slap on the wrist." Most important, they failed to affect the one key commodity that could have made an impact on Italy's invasion, oil. Great Britain and France feared that depriving Italy of oil would make Mussolini target oil reserves in Europe. Consequently, the United States and President Roosevelt simply ignored Emperor Selassie's pleas for the assistance that might have saved Ethiopia.[104]

In fact, isolationist American politics and domestic priorities had played a large part in sealing Ethiopia's fate from the beginning. Unfortunately for Ethiopia, 1935 was in fact "the high-water mark of American isolationism" and apathy. Ever the politician, Roosevelt, who showed even some "admiration" for Mussolini to court Democratic votes from Italian Americans, was most of all concerned about reelection in 1936. Therefore, a neutrality resolution was passed not long after Italy's invasion, excluding arms shipments to not only Italy, but also to Ethiopia. With both Great Britain and France refusing to supply arms to Selassie, Ethiopia's defenselessness against the full weight of Mussolini's aggression was additionally assured.

At this time, Americans feared overseas involvement, especially in European affairs, after the nightmare of World War I. Most of all, Ethiopia was a victim of the ballot box to ensure the reelection of America's Democratic leader, Roosevelt. After all, millions of Italian Americans across the United States, including many recent immigrants, were strongly pro-Mussolini. Il Duce was their idol and "folk hero." Clearly, European leaders and politicians were not the only cynics motivated by self-interest and political agendas.[105]

In order to upstage an equally ambitious Hitler, Mussolini saw glory in an over-powering advance, to capture Addis Ababa and end the conflict as soon as possible. Therefore, Mussolini went against the advice of leading members of the Italian general staff who advocated a halt at Makalle to consolidate extensive gains, after penetrating around seventy-five miles into Ethiopian territory in only a few days. Consequently, an impatient Mussolini replaced Marshal De Bono with Marshal Pietro Badoglio. Ironically, Badoglio would lead the coup that would eventually overthrow Mussolini, after Italy was invaded by Allied forces during World War II.

Another serious Ethiopian setback occurred when Ras Haile Selassie Gugsa, whose capital was Makalle, defected to the Italians. Such deep internal rifts were masterfully exploited by European aggressors.[106]

This sudden change of command boded ill tidings for Ethiopia. Marshal Bado-glio was Italy's most famed and capable commander. He now mustered additional strength and resources for a final push south toward Addis Ababa that was to be-gin in the new year. With Marshal Badoglio in command, Mussolini was convinced that he had the right man for the job. In addition, this much-respected marshal possessed his own personal reasons to reap revenge on Ethiopia—Badoglio had sur-vived the 1896 fiasco at Adowa.[107]

Marshal Badoglio's arrival in Ethiopia, combined with Mussolini's demands for a quick and decisive victory by any means, ensured that the Italians would wage an even more ruthless war without mercy, and with a brutality that shocked the world.[108] Even more than previously, consequently, the full might of Italian air power would be unleashed in this increasingly vicious conflict. Writing home, one confident Italian soldier bragged, "With our Air Force, Italy can never lose. As the planes go forward and explore the ground not even an ant can escape them."[109]

Additional Ethiopian military setbacks followed in the southern front's burnt deserts in early November, repeating reversals along the northern front. These de-feats in the south, despite spirited resistance in vain, caused one defiant Ethiopian leader to declare: "Every square metre and every tukul will be defended to the last drop of our blood." The battered Ethiopians, including Imperial Guard troops, withdrew under the relentless punishment of Italian bombers. But the steady Ethi-opian withdrawal was suddenly turned to victory in a surprise counterattack that forced the Italians to retreat. The overall tactical situation on the southern front however, remained shaky. As on the northern sector, other Ethiopian war chiefs be-gan to defect to the Italians as the fragile fabric of Ethiopian nationalism gave way to tribalism. At this critical moment, however, Ethiopian resistance in this sector was suddenly fortified after Robinson flew Emperor Selassie to the southern front to inspire confidence among his out-gunned warriors.

Robinson descended from the blue skies to land with the emperor in the Ogaden Desert town of Jijiga. Selassie, Robinson, and other high-ranking leaders, then drove across the desert flats to the sand-blown town of Dagghabur on the Tug Jerrer. The emperor's arrival was timely. His presence raised his troops' morale on the southern front, ensuring more determined resistance against the invaders from Italian Somaliland. Completing his mission, Robinson then flew Selassie back to Addis Ababa without incident.[110]

Stabilization along the southern front—and the northern front as well—was only temporary, however. The most significant indication of the dramatic change in the war's nature, after General Badoglio's appointment, would be revealed in the Italians' unrestrained use of the greatest horror of World War I's trench warfare, dichloroethyl sulfide, or mustard gas. Mussolini informed General Badoglio in no uncertain terms: "I authorize you to use gas, even on a large scale." And in Ethiopia, this rain of death would be delivered with merciless regularity by the seemingly countless aircraft of the Regia Aeronautica that commanded the skies.

By this time, the Italians, despite enjoying overwhelming strength of sixty thousand troops, launched no major offensive from Italian Somaliland. Here, the Italians counted heavily on black allies to do most of the fighting. These were the Islamic Somali war clans of the arid lowlands, consisting of warriors who were determined to continue their centuries-long struggle against the black Orthodox Christians, the Ethiopians of the cool highlands.

In the bitter fighting in the Ogaden Desert region, the Italians had first dropped mustard gas on both Ethiopian troops and civilians even before mid-October. Mussolini had sent a top secret telegram to his commander, General Rodolfo Graziani, of that region southeast of Addis Ababa: "Authorized use [of] gas as last resort in order to defeat enemy resistance and in case of counterattack."[111]

For the war's remainder, the Italian Air Force would slaughter Ethiopians, both soldiers and civilians, by the thousands with mustard gas. In total, at least eighteen poison gas attacks were unleashed from the air. A horrified Emperor Selassie denounced the Italian's most lethal aspect of modern warfare: "In order to kill off systematically all living creatures . . . the Italian Command made its aircraft pass over again and again. The very refinement of barbarism consisted of carrying ravage and terror into the most densely populated parts of the territory [in order] to scatter fear and death over a great part of the Ethiopian territory."[112]

Meanwhile, with the promise of heavy fighting when Marshal Badoglio pushed south toward Addis Ababa, Robinson continued to labor tirelessly, but against ever-increasing odds for success. For the first time in his life, Robinson was now encountering an unprecedented degree of frustration. After all, this young man with the can-do attitude was familiar with encountering obstacles that seemingly could not be overcome.

Before the Italian advance in the north on Addis Ababa, a lull occurred while the Italians consolidated their gains, dealt with logistical problems, and reorganized their forces in preparation for the final offensive effort. After advancing around seventy-five miles into Ethiopia's mountainous depths, Italian forces rested before the four-hundred-mile final push south to the Ethiopian capital. Good roads had to be constructed so that mechanized Italian columns could advance through the formidable mountain ranges, which now seemed to protect Addis Ababa like a gift from God.

This relatively quiet period—the lull before the storm—presented Robinson some time for reflection and the opportunity to write a few letters back home. By this time he was a changed man, having evolved from the romantic idealist who had first landed in Ethiopian less than six months before. On November 21, a supremely frustrated Robinson wrote a long letter from his headquarters of the Imperial Ethiopian Air Force at Addis Ababa, to Claude A. Barnett, the Director of the Associated Negro Press (ANP) of Chicago. His letter to Barnett was written on official military stationary, carrying the title of the "Imperiale Ethiopienne Air Force," and with his name and rank, "Col. J. C. Robinson."

The royal seal—an African lion carrying an imperial flag with a long staff distinguished by a Christian, or Latin, cross at the end, and wearing a crown (the same style that had been worn by Emperor Selassie during his coronation) topped by a Latin cross—dominated the top of the page.[113]

Robinson was even more convinced that only American pilots in modern American aircraft could transform his air force into a fighting force capable of defending the capital. He made additional efforts to secure black aviators, friends, and acquaintances from Chicago to create the invaluable cadre of experienced, well-trained flyers who hopefully would serve as the solid nucleus of the Imperial Ethiopian Air Force.[114]

Robinson's hopes improved slightly when the League of Nations half-heartedly placed mild sanctions upon Italy in December 1935, with the Sir Samuel Hoare-Pierre Laval plan. To appease Mussolini, so that he would not ally himself with Hitler's Germany, this cynical secret plan gave Italy two-thirds of Ethiopia, while Emperor Selassie retained only the interior highlands. Weapons and war materiel could no longer be shipped to Italy, but that now made no difference as, unlike Italy, Ethiopia had no manufacturing base. Therefore, the arms importation sanctions more severely negatively affected Ethiopia, whose armies continued to fight with only a few old artillery pieces captured at Adowa in 1896.[115]

Additional aircraft gained by Robinson were not useful without experienced pilots, emphasizing the need for well-trained African American volunteers. In Robinson's words to Barnett indicating his frustration about the lack of support, especially the extreme difficulty in obtaining African American pilots, "I told my fellow pilots [in Chicago] that I would do everything I could to get them in the [Imperial Ethiopian] air force here. Last Saturday, I cabled for six of them. I asked Mr. [Cornelius R.] Coffey to answer me at once by cable and I would cable the fare [for the trip to Ethiopia] at once to them. This was one week ago and I havent [sic] had any reply. All of these men asked me before I left there to please get them jobs here. Every one of them have failed me so far, which means the last time I will ever ask The Emperor [sic] permission to send for any one else."[116]

Consequently, Robinson continued to be increasingly frustrated. Both before and after the war's outbreak, many foreign assistants, volunteers, and mercenaries, including some white Americans but especially the French, had fled Ethiopia in droves, leaving Robinson more or less on his own. Even the *New York Times* recorded how "all foreigners in the army save the professional Belgian soldiers on long contract, are dissatisfied with . . . the war and appear to want to quickest and most honorable way out."[117]

Unlike the majority of Western volunteers, however, Robinson was determined to honor his solemn pledge and one-year commitment to the emperor. He would not abandon Ethiopia or "the great army of the Conquering Lion of Judah" during their darkest hour, despite feeling a sense of abandonment by the exodus of foreign volunteers after the war erupted. And for those relatively few remaining volunteers in Ethiopia, the already sagging "morale of foreign freedom fighters worsened when a rumor spread that the Emperor himself had made plans to flee the country."[118]

Worst of all, Robinson was beginning to discover that his strong spirit of Pan-Africanism and the idealistic commitment to Ethiopia were not matched by his friends, especially Coffey, and the other black aviators in Chicago. Nor was black America responding to Ethiopia's assistance with either manpower or financial support. As fate would have it, Robinson would receive no help from his friends and associates in Chicago, or elsewhere, while in Ethiopia. He was becoming increasingly disillusioned. He now discovered that he was as thoroughly abandoned by other African Americans, just as Ethiopia had been abandoned by the world.

Robinson's old friends and associates in Chicago had made their personal commitment to serve Ethiopia before the war's outbreak. Now that war had gone against Ethiopia, they had changed their minds. Foremost among those who had a sudden change of heart was Robinson's friend Coffey. Like other Chicago aviators, Coffey had completely washed his hands of the idea of ever going to Ethiopia. Robinson was beginning to feel betrayed by his closest friends and members of his Challenger Air Pilots' Association.[119]

On November 21, Robinson described his bitter frustration in a letter: "New airplanes were ordered for the six [African American] pilots [in Chicago] I cabled. These airplanes cost over 30,000 American dollars each. They are coming from England. I first ordered some American airplanes, but the order was turned down on account of the American embargo on airplanes being sent here."[120]

In time, these six aircraft from England would arrive to eventually bolster the Imperial Ethiopian Air Force to its peak strength of two dozen aircraft. But the African American aviation volunteers that Robinson so desperately needed would never depart the United States for reasons other than simply cold feet. With the Ethiopian Embassy's assistance, Robinson had secured his own personal passport before the war's outbreak. Several months even before the war opened, a good many African American citizens, including those from Robinson's native Mississippi, desired to volunteer to serve in Ethiopia, because, in the words of a prospective black volunteer from Baltimore, Maryland, America and the West would "not help Ethiopia because she is black." To Robinson, seemingly all that was now needed was the issuing of passports and for the Ethiopian government to pay transportation costs for American volunteers to reach Selassie's Motherland for "the defense of the African Race." But these zealous American volunteers desiring to assist Ethiopia were denied passports, because the Neutrality Act had been invoked by President Roosevelt.[121]

One angry prospective African American volunteer wrote a letter directly to President Roosevelt: "Why can't the black people fight against Italy?" In addition, Ethiopia was not ready to accommodate those African American volunteers desiring to defend the "ancestral homeland." And no organized Ethiopian recruiting effort had been established in the United States by the Ethiopian government.[122]

Robinson thus remained largely on his own. Tecie N. Hawariat, an Ethiopian diplomat in the United States, emphasized that Ethiopia needed "technical, flying, and medical units," but the lack of funds also thwarted such possibilities. Indeed, many African Americans "wished to join the fighting but recruitment of blacks for service in Ethiopia was discouraged because of the cost." And a cash-short Ethiopia was unable to provide funds for the transportation of volunteers to the Horn of Africa like they had for Robinson. But perhaps most of all, the early Italian string of successes greatly discouraged a good many prospective American volunteers, both black and white.

Robinson also continued to be frustrated by the inability to obtain additional aircraft from the United States. As Robinson later explained: "The emperor tried to purchase modern planes, but was unable [as] Americans would not sell to him, nor would the other great powers except England, who sold him old planes at the cost of $30,000 each."[123]

Meanwhile, black newspapers in the United States, such as the *Afro-American* on October 12, 1935, implored the League of Nations to "approve the sale of modern arms [especially aircraft] to Ethiopia, so that this ancient nation may put up a real defense against the cut-throat brigands now invading its firesides."[124]

From his headquarters in Addis Ababa, Robinson deplored the fact that his ambitious aviation plans were steadily thwarted by politics, fate, and apathy: "I am sorry the boys [in Chicago] dident [*sic*] answer my cablegram after the [Ethiopian] government went to so much trouble to get these airplanes especially for them. There are many [white] European pilots here trying to get jobs in the [Imperial] air service. They came here at their own expense and have been two or three months trying to get work. I am sure they will be given work now because it seems impossible to get colored Americans. There are many white American pilots that send cablegrams and many letters every day wanting to pay their way here if they are promised a job when they get here. Up to the present day they have been turned down," because Emperor Selassie still wanted an all-black Imperial Ethiopian Air

Force. Robinson had no choice but to abide by the emperor's wishes based on war-related decisions, regardless if good or bad.[125]

Ironically, Selassie's overly optimistic dream of an all-black Imperial Ethiopian Air Force meant that new white aviation volunteers were yet unwelcome. In a bid to secure French support by ensuring that no international incident would result with Frenchmen flying and dying in this war, the emperor sent away the few remaining French airmen in Colonel Robinson's command.

As a dismayed Robinson explained: "All of the French aviators are leaving at the end of this month [November and] this is a very good move on the part of the government [for political considerations and] the boys there [in Chicago] can't say they dident [sic] get a chance because the door was thrown wide open to them and they failed to walk in."[126]

But most of all, Robinson was shocked by encountering racial prejudice among many Ethiopians, despite his firm commitment to their cause and nation. Robinson was now experiencing greater disillusionment about the concept of cooperative Pan-Africanism. In fact, cultural differences were so wide that many African Americans were long unable to find "the promised land in Ethiopia." Since Ethiopians in general were strongly xenophobic, especially toward Westerners regardless of color, and provincial in their isolated feudal cocoon amid the remote highlands, they often believed the worst white racial stereotypes about African Americans.

Robinson, therefore, was surprised by an entirely new kind of prejudice that he never dreamed possible: African people's disdain for African Americans. Despite having studied in Europe or America, the leading Ethiopian intellectuals of the Young Ethiopian Movement were known for their anti-foreign sentiment. This racism shattered some of Robinson's naive idealism about Mother Africa and the romanticized sense of brotherhood that existed between African Americans with the Ethiopian people. But ultimately, Robinson blamed pervasive white cultural influences for this phenomenon rather than homegrown Ethiopian prejudice, reflecting his experiences in the Deep South, Detroit, and Chicago. As an incredulous Colonel Robinson wrote from Addis Ababa: "The white influence over here is very, very, strong [and consequently] the[y] have posined [sic] the minds of the Abyssinian against American Negroes."[127]

But in fact most Ethiopians viewed themselves as closer racially to whites than to African Americans partly because of their ancient cultural heritage and the amount of white blood that ran through their veins. Stemming from another kind of xenophobia in the United States, this perception of Ethiopian whiteness was so prevalent in black America that it diminished overall African American support for the Ethiopian cause. Attempting damage control, one Ethiopian official in the United States officially addressed this sensitive issue: "I have learned of the mischievous propaganda to the effect that Ethiopians do not want your help, that they consider themselves of the white race. It is said that we despise Negroes" of the United States.[128]

Even Europeans visiting Ethiopia complained of "indignities" suffered at the hands of proud Ethiopians, who "persisted in behaving as superiors; it was not that they were hostile, but contemptuous," wrote Evelyn Waugh. Clearly, Robinson was now caught between two xenophobias and two discriminatory worlds that helped to sabotage his best efforts: that of African Americans in the United States and of the Ethiopians themselves who failed to live up to the central beliefs of Pan-African unity. As Robinson discovered, the cultural gap between Ethiopians and African Americans remained shockingly wide even when they were united against the Italian invasion. And the war's stresses only widened the gap.

Before journeying to Ethiopia, Robinson had not known that Ethiopians in America hated to be classified as "Negroes." The Ethiopian people "were always careful to distinguish their civilization" from other blacks, including African Americans. Marcus Garvey was especially critical of such Ethiopian open breaches in racial solidarity, which raised "doubts about Ethiopia's commitment to the concept of black brotherhood." At times, therefore, Robinson found himself in the seemingly surreal position of facing the same kind of prejudices from Ethiopians that he had encountered with white Southerners, even though he was risking his life to defend their ancient homeland. But despite his growing sense of disillusionment and frustration, Colonel Robinson continued to turn negatives into positives. He believed that such prejudice—from either blacks or whites—could be overcome by both his own superior performance and more evidence of his unfailing personal commitment to Ethiopia's life-and-death struggle. Robinson was now even more determined, in his own words, "to let the Ethiopians know that the American Negro is not at all as bad as the White race try to picture him to be."[129]

Providing increasing disillusionment for Robinson, however, was the fact that far more white volunteers had actually rushed to Ethiopia's assistance than black American volunteers. As could be expected, this surprising realization made Robinson rethink his own beliefs in regard to the complexities of race, people, and politics. Robinson lost more of his innocence and faith in the idealistic concept of Pan-Africanism from his hard-learned experiences in Ethiopia. Robinson saw not only white military volunteers in Ethiopia, but also a good many white civilians, primarily Red Cross workers, coming to Ethiopia's aid. From all across Europe, many white military volunteers continued to reach Addis Ababa to defend Ethiopia against their fellow white Europeans. Robinson wrote on November 21 with a degree of admiration how "their [sic] are many Swiss men [and Belgium volunteers] coming in to serve in the army as officers." And, as revealed in the same letter, he was proud of the fact that Egyptian physicians and "nine new English Doctors have just arrived for redcross [sic] work."[130]

But by far the greatest personal blow dealt to Robinson's sense of black solidarity was in regard to his best friend, Coffey, who refused to join him as promised. This betrayal tore at Robinson's heart and soul. Bragg regretted that "Cornelius Coffey and Robinson were never so close again."[131]

Coffey possessed another good reason for not rushing to Ethiopia's assistance. By this time under the bright lights and all-night entertainment of "Bronzeville," he began a passionate relationship with pretty Willa Brown. She evidently had been Robinson's girlfriend, before he left for Ethiopia, while a member of the Challenger Air Pilots' Association—an early indication of troubles in Robinson's relationship with his wife.[132]

Increasingly disillusioned with the United States' lack of support for Ethiopia, Robinson was becoming frustrated with American humanitarian organizations as well. In his November 21 letter, Robinson wrote with some disgust how, "There [sic] are many Red Cross units coming here from all parts of the world except America."[133]

Robinson's November 21 letter also revealed his growing frustration in attracting more black aviators. Robinson wrote, "I am sorry Mr. Ray could not come over, as I had gotten permission for him to be in charge of the regiment station at Addis Abeba to protect the city. He was also to start a new program for the war training of the army [after the departure of French trainers]. Well after we could not get him, a Belgium officer was sent for; he came at once [evidently from the Belgian Congo], and after, one week here he sent for fifteen other Belgium men to assist him. They all came at once."[134]

Some of Robinson's frustration was misplaced, however. He did not know that the six black pilots from Chicago would have been refused passports by the U.S.

government on the grounds that Ethiopian Army service violated neutrality laws. It is not known if any black aviators had attempted to join Robinson, or had simply concluded, like Coffey, that a faraway, dangerous war in East Africa was simply too risky.[135]

Ironically, unlike Herbert Julian, who became an Ethiopian citizen, Robinson maintained his U.S. citizenship while serving in Ethiopia. This proved a wise decision, and guaranteed Robinson's access to the United States embassy in Addis Ababa, where he sought America's support for Ethiopia's defense. Here, one American consul "assured me that he was proud of me as an American citizen, and hoped that I will always remain one [and] that the American government is behind me one hundred percent," wrote Robinson on November 21, 1935.[136]

By this time, however, Robinson was only too aware of the American racism that ensured Ethiopia's abandonment. This realization was expressed by his friend of Jamaican American descent, now in Ethiopia, newspaperman Joel Augustus Rogers, who wrote: "The two great democratic nations, Britain and America, while condemning Fascist and Nazi doctrines, and proclaiming equal justice for all, were using 'race' as a fetish to keep their own citizens and subjects divided."[137]

Worst of all, Robinson also possessed ample reason to feel gloomy about prospects for Ethiopia to successfully maintain its independence. Many prominent politicians in the West, including Winston Churchill, admired Mussolini and Fascism. The Ethiopian representative to the League of Nations, Wolde Mariam, declared how his ancient independent Christian nation "cannot believe that the Ethiopian people will be abandoned and delivered over to its cruel enemy [but if so then] what Ethiopia asks is that, in mere justice, she should be given facilities to acquire more complete and more up-to-date defensive material than she now possesses."[138]

Tragically, however, the requested vital military assistance would never be sent from either the United States or the West. Nor would any nation, including the United States, extend the all-important financial credit necessary to Ethiopia to adequately defend itself and survive. It was only a matter of time before Ethiopia was subjugated, and Robinson gradually began to realize as much.[139]

Equally disheartening for Robinson was the fact that the conflict had also become a civil war. Black Ethiopians now fought against black Ethiopians, despite that fact that the Italo-Ethiopian War was also very much a racial conflict. Italy employed large numbers of black troops, especially Muslim warriors from Somalia, against the Christian Ethiopians. An especially harsh realization for Robinson was the fact that blacks now slaughtered each other because one side served the imperial designs of a racist European power. This haunting irony helped to destroy the last lingering illusions and idealism about Pan-Africanism in Robinson's mind. Robinson described the bitter reality of this increasingly brutal struggle: "Blacks were pitted against blacks in the most tragic contest in African history." Even worse for the Ethiopian people's morale, "the Emperor was tricked by the rebellion of 80,000 soldiers [of Ras Gugsa] who turned on him" and joined the Italians. These Galla warriors nursed old tribal grievances against Emperor Selassie, a member of the Amhara tribe as were most of his people, which controlled the government and held power.[140]

On the northern front, Ras Gugsa's defection was an especially severe blow to morale and to the resistance effort. Italy benefited from its clever policy of divide-and-conquer, sowing seeds of dissatisfaction and reaping a bountiful harvest. An angry Emperor Selassie wrote how Ras Gugsa "betrayed his mother country [and went] over to the Italians. In consequence, We made Dessie Our headquarters" on the northern front.[141]

Near the end of November 1935, Robinson described the complexities of the Ethiopian resistance effort, which was also hampered by the religious divisions among the defenders of their ancestral homeland: "On the North East and South East frontier most all the Ethiopians are Mohammedan [sic] and they are putting up a good fight. The Italians are having a real hard job fighting them. It is strange to say, but it is true, the Christians in the north are the worst fighters. When it comes to battle the Italians kick them around like nothing."[142]

But thousands of Italian troops hardly needed black allies to subjugate Ethiopia. Italian commanders, especially General Rodolfo Graziani, had learned how to wage a new kind of twentieth-century warfare without mercy or pity, after ruthlessly crushing the Islamic revolts of a northern African people in Libya, which Italy had subjugated.[143]

Meanwhile, the Italians retained total command of the air across Ethiopia. Well-trained aviators of the Regia Aeronautica continued to launch strategic bombing campaigns with their big Caproni bombers. Without the traditional strategic bombing targets of industrial networks, or supply and communications lines in this feudal land of mostly farmers, peasants, and herdsmen, Ethiopia's population became a primary bombing target. By design, the terror bombing of the civilian populace was calculated to destroy the Ethiopian will to resist, appalling even the Italians themselves.[144]

Thanks to effective reconnaissance flights, the Regia Aeronautica soon ascertained the location of vital military, political, and civilian targets at the town of Dessie. About halfway between the Eritrea border and Addis Ababa, this was now Emperor Selassie's imperial headquarters and the mobilization point of the Ethiopian resistance effort on the northern front. Dessie was first bombed on December 6. The Italian Air Force now hoped to eliminate Selassie in one blow. A *Chicago Defender* correspondent described the devastating Italian air attack: "A fleet of Fascist bombing planes poured death and horror on the Imperial headquarters of the Conquering Lion of Judah. The streets became a veritable sepulcher with 100 dead and nearly 400 wounded. . . . With their machine guns spouting bullets and their engines thundering, thirty powerful tri-motors dropped more than 1,000 bombs during the 30 minute assault [and then] they roared onto the horizon."[145]

Thereafter, Dessie was bombed with lethal regularity by swarms of the lumbering Caproni bombers. As Emperor Selessie explained: "The first bombs at Dessye were bad enough, but at least the Italian planes went their way after the raid [but] afterwards, aeroplanes would begin bombing at dawn and the raid would succeed throughout the day. Bombs, and bombs and more bombs, without intermission or end."[146]

The imperial headquarters and the Ethiopian army were not the only targets of the Italian air force at this time. The Caproni bombers pounded the civilian population of Dessie. Even Dessie's international hospitals, including the American infirmary, fell under the bombardment's wrath. Clearly, by this time, "unable to make progress on the ground, 'victories' were [now] provided for the home population [of Italy] by hit-and-run attacks from the air."[147]

During these repeated bombardments, Selassie's life was in peril. Because it had been too risky since the Italians were alerted to his impending move north, Robinson had not flown the emperor to Dessie on November 28, only a week after he had ferried the emperor back to Addis Ababa from the southern front. When Emperor Selassie left for the capital, he described an especially close call for him at Dessie during the bombardment: "Thank God I was never struck but men a few yards away from me were" hit.

Here, at Dessie, along the eastern rim of the high plateau in the central highlands, the emperor, like Robinson before him at Adowa, witnessed the bombardment's horrors. Incendiaries were dropped on Dessie, causing widespread destruction and sparing no one.[148]

Finally receiving new orders, Robinson hurriedly departed Emperor Selassie's headquarters, now located in the old Italian Consulate building which was Dessie's only modern structure. He flew back to his own Imperial Ethiopian Air Force headquarters in the capital, taking the emperor with him, to safety. Throughout December, Robinson repeatedly flew back and forth the nearly 250 miles from Addis Ababa to Dessie. He had evidently also flown Everett Colson, Selassie's trusted American advisor from the State Department, who had helped to convince the emperor to appeal to the League of Nations, to Dessie to confer with Selassie, before flying the emperor back to Addis Ababa. Robinson also orchestrated deliveries of precious medical supplies and war munitions to Dessie and other front-line troop positions.[149]

Now assigned to permanent duty in Addis Ababa but occasionally flying to Dessie to communicate military orders from Emperor Selassie, Robinson remained at considerable risk during these lengthy flights to the front. By this time, however, he had become more war wise and accustomed to danger.

Robinson spent much of his time at his busy headquarters of the Imperial Ethiopian Air Force at the airport at Addis Ababa. Here, he continued to train young Ethiopian pilots. From beginning to end, Robinson dealt with a host of logistical and manpower problems that seemed insurmountable. And he tackled an increasing number of mechanical and technical difficulties as well. Despite his rank and title, Robinson was the most experienced mechanic in his air force, doing much of the technical work himself. This heavy workload, especially when combined with the deteriorating war situation, took an increasing toll on Robinson's can-do attitude and optimism, and perhaps even his health.

By this time, he was almost overwhelmed by the burden of command and the responsibilities imposed upon him. An increasingly cynical Robinson wrote: "We have ordered some new airplanes from England [but] now the English company is asking us to employ English mechanics and English Pilots. They also want the director to be English. It seems to me that the same English Policy that happen[ed] in Egypt [which Great Britain controlled in customary colonial fashion] some years ago is beginning [sic] to happen here."[150]

Clearly, Robinson had embraced some of the anti-foreign views so prevalent among Young Ethiopian Movement's members. Utilizing English pilots ran contrary to the emperor's desire for an all-black air force, however. In addition, Robinson had personally experienced the ugliness of English colonialism on the African continent.[151]

Robinson, and evidently Emperor Selassie, viewed the English as attempting to gain not only military influence in Ethiopia, but also political influence. Robinson explained how the proud Ethiopians carefully guarded their national integrity by refusing to compromise with Europeans: "All a person can here [sic] now is the English People is this and is that. When I first came it was French this and French that. Really I often wonder what the hell they [the Ethiopians] will be saying next."[152]

Robinson now realized that the Ethiopians could be their own worst enemies, sabotaging their own war effort. Consequently, he became increasingly intolerant toward uncooperative Ethiopians, who seemed to prefer nationalistic pride and an outdated sense of honor instead of everyone working together to preserve their nation's independence. Robinson remained close to the emperor's cousin Malaku E. Bayen. Helping the wounded on the northern front with his Howard University medical training, Dr. Bayen served as Selassie's personal physician while also holding a position on Selassie's staff, and serving as a member of the Ethiopian Red Cross. He had first recruited Robinson for Ethiopian service in what now seemed like a lifetime ago to the native Mississippian.

Growing more discouraged, Robinson increasingly saw that the Ethiopians seemed more willing to lose their war against Italians rather than embrace whites and African Americans as allies.

A mixed race people with white Semitic ancestry since ancient times because Ethiopia had long stood at a crossroads of not only east and west but also north and south, the "Amharic people made careful distinction between themselves and Negroid people," in part because Ethiopians had long enslaved Negroid peoples, especially Muslims to Sudan's south. Like the Ethiopians themselves, white writers also made clear distinctions. They emphasized that Ethiopians, with white features, descended in part from Caucasians, and that these Hamitic people of northern Africa were superior to the darker Negroid people of the Sudan and African Americans. Many Sudanese, who were as dark as Robinson and with similar features, yet served as slaves in Ethiopia: certainly another culture shock for Robinson.

As in African American culture, ironically, variations in the shading of skin color were factors in Ethiopia that not only determined a degree of social status but also perceptions of beauty and intelligence. Light-toned Ethiopians felt entitled to the services of darker-hued servants. This peculiar kind of prejudice—existing in both America and Ethiopia—was exploited by some white American journalists, who sought to malign the spirit of Pan-Africanism.[153]

Because of his use of foreign advisors, even the emperor himself had been criticized by xenophobic Ethiopians, who wanted no foreign military advisors in their country. This anti-foreign attitude continued to cause Robinson many problems, complicating his mission and sapping his morale. Even the emperor was admonished by his Minister of War, Ras Mulugueta, "You take too much notice of foreigners and their worries. This is foolish and against tradition. Rely on your own countrymen!"[154]

As his revealing November letters indicated, Colonel Robinson was more or less on his own, with a wider gulf growing between him and the Ethiopians, as well as with African Americans back at home. In his own words, Robinson was by now "the only American in the whole outfit."[155]

But the most disillusioning of all aspects of Ethiopian life for Robinson that punctured his romanticized concept of Pan-Africanism and sense of black unity was the ugly reality of slavery, which was still alive and well in Ethiopia. Slavery had existed in Ethiopia since ancient times, stemming not primarily from an organized slave trade but mostly as a consequence of the centuries of warfare between black Christians and black Muslims, primarily from the Sudan, the captives who became slaves. In fact, slavery had expanded in the early twentieth century, when Ethiopia extended its borders and conducted successful slave raids. Slavery existed across Ethiopia to fulfill the menial requirements of the ancient ruling class. Some members of the Ethiopian nobility owned thousands of slaves. Selassie lamented how slavery in Ethiopia "had yet remained firmly established by [ancient] custom."[156]

After launching slave raids from the cool central highlands and down into the steamy lowlands of neighboring countries to the south and west to capture the Negroid peoples of the lowlands, Ethiopian slave traders had exported slaves to the great slave markets of Persia and Arabia for centuries. Despite his own efforts, Emperor Selassie could not end the brutal institution that even included slave breeding, because large numbers of slaves were owned by the most influential Rases, various warlords of a feudal society, and by the Ethiopian Orthodox Church. Selassie needed their support, especially when the Ethiopian nation was battling fiercely for its life. Great Britain had refused to vote for Ethiopia's entry as a member of the League of Nations because of the curse of slavery. Mussolini in part justified his invasion as a "civilizing" mission to end slavery in Ethiopia.

Even though some blacks were virtually enslaved in Italian Eritrea, Ethiopia now paid a high price for harboring slavery—the arms blockade on Ethiopia had been imposed in part to stop the slave raids. This penalty "eventually made Ethiopia defenseless in [the] face of Italian aggression." Probably the greatest irony of Robinson's further disillusionment was his realization that the Italians had launched their invasion of Ethiopia in part as a moral mission to end slavery. Ironically, in a byproduct of one of the most brutal wars in the twentieth century, white Catholic troops from a faraway foreign land would eventually bring to an end forced servitude for thousands of blacks in Ethiopia.[157]

7

THE GODS OF WAR TURN AGAINST ETHIOPIA

ROBINSON CONTINUED TO PRESS in vain for more black pilots from America. As he wrote to Barnett (original orthography here and in later passages is preserved):

> I had money given me to arrange for the passage of six of the fellows from Chicago. Now the English is asking the [Ethiopian] government to favor English aviators (I mean the English company we have ordered the new airplanes from). Now the [Ethiopian] government dont know what way to decide. They told me to hold the passage money up for a few days. Japan wants to send as many airplanes as they want or any thing else that they might need. The government is afraid England wont like it, if Ethiopia excepts to many things from Japan. You see how childish these [Ethiopian] officials are and how frighten[ed] their attitude is getting. I am begining to get fed up in fighting here, because of the attitude of the officials.[1]

As time passed without any amelioration of his circumstances, Robinson observed: "I think they [Ethiopian officials] should take a definite stand win or lose. If we all have to die, I think we should all die like men and have it over with."[2]

Despite seemingly everything going wrong around him and facing discrimination himself from Ethiopians, Robinson was fully prepared to fight and die to the bitter end, if necessary. His frustration with Ethiopians, Japanese, Italians, and Americans, black and white, vented for the moment, Colonel Robinson continued to plead for additional assistance from Barnett in his letter:

If they cut out these childish [examples of bad behavior] and have me send on for the [African American] men [from Chicago, then] I would like very much if you would let me send the passage money to you, so you could arrange for the men's tickets. You see if you will do this for me I know their wont be any hitch in the fellows getting their tickets ok. They would have to first come to France or England, then get their tickets from one of those points to here.[3]

Robinson would have been even more disillusioned had he known that by this time plenty of support for the war effort now existed in the United States. Black communities raised funds and collected relief supplies for the Ethiopian people. Medical supplies were gathered through an organization known as the Medical Aid to Ethiopia. Protests of Italy's invasion were sent from such organizations as the Ethiopian Pacific Movement. The Ethiopian World Federation published *The Voice of Ethiopia* to report war news to the American people. Other support and assistance organizations were formed, such as the Council of Friends of Ethiopia.

Additionally, thousands of African American volunteers had rallied for military duty in Ethiopia. An estimated eight thousand black men trained for military action in Ethiopia, thanks in part to the black newspapers reporting of Robinson's military service in Ethiopia. Another one thousand African Americans had trained in New York City. Significantly, thanks to newspapers like the *Chicago Defender*, many more African Americans in Chicago than New York City—an estimated eight times—were prepared to fight in Ethiopia. Another estimated five thousand African Americans trained for Ethiopian service in Detroit, while an estimated two thousand black volunteers made preparations in Kansas City, Missouri.[4]

But U.S. neutrality laws forbid direct aid and assistance to Ethiopia from America, especially volunteers. Moreover, American oil companies were reaping huge profits from supplying the Italian war machine. During the fall of 1935 American oil shipments to Italy tripled. [5]

Indeed, "as long as the United States continued to sell oil to Italy, a League [of Nations] embargo would be ineffective. America had no intention of penalizing Italy for her aggression."[6]

Unfortunately for Ethiopia, the sanctions placed on Italy by the League of Nations had only forced Mussolini to trade for oil with the United States, which was not a League of Nations member. The sanctions thus became "a gold mine for American business." This lucrative trade included American shoe and meat companies that supplied Italian soldiers on the march toward Addis Ababa. General Graziani had unleashed his offensive thrust from Italian Somaliland, after buying American "caterpillar" diesels and troop carriers directly from the United States. This flow of oil and gasoline from America were necessary to keep not only the Italian war machine on the move, but also the Regina Aeronautica operating in Ethiopian skies. Hundreds of Italian Air Force aircraft in Ethiopia needed 150 tons of gasoline per day. Because of sanctions, Italy was also forced to increase trade with Germany, drawing the two nations closer.

Little support for Ethiopia was because of racism. Such typical attitudes of white America can be seen in the words of W. D. Hubbard, a white newspaper correspondent, who admitted: "I firmly believed that it wasn't right that Whites should be defeated in Africa."[7] Indeed, the "assumption of white, western superiority was the biggest obstacle the Ethiopians had to overcome."[8]

An ever duty-conscious Robinson, revealing that he was a man of honor even in the face of mounting discrimination difficulties and apathy, wrote in November: "My present agreement will be up in May 1936, at that time I think I will have done my part to help Ethiopia, and also to let the Ethiopians know that the American Negro is not at all as bad as the white race try to picture him to be."[9]

Incredibly, despite all the setbacks, Robinson was still committed to the Ethiopian cause, even though he admitted to Barnett some of his darkest, innermost feelings: "Really Mr. Barnett it looks like the begining of the end for this country to me. The officials have begin to loose their boisterous idea about Ethiopia can beat the Italians at any time. They [belatedly] realize now that they have been [a]sleep for the last forty or more years. They are wondering who will save them from the Italians, instead of let[ting] the Italians come that they could beat them."[10]

The extent of Robinson's increasing gloom over Ethiopia's prospects can be partly glimpsed in his signature at the end of his November 28 letter to Barnett. In humble fashion, resigned to his fate, and as if the priorities in life were now in order, he simply penned "Johnny," as opposed to the lofty colonel's rank as the Imperial Ethiopian Air Force's commander as in his previous letters.

But in this same letter, perhaps the most revealing words that indicated the full extent of Robinson's disenchantment was the fact that he was already looking beyond this ill-fated war without solutions or glory, thinking of his future life upon his return to the United States, if he survived this war. He wrote: "Please let Mr. [George L.] Washington at Tuskegee [Institute and the head of the Department of Mechanical Industries] know when you write him next; that if I [will] be able to live through this little war, I would still like to get my job at Tuskegee."[11]

Some question remained, however, about whether Robinson could even "live through this little war" so far from home. As commander of the Imperial Ethiopian Air Force, he was a prime target of the Italian airmen.[12] Indeed, by this time, he had experienced enough close calls to know how easily he could be shot down. Robinson's only consolation when not working at headquarters or flying to the front was that he lived well and enjoyed prestigious royal connections. He had come a long way from the lowly boy spit-shining the shoes of whites at the Gulfport Railroad Depot in south Mississippi.

With some exaggeration, an American journalist described Robinson's life in Addis Ababa as that of a "royal courtier."[13] As the Imperial Ethiopian Air Force's commander, Robinson lived in what was considered a luxury home—by Ethiopian standards—in Addis Ababa. Robinson's house was even staffed with six Ethiopian servants. Robinson later stated that it was "strictly just like a flat in New York."[14] But Robinson was not corrupted by his close connections with Emperor Selassie and the royal family: "Those kind of things are kind of artificial to me. I never let it become a part of me. I always liked to do things for myself. Yes, it was very nice. I had six servants and lots of times they wouldn't even let me carry my brief case."[15]

When not laboring overtime to create his air force for the emperor, Robinson explained how "his majesty gave me an automobile and I also had the privilege of riding any of his horses when I was off duty. And I had many costly gifts given to me by the different rasses and things."[16]

Robinson faced relatively few health concerns. Fortunately Addis Ababa was a healthy, "cool and pleasant" location with its high altitude and relatively modernized standards compared to the rest of the country.[17] Living amid the cool, green highlands, Robinson escaped the ravages of diseases that especially plagued the wet lowland regions infested with deadly tropical diseases, from malarial mosquitoes and the tsetse fly. He felt fortunate not to have been headquartered far outside the capital, where "an awful lot of sickness: malaria, and things . . . in the interior, not in Addis Ababa. This is a very healthy place, ordinarily."[18]

During this hectic period, Robinson enjoyed the popular national cuisine of Ethiopia. *Injera* was a pancake-like bread made of flour. A spicy stew, *wat*, was well seasoned and peppery like the Creole foods of Robinson's native Mississippi Gulf Coast. Chicken, goat, pork, lamb, beef, and even camel were meat dishes for those, like Robinson, who could afford such luxuries. A wide variety of vegetables were available at the busy open-air markets. But there was nothing quite like Ethiopia's rich and full-flavored coffee, which helped to stimulate Robinson's work activities, mind, and endurance.[19]

Robinson's best times were experienced primarily during the early period of Ethiopian service. As the war lengthened, he was away from Addis Ababa for ever longer periods. As Robinson described, "Sometimes I have to fly for two weeks without pulling my shoes off, and with very little sleep in between time; this is when I am along the Northern front, but I am only too glad that I am doing my part to help [but] these conditions might help to finish my flying career," thanks either to the Italian pilots or fatal disease.[20] On occasion, Robinson also flew missions of mercy. When Dr. F. Hylander was injured on the southern front during an Italian bombing raid, he was flown back to Addis Ababa in a Fokker, named "Abba Dagnew," which Robinson had converted into a flying ambulance.[21]

During the second week of December, Robinson finally gained an opportunity to strike back at the Italian Air Force on a flight north from Addis Ababa to Dessie. During this mission, he was delivering medical supplies to both soldiers and civilians on the northern front. Robinson suddenly spied a large Caproni bomber, flying on its own without protective fighter support. Robinson dove straight at the Caproni bomber. He was now especially eager to strike, because this Caproni was like the ones he had seen raining down destruction upon the Ethiopian people for so long. At close range, Robinson raked the Caproni with a burst of machine gunfire. He then turned, swinging wide to set up his next attack. From a high altitude, he once again bore down on the Italian bomber at full speed. He unleashed a steady stream of fire from his machine gun. A sheet of bullets tore through the slow-moving bomber, whose shocked crew was defenseless, and not expecting an attack.

Robinson disengaged only after he inflicted extensive damage on the bomber. He evidently ran out of ammunition, and Italian fighters flew to the bomber's rescue. They aggressively pursued Robinson, but his flying skills proved more than a match for them. Even though his plane was raked and hit by machine gun fire, he escaped without injury. Despite another close call, this aerial clash was no insignificant combat for Robinson. It would be nearly a decade before the next African American pilot would attack an enemy bomber: well-trained young Tuskegee Airmen who struck German bombers during World War II.[22] Thanks to Robinson's efforts, additional aircraft were obtained to replace those that became unserviceable, maintaining in a peak strength of two dozen. Consisting of six Potez 25s, the three Junkers, three Fokkers used for Red Cross missions, one Breda, the Beechcraft, two Farmans, two De Havillands, one Heinkel, and the Weber Meindl van Nes A.VII Ethiopia I, which was the modified De Havilland Moth, and other aircraft, these were either secured from the illegal trade with neutral nations, the Red Cross, private citizens, volunteers flying to Addis Ababa, or from aircraft bringing in supplies—both medical or war munitions—from the outside world.[23]

But the end was drawing ever nearer for Ethiopia. All the while, Robinson saw additional service at the front and had more close calls because the Italian Air Force enjoyed absolute air superiority. Robinson emphasized the many missions that he flew to the front at considerable risk: "I had 700 hours in the air between June 15 [1935] and April 3 [1936]."[24]

As before, these missions included flying Emperor Selassie to meet with his warlords and to inspect their warriors, fortify resolve, and discuss strategy. As Robinson explained, "during the time his majesty was flying, I flew him to the front. He wanted to know all about the plane—it was an eight-passenger Fokker—and sat in the co-pilot's seat with me in the cockpit. I only flew him to the front three times, there were always so many [Italian] planes after you and so many spies."[25] These "spies" were informants who relayed exact details of Robinson's flights to the Italians, especially those of the air force.

Another one of Robinson's close calls came when the Italian Air Force dropped mustard gas on Ethiopian troops. In Emperor Selassie's words, "They began to drop, in casks, the poison gas called yperite. As they fell, they would explode like a bomb and the poison would be splashed, killing everybody nearby."[26]

During one mustard gas raid from the air, a vulnerable Robinson was caught on the ground. Unlike the bombs that exploded in Adowa, these bombs were deceptive, hitting the ground with a dull thud, before releasing their deadly contents. Unable to find shelter from the surprise attack, Robinson became a victim of mustard gas. Robinson stated that he was "gassed" by the low-flying Italian planes, but he survived the attack, even though his breathing would be impaired for years to come.[27]

But this would not be Robinson's only exposure to mustard gas, as he survived every attack "in spite of the three gassings he suffered."[28] An unprecedented level of death and destruction rained down on the Ethiopian Army. As Emperor Selassie explained the horrors that he had seen: "My men could endure the bombing and the shells, even the gas. Only when the enemy planes dropped the burning rain upon us did it become unbearable. The Italians used Yperite which fell like water on us. You felt it like a gentle rain, then you would experience a damp humidity, and if you were not fast in getting off your clothes you were burned."[29]

But Robinson suffered an even closer call when he became the world's first black pilot and air force commander wounded in combat. He was fortunate to come away with only an "injured arm and hand [which were] sustained in another air raid," by the Italian airmen who ruled the skies.[30]

Robinson's most serious injury resulted from when he flew too close to the front during a relative lull in the fighting on the northern front. He was flying one of the old French Potez biplanes, which were armed for self-defense but only limited combat. Caught by surprise, Robinson's Potez was jumped by two Italian fighter-reconnaissance aircraft, Imam biplanes. Robinson's only chance for survival was to take evasive action by flying at full speed into the safety of a nearby cloud bank before the Italians blasted him out of the sky with a hail of machine gun fire.

He, therefore, opened up the throttle lever so that the maximum amount of fuel would rush to the engine for top speed. Robinson flew fast to reach the cloudbank above the mountaintops, gaining higher altitude in a race against death. Italian machine gun fire, meanwhile, ripped through his biplane during his ascent. A hail of Italian bullets tore through both wings and the tail section of Robinson's French Potez. One bullet smashed into the lower portion of Robinson's left arm, drawing blood and leaving a nasty-looking wound. Utilizing his years of flying experience, Robinson only escaped by a skillful rolling maneuver, slipping into the white blanket of clouds to evade the fast-pursuing Italian fighter aircraft.[31]

Fortunately, Robinson's wound was mostly a flesh wound with no broken bones, but the injury was extremely painful because the bone was chipped by the bullet. Nevertheless, Robinson was able to land safety at the Imperial Ethiopian Air Force base at Janoy Meda Akaki. Ironically, he had first reached Ethiopia with a broken arm, and now only a few months later he had yet another arm injury. Only the world's second black military pilot in aerial combat in history after Bullard of World War I fame, Robinson now possessed his own "red badge of courage."[32]

Later, newspaperman A. E. White, emphasized how Robinson "had brought honor to his people and had shed his blood in the defense of Ethiopia and the Emperor of the black peoples of the world."[33]

Against the odds, meanwhile, Robinson had done all in his power to create an air force before time ran out for Ethiopia. He had collected all available aircraft in the country or managed to secure others, either legally or illegally and by almost any means possible, until: "the Ethiopian air force consisted [at peak strength] of twenty-four planes, unfit for combat service, but useful in scouting, conveying messages to the front and supplies to the Red Cross."[34]

All the while, Robinson's aerial exploits and close calls in Ethiopia's skies were widely covered by the black press, especially the *Chicago Defender*, which generated support across America for the Ethiopian struggle for freedom. Though a rarity, Robinson even occasionally garnered recognition beyond the black newspapers. On October 5, 1935, Robinson's Ethiopia's exploits were described in an article published in the *New York Times*.[35] This article was the most extensive recognition for Colonel Robinson in a major white newspaper of America's largest city during his lengthy service in Ethiopia.[36] But generally Robinson's role in Ethiopia was widely ignored by white America. In contrast to the *Chicago Defender*, for instance, the *Chicago Tribune* and *Time* magazine were openly sympathetic to the Italian invasion.[37]

More details of Robinson's activities came to light thanks in part to the journalism of Joel A. Rogers, war correspondent, historian, lecturer, and prolific writer, who had attended Emperor Selassie's coronation in 1930. He was dispatched to Ethiopia by the *Pittsburgh Courier*, a leading black newspaper. Robinson and Rogers, now among the few African Americans in Ethiopia, became close friends. Rogers never forgot "his frequent talks with Colonel Robinson in Ethiopia, of how the Colonel arrived in Ethiopia with a broken arm, but persisted in his mission, [and of] having flown over the battle front with Colonel Robinson and of the dexterity with which the aviator handled his plane. No map of the country being available, Colonel Robinson was called upon to exercise every bit of ingenuity he possessed in making the many flights he was called to make" in Ethiopia.[38]

With his revealing newspaper articles, Rogers spread the word about both Ethiopia's struggle and Robinson's achievements in the skies over Ethiopia. Robinson was described quite accurately as possessing a rare blend of "balance and good judgment." Most of all, Rogers told the truth about an unjust war. Rogers viewed this war "as a fire set by Fascist looters." Meanwhile, Rogers wrote stories about Robinson's achievements as the Imperial Ethiopian Air Force's commander and his numerous close encounters in the air, capturing the imagination of black America.[39]

But Robinson's rising reputation also reached Italian Americans in the United States, the people of Italy, and the Italian military. Regia Aeronautica pilots had already seen his daring flights and skillful maneuvers. By this time, Italian fighter pilots knew about Robinson because of his growing reputation as Ethiopia's top military air commander.[40] Also, "because of his success in carrying vital military dispatches to the front lines, Robinson had been selected by Italian fighter pilots as a prime target."[41]

Robinson, however, was also targeted by the Italians for other reasons. Because the young black aviator represented an inspirational symbol of a high-ranking American volunteer battling against the march of fascism to both the Ethiopian people and African Americans, the Italians felt they could claim a propaganda and psychological victory in destroying this most visible symbol of Pan-African cooperation in Ethiopia. In addition, by killing Colonel Robinson, the Italian aviators could demonstrate what would be in store for other American volunteers, black and white, if they served in Ethiopia. And, according to correspondent Rogers, the Italian pilots of the Regia Aeronautical were also "seeking revenge for the agitation against them by the people of Robinson's race in America, and for the humiliating defeat inflicted upon the mammoth Italian boxer, Primo Carnera, by the black heavyweight contender, Joe Louis, on June 25, 1935."[42]

Meanwhile, Robinson continued to fly missions to deliver supplies in the big JU-52 Junkers tri-motor aircraft and also to fly the emperor in the American Beechcraft and the Fokker. One photo shows a jaunty Colonel Robinson standing in front of a JU-52 tri-motor transport plane, apparently just before a mission to the front. This photo depicts a confident Colonel Robinson, handsome, and fit, wearing a white flight suit and white flying scarf for dramatic flair. Looking like an aerial swashbuckler, he posed proudly in front of his German-made aircraft near his headquarters at the flying field, Jahoy Meda Akaki, where he commanded the Imperial Ethiopian Air Force. This aircraft, as indicated by Robinson's handwriting at the bottom of the rare photo, was part of his "Ethiopian Air Force."[43]

In early 1935, Mussolini was still concerned about sanctions imposed on Italy. He had not yet unleashed the full wrath of his military machine upon Ethiopia. Italy had the military muscle in place, nearly half a million Italian troops and a mighty air force well within Ethiopia's borders to eliminate every Ethiopian army and the imperial rule of Emperor Selassie. One American newspaper correspondent, Herbert Matthews of the *New York Times*, made the romantic analogy of comparing Mussolini's troops to "Caesar's legions [in] conquering Gaul."[44]

By this time, Robinson would have been surprised to learn that he was making news even back at his old alma mater. Tuskegee's newspaper, the *Campus Digest: The Voice of the Tuskegee Student*, ran a number of stories about Colonel Robinson's aviation and military exploits in Ethiopia. The September 28, 1935 issue—before the publication of Robinson's write-up in the *New York Times*—carried a story with the eye-popping headlines for rural, black Southern students about one of their very own who had made good on the world stage: "Tuskegee Graduate Heads Ethiopian Air Force."[45]

Robinson's uplifting example played a role in extending the spirit of Pan-Africanism and pride for an unprecedented example of black military service in wartime to the young men and women of Tuskegee Institute during the period of Jim Crow. Robinson's influence was more than a source of black pride, embodying political and social significance to young African American men and women by providing an inspirational example of dreaming big and achieving what others thought impossible.[46]

The words from the September 28, 1935 issue of Tuskegee's school newspaper reflected the deep psychological and emotional impact of Robinson's leading military role in Ethiopia and what it meant to African Americans, young and old, rich and poor, across the United States: "It is unnecessary to state the degree of pride with which the whole Tuskegee family regards Mr. Robinson. He is more than a race pioneer in the field of aviation, he is a link in that chain which binds us to Africa."[47]

These were radical words for a Deep South educational institution and its founder, Booker T. Washington, which had been widely criticized by many black activists as having been too conservative and accommodating. Thanks to Robinson's moral role of standing up against fascism in Ethiopia, Tuskegee's faculty and students were presented simultaneously with inspiring examples of the spirit of Pan-Africanism and an enlightened vision of future possibilities for blacks in military aviation in a wartime environment: an early vision of a bold dream that was destined to reach maturity with the Tuskegee Airmen of World War II fame.[48]

And the fact that Robinson and his military exploits were publicized in the school newspaper provided proof of Tuskegee's extreme admiration and "emphatic endorsement of Robinson and his service in Africa."[49]

Additional articles about Robinson appeared in Tuskegee's school newspaper. One published on October 26, 1935, honored "the fine qualities that make him great in the eyes of the world," and emphasized that he was "An Aviation Hero" for Tuskegee, black America, and a new generation of youth.[50]

In 1936, Rogers published a pamphlet entitled *The Real Facts About Ethiopia*. In this brief work, Rogers gave Robinson wider recognition across America. With some understatement, however, he only briefly described how Emperor Selassie "has made John Robinson of Chicago one of his principal aviators" in the war against Italy.[51]

The first mention of his sobriquet, the "Brown Condor of Ethiopia," had appeared in the August 23, 1935, issue of the *New York Times* and not in what has generally been considered his nickname's first mention in the October 12, 1935, issue of the *Chicago Defender*.[52]

Robinson's nickname possessed symbolic meanings not fully appreciated by most Americans. No bird of prey in nature displayed more sheer majesty and grace in soaring flight and long-range endurance than the mighty condor. Robinson had been named after the largest African condor, or vulture, in Africa. This was the Nubian Vulture or the African Fared Vulture. The condor was chestnut brown in color. Hence, the name brown condor was appropriate for the African American aviator during a time when the most famous fighter in America, Joe Louis, was known as the Brown Bomber. Most important, the Ethiopian condor was known for its aggressiveness and tenacity, especially in struggling for its share of prey.

To his life's end, Robinson would be forever known as the "Brown Condor," though he was also known as the "Flying Colonel" of Ethiopia.

While serving in Ethiopia, Robinson also contributed factual war stories as a journalist. He wrote for the Associated Negro Press in order to generate support from African Americans in the United States. Robinson submitted his dispatches about life and wartime events in Ethiopia under the pen name of Wilson James.[53]

Month after month, meanwhile, African Americans across the United States, including the students and faculty of Tuskegee Institute, followed the stories of Robinson's military exploits and close calls in Ethiopia.[54] He became better known in the United States while absent from the country in 1935–1936 than when he had been flying as a black aviator in the own homeland. Robinson's role in Ethiopia catapulted him to center of an international stage, earning him widespread recognition in African American communities across the country.

As Robinson was serving in Ethiopia in 1936, aviatrix Willa Brown, who was by now Coffey's attractive lover back in Chicago, and the second black female student in Robinson's Curtiss-Wright Aeronautical School Class of 1931, was making a name for herself as well. Inspired by Bessie Coleman's aviation legacy and Robinson's example, she boldly introduced herself to the *Chicago Defender* city editor, Enoch Waters. She played a role in promoting not only Robinson but also his Challenger Air Pilots' Association.[55]

Besides his own deeds in the skies over Ethiopia, Robinson played another overlooked role in the Italo-Ethiopian War: that of an active propagandist, beyond that of a newspaper article writer, who generated greater sympathy and support for Ethiopia's struggle against the foreign invader. He dispatched a host of scathing reports back to the black press, one published as early as October 10, condemning the indiscriminate bombing of civilians and Red Cross volunteer physicians and medical assistants by the Italians.

Robinson realized early on that the only way that Ethiopia might succeed in maintaining its independence was through a massive amount of foreign assistance. Therefore, with his deluge of reports, Robinson explained the situation in faraway Ethiopia to rally more support across black America as well as white America.

During the third week of November, Robinson sent a personal letter directly to Claude A. Barnett, intended for publication in the *Chicago Defender*. He wrote: "I am sending a book along with this letter. It gives the details [and] arguments between Abyssinia and Italy from the begining to the end. I think you might be able to use some good information out of it. It has articles . . . and many other things that has happen[ed] in regards to the League [of Nations] decisions since I have been here."[56]

Naturally Robinson was heartened by the support forthcoming from the congregation of his own South Park Baptist Church in Chicago, which donated money to the Ethiopian's struggle. The people of Robinson's South Side church even contributed a "field hospital to the warfront," which was greatly appreciated by Emperor Selassie.[57]

But all the support from Bronzeville and other African American communities across the United States was far too small to assist Ethiopia, which was about to succumb to a tragic fate.

Meanwhile, during his missions across Ethiopia, the greatest threat posed to Robinson was the finest biplane fighter of the period between the wars, Italy's Fiat CR.32 Falcon, designed by Celestino Rosatelli. One of the last biplane fighters constructed in the period between the wars, this Italian fighter was first built in

1933 and noted for its superior performance capabilities—the Fiat Falcon was fast, sleek, and light. Loved by veteran Italian pilots, this single seat biplane was made of the best light metal available. To enhance maneuverability and to reduce overall weight, the Falcon, with an open cockpit, had light fabric covering aft and along both wings.[58]

The swift Falcon and the "Brown Condor" would meet and maneuver against each other above Ethiopia's mountains and plateaus on numerous occasions. Robinson prevailed in these aerial maneuvers and lengthy chases, even when not flying the fast Beechcraft. Robinson's skillful evasiveness was no small accomplishment since the Falcon could reach a top speed of 270 mph. This biplane was often painted dark, which allowed the large white Italian Latin Cross to be displayed vividly on the vertical tail assembly, the empennage, of this sleek fighter aircraft.

While Robinson was evading the darting Italian Falcons as best he could, Emperor Selassie emerged as a world figure of symbolic importance. The emperor displayed moral courage by battling fascism, while his nation had been abandoned by the West. Through his eloquent, stoic appeals to the impotent League of Nations, Emperor Selassie stood up to racism and oppression, gaining admiration around the world.

Month after month, meanwhile, Robinson continued to work closely with Selassie, who had suddenly become "the first black African to be a world statesman."[59] The January 1936 issue of *Time* magazine was graced with a regal portrait of Emperor Selassie on its cover in tribute for the "Man of the Year." This widespread international recognition was the first time any African's portrait had ever graced the magazine's cover.[60]

Meanwhile, from his Dessie headquarters, Emperor Selassie concentrated additional forces against the Italian offensive. One Ethiopian army gathering on the northern frontier was commanded by Ras Imru. This ill-equipped army of twenty-five thousand troops had marched more than six hundred miles from the south to reach the town of Dabat, north of Gondar, which was located just north of Lake Tzana, the source of the Blue Nile, in the Simien Mountains, and southwest of Adowa. But the Ethiopian army was hard hit by the attacks from the Italian Caproni bombers. Ras Imru lost half of his army from both casualties and desertions in short order in early December.[61]

At this time, Ras Imru's battered army was in a critical situation, in part because it was now isolated and situated in the mountainous territory of another

Ethiopian warlord, Dejaz Ayalew Birru. Emperor Selassie had ordered Birru to attack the Italians in the lowlands of western Eritrea. Earlier, one of Robinson's missions had been to fly a Swedish physician from Addis Ababa to the northern frontier to administer to Birru.[62]

Robinson was operating far north of Addis Ababa by late December 1935. Departing Dessie, where he had been with the emperor at his imperial headquarters in the field, Robinson flew a French Potez northwest over some of the highest peaks of the Simien Mountains to Dabat with critical military orders from Selassie. Robinson relayed orders for Birru to cease his raids and independent offensive actions, and to join his forces of around ten thousand men with those of Ras Irmu. Then, the united Ethiopian armies would attack the Italians in the Takkaze River Valley. Selassie planned to concentrate as much of Ethiopia's forces on the northern frontier and make one final offensive effort—the first major Ethiopian counterblow—in an ambitious attempt to regain the initiative and to sabotage Italian plans to advance south upon a virtually defenseless Addis Ababa.[63]

Therefore, Robinson remained especially busy, and "upon numerous occasions he [took] Haile Selassie to the front line and delivered personal dispatches to the chieftains."[64]

Birru's offensive had caught the Italians by surprise. The attacking Ethiopians eliminated outposts, overran camps, and even disabled a number of tanks. At one point during the vicious hand-to-hand fighting, the Italians were nearly encircled by the sword-carrying warriors of Ras Irmu. Motivated by the war cry, "Don't let these dogs escape," the attacking Ethiopians reaped sufficient tactical success that the Italians requested air support from the newly established air base at Axum, the ancient Ethiopian capital and holy city, which they had captured earlier. Then, chanting ancient war songs, Ras Irmu's men linked with Birru's troops. The combined forces pursued the retreating Italians for five miles to the town of Enda Selassie. In the mountains rising above the Takazze River valley, the Ethiopian's successful counterattack brought them within only thirty miles from the ancient holy city of Axum, northwest of Makalle and just southwest of Adowa.

Then Birru's and Ras Imru's combined armies surged toward Axum. They ambushed an Italian Blackshirt column of ten tanks and transports dispatched from Axum to launch a counter-stroke. Sensing another Adowa-like success as in March 1896, the elated Ethiopians continued onward to exploit the tactical advantage. With Axum only a dozen miles away, a dramatic Ethiopian success seemed in the making by December's end. However, General Badoglio ordered an attack by twelve thousand troops, "because Ras Imru had to be halted at all costs before he invaded Eritrea, destroyed the supply depot, and cut Second Corps' line of communications." But even this counterattack was insufficient to contain the Ethiopian advance elements from making raids on the main supply depot of the Second Corps at Adi Quala in Eritrea.[65]

With the Italians getting the worst of it, the presence of Regia Aeronautica aircraft now proved decisive. In the words of Major Ralph F. Stearley, who later analyzed the vital role played by the Italian Air Force in a 1939 study for the United States Air Corps: "Here we have one of the most interesting and spectacular uses of the air force in the entire campaign [with the Italians on the verge of defeat]. It looked like another Adowa [but] the air force was the Italian's ace in the hole. It was the only thing they could use to check the hordes of Negroes advancing on Eritrea. Had it not been for this splendid action by the Italian Air Force, the campaign might have had a different ending."[66]

By this time, Ras Imru's main forces, now on the verge of overrunning the Italian army's supply depots at Adi Kwala, were swarming through the wide, open valley of the Takezze, an ideal target from the air. General Badaglio's decision to unleash his aircraft in a massive aerial offensive altered the war's course on the northern front. This vigorous Italian air offensive included dropping cylinders of mustard gas. In fact, the Italian "air force carefully refrained from using machine gun fire or bombs on the advancing mass" of Ethiopians. The deadly effects of the gas destroyed masses of Ethiopians and shattered their morale, as hundreds of stricken men lay dying and gasping in vain for life. Such severe punishment forced the hardhit Ethiopians to retreat.[67]

Emperor Selassie lamented how "no people on earth, even if they are a people descended from lions, could resist if they did not possess the technical means necessary" to win victory against a modern military machine.[68]

Twentieth-century modern warfare was vanquishing a feudal people and society with ruthless efficiency and in the most brutal fashion. More than anything else, it was the Western world's "modernity [that] defeated Ethiopia—it was that simple."[69]

At this time, Robinson was still in the Takezze valley with Ras Imru's army on standby after conveying additional orders from Emperor Selassie at Dessie, or to report on military developments in this foremost sector to assist the emperor in formulating strategy. Near the front, Robinson was impressed by the extent of the Ethiopians' success. As he later related to a newspaperman: "Selassie's soldiers started out in the war with as few as sixty bullets each. They fought for the most part with swords, not spears, as was publicized. The 'irregular soldiers,' those trained in the country's traditional war tactics, never lost a battle."[70]

Here, in the northern front, the mustard gas attacks in the Takezze Valley upon Ras Imru's army was almost certainly where Colonel Robinson suffered under another gas attack.[71]

This first successful Ethiopian offensive perhaps would not have been possible without Robinson's efforts in swiftly relaying Emperor Selassie's military orders over mountainous terrain—which would have taken days by foot—to communicate to the front for a coordinated offensive effort that reaped considerable tactical success. Even though lacking in offensive capabilities, Robinson and his aircraft of the Imperial Ethiopian Air Force had made important contributions in enhancing both the Ethiopians' defensive and offensive efforts. Thanks to Robinson, air communications had given Selassie's forces an advantage by way of timely intelligence, reconnaissance, and surveillance.[72] But the Ethiopians' tactical success had been brief. General Badoglio knew better than anyone else that the end was near for Selassie and his under-equipped armies of enthusiastic warriors, because "whether the Negus attacked or whether he awaited my attack, his fate was now sealed."[73]

ONE FINAL DESPERATE OFFENSIVE

Robinson had been fortunate in having survived so many close calls by this time. Nevertheless, this brutal war had taken a serious toll—physically, emotionally, and psychologically—on the young colonel so far from home. In a letter to his friend Harold Hurd of Chicago, Robinson wrote: "I am trying to do my best in what ever mission or duty. We are having a hard fight over here with our limited amount of modern war equipment, but every man, woman, and child is doing their part to help" in the struggle.[74]

Despite the considerable setbacks on the military, political, and diplomatic fronts, Robinson still hoped for the best, when he allowed himself to be optimistic by drawing upon his religious faith. As expressed in this same letter to Hurd: "I am sure [that] with God's help and our courage we will come out OK in the end."[75]

Hurd was one of Robinson's first students at the Curtiss-Wright Aeronautical School, a member of the Challenger Air Pilots' Association, and a lieutenant of the Military Order of Guard Aviation Squadron. Hurd was also one of the volunteers who Robinson had expected to join him in Ethiopia. At this time, Robinson still hoped for their arrival, but the passports of the seven African Americans, all members of Robinson's Challenger Air Pilots' Association—Hurd, Coffey, Earl Renfroe, Albert Crosby, Dale White, Clyde Hampton, and Willa Brown—were never issued by the U.S. government, which enforced the Neutrality Act. Others never applied for passports.[76]

Meanwhile, Emperor Selassie followed tactical developments from the imperial headquarters at Dessie. He now dispatched new orders—evidently relayed by Robinson and his top air lieutenants—to all of his ras for an united effort to encircle the Italians at Makalle: a masterful tactical plan that seemed to promise success. After Ras Desta's defeat in the south, Selassie planned for a total effort in the north to save his nation from conquest.

Initially, the emperor had planned for a concentration of his forces at the mountainous stronghold of formidable Amba Alagi. But the situation called for new dispositions and a new offensive strategy before a final desperate attempt could be launched to reverse the war's course. Therefore, Ras Mulugueta, the emperor's War Minister and Commander of the Army of the Centre, and seventy thousand men were dispatched to hold the mountainous plateau known as Amba Aradam, located some thirty miles north of Amba Alagi.[77]

Just to the southwest of Mount Aradam lay the great mountain pass of Amba Alagi, which guarded "the gates of central Ethiopia." Departing the Amba Alagi, Ras Kassa, Ras Seyoum, and Birru, with lesser warlords and their forces, had reinforced the army of Wag in the valley of the Takkaze River northwest of Amba Alagi: a force of more than 100,000 Ethiopian warriors. This potential threat on the northwest, or right flank, of General Bagadolia at Makalle had to be eliminated by the Italians, before a full offensive effort could be launched from Makalle and toward Addis Ababa.

Not realizing that they faced such sizable numbers of Ethiopians, the Italians attacked and were beaten back in the struggle in the Simien Mountains near the Warieu Pass. But it would not be another Adowa. Thousands of Ethiopians would never stream through Warieu Pass to gain the Italians' rear behind Makalle. Large numbers of Ethiopians fell in futile assaults against Italian entrenched positions, machine gun nests, and concentrated artillery. Because of an overreliance on massed attacks in the Ethiopian warrior tradition and against Emperor Selassie's advice to wage a guerrilla war, the second Ethiopian offensive—the first battle of Tambien of January 20–24—on the northern front came to a bloody end.[78]

Now, to exploit the tactical advantage with the Ethiopians' repulse, the Italians took the offensive. The first target was Mount Aradam now held by the forces of Ras Mulugueta. From Makalle and supported by an air armada of more than 170 aircraft, the main Italian force of seven divisions of 70,000 troops advanced south toward Addis Ababa on February 10. Marshal Badogio hurled "the largest mechanized column [ever] thrown out by history." Ill-armed and barefoot, around 80,000 Ethiopians of Ras Mulugueta were situated in a lengthy line of defensive positions atop formidable Mount Aradam. A seemingly impregnable rock fortress, the towering plateau known as Mount Aradam, consisting of a lengthy outcropping of solid rock, was located a dozen miles south of Makalle. This strong point defended the twisting, dirt road leading to the capital.[79]

In preparation for the final offensive, more than 170 Italian aircraft flew into action. Heavy bombardments, including the dropping of the gas cylinders, smashed into the Ethiopian positions along the six-mile length of Mount Aradam and along its flanks held by the doomed ebony warriors. In addition, massed rows of Italian artillery simultaneously pounded the mountain position held by Selassie's men. More than 25,000 bombs, with a total weight of more than 381,000 pounds, were dropped on the Ethiopians. In one day alone, the Regia Aeronautica flew 90 missions, unleashing more than 60,000 pounds of bombs. To escape the storm, the emperor's soldiers found sanctuary in caves.

The Ethiopians naively believed their mountain perch was unassailable, even while thousands of Italian soldiers struggled up the steep slopes in a double encircling movement. General Badogolio wisely decided against a frontal assault on the mountain fortress. He, therefore, caught the Ethiopians by surprise with his alternative flanking tactics. This former World War I general utilized his best soldiers, the crack Alpine troops of the Valpusteria Alpini, to overwhelm the Ethiopian mountain fortress with an indirect approach. In what was the collapse of the central sector of the northern front, the Ethiopians were swept off Mount Aradam, as if pushed away by a giant broom. These new Romans reaped a most impressive victory during the second battle of the Tambien, or Amba Ardam.

Then ensued a wild flight of the surviving Ethiopians to escape an Italian encircling movement, retreating rapidly south through the mountains toward Addis Ababa. This now presented a real opportunity for the Italian bombers to reap a whirlwind of devastation upon the hapless Ethiopians. During three awful days— a living nightmare for Selassie's unfortunate warriors—Italian aircraft dropped nearly four hundred tons of bombs on the fleeing Ethiopians. The bombing wiped out untold numbers of Ethiopians in an unparalleled slaughter that foreshadowed World War II: "the most intensive aerial bombing the world had known until that time."[80]

As if conventional bombing was not enough, the Italian aircraft applied the fatal coup-de-grace by dropping mustard gas. The gas fell from the skies to wipe out thousands of Ethiopia's proudest warriors with deadly efficiency. Ethiopia's young men now found a grisly death and eternal peace instead of Adowa's glory during "one of the great slaughters of modern times."[81]

Most of the massacre occurred in the pass of Amba Alagi. This undefended pass was hit by wave after wave of Italian strafing, bombing, and gas attacks more than five hundred times day after day, while the Ethiopian survivors, which did not include the forces of Ras Mulugueta, attempted to escape south to Quoram.[82]

After the slaughters at Amba Aradam, the pass of Amba Alagi, and along the gory Imperial Road leading to Quoram and Dessie, what little remained of Ras Kassa's and Ras Seyoum's armies prepared to once again make a defensive stand in what they believed was an impregnable position. Here, on the Golden Mountain, Worq Amba, the Ethiopians took new defensive positions against the inevitable Italian onslaught.

Italian Alpine troops scaled the mountain's northern face on February 27. With ancient war cries and broad swords from a bygone era, the Ethiopian warriors attacked more than a dozen times to hurl the Italians off the commanding peak. Unfortunately the Ethiopians relied not only on the same weapons but also the same aggressive tactics as at Adowa. Instead of waging a guerrilla war, the Ethiopians continued to fight according to warrior tradition, which was much like conventional European warfare: the tactical offensive. Now the massed Ethiopian attacks against a strong position, defended by modern weaponry, were suicidal, hastening the war's end and Ethiopia's untimely death. Another Ethiopian defeat and disastrous retreat resulted, and, of course, more slaughter, thanks to the relentless Italian Air Force. Italian aircraft swept the defenseless columns of withdrawing Ethiopians with machine gun fire, bombs, and mustard gas. One airborne Italian never forgot how "the [retreating] Ethiopians straggled along in disorder. Our plane swooped down, sowed its seeds of death, and zoomed upward."[83]

Emperor Selassie was horrified by the slaughter. He described how "as usual, many aeroplanes arrived wiping out the Ethiopian forces by spraying mustard and yperite poison. The Italians had begun to send out week by week a very large number of planes and to set on fire, with incendiary bombs, provincial towns."[84]

Eager to ascertain more easy targets, ingenious Italian airmen continued the slaughter even at nighttime, dropping flares to illuminate the holocaust in order to reap even more destruction from above.[85] Beaten Ethiopian survivors fled south toward Quoram, north of Dessie, to escape. All the while, the massacre continued unabated. Ethiopia had become hell on earth for Selassie's solders, who battled against a cruel fate. Then, employing strategies at February's end that would systematically destroy each new Ethiopian Army he faced, Marshal Badoglio turned his forces on the army of Ras Imru, reinforced by Birru, in the third phase of his "battle of annihilation." Ethiopian resistance was fierce, but not enough to stop the powerful onslaught. Once again, the Ethiopians could not resist the temptation of launching massive frontal assaults in the ancient warrior tradition, and with the same predictable bloody results.

The inevitable Ethiopian defeat and subsequent retreat once again brought "the familiar consequence of wholesale massacre." Ras Imru's army of holy warriors was virtually wiped out by an avalanche of incendiary bombs and mustard gas, especially when the Ethiopians attempted to cross the muddy Takazze River to escape. The worst slaughter occurred here, at the fords of the Takazze, because these vital crossing points were specifically targeted by Italian bombs and gas. Mass desertions took place until Ras Imru's army was no more. Ethiopia was caught amid the grim process of being "defeated, its armies massacred, and dispersed" to the winds. By this time, the Imperial Guard, well trained, uniformed, and armed with modern weapons, was counted upon to stand firm by Selassie.[86]

In effective but brutal fashion, General Badoglio had successfully "used air power and poison gas to separate, flank, and destroy the Ethiopian armies one by one."[87]

By mid-March 1936, Robinson was with the emperor at Quoram, and on the road leading south to Addis Ababa. Emperor Selassie had reached Quoram by mule from Dessie on March 1, after the series of defeats on the northern front. And now Quoram, situated along the eastern rim of the rugged plateau, served as the imperial headquarters. Here, Emperor Selassie had attempted to rally as much of the scattered troops as possible to firm up resistance. After the destruction of one Ethiopian army after another, the emperor could now only count on Ras Kebbede's army and his faithful Imperial Guard.

Robinson's airmen and aircraft performed overtime throughout this period. Colonel Robinson ordered Count von Rosen in a big tri-motor Junkers transport to deliver Red Cross supplies and equipment to Quoram. Here, during the late evening at on March 16, Robinson landed at Quoram in the "emperor's aircraft," just before von Rosen set down. Like Robinson during his past escapes, von Rosen was fortunate. The Swede had earlier evaded two Italian aircraft, whose pilots failed to spot von Rosen's plane in time. Later, Robinson's two aircraft, the tri-motor German Junkers and one of his most swift aircraft, were parked side by side on relatively level terrain of this mountainous region. Here, they were camouflaged by soldiers upon the emperor's orders, evidently at Robinson's suggestion. This precaution was wise. Striking hard, the Italian bombers returned the next morning, on March 17, to heavily bomb Quoram.[88]

After the Ethiopians withdrew from Dessie, the imperial headquarters was located in a sheltered cave complex at Quoram for protection against Italian bombing raids. And these air strikes came with more regularity. With von Rosen on his flight was a Swedish physician, Dr. Marcel Junod. The doctor immediately ascertained that mustard gas had been dropped over the area. And because he had landed only a short time before on this spot, Robinson was again exposed to this contamination.[89]

But a greater danger was yet to come. Suddenly, a trio of Caproni bombers struck, after appearing seemingly out of nowhere. The Capronis flew yet another raid over Quoram in an attempt to destroy the imperial headquarters and kill Emperor Selassie. The rain of bombs began to drop from the skies. By this time, Robinson was sheltered in one of Quoram's caves. Seeing through the thin camouflage, the Italian pilots and bombardiers immediately targeted the aircraft of the "Brown Condor"—a rare target of opportunity for the Italian airmen. One of the first exploding bombs destroyed Robinson's aircraft in a fiery blast. This was the inglorious end of one of the best aircraft of the Imperial Ethiopian Air Force. Von Rosen's Junkers was also destroyed. Mustard gas again fell from the bombers and then eerily rose from the ground in a hellish mist.

This was Robinson's third, and last, exposure to the deadly gas in a relatively short period of time. Robinson, von Rosen, and Junod were now forced to make a lengthy overland journey of more than four hundred miles south to Addis Ababa.[90]

As an indication of the conflict's close coverage by the black press, the *Chicago Defender*, reported the destruction of Robinson's plane: "Italian airmen destroyed another Ethiopian airplane—a Red Cross ship—which was wrecked at Quoram."[91]

Emperor Selassie gained some measure of optimism when he was joined at Quoram by the remains of armies of Ras Seyoum and Ras Kassa on March 19.[92] On the following day, the emperor moved his imperial headquarters to the forward slopes of the mountain perch overlooking Lake Ashangi and the Italian defensive positions at Mai Ceu. Two days later, as if knowing the end was near, on March 21, he dispatched a radio message to his wife in which he emphasized that "God is [now] are only help."[93]

With this concentration of Ethiopian forces in the northern front—an estimated 300,000 troops—and with the emperor present, morale lifted among the remaining defenders of their ancient native homeland. Ethiopian confidence rose "in spite of the fact that Italian aerial bombs have leveled a goodly number of Ethiopian towns whose traditions are dear to the natives."[94]

Even though Robinson was now absent from the northern front, the airmen and remaining operable aircraft of the Imperial Ethiopian Air Force continued to perform as ordered either by Robinson or Emperor Selassie, or both. On March 22, Colonel Konovaloff and a trio of Ethiopian graduates from the French military academy St. Cyr, took flight to reconnoiter Italian positions at Maychew. They gained intelligence about the tactical weaknesses that they spied in Italian troop dispositions.

Based upon this valuable intelligence gained by Robinson's flyers, Emperor Selassie developed a plan of attack for the night of March 22 to exploit the enemy's vulnerabilities. The emperor delayed his final decision, however, on the advice of his top commanders, who were overly cautious, if not defeatist by this time. Thus, the timely intelligence gained by Robinson's air force was wasted. This delay in launching an Ethiopian attack allowed the Italians time to readjust their defensive lines to cover weak spots, build up their strength, and to punish the Ethiopians with repeated strikes from the air.[95]

Luckily, Robinson escaped one of the war's last slaughters at March's end. By this time, the conflict had turned into little more than genocide. Out of desperation and in one last gamble to save his capital and his nation for the invaders, Emperor Selassie planned to launch an audacious attack into Mai Ceu's valley with the last large organized force of Ethiopian warriors less than twenty miles north of Quoram, because, in his words, "our trust is in our Creator and in the hope of His help . . . we have decided to advance . . . and since God is our only help."[96]

In person, during the early morning hours of March 31, which was a day named in honor of Ethiopia's revered patron saint, St. George, the emperor made

Robinson in 1935 as the co-commander of America's first all-black military aviation unit officially known as the Military Order of Guard, Aviation Squadron, in Chicago, Illinois. *No. 87-15491 Smithsonian National Air and Space Museum*

Robinson in the cockpit of a Buhl Bull Pup at his airport in Robbins, Illinois. *No. 87-15493 Smithsonian National Air and Space Museum*

Robinson's airport in Robbins, Illinois, and members of the Challenger Aero Club. *No. 87-15492 Smithsonian National Air and Space Museum*

On wartime duty as the tireless commander of the Imperial Ethiopian Air Force, and standing before one of the transport aircraft, a Junkers-52 from Germany, of his air force at the capital of Addis Ababa, Ethiopia, on February 24, 1936. *No. 99-15423 Smithsonian National Air and Space Museum*

Colonel Robinson upon his return to the United States from the Italo-Ethiopian War, overwhelmed by his reception and suffering from war injuries. *From the collection of Sidney L. Rushing*

Robinson with leading members of the African American community in Jackson, Mississippi, 1937. *From the collection of Sydney L. Rushing*

Robinson (at the rear of the table, on the right) and friends in a black nightclub on the South Side of Chicago, 1941. *From the collection of Sydney L. Rushing*

Robinson and friends socializing on the South Side of Chicago, 1941. *From the collection of Sydney L. Rushing*

Robinson (back row, second on the right) and his military aviation team of technicians from the United States in Addis Ababa during the later years of World War II. *From the collection of Sydney L. Rushing*

Wearing the insignia of the commander of the Imperial Ethiopian Air Force, the war-weary Col. John Charles Robinson poses for the camera on May 18, 1936, in New York City, just after his arrival from Ethiopia. *From the collection of Sydney L. Rushing*

Robinson bestowing an honor on a woman, perhaps his own mother, during a celebration of his arrival among the African American community in Gulfport, Mississippi, in the early summer of 1936, after his return from Ethiopia. *From the collection of Sydney L. Rushing*

his final preparations to lead the last desperate attack in defense of his "Christian Empire and its independence."[97]

At the end of March, the attacking Ethiopians, including Emperor Selassie and his Imperial Guard, surged toward three Italian Divisions situated in strong defensive positions. Thanks to intercepted radio messages, the Italians knew exactly when and where to expect the attack.

Like other Ethiopian men of war during this desperate offensive, the elite Imperial Guard, carrying flags depicting the Lion of Judah, also met with disaster in the face of an overwhelming array of modern weaponry. Repeated Ethiopian charges resulted in thirteen hours of bitter fighting during the battle of Mai Ceu. Sixty Italian aircraft bombed and strafed the Ethiopians caught out in the open and in inadequate defensive positions, including the imperial headquarters at Mai Ceu, without mercy.

Another Ethiopian retreat back to the rocky slopes of Quoram resulted in additional slaughter of Emperor Selassie's troops in the same old bloody scenario. Day after day, the Ethiopian warriors were unmercifully "hammered by our entire Air Arm," wrote one Italian with pride. After this crushing defeat, the fall of Addis Ababa was imminent. Fascism had triumphed in Ethiopia.[98]

Robinson had accomplished all that he could do in Ethiopia's defense by way of attempting to create a viable air force. In the end, however, "the Emperor's tiny air force could do little to counter the waves of modern Italian fighter bombers dispatching bombs and tons of dichlorodiethyl sulfide (mustard gas) over battlefields, towns, cities, and countryside, all done with Mussolini's explicit approval."[99]

Indeed, despite Colonel Robinson's best efforts, the Imperial Ethiopian Air Force, in one historian's estimation, was simply "too small and ill-equipped to do more than ferry senior officers, munitions, and medical supplies around the country."[100] But it would have been much harder, if not impossible, to accomplish these vital missions without the much-overworked air force that Robinson had built up.

Regardless of the odds against it, this tiny, fledgling Imperial Ethiopian Air Force had repeatedly engaged in aerial combat with swarms of Italian fighters. Robinson himself was "cited several times for bravery. He was in twelve actual flying battles and in one he narrowly missed shooting down the plane of Mussolini's son."[101]

Indeed, Robinson's most celebrated dog fight in the skies over Ethiopia was notable because the opponent he faced was Vittorio Mussolini, the Italian dictator's oldest son. Callous and heartless, he viewed killing Emperor Selassie's people, both soldiers and civilians, as "great fun" like his brother Bruno, who found the slaughter to be "most entertaining." As the pampered upper class representative of Italy's elite who visited Hollywood in 1937 at Hal Roach's invitation and wined and dined with leading actresses such as the beautiful Dolores del Rio, Vittorio hailed from a glamorous world that Robinson could not even imagine. Therefore, this dramatic clash between Robinson and Vittorio Mussolini in Ethiopia's skies also symbolically represented a class, racial, and social contest. Both men survived the encounter, living to tell the tale.[102]

Robinson had larger strategic concerns and priorities than his dogfight with Mussolini's son. From beginning to end, the fact that the United States failed to supply Ethiopia with aircraft and because African American volunteers were not forthcoming doomed Robinson's dream of creating an air force that could offer serious resistance. The lack of black volunteers from America caused one frustrated Chicago citizen to angrily write to the *Chicago Defender*: "It is time for us to awake and help to face the difficulty with our brothers, the Ethiopians, [and] to help save Ethiopia from being confiscated by the plunderers. As a race we have shed our blood on every battlefield here and abroad to save lives and wealth of other nations—why not do the same for our race" in Ethiopia?[103]

In a last-ditch effort to stave off defeat and at Colonel Robinson's urging, the Ethiopian ambassador to England, Workneh Martin, whose two sons served in Robinson's Imperial Ethiopian Air Force, had negotiated "a $50,000 loan in order to purchase a hundred bombing and pursuit planes" from the English aircraft industry. But not enough time remained for Robinson's effort to build an air force.[104]

The ill-fated month of April 1936 brought more disaster for Emperor Selassie and his reeling nation. During the retreat south toward the capital, more than 150 Italian aircraft continued to drop bombs and mustard gas on the troops fleeing across the Golgola plain to escape. Taking a terrible pounding, the Ethiopians lost thousands more men during the two days of withdrawal than at the battle of Mai Ceu.[105]

By this time, the Regia Aeronautica was demonstrating its awesome lethal capabilities never before seen. An amazed United States Air Corps officer, who later analyzed the decisive role played by the Italian Air Force in this conflict, summarized the campaign in the north: "The Air Force in this campaign had over 20,000 flying hours; it dropped over 2,000 tons of bombs and fired over 300,000 rounds of ammunition. The Air Force played a major role in the conquest. . . . The extensive use of aircraft and mechanized forces . . . made it possible to advance with a rapidity never attained even on European battlefields and to conduct an offensive war in a roadless, mountainous country, whose forbidding heights resemble those of the Alps": the theortical concept of blitzkrieg had been vindicated. Clearly, this was a lesson not lost to Hitler and Nazi Germany in the years ahead.[106]

During this war, the Italians proved to be in the "forefront of military ideas in the way they used aircraft as airborne 'cavalry' in this new form of open warfare [because] Italian planes harassed Ethiopian supply lines with considerable success and helped break the morale of the enemy infantry."[107] Additionally, Douhet's bold promise of strategic bombing's decisiveness against an opponent's support systems was fulfilled. As Emperor Selassie explained the national tragedy, the Italians "changed their tactics and started bombing rural areas and grazing cattle and thus broke the heart of the people in the country [because] the Italian aeroplanes, which were spreading this poisonous mist in order to destroy the Ethiopian people as well as animals living on mountains and in the fields, were going to and fro from morning till evening and set out to exterminate man and beast."[108]

THE END OF A DREAM

By this time, the Ethiopian struggle to maintain its cherished independence was coming to a tragic end, the nation all but vanquished with its major armies crushed and dispersed to the hills. Addis Ababa was defenseless both from the ground and from the air. Thanks to the Regia Aeronautica's effectiveness, Ethiopia's rugged mountains no longer protected the capital against invaders, as it had in the past. Robinson learned the disturbing news on April 16 that Dessie had fallen. Few knew whether Emperor Selassie was alive or dead.

Already, most foreign advisors and correspondents had long since departed from the capital. And now the Belgian advisors were boarding the train for the port of Djibouti. At this time, not a single Ethiopian army lay between the invaders and Addis Ababa.

One last desperate plan was developed to stave off defeat, however, a bold plan that was evidently Robinson's brainchild, and agreed upon by Selassie. In early April, Selassie had stationed his forces to guard the four key mountain passes immediately north of Addis Ababa, but these troops had been easily pushed aside.

Since no bombers existed in the Imperial Ethiopian Air Force, some aircraft had been modified—upon Robinson's orders—to be loaded with explosives for a final desperate mission to attempt to blow up and block the mountain passes to stop the Italian drive south on the capital.

Robinson very likely utilized his largest aircraft, the German Junkers transports, for this purpose. During the mission, a large supply of bombs, either captured from the Italians or smuggled through the embargo, were to be pushed out of the transport aircraft's open doors. Robinson prepared "to lead a squadron of special bombing planes [that had been modified] in an assault on certain mountains which are to be blasted [in order] to halt the advance of the Italians on Addis Ababa."[109]

Robinson also planned to strike behind the lines and target the rear supply depots that fueled the Italian army's advance toward Addis Ababa. Indeed, "military experts gasped at the audacity of the plan, many calling it as strategic and feasible a maneuver as was the trick Hannibal of Carthage on the ancient Romans."[110] With this audacious strategic plan, Emperor Selassie had ordered the destruction of bridges leading to the capital and "decided to blow up the mountains as a last resort to save his kingdom" from certain destruction.[111]

For whatever reason, either this final desperate mission of the Imperial Ethiopian Air Force, as ordered by Selassie, was never undertaken, or perhaps it simply failed. Robinson was later cited for bravery, and it might have been for this last desperate effort to save the day and the capital.[112]

By April 28, the disturbing news that the unstoppable Italian advance was less than forty miles from the capital caused a wave of panic to sweep through the doomed city. Weary and discouraged, the emperor reached a panic-stricken Addis Ababa on April 30. He somehow escaped death during the relentless bombings, gas attacks, and strafings by the Italian aircraft of everything that moved along the road south to Addis Ababa. The Italian army would march into the capital in less than a week.[113]

Robinson's final mission for Selassie evidently occurred on April 29, as the *Chicago Defender* first mentioned it on April 25 as an upcoming effort of sheer desperation. At that time, an unidentified pilot was sent forth from Addis Ababa to locate and drop orders to two battalions under Lieutenant Bouveng (first name unknown), a French advisor, to move forward to face the Italian onslaught in a last-ditch attempt to slow the relentless advance.[114]

On the next day, Thursday, April 30, Robinson was reminded exactly how close the end was for the fast-fading life of an independent Ethiopia. In a strange twist of fate, Robinson and Count Ciano, Mussolini's son-in-law, were about to meet again. Eager to win ever-lasting fame, Ciano wanted to make a dramatic landing at the airport to officially claim the capital for Italy. Desiring to match his father's World War I heroics, Ciano descended and his plane touched down on the runway of the Janhoy Meda Akaki airport, where Robinson had headquartered his air force. But a hail of machine fire opened up on the Italian plane. Robinson and his airmen were now alerted to the fact that an Italian warplane was attempting to land at their own airfield. A total of twenty-five bullets tearing through Count Ciano's plane convinced him to pull up on the throttle. His landing in an audacious bid to lay claim to the Ethiopian capital had been thwarted.[115]

Before he departed Addis Ababa, Count Ciano, with a flair for the dramatic, dropped the colorful pennant of his unit, La Disperata, the 15th Bomber Squadron, on the capital's main square, however. For this act of bravado, Ciano was heralded as a war hero across Italy. An impressed Mussolini telegraphed from Rome: "I am very proud of your flight over Addis Ababa." The daring Ciano would win a silver medal for bravery for his bold exploit.[116]

Clearly, the bitter end was drawing ever-closer for the dying Ethiopian nation, when another Italian aircraft "flying over Addis Ababa, dropped leaflets written in the native Amharic, begging the inhabitants to surrender without resistance." The propaganda leaflets delivered a grim warning: "If Addis Ababa is delivered without resistance, we will not bomb the city. Otherwise we will destroy it all."[117]

But the Ethiopians remained defiant to the end. One *Washington Post* journalist described how, "Increasing indications that Addis Ababa is not to be surrendered without a struggle to the death spread further panic through the city."[118]

Italian indignation ensured that severe punishment was soon forthcoming from the air. Among the initial targets hit by the Italian bombers were the last few remaining aircraft of Robinson's air force, which were destroyed on the ground.[119]

On April 30, after having been granted permission, since Emperor Selassie himself planned to depart the capital, Robinson made his final preparations to leave Addis Ababa, and Ethiopia, by train. However, he only did so after having been "advised by higher authorities that it would not be safe to remain at the nation's capital."[120]

For Robinson and others, including the emperor, Count Ciano's attempt to land in the capital and the recent bombing raids were the final proof that convinced them to leave as soon as possible. After all, by this time, "there was nothing between the Italians and the capital." Robinson fully realized that he would be executed if he remained in Addis Ababa. Leaving behind his worldly possessions including a number of expensive gifts from Ethiopian leaders, including from the emperor, Robinson rushed to the sprawling main railroad station before it was destroyed by bombs. With no illusions remaining, he departed the chaos of "Addis Ababa [only] two days before Haile Selassie."[121]

In the April 23, 1936 issue of the *Washington Post*, a war correspondent who assumed incorrectly that Robinson had already departed the doomed capital at this time, described the latest news about the final collapse of resistance and the capital's inevitable capture: "Foreigners continued to evacuate. John C. Robinson, Negro aviator of Chicago, who served with Ethiopia's pathetic air force until bombers destroyed Emperor Selassie's few planes, left by train for Djibouti with Capt. John Meade, military attache of the American Legation."[122]

Why Robinson decided not to earlier fly out of Ethiopia is open to conjecture. He still possessed some serviceable planes, especially the swift Beechcraft, before the air raids on the capital. But leaving the capital by air meant risking interception by Italian fighters. At least one of Colonel Robinson's flyers, Mischa Babitchev, flew out of Addis Ababa on May 1, however.[123] And two days later, on May 3, Ludwig Weber, who would be killed just before escaping the capital, and three other armed Germans, who evidently were the volunteers who had flown the three Junkers transports to Ethiopia from Germany in July 1935, planned to leave Ethiopia in a Junkers—the only one that remained—at Janhoy Meda Akaki.[124]

By this time, as reported in a *New York Times* article, the "Ethiopia air force [had] boasted a fleet of about seventeen planes, but all of these except two were destroyed or taken [and Robinson's] last plane was a Beechcraft."[125]

As a strange fate would have it, the last volunteer airman who was to have joined Robinson's Imperial Ethiopian Air Force would arrive much too late. He was Ene Drouillet, a World War I Ace. "Against the orders of the French government" he departed Paris on May 1. He flew a new $15,000 aircraft built in and recently arrived from the United States, but by the time that this famous "French flying ace" and Selassie's "technical advisor" reached Ethiopia with funds and "a cargo of light provisions [for] the Emperor," Colonel Robinson was already gone.[126]

On Thursday, April 30, just after Robinson's return to Addis Ababa and on the day he departed, a council of Ethiopia's top leaders was held. Here, "it was decided, upon the basis of advice proffered, that it would be well for the Emperor to go to Europe and to inform the League of Nations, by his own voice, of all the violence Italy had perpetrated against us."[127]

Robinson, who had committed his heart and soul to Ethiopia and her desperate struggle for survival, possessed no regrets about his escape from the capital. Fortunately, the iron railroad tracks to the Red Sea port of Djibouti were still open. The westward advance of the ruthless General Graziani, known as the "Butcher of East Africa," continued toward Addis Ababa and approached the railroad, however. Robinson's chances of slipping out of Ethiopia safely were yet in jeopardy.

After many tense hours had passed, Robinson finally reached the Gulf of Aden port of Djibouti on May 2, after a nerve-racking trip of nearly five hundred miles. Feeling most fortunate to have escaped disaster and almost certain death, he arrived "with just the clothes on his back."

In a sad departure, Emperor Selassie left his beloved capital on the last train out of Addis Ababa early in the early morning hours of May 2. On May 3, he reached Djibouti only one day after Robinson.

Meanwhile, Addis Ababa fell to the Italians on May 5. *New York Times* reporter Matthews cabled back to New York City the astounding news on this day: "ERA OF INDEPENDENCE THAT LASTED SINCE BIBLICAL TIMES ENDED FOUR THIS AFTERNOON WHEN ITALIANS OCCUPIED ADDIS ABABA."[128]

Indeed, "Italy's invading army marched into this capital today in the shadow of great aerial squadrons," whose veteran airmen had so often pursued Robinson through Ethiopia's skies in wild chases. This dramatic story was reported in the *Chicago Defender* beside a photograph of a brutal lynching of a black man in Georgia and a triumphant group of gloating Southern white males around the unfortunate victim: symbolically and perhaps appropriately, the story of the tragic death of the oldest black Christian nation in Africa was printed beside a grisly photograph that displayed the horrors of American racism in the Deep South.[129]

Emphasizing the analogy between these lynched African Americans and Robinson's role in Ethiopia's struggle, an address delivered by actor Clarence Muse in Los Angeles explained how "Colonel Robinson, a young colored aviator from Chicago, is at the head of his air fleet. He gave up his citizenship to help Ethiopia [at a time when there were] sixteen lynchings. Evidently there were many good American citizens that can and will make great soldiers in the defense of peace in this land!"[130]

By the time Robinson reached the Gulf of Aden, all that remained of the Imperial Ethiopian Air Force was a single operable aircraft—the Beechcraft—undestroyed. The Italians at the Janhoy Meda Akaki air field captured the Beechcraft and a slightly-damaged French Potez 25, with an Amharic inscription written across the fuselage in large letters, "Bird of the Crown Prince."[131]

As early as November, Robinson wrote that it was "the begining of the end for this country." Nevertheless, he had continued to faithfully serve Ethiopia and Emperor Selassie for more than the next six months. All the while, he had performed everything asked of him and much more regardless of the circumstances. As Robinson wrote of his resolve in November 1935: "My present agreement will be up in May 1936, at that time I think I will have done my part to help Ethiopia" in her ill-fated struggle against the odds.[132]

At Djibouti on the Red Sea, Robinson basked in his good fortune of having escaped from the capital just before its fall. With certainty, he realized that "the Italians might have shot me first and investigated afterwards."[133]

This was no exaggerated fear. One of Emperor Selassie's trusted aides was summarily executed by the victors. For foreign military advisors, and especially if one was black, "it was possible that the Italians might have been hard, indeed savage, with any who fell into their hands."[134]

One air force member killed in the chaos of the nation's collapse was German airman Ludwig Weber, on whom Robinson had relied countless times. Airman Count Hildaire du Berrier was captured just before the capital's fall. The fates of other members of Colonel Robinson's Imperial Ethiopian Air Force were not known.[135]

Not long after the capture of Addis Ababa, the Italians began systematically executing Ethiopians, especially leading chieftains, in order to crush potential organizers of resistance and to reduce the possibilities of having to fight a guerrilla war now that they occupied Ethiopia.[136]

Mussolini's May 3 orders specified a dark future for the subjugated Ethiopian people: "When Addis Ababa is occupied [anyone] caught with arms in hand will be summarily shot. All those who within twenty-four hours have not given up their arms and munitions be summarily shot."[137]

So hurried had been his departure from the capital that Robinson left with no baggage. He found himself stranded in Djibouti without money or resources of any kind. Somehow, however, Robinson boarded a steam liner that carried him northwest up the Red Sea, up the Suez Canal, and toward the eastern edge of the Mediterranean Sea. But this lengthy journey by sea was not without peril. Indeed, "Colonel Robinson tried to land at Port Said [Egypt] but because it was thought that his presence would cause trouble among the Italians, he was refused admittance and had to continue over to Marseille [France] and thence to Cherbourg [France] from which place he sailed for the United States."[138]

In total, "at least six attempts to assassinate Colonel John C. Robinson by Italian spies [were made] since his departure from Addis Ababa [and the] most significant attempt to kill him was on the ship which brought the flyer to Marseille, France. While on deck, Colonel Robinson was warned by an Egyptian that several men were after him. Shortly afterwards . . . three men started after him with a dagger, but the plot was nipped by two sailors."[139]

Feeling that he had once again defied fate by a narrow margin, Robinson made his way to Paris, after disembarking at the bustling port of Marseille, which had grown wealthy from selling slaves—perhaps his own ancestors—to the New World, especially the French West Indies, in the eighteenth century. From there, he telegraphed Coffey for funds to secure passage for the trip back across the Atlantic. Since Coffey did not have excess cash, he sold—perhaps out of guilt for failing to join Robinson in Ethiopia as promised—a Great Lakes Trainer biplane that he had purchased and repaired. He also raised $500, and sent the money to Robinson, who remained in southeast France until the funds arrived.[140]

Foremost on Robinson's mind was concern that there might yet be additional attempts by Fascist agents to kill him. Nevertheless, by the time he neared New York City by steamboat, a much-relieved Robinson fully realized how "it is just pure luck that I am still alive."[141]

Another nagging regret for Robinson was that Addis Ababa's fall cost him the emperor's official recognition. Indeed, "Robinson [was] cited several times for bravery [but] the fall of the Ethiopian empire and the fleeing of Selassie caused him to miss being decorated for bravery."[142]

Ethiopia's defeat left an enduring legacy, paving the way for additional Fascist aggression and World War II. Mussolini's conquest of Ethiopia was destined to become the most crucial single factor resulting in the collapse of the spirit of the Western democracies' collective security to maintain world order and peace. Therefore, this often-overlooked war in faraway East Africa was a "crucial turning point" in world history. Ethiopia's subjugation set the stage for the formation of the Italy–

Germany Axis alliance, the further decline of the League of Nations, and additional Italian and Nazi aggression. "The real death of the League was in December 1935," just after the Italian armies swept into Ethiopia, while the apathetic West and the League of Nations could only watch Ethiopia's sad demise.[143]

Robinson's friend, war correspondent, Joel A. Rogers, wrote: "The second world war began as a fire set by Fascist looters in a black neighborhood (Ethiopia) which then spread into the white one (Europe) where they and the Nazis had more to loot."[144]

A gloomy editorial in the *Chicago Defender* described the bitter mood of African Americans all across the United States with Ethiopia's tragic death, lamenting the "Duce's rape of defenseless Ethiopia. Lack of concerted activities on our part morally and financially in behalf of Ethiopia makes one's heart shudder with disillusion, contempt and bitterness. [America's] tardy disposition toward aiding Ethiopia will forever hang like a macabre curtain over our very existence" in the future.[145]

Even though he had been forced to flee the ancient East African land that he loved, Robinson could yet hold his head high and feel pride in what he had accomplished in attempting to save Ethiopia against the odds. He was the only American, black or white, who served in the Italo-Ethiopian War from its beginning to end. And in the words of one *Chicago Defender* reporter, "Col. Robinson literally covered himself with glory, trying to preserve the independence of the last African empire" in the world.[146]

8

RETURNING A WAR HERO

AS ROBINSON SAILED for home aboard the North German Lloyd luxury liner the *Europa*, he journeyed through the Atlantic's waters along what had been called the Middle Passage, by which his West African ancestors had been transported to America so many generations before.[1]

Robinson was unable to realize how the abundant publicity about his wartime role as the Brown Condor of Ethiopia had so thoroughly captured the imagination of black America. By this time, "John Robinson's involvement in the Ethiopian conflict raised more interest within the Negro community in the political status of African-ruled nations than any other activity since Marcus Garvey."[2]

Robinson was surprised when David W. Kellum, a *Chicago Defender* reporter, and later nearly two dozen other newspaper correspondents from leading black newspapers, managed to get aboard the *Europa*, when the ship steamed into New York harbor on May 18, 1936. But the enterprising Kellum was the first to gain an exclusive interview with him. Because the ship was delayed in docking, Claude A. Barnett, who had just arrived from Chicago, cleverly utilized a U.S. Coast Guard cutter to take himself and the correspondents to Robinson's liner.[3]

Kellum "stepped out and scored another journalistic triumph when he effected a coup in New York which sent him down the bay in a U.S. Coast Guard cutter to be the first newspaper reporter to greet Col. John Robinson on his return to America from Ethiopia."[4]

Along with a horde of newspapermen and photographers, Kellum and other reporters requested the finely uniformed Robinson to pose on the ship's wooden deck for the camera. Only when a good many camera flash bulbs began popping did Robinson realize that his arrival from Ethiopia was going to be big news across America. Yet he felt more embarrassed than anything else by the reception.

It was not until he walked down the wooden ramp to the dock, however, that Robinson realized the full extent of his popularity. Not only was he greeted by a crowd of two thousand people, but also by United Aid for Ethiopia Society members. The noise from the cheering throng of black New Yorkers was deafening. This widespread adulation for the young Imperial Ethiopian Air Force commander, who had served for nearly a year in Africa, was comparable to white America's hero worship of Charles Lindbergh.[5]

Feeling equally fortunate that he had so often cheated death in Ethiopia, Robinson was more than happy to return to America. In one reporter's words, "Monday marked the first time that the flyer's feet have touched American soil. That he was happy was evidenced by the 'million dollar' smile he gave his admirers as he stepped from the ship."[6]

More than any other African American aviator—military or civilian—in American history, Robinson was now fully embraced by the African Americans as the "colored Lindy." By this time as the second African American military pilot who saw combat in history, Robinson was acclaimed across the United States as "the No. 1 Flyer of His Race."[7]

At the crowded dock, Barnett, who came ashore with Robinson, was part of a reception committee that included Dr. William Jay Schieffelin, the president of the Tuskegee Institute Board of Trustees, and Dr. P. M. H. Savory, who was the chairman of the United Aid For Ethiopia organization of New York City.[8]

An excited throng consisting of hundreds of African Americans who were primarily from Harlem welcomed this new "American hero of the short war." African Americans of all ages and backgrounds wanted to get a glimpse of the famed Brown Condor in person.[9] By now, the name John C. Robinson "was approaching [the] status" as a household word in major black communities across the United States, and especially in two of America's largest cities, New York City and Chicago.[10]

Robinson's exuberant reception at the New York Harbor pier was only the beginning of the cascade of honors and tributes in the months ahead. He was then driven to Harlem's YMCA where he gave a speech about Ethiopia. He emphasized his desire of launching a flying school to generate more interest in aviation among black youth and to train a new generation of African American pilots and mechanics. In fact, so many speaking engagements and banquets were set up by the United Ethiopian Aid Society to honor Robinson that he was unable to accommodate them all.[11]

According to one white Associated Press journalist's account, "They are making whoopee in Harlem over a new hero—flyer Colonel John C. Robinson."[12]

At this time, Robinson certainly looked the part of a genuine black aviation war hero, the first since Bullard's service for France in WWI. Moreover, and unlike Bullard, Robinson was also America's first war hero in the moral struggle against fascism and to defend a weak, unoffending nation. He proudly wore the full uniform of the Imperial Ethiopian Air Force's leader. Robinson also wore a dark pith helmet with the winged insignia, indicating a colonel's rank in the Imperial Ethiopia Air Force. Robinson, with a pencil-thin moustache, looked especially dashing and stylish in a fine leather jacket, which had the gold-embroidered insignia of the Royal Lion of Judah on the chest. Under the jacket, he wore a white sweater with a large-sized imperial insignia—the lion's face of the Lion of Judah, with royal crown, flanked by the golden wings of the Imperial Ethiopian Air Force. All in all, the self-assured Robinson looked more like a Hollywood movie star, a black Clark Gable, than a hardened war veteran who had so often cheated death.

An Associated Press journalist described Robinson's jaunty appearance. He was now "sporting a stubby little beard which made a black fringe under his chin. He was attired in [a] leather jacket emblazoned with the [royal] insignia of the 'Conquering Lion of Judah'—a lion rampant with crown and flag, a gift from the emperor—light brown shirt, tan tie, and Khaki trousers and shining leather boots."[13]

Robinson seemed slightly embarrassed by the enthusiastic response. Such modesty was not what Associated Press journalist Charles Norman expected: "Despite his impressive apparel, his bearing was modest, almost shy. Modest, too, was his account of his experiences in war-torn Ethiopia for which Harlem has named him the 'Brown Condor.'"[14]

The night of Robinson's arrival in New York City, a banquet was held in his honor in Harlem. Here, Robinson was introduced by Dr. William J. Schieffelin, who was the chairman of the Board of Trustees of Tuskegee Institute, and Barnett, a Tuskegee trustee. Barnett had brought a Chicago contingent of Tuskegee alumnus to New York City to welcome Robinson back to America.[15]

Robinson's arrival even made the front page of the *New York Times* on May 18: "John C. Robinson, the Chicago aviator who acted as aide and personal aviator to Emperor Haile Selassie during Italy's invasion of Ethiopia will return today on the North German Lloyd liner *Europa*, his representatives amassed last night. Robinson, known in Africa as 'Ethiopia's brown condor,' was credited with carrying many of the Emperor's dispatches by plane, despite the Italians' control of the air . . . After a visit to Chicago Mr. Robinson will visit Tuskegee Institute, where he has been named director of the first aviation school under Negro auspices."[16]

Recognition and appreciation for Robinson and his distinguished role in Ethiopia continued unabated in the days ahead. But the climax of Robinson's reception came on Saturday night, May 23.[17] Organized by the United Aid of Ethiopia organization, a rally of more than five thousand ecstatic citizens was held at Rockland Palace, Harlem, "in honor of the victorious return to America of Colonel John C. Robinson noted airman and the recent chief of Ethiopia's Air Corps."[18]

This festive event was "one of the most spectacular and thrilling held in New York," wrote newspaperman A. E. White.[19] Such a demonstration of admiration merely indicated the extent of Robinson's popularity among black America on the East Coast. In a carnival-like atmosphere, this "big mass meeting was attended by thousand of New Yorkers."[20]

Reverend William Lloyd Imes, a leading Harlem religious leader, wrote a new song entitled "We'll Sing Ethiopia" to "commemorate [Robinson's] valiant efforts in support of Ethiopia's struggle to maintain her independence against the invading Italians."[21]

Many "copies of the song were distributed among the Rockland Palace audience and for the community at large":

WE'LL SING ETHIOPIA

We'll sing Ethiopia, sing her praise,
We'll sing of her courage the rest of our days.
And we'll shout our defiance at cowards we know
Who killed women and children, instead of the foe,

We'll sing Ethiopia, proud of her blood.
All Afro-Americans one brotherhood
And we'll ring our defiance against this foul crime,
With firmest reliance, awaiting God's time.[22]

Speakers, including Barnett, praised Robinson to the assembled crowd of New Yorkers, mostly from Harlem. Barnett was generally recognized as the man "responsible for Robinson's venture to the African Empire."[23]

Savory also spoke and presented an address entitled, "Patriotism, Loyalty and Sacrifice." He emphasized the spirit of the Pan-African message that Robinson had demonstrated by serving Emperor Selassie and defending Ethiopia in its darkest hour, "Not Patriotism of a national kind but patriotism of your race [which] transcends all other patriotism and knows no bounds."[24]

Walter E. Blair also praised "the intrepid young aviator for the forward step he had taken and in offering his services to the harassed empire [and] urged the mighty throng to take a lesson from Colonel Robinson's life and dedicate their own lives to the establishing of [Dr. Savory's] three virtues so necessary to the success of the black peoples the world over."[25]

Other respected individuals sang Robinson's praises to the crowd, including religious leaders of the African Orthodox Church, "but it was Robinson the crowds wanted, and each mention of his name during the evening brought roars of cheers and salvos of applause."[26]

As reporter White described the frantic scene: "A standing ovation greeted Colonel Robinson as he walked to the microphone. Clad in his aviator's uniform, his figure erect in spite of the three gassings he suffered and the injured arm and hand sustained in another air raid, the Colonel was an imposing figure as he addressed his hearers. Intense attention was directed at the young Negro as he stood at ease in front of the mike."[27]

After the deafening fifteen-minute standing ovation, Robinson then began to relate his war experiences to a spellbound audience.[28] Afterward, he was presented with a token of appreciation from the Tuskegee Club of New York City. He was also given "a magnificent souvenir, a plane resting atop two beautiful columns, silver with a fine bloodstone in the base and a suitable inscription."[29] Then, "the entire group tried to shake hands with the 'Brown Condor' who had brought honor to his people and had shed his blood in the defense of Ethiopia and the Emperor of the black peoples of the world."[30]

Robinson would take with him lifelong reminders of this unexpected outpouring of admiration from the warmth of New Yorkers, who he had never seen before. At another banquet, Robinson was presented with a beautiful twenty-two-inch silver trophy. The engraved inscription spoke eloquently of the high esteem held for

Robinson and his symbolic and inspirational wartime contributions in a faraway land: "Presented by the people of Harlem to Colonel John C. Robinson, in honor of his heroic service in the defense of Ethiopia and the honor of the Negro race."[31]

In contrast to the leading newspapers across black America, Robinson garnered some minor recognition from white newspapers, many of which were not only anti-black, but also had openly admired Mussolini. But any mention of Robinson was almost always short and cursory at best. In addition, such articles by white journalists seriously underplayed and minimized Robinson's wartime activities and contributions.[32]

In the May 25, 1936, issue of the *Star*, Robinson's name did not even appear in the story's headline about his arrival from Ethiopia. He was only described in the headline as simply a "Colored U.S. Mechanic," instead of either a black pioneer aviator, the Imperial Ethiopian Air Force's commander, the second African American pilot to engage in aerial combat in history, or the wartime personal pilot of Emperor Selassie.[33]

Another white United Press journalist described the returning war hero of black America as simply "a former Chicago garage man."[34]

But Robinson received favorable coverage from some of the top white radio announcers of the day. Ohio-born Lowell Thomas, the most famous of these reporters, mentioned Robinson over NBC's airwaves. Also, other major radio networks, including the Mutual Broadcasting System, likewise carried brief bulletins about Robinson and his wartime exploits.[35]

While everyone was celebrating his arrival, Robinson was little more than a physical wreck. At only age thirty-one, he had suffered considerable mental and emotional fatigue from the strains of combat during nearly a year of hectic activity. One reporter wrote candidly about Robinson's deteriorated condition, depicting a war-weary combat veteran: "Colonel Robinson seemed quite disturbed as he talked. He was not feeling well although he tried to appear so. He was having trouble with [mustard] gas and desired to see a doctor after the ship docked."[36]

As another reporter described this black combat veteran, who had amassed a total of 728 flying hours in multiple war zones during 1935—1936, "Col. Robinson in telling of his flying exhibited two scars on his right and left hands which he had received in actual warfare. He was [also] gassed, he said when one of the Italian planes dropped poison gas and liquid fire near a Red Cross station."[37]

Incredibly, Robinson had flown 128 more hours in less than twelve months in war-torn Ethiopia than in all the years of peacetime flying in Chicago. Therefore, he admitted with some understatement: "I'm a little worn out by the war. It was quite a strain on me. I had 700 hours in the air between June 15 and April 3."[38]

But Robinson revealed relatively little of his inner anguish and trauma. After all, he looked good, trim, in shape, and handsome in uniform. His splendid outward appearance betrayed his poor physical and mental health. As reported in the *Chicago Defender*, "Before going to Ethiopia, Colonel Robinson weighed 157 pounds and now, even with the two wounds and having suffered from the poison gas, Colonel Robinson weighs 164 pounds."[39]

Nevertheless, Robinson was now in serious need of a long period of rest and recuperation, if not hospitalization. As revealed by a New York journalist, Robinson had been "severely gassed. He also suffered a broken collar-bone. He says he was shot twice while in combat with the Italians. It was arranged that he should get a few days rest and then see a doctor before he attempts to travel back to Chicago, his old home, and to St. Louis to visit his mother, Mrs. Celeste Robinson."[40]

Only much later after a full recovery would Robinson look upon his searing wartime experiences in a more positive light. By the summer of 1937, for example, a journalist would report how "Those Italian bullets whizzing by him in the air—three of them struck him—gave him his most-thrilling experiences since he has been flying, the colonel said."[41]

CHICAGO AGAIN

The day after the reception at Harlem's Rockland Palace, Robinson, along with Barnett, boarded a Trans-World Airlines plane to Chicago. To Robinson's surprise, the Chicago reception, especially in Bronzeville, was even grander than that in New York City. A Chicago reporter described the feeling among African Americans on the South Side: "This mammoth open air theatre [Chicago Municipal Airport] is in turmoil. It is seething with action, but tense action . . . because Col. John C. Robinson, Chicago's own, is winning his way back to town after 13 dreary months in Ethiopia. Everybody knows the colonel is coming home! [A] giant twin-motored plane [was] bringing the 'Brown Condor' home" to Chicago.[42]

On Sunday, May 24, more than five thousand people of the South Side greeted Robinson upon his arrival in the Windy City. As he deplaned, two young women—one being Janet Harmon Bragg—of the Challenger Air Pilots' Association, pre-

sented him with bouquets of flowers. The women wore military-like attire, including leather boots and flying caps. Other Challenger Air Pilots' Association ladies
attending were Doris Murphy, Billie Renfroe, Willa B. Brown, and a Mrs. James.
As described by one reporter: "Two beautiful bouquets of peonies were presented
Col. John C. Robinson as he stepped from the TWA plane Sunday afternoon by
two aviatrixes. Attired in snappy air pilots uniforms, these young women rushed
to Colonel Robinson, shook his hand, then presented him with flowers, the gift of
the Challenger Air Pilots Association, the organization founded by Colonel Robinson." Wearing a stylish commander's flying cap, Robinson arrived in Chicago wearing his finest uniform. He now wore the resplendent dress uniform of an Imperial
Ethiopian Air Force colonel. This decorative uniform was far more impressive than
the more informal uniform that Robinson had worn when he arrived in New York
City. More photos were snapped, while the cheers and applause rose from the large
crowd. All of a sudden, "police lines were broken by the admiring throng which
rushed to the ace war pilot and showered him with flowers, kisses, handshakes, and
words of cheer."[43]

All the while, the crowd grew even larger with everyone eager to see the Brown
Condor. Then, Robinson, in an open limousine, led a procession of five hundred
cars from the airport to the South Side. Robinson's car, draped in Ethiopian flags
and with the mayor of Bronzeville inside, led a parade through the black community. The "word of Colonel Robinson's arrival had spread over the city like wildfire
and streets along the way were jammed with admirers who let out cheers and roars
of welcome." Hundreds of automobiles, honking their horns, followed the parade
led by Robinson's car.

Wearing neat military uniforms, Chicago black veterans of World War I
then took Robinson to the Grand Hotel. Here, from the hotel's balcony, Robinson spoke to a cheering crowd of more than eight thousand people. This throng
stood around the large bronze statue of General George Washington on horseback
during a "mammoth celebration" in Washington Park. In humble fashion, Robinson spoke, spontaneously and from the heart: "While I am glad to be back in my
own country, I yet regretted very much that the war ended as it did. I had hoped
of course that Ethiopia would have been victorious in her struggle to maintain her
standing in the family of nations. This was impossible because the League of Nations failed her and in addition thereto, the very people upon whom Ethiopia depended believing them to be the most patriotic of her tribes turned traitor at the

crucial moment." Robinson blamed both black and white alike for Ethiopia's martyrdom.[44]

A *Chicago Defender* reporter wrote without exaggeration how never had "Chicago welcomed home its hero of the Ethiopian war Sunday afternoon when more than twenty thousand men, women, and children joined in a rip-roaring reception for Colonel John C. Robinson, the 'Brown Condor' of Emperor Haile Selassie's Royal air force. Not in the history has there been such a demonstration as was accorded the 31-year-old Chicago aviator who left the United States thirteen months ago and literally covered himself in glory, trying to preserve the independence of the last African empire."[45]

From the hotel's balcony, Robinson spoke to "a sea of faces which filled the entire boulevard." It seemed as if all of black Chicago had turned out to greet the Brown Condor. A large Ethiopian banner, flanked by two larger American flags, was displayed in decorative fashion below him. The immense crowd jammed the plaza around the Washington Monument in front of the Grand Hotel, cheering his words that echoed the hard realities of a distant struggle for survival.[46]

The next day, Robinson spoke at Binga's Arcade Building, where another banquet was held in his honor. Symbolically, the "members of the Curtiss-Wright Aviation school of which Colonel Robinson is an alumnus, were out in a body." The following day, Robinson described his wartime experiences to several thousand citizens at Du Sable High School, which was named in honor of Jean Baptiste Pointe Du Sable, the black pioneer founder of Chicago. Here, the aviator described how "Italy can hardly call the taking of Addis Ababa a military victory [as] it was a military march from Dessye" by the Italian military machine.[47]

Robinson was amazed by the widespread recognition. He would have been more astounded, however, had he known that his aviation role in Ethiopia had not only thrust him into the national spotlight but also had catapulted his fame far beyond any other African American aviator in America at this time.

Robinson was now only beginning to understand the extent of the gaping void that he had filled for black America, which had long desired to embrace a black Lindbergh. Indeed, ever since "Lindbergh's flight [in 1927], black America's hopes for an air hero continued to loom large."[48]

While other African American aviators laid claim to more civilian records, none possessed a more inspirational and meaningful dual reputation as both a race barrier–breaking civilian aviator and the authentic war hero of a moral struggle.

Like no other African American of his day, consequently, Robinson "provided the Negro press and Negro America with a bona fide hero with the stature of Joe Louis and Jesse Owens."[49]

Robinson received yet another warm reception in Washington, D.C. During the second week of June, he made a speech before a large audience at the Metropolitan Baptist Church. Here, the Brown Condor was presented to the crowd by the head of the Ethiopian Research Council, Dr. Leo Handsberry, who was also a respected professor of African Studies at Howard University. But Robinson was not merely basking in his newfound fame. He had founded the John C. Robinson Aviation Fund to promote aviation among a new generation of black youth and to purchase an aircraft. In part, this event in Washington, D.C., was to benefit that fund.[50]

Robinson's fame made black America more conscious about the possibilities for blacks to play leading military aviation roles in wartime, inspiring a new generation of African Americans, who would become the famed Tuskegee Airmen of World War II. Historian Robert J. Jakeman placed Robinson's role in a proper historical perspective: "When Robinson entered the service of Haile Selassie, no black aviator had achieved the right balance of flying expertise and public acclaim to become the nation's 'black Lindy,' but now that had changed forever with Robinson's dramatic emergence "from his Ethiopian adventures as a bona fide air hero."[51]

Indeed, "For five long years after Lindbergh emerged as the hero of the machine age, black America waited for the appearance of a 'colored Lindy': Bullard had abandoned flying and was forgotten; Julian was an embarrassment; Bessie Coleman [met an] untimely death."[52]

Ironically, while Robinson was showered with applause, received widespread recognition, met thousands of worshipers, and was hailed as a national hero in black newspapers across the United States, another esteemed American aviation colonel received a May 25, 1936, letter from Major Truman Smith, the military attaché to the American embassy in Berlin, Germany, who extended to him, "in the name of General [Herman] Goring and the German Air Ministry an invitation to visit [Nazi] Germany and inspect the new German civil and military air establishments."[53]

In the late spring of 1936, the letter's recipient, the quiet Charles Lindbergh, was the most worshiped aviation idol of white America. A number of interesting parallels existed between the lives of Lindbergh and Robinson: early mechanical inclinations and talents; love of automobiles, racing, and speed; interests in automobile engines; daredevil motorcyclists; obsessions with becoming a pilot, early aviation visionaries, and, perhaps, most of all, both men were idealistic dreamers, who followed their dreams and made them come true.[54]

In a surprising turn of events, an obscure, young black aviator from south Mississippi became a hero of black America by making a bold moral stand against the evils of fascism, while Lindbergh would eventually fall from grace in moral terms for "appeasement of history's most barbaric tyrant," Adolf Hitler.[55]

For black America, the striking contrast between Lindbergh and Robinson was even more significant and poignant from a racial perspective. Fascism's followers viewed blacks as inferior beings who were destined for enslavement in their new world order. African Americans, consequently, saw fascism as the same as racism. Lindbergh and Robinson moved in opposite directions, because of their radically opposing moral responses to the growing threat of fascism's expanding dark shadow. While Lindbergh shook hands with Hitler and openly admired Nazi Germany, Robinson demonstrated in Ethiopia that America could and should take a strong moral stand against tyranny.[56]

Robinson had also struck a highly visible blow against the ugly racial stereotypes held by whites, who were convinced that blacks could become neither technically proficient nor aeronautically competent, much less demonstrate courage as military aviators and leaders in wartime.[57] Sadly, in his popular 1927 book, *We*, Lindbergh himself promoted such popular stereotypes about blacks.[58]

After Ethiopia's fall, Dr. Bayen, who had helped to facilitate Robinson's mission to Ethiopia, traveled back to the United States as Emperor Selassie's special envoy to the western hemisphere. With a war of liberation against the occupying Italians on his mind, he met with black leaders in New York City. In the words of historian Joseph E. Harris: "This was a historic moment, marking the first result of a mission designed and carried out entirely by African Americans for the purpose of challenging aggression of a European power was embarked on in Africa with the support, or at least the acquiescence, of the most powerful countries in the world [and Dr. Bayen now] represented the emperor and was going on to work closely with black Americans for Ethiopia's liberation" from Italian occupation and rule.[59]

Bayen attempted to establish a black power base in America for Ethiopia's liberation from fascism. At Harlem's Rockland Palace Bayen presented a stirring address in which he especially "praised Colonel Robinson" and for his many accomplishments on multiple levels in the war against the rising tide of fascism.[60]

Robinson actively supported Bayen's efforts and those of the Ethiopian World Federation, founded by Bayen, to rally support in America for Ethiopia's future liberation. Robinson flew to New York City, and helped to rally support for the Ethiopian cause. On one occasion, he "served as head of the marching unit [of the Ethiopian World Federation] and of more than one athletic group."[61]

At this time and despite his harrowing experiences from 1935 to 1936, Robinson was "still willing to risk [his] life for Ethiopia." Support for the Ethiopian World Federation grew because of Robinson's influence and efforts. At one popular event, he organized and led a parade of participants of a large conference from an auditorium to a Methodist Church in Harlem in a special service honoring Emperor Selassie. When Bayen died in May 1940, Robinson filled the large gap left by this spiritual and inspirational leader of the Ethiopian World Federation. Clearly, Robinson's personal war against the relentless march of fascism and its evils was far from over.[62]

9

AVIATION VISIONS BURN BRIGHTLY

EVEN THOUGH HE WAS back in America, Robinson's heart, soul, and spirit remained in Ethiopia. He served as a powerful anti-fascist voice, working to keep the dream of Ethiopian independence alive. He helped organize the Chicago branch of the Ethiopian World Federation, headed by Dr. Bayen. In addition, Robinson continued to work closely with the United Aid for Ethiopia organization, based in New York City. All the while, he hoped for Emperor Selassie's return to a free Ethiopia, if the British could defeat the Italians.[1]

Meanwhile, Robinson attempted to return to the world that he had known and the life that he had lived before. Like many combat veterans, Robinson had become more fatalistic and cynical. He now saw life as precious and fleeting. Robinson was not entirely content to resume life exactly as it had been, however. He wanted more than to simply manage his garage and repair automobiles with his wife, Earnize, or even to enjoy a quiet life on the South Side of Chicago.

Robinson more seriously contemplated returning to Tuskegee. When interviewed by journalists not long after his return to New York City, Robinson declared that he was "now considering an offer from Tuskegee Institute, Alabama, to teach aviation." A *New York Times* article from May 18, 1936, stated that Robinson had already been "named director of the first aviation school under Negro auspices," but in fact Robinson hesitated before making his final decision.[2]

The next day, May 19, the *New York Times* also reported how "the 31-year-old flyer has returned to become an instructor in aviation at Tuskegee Institute."[3] But, despite a healthy outward appearance, Robinson continued to be in overall poor physical, and perhaps psychological shape, during the summer of 1936. As a sympathetic white journalist observed: "He also needs to be hospitalized, he said, for treatment after being gassed."[4]

His youthful fascination with the sleek aerodynamic beauty of streamlined aircraft and the sheer majesty of flight in endless skies of blue had been transformed, now representing something altogether different to him: death and destruction. As Robinson, with a gift for understatement, told United Press correspondent Jack Diamond in May 1936: "Even now, when a plane goes by I feel like I've got to get under something" and seek shelter.[5]

Robinson's most severe postwar trauma stemmed from the memory of the mustard gas attacks, when the chemical—dichloroethyl sulfide—floated down in a lethal spray from low-flying Italian military aircraft. In fact, Robinson's breathing would continue to be impaired for years to come.[6]

Attempts to profit from Robinson's widespread fame had begun even before his arrival back home in America. For instance, Tuskegee trustee Claude A. Barnett, a master publicist, had notified President Frederick Douglass Patterson at Tuskegee Institute of what he viewed as a golden opportunity to capitalize on the Brown Condor's return, and therefore, set up the wide-ranging publicity campaign that Robinson now embarked upon.

Additionally Barnett had also recommended an aviation event to be held at Tuskegee Institute to welcome Robinson back home. Not only had all of this activity begun before Robinson's return, but also without his knowledge or approval. As the key part of this promotional campaign and as Robinson had believed, Tuskegee Institute would have an instructor's position open for him in its Department of Mechanical Industries upon his return. But in fact, this plan was more fantasy than fact. The money-short institute in the Deep South possessed neither planes, nor airport, nor landing strip, nor aviation facilities of any kind. For the most part, therefore, Robinson's Ethiopian fame was exploited solely to promote, for a new generation of African Americans, Tuskegee Institute itself, rather than aviation, and for the benefit and evidently financial gain of trustees like Barnett.[7]

Before Barnett met Robinson in New York City, he issued press releases announcing the Brown Condor's arrival, emphasizing that Robinson would join Tuskegee's faculty to create "the first aviation school under Negro auspices."[8]

As in Ethiopia, his fame made him little more than a commodity. Robinson, consequently, began to resent such exploitative attempts, and ever the individualist, he was determined not to be turned into a pawn and commercial product. Therefore, Barnett, President Patterson, and the head of the Department of Mechanical Industries, G. L. Washington, were surprised, if not shocked, when they discovered "that the Brown Condor had his own ideas about how to use his newfound fame."[9]

But Robinson, hoping that he could still be allowed an opportunity to develop an aviation program at the institute, had yet to give Tuskegee his final decision. Meanwhile, he continued to speak about his war experiences throughout Chicago. During the summer of 1936, billed as "Ethiopia's Ace of the Air," Robinson lectured to a large crowd at Poro College, in Chicago, which was headed by Anne T. P. Malone, the school's founder. During the "chapel exercises in the parlors" a poem about the Brown Condor was read in Robinson's honor.[10]

Robinson's public appearances raised great interest in aviation in black communities, and thus paid dividends. On June 13, a *Chicago Defender* journalist recorded how "with pledges and cash still pouring . . . indications are that public spirited citizens of Chicago will go over the top in their drive for the purchasing of a plane for Col. John Robinson, ace Ethiopian flyer, who is resting in Chicago before leaving for Tuskegee Institute where he is to become an instructor in aviation."[11]

These donations were for the Colonel John C. Robinson Aviation Fund. Money had been collected from Robinson banquets and other Brown Condor events held by the Challenger Air Pilots' Association. Funds poured in from across Chicago, including from white contributors, and African American organizations like the Military Order of Guards and the Graduate Nurses Association. Small private black businesses, such as The Garden Dress Shop and the Johnson Shoe Store of Bronzeville, donated money to the fund. Even the Rosenwald Glee Club, a group of Jewish singers, contributed donations. Since Robinson's return, money had been gathered for the fund primarily through three organizations: the Tuskegee Club of Chicago, consisting of Tuskegee graduates, the Challenger Air Pilots' Association, and the Friends of Ethiopia.[12]

Robinson gained widespread support for his fund, because in the words of an *Amsterdam News* reporter, he "will do big things in aviation which will reflect credibility on the Negro. His type needs the boosts rather than the glib dramatic posers who bring us such humorous headlines and accounts in the white press."[13]

By this time, Robinson had already outgrown Chicago in many ways. Even though Robinson was increasingly disenchanted, Barnett continued to set up a large number of speaking engagements and fund-raising events throughout the summer of 1936. Robinson appeared at speaking engagements in Brooklyn, New York,

Pittsburgh, Pennsylvania, Tuskegee Institute, Washington, D.C., and Kansas City, Missouri.[14]

This fast-paced promotional tour provided a good opportunity for Robinson to return to the Deep South. He took off in a SR-7 Sprint Reliant single-engine monoplane and flew south from Chicago on a warm late June day in 1936.[15]

Robinson landed in Cairo, Illinois, at the state's southern tip, after following the brown-hued Mississippi River southward. From Cairo, he continued flying down the "Father of Waters," until turning southeast toward Alabama. At Birmingham, in northwest Alabama, Robinson landed for refueling.[16] He then headed straight for Tuskegee Institute. Besides promoting aviation, the Tuskegee trip was planned to finalize plans for Robinson's future role as an instructor at the institute for the fall of 1936.

As he had on that warm May 1934 day when he first flew to Tuskegee Institute more than two years before, Robinson landed in a sprawling oat field. After an enthusiastic reception, he then met with Tuskegee s president Patterson. On the next day, Robinson addressed the students and faculty. The institute's printed voice, the *Tuskegee Messenger*, recorded how "In presenting Colonel Robinson, President Patterson referred with pride to the fine record of this Tuskegee graduate in blazing the trail for Negro youth in a new field of endeavor and proving to the world beyond doubt the Negro's capacity for accuracy, endurance, skill, and courage."[17]

After the speech, the issue of Robinson's potential employment was seriously discussed in person with institute officials and at some length. But soon Robinson, to his dismay, learned from school officials that Tuskegee lacked not only the financial resources to support an aviation program, but also the necessary facilities. Indeed, "none of the school's resources were committed to operating expenses" of an aviation school. Tuskegee president Patterson and other institute officials naively believed that, despite the Great Depression, sufficient money could be donated for building aviation facilities and for the purchase of aviation equipment at Tuskegee in time for the fall 1936 classes. This badly misplaced optimism reflected the ignorance of Tuskegee's administrative leaders, who knew little, if anything, about what it took to launch an aviation program.

Clearly, it would be some time before Tuskegee Institute would be able to develop an aviation program. During this severe economic downturn, black schools like Tuskegee were especially hard-hit. Consequently, Robinson estimated that Tuskegee's future prospects for an aviation program were remote at best, but he had already established the conceptual vision and instilled the wisdom of teaching aviation at Tuskegee, setting them firmly in place. However, the demands of a world war, coupled with extensive government support, would be required to make the dream of aviation come alive at Tuskegee Institute in the future.[18]

Robinson flew away from his alma mater with a heavy heart. He had much to think about. The offer to teach aviation at Tuskegee in the fall 1936 semester was still on the table—if Tuskegee was somehow able to establish an aviation program by then. Relying on compass and flight maps, Robinson headed west to his native state of Mississippi. Along a small, dusty airstrip known as Key Field, he landed at Meridian where Lindbergh had flown during his barnstorming days in 1923. An estimated four thousand African Americans waited at the Meridian airport for Robinson's arrival. Like in Harlem, it seemed as if all of black Meridian received Robinson as a returning war hero.[19]

He then flew west to the capital, Jackson, and nearby Tougaloo University, a coeducational liberal arts college. Annie Mae Gaston, who grew up only three blocks from Robinson in Gulfport, never forgot the moment when he landed on Tougaloo's football field. The American Missionary Association of New York had organized this respected black educational institution in 1869, to train young African Americans just freed from slavery to become full American citizens.

Thirteen years Robinson's junior, Annie Mae Gaston "always had a crush on the handsome pilot [as a Gulfport teenager, but it] wasn't until she was a student at Tougaloo University that he noticed her," for obvious reasons. She recalled: "One of the things that I remember about John is that after he went to Chicago he came to Tougaloo and landed in the football field. He inquired about me, and I was on cloud nine [as] I was crazy about him." After reminiscing about the good old days, Robinson asked Annie Mae to join him on his return to their mutual hometown of Gulfport. This was a dream come true for young Annie Mae because she "admired him so much." She excitedly called her mother to inform her of the good news. Reflecting the conservative, traditional values of a black Deep South community, Annie Mae's mother absolutely forbade her daughter from joining Robinson. Evidently his reputation as a ladies' man was alive and well in Gulfport. Annie Mae remembered how hurt she was by her mother's decision. Clearly, Annie Mae and a good many other young women were simply "crazy" about the dashing, personable war hero with the winning smile and ways.[20]

After departing Jackson, Robinson flew directly south for the Mississippi Gulf Coast. By this time, Gulfport was proud of its small airfield, amid the open, level fields lying just north of town on the other side of the railroad tracks. The little air field had been built to accommodate regular air mail flights. When Robinson departed Gulfport for Tuskegee Institute in the late summer of 1920, no airport existed. Clearly, Gulfport was now less isolated than in Robinson's younger days. After he landed in his hometown, Robinson was at last reunited with his family, stepfather Charles C. Cobb and mother Celeste, for the first time since returning from the war in Ethiopia. He had much to talk about with family members and old friends at his old two-story home at 1905 31st Street.[21]

The African American community of Gulfport welcomed Robinson with open arms. He was not only the African American Lindbergh but also the native son hero of Gulfport's Big Quarter. On the first Sunday back home, Robinson attended special religious services and social activities, including a picnic, honoring him. The St. Paul African Methodist Episcopal Church, where he attended services as a younger man, and the Bethel Baptist Church had sponsored this community event.[22]

Robinson was less warmly welcomed by some of Gulfport's white citizens. The sight of such a confident young black man in a resplendent colonel's uniform walking down Gulfport's streets with the dignity of a wartime veteran, who was furthermore respected by a foreign nation's emperor and idolized all across black America, caused considerable dismay among many white Mississippians. After all, many of them were themselves the sons and daughters of slave owners.[23]

Less than twenty years before, another equally proud young black man, the brother of Robinson's friend Katie Booth, also had once walked these same Gulfport streets with a comparable upright military bearing. A veteran of the Great War, he refused to take off his U.S. uniform when ordered to by appalled whites. When some local toughs tried to tear off his uniform, he resisted. Tragically, this young veteran, who had served his country with honor, was lynched in Gulfport, while still wearing his uniform. This tragedy was only part of a larger, national postwar backlash, including anti-black riots and an upsurge in lynching, against African Americans, who had served their country proudly.[24]

Robinson also gave an interview to the local newspaper. This story, however, failed to include his full name. On June 26, 1936, the article appeared under the headline: "Gulfport Negro Who Piloted Emperor Haile Selassie Visits Home; Relates His Experiences in Wartime Flying." The white journalist who interviewed Robinson wrote:

> J.C. Robinson, Negro aviator who gained worldwide fame as Emperor Haile Selassie's official air pilot and who was in charge of the entire [Imperial] Ethiopian Air Force, is in Gulfport visiting his stepfather and mother, C[harles] C. Cobb and wife who reside at 1905 Thirty-first Avenue. Robinson called at *The Herald* Office this morning wearing the Ethiopian official uniform. His rank is Colonel and his uniform carries the official emblem of the emperor, "The Lion of Judah," worked in gold mined from the gold mines of Ethiopia from which King Solomon was supposed to have secured much of the gold for his famous temple at Jerusalem. He was employed by C.A. Simpson in Gulfport at one time and went from Gulfport to Chicago where he worked for six years with the Curtiss Flying Service. Ethiopia had 24 airplanes during the war, he said, and all but three of them were shot down. During this thirteen month's service in the Ethiopian air service, he was wounded three times and gassed twice.[25]

Sunday's activities honored the hometown hero at the tiny Gulfport airport. Black church and community leaders spoke at length. Robinson's parents were introduced to the crowd. Celeste, John's mother, was beaming with pride for her son. Even the more liberal whites in town were present, including Gulfport's mayor. Robinson had brought together a mutual community spirit and newfound sense of solidarity between the races. Robinson spoke only briefly, but he mentioned his dream of starting an aviation school in Chicago for African American youth.

Robinson then displayed his flying skills in the new, swift Stinson, thrilling the crowd. He took a lucky female passenger up in flight despite the concerns of her father, Will Gaston. She was Annie Mae Gaston's sister, and had won a drawing for the coveted honor of flying with Robinson. With a stern voice, Will Gaston emphasized to Robinson, "You take care of my daughter." Robinson then assured him that he would at all costs. Later, other Gulfport passengers flew with Robinson, including the mayor, who apparently had never been on a plane before.[26]

What Annie Mae Gaston's brother, Albert, most recalled about Robinson was not his flying skill but that he was so "ambitious." Young Albert was awestruck because, "What impressed me most about Robinson was that he was [so] interested in business." Even at this time, the forward-thinking Robinson expounded upon bold ideas about creating his own airlines, the first black airline in history. Albert Gaston never forgot how Robinson now contemplated what was almost incomprehensible to the people, both black and white, on the Mississippi Gulf Coast, because he "wanted to start a commercial line."[27]

Indeed, this young visionary possessed a host of aviation dreams by this time, all of which still burned brightly. Annie Mae recalled that Robinson "wanted to start a [flying] school" for black youth. Annie Mae also remembered that Robinson, desiring to regain his passion for motorcycling as he had before he went to Ethiopia, "wanted to buy a motorbike."[28]

In addition, Robinson had not yet given up the hope that he could still "go to Tuskegee Institute . . . and begin preparations for the new course of study in aviation, which he will teach during the fall and winter school term," wrote a *Chicago Defender* reporter.[29]

THE FINAL TUSKEGEE INSTITUTE DECISION

Upon returning to Chicago, Robinson carried a written agreement from Tuskegee for him to begin teaching aviation classes in the fall, but he hesitated before signing the contract, in part because he felt he was being manipulated.

He read the contract in detail, going carefully over every word like a lawyer on his first legal case. He did not like what he saw. Besides the lack of money and aviation facilities at Tuskegee Institute,[30] he explained to Barnett on July 1, "I have not been satisfied . . . as to how things have been handled [by Barnett and his cronies who had made their own decisions about the aviation program] instead of using my thoughts that are seasoned with much experience in aviation."[31]

Additionally, Robinson was perplexed to discover that Barnett, and not himself, could use the donation monies of the John C. Robinson Aviation Fund. Indeed, Barnett refused to release funds so that Robinson could purchase an airplane, which was the fund's primary purpose so that he could better promote aviation to black youth. Robinson emphasized that in the future he alone should determine the future direction of the John C. Robinson Aviation Fund and not Barnett, though he hoped that he and Barnett could remain on good terms despite this.[32]

Then, after careful scrutiny, Robinson sent the contract back to Washington unsigned. Robinson had made up his mind. Always a pragmatist, he simply could not base his future aviation plans upon the unrealistic possibility of success at money-short Tuskegee during the Depression. Robinson was incredulous by the agreement's wording, which clearly indicated that "none of the school's resources were committed to operating expenses" for the first projected aviation program at Tuskegee![33]

The document revealed that Washington was, in fact, only making a token gesture at launching an aviation program, revealing an overall "reluctance on the part of Tuskegee to support fully an aviation training program." This perhaps was natural, because the field of aviation was yet an area of expertise that the school's conservative leaders and faculty, including Washington, knew little, if nothing, about.[34]

Virtually on his own and without financial support, adequate assistance, a firm commitment, or even a vote of confidence from Tuskegee officials, Robinson would have been almost solely responsible for the success of the new, poorly supported infant aviation program when the Southern and national economy were in bad shape: a recipe for almost certain failure. Indeed, Robinson would have to "initiate and carry on the program" on his own, but without the necessary resources—unless he supplied them himself—to successfully accomplish this mission. Protecting themselves and their reputations, Tuskegee Institute's officials had ensured that no blame would fall upon them if such an aviation program at Tuskegee failed, or in the case of fatal aircraft accidents, especially liabilities, in regard to the possible loss of white lives and property.[35] Consequently, Tuskegee Institute would provide only "limited support [as the success of the aviation training program at Tuskegee] depended on Robinson's willingness [and ability] to cultivate financial support from sources outside the institute."[36]

Barnett and Tuskegee had unashamedly exploited Robinson's immense popularity as a war hero, even before he reached New York City, to announce the start of an aviation program at Tuskegee without realistic plans, the necessary finances, adequate aviation facilities, including an airport and runway, or the all-important political or local support necessary for a successful aviation program. Indeed, according to the complex agreement, Robinson would be solely responsible for every aspect of the new aviation program at Tuskegee, including finances.[37]

Evidently this lack of support and commitment was Tuskegee's way of applying pressure to force Robinson to utilize the resources of the John C. Robinson Aviation Fund, which had been established with Barnett, to start an aviation program at Tuskegee from scratch. Apparently, Barnett and Tuskegee believed Robinson had been handsomely paid in gold by Emperor Selassie for his services in Ethiopia.

Because of Tuskegee's failure to make a serious commitment to an aviation training program, Robinson felt the Tuskegee faculty and trustees lacked confidence in him to handle such responsibility, or held an elitist opposition barring him from the ivory tower world of Tuskegee's faculty. The educators seemed to doubt his abilities as an instructor and administrator, viewing him—like whites—more as an auto mechanic. Tuskegee's officials did not take Robinson seriously in part because they incorrectly considered him merely a popular, if not romanticized, war hero without substance. To these respected educational members of black America, how could a young man called the Brown Condor of Ethiopia be taken seriously in the academic community?[38]

Perhaps these conservative educators were a bit intimidated by the outspoken Robinson. With his unprecedented expertise and his many achievements on both sides of the Atlantic, Robinson must have seemed larger than life. After all, he had made a name for himself at the most prestigious aeronautical school in the country—Curtiss-Wright in Chicago—and had created a life for himself in the North by relying upon his technical expertise, intelligence, and ability. Robinson was a self-made man, an aviation pioneer, and a war hero. Robinson had hobnobbed with world leaders, far exceeding the relatively narrow experiences of Tuskegee's provincial faculty. Indeed, Robinson was far more progressive, if not radical, as an advocate for black equality both in aviation and American life. In truth, he was well qualified for high placement at Tuskegee Institute, including as the head of Tuskegee's Department of Mechanical Industries, or even Washington's position.

After all, Washington possessed no aviation background, and "lacked the technical expertise to establish and conduct an aviation program himself." Without Robinson at Tuskegee Institute, Washington was able to rise higher in the years ahead. Eventually taking a high-level position that should have been first offered to Robinson, he would become the Director of the Division of Aeronautics, and would make the 1939 initiatives—inspired by Robinson's influence and aviation vision—for Tuskegee to become part of the Civilian Pilot Training Program, (CPTP), later the War Training Service Program (WTSP), that transformed African American students into Tuskegee Airmen. Perhaps these reasons also explain the halfhearted support Washington and Tuskegee Institute offered to Robinson.[39]

Therefore, Robinson made a novel proposition in an attempt to guarantee himself a long-term, serious commitment at his alma mater and to ensure that Tuskegee Institute became seriously committed to an aviation-training program with a real future. Robinson proposed the establishment of an autonomous school of aviation independent at Tuskegee Institute, the John C. Robinson School of Aviation.[40]

Robinson understood better than any of Tuskegee's officials that any hope for an aviation-training program to succeed required a serious commitment of resources, manpower, and facilities. To Robinson, this objective could only be accomplished if the aviation school acted autonomously from the institute. This was much like the argument of U.S. military air power proponents like General "Billy" Mitchell, who had long advocated that an air arm independent—instead of remaining part of the United States Army and subordinate to ground priorities—was necessary before modern air power could reach its full potential in wartime.

Robinson was fully prepared to utilize the John C. Robinson Aviation Fund monies for an aviation school at Tuskegee, as opposed to Tuskegee's officials using his fund for other departments, such as Washington's Department of Mechanical Industries. Robinson's proposed aviation school, however, especially if successful, would pose a direct threat to Washington, his department, and, most important, his promising future.

As could be expected, Washington rejected Robinson's proposal. Washington's final decision put an official end to Robinson's vision for an aviation school at Tuskegee in the 1930s, before wartime requirements would force the issue a half-decade later.[41]

Robinson had become thoroughly disillusioned with the self-serving motivations of Barnett, Washington, and other school officials. As with everything else in his life, Robinson would accept nothing short of total commitment to aviation, as he himself had been committed totally to building an airplane on his own, learning to fly, entering the Curtiss-Wright Aeronautical School as the first African American student, breaking racial barriers by becoming the first black instructor at the same prestigious institution, forming his aero clubs for black youth in Chicago, constructing an all-black airport almost from scratch, and faithfully serving Ethiopia and Emperor Selassie during a brutal conflict.

If Tuskegee Institute could not make the kind of total and serious commitment that Robinson knew was absolutely necessary, then he would go it alone. If he had to start an aviation program at Tuskegee Institute from scratch, with his own money, without adequate support, and based upon his own expertise and abilities, then why not start his own aeronautical school in a more favorable environment in the North? Most of all, he would not allow Tuskegee Institute, Barnett, Washington, or anyone else defer his great aviation dream—founding the John C. Robinson School of Aviation to reach a new generation of black youth.[42]

By this time, Robinson was a changed man, especially after his war experiences, brushes with death, and narrow escapes in Ethiopia. Tuskegee Institute had already lost some appeal to him. He evidently felt like it would be returning to the past if he taught at his alma mater, because he would have to endure the harshness of racial realities in the Jim Crow South.

Robinson had already accomplished too much both in his personal life and in aviation, seen too much of the world, and possessed too many varied experiences, to once again become a second class citizen in the Deep South. And after having been a longtime proven leader in both the civilian and military worlds, he was not prepared to start at the bottom at Tuskegee Institute as a new instructor, under the control of jealous senior instructors and administrators who knew nothing about aviation, war, or life, both in the North and overseas.

Therefore, by the summer of 1936 and at only age thirty-one, Robinson faced yet another key turning point. He now had a number of key decisions to make, even while suffering in health and some psychological trauma, attempting to readjust to American life, and dealing with his newfound fame. His private business—the automobile garage at 47 East 47th Street in south Chicago—was going well, and he sought stability in his personal life, after his return from Ethiopia. He evidently continued his married life with Earnize, who had operated the automobile repair shop in his long absence, in Bronzeville. Long familiar and content with Chicago life, Earnize had no desire to be torn from a more tolerant urban environment and to be suddenly—and perhaps for the first time—thrust into one of the most segregated and rural sections of the Deep South. The lives of both Robinson and his wife were firmly rooted on Chicago's South Side.

In addition, political and philosophical factors might well have existed in Robinson's mind by this time. Tuskegee Institute's image had become somewhat tainted in the eyes of black America. Booker T. Washington's policy of accommodation now seemed outdated and obsolete to more progressive, and especially activist and radical, African Americans. Some critical black leaders were even convinced that Washington and Tuskegee had sold out to the white man's world. One Chicago critic of Washington, who was now a Republican, was Julius F. Taylor, the editor of the free-swinging newspaper appropriately entitled, the *Broad Ax*.[43]

An angry Taylor criticized Tuskegee's founder as "the greatest white man's 'Nigger' in the world." He also called him "the Great Beggar of Tuskegee," because of his ceaseless efforts to solicit funds.[44]

Quite likely, Robinson possessed a comparable view. Like others, Robinson no doubt felt that Tuskegee's top priority was no longer the advancement of black youth. If so, this realization would also explain why Robinson decided not to teach aviation at Tuskegee Institute, the education aspiration of his childhood. Robinson fully understood that the real potential for black aviation and its future success in peacetime lay in the North.

ANOTHER AVIATION DREAM FULFILLED

Robinson now invested all his money and energy in the establishment of his own flying school to train both pilots and aviation mechanics and to support charter air services in the Chicago area. By late 1936, Robinson possessed one such designated aircraft, a four-seat Curtiss Robin, marked "John Robinson Airlines" across the fuselage. To ensure that Chicago would remain a vibrant center for black aviation, he planned to christen the new school of aviation and automobile instruction the John C. Robinson National Air College and School of Automotive Engineering, to be located at 44th South Parkway, now King Drive.[45]

Robinson possessed sufficient money from his speaking engagements and his automobile garage business that Earnize had operated efficiently for more than the past year, but to open his school, he now needed to tap into the resources collected in the John C. Robinson Aviation Fund. Robinson had been forced to bluntly confront Barnett because he refused to release the fund's monies to Robinson. Evidently, at some point during the summer of 1936, Barnett finally acquiesced, releasing the funds.[46]

In preparation for launching his aviation school, therefore, Robinson purchased a new training plane, a Cub, for more than $1,600. Robinson also invested much of his remaining monies in a down payment for a new SR-7C Stinson Reliant, a top-of-the-line blue and gray monoplane, NC 16161.

This recent model was a real beauty. Robinson would employ both new aircraft as trainers for his new flying school. In addition, Robinson used the Stinson for flights across the country on recruitment campaigns to solicit students and donations for the new school. Janet Harmon Bragg described Robinson's most prized aircraft as a "gull wing Stinson."[47]

To raise additional funds and to seek prospective students for the John C. Robinson National Air College and School of Automotive Engineering, Robinson continued his barnstorming campaign in the Midwest and South during the summer of 1936.[48]

While Robinson was busy establishing his own school, the menacing tide of fascism continued to rise unabated. In contrast to Ethiopia where Robinson fought as the lone African American from the conflict's beginning to end, the Spanish Civil War saw the participation of large numbers of American volunteers, both black and white, in the Abraham Lincoln Brigade. This bitter conflict erupted in the summer of 1936, just after Robinson's return to the United States. Fascist Dictator Francisco Franco overthrew the democratically elected republican Spanish government, and the people of Spain rose up. Both Hitler and Mussolini supplied thousands of men and aircraft to the Spanish fascists by the spring of 1937. Meanwhile volunteers—including many both black and white Americans—from the Western democracies went to Spain's aid in a people's struggle for democracy.

African American volunteers, including James Yates and Oliver Law, who commanded the racially integrated Abraham Lincoln brigade at one time, hailed from Chicago. Drawing the appropriate analogy that Robinson early and well understood, one volunteer emphasized that, for African Americans and freedom-loving people everywhere, "Ethiopia and Spain are our fight." However, this realization was accepted around the world primarily after Ethiopia's fall. Such common attitudes now contrasted sharply with those prevalent during the Italo-Ethiopian War, before white public sentiment and opinion had turned against fascism. And like Robinson's role in Ethiopia in 1935–1936, the struggle of black American volunteers in Spain was against the dual threat of "racism and fascism."[49]

Throughout the summer of 1936, meanwhile, Robinson continued to raise money with barnstorming flights around the United States. Finally, toward the end of September, yet another one of Robinson's aviation dreams became a reality. Officially certified by the Illinois Department of Commerce, the John C. Robinson National Air College and School of Automotive Engineering officially opened on September 28, 1936 on Chicago's South Side. Offering technical courses on all aspects of an aviation ground school, including aircraft engine mechanics, automotive mechanics, and flight instruction, this black technical and aviation educational institution broke new ground, being "the first of its kind for African Americans in the country."[50]

Robinson's school operated in buildings on the grounds of Poro College. His instructors were highly qualified, appealing to a wide range of students with various backgrounds. One instructor Robinson had chosen presented lectures in Spanish and French. The grand opening of Robinson's dual automotive and aviation school was leading news across black America. A top black New York City newspaper, the *Amsterdam News*, carried the headline to the people of New York City and Harlem: "Col. Robinson Starts own Aviation College,"[51] and the *Chicago Defender* entitled its story about the school's opening in the cool, early autumn weather in Chicago: "Col. Robinson's National Air College Stages Gala Opening."[52]

As Bragg wrote with pride, Robinson's new school was "located in the coach house behind Poro College for beauticians, operated by Anne Malone. [Cornelius R.] Coffey sometimes taught evening classes there, continuing his own flight instructions at Harlem Airport. Robinson, Walter Murray (a student), and I flew south in Robinson's [five-seat] gull-wing Stinson on a recruitment trip for the school. We had a forced landing in western Tennessee, but no one was injured and the plane was not damaged. The four-day flight created considerable interest among potential black students."[53]

Anne Malone, the enterprising African American millionaire who invited Robinson to move his school to her school's grounds, had opened Poro College in St. Louis in 1917. Her success stemmed from the lavish sales of her beauty products for black women. Seizing the opportunity, Malone's enterprise had been the first American company to tap extensively into this lucrative market. After relocating from St. Louis to Chicago's South Side in 1930 as its business expanded worldwide, the college thrived as a black cosmetics company that trained African Americans to distribute and sell the popular Poro line of products. Clearly, Robinson made a savvy business decision to locate his school in the large carriage house behind a stately Victorian mansion situated on the tree-lined grounds of Poro College. At this time, the college served as a busy social center for African Americans from Chicago and from across the United States. Malone was impressed by Robinson and his goal of opening the world of aviation to black youth, both men and women, and wanted to help him and a new generation.

Robinson's school was now accomplishing in Chicago what Tuskegee Institute was unable to do in the Deep South. Besides his own aviation expertise, Robinson could count on excellent technical and aviation support from key personnel in Chicago, many trained by him, unlike what would have been available to him at Tuskegee.

Robinson's school thrived thanks in part to six well-qualified aviation instructors, including Coffey, who taught courses by the following summer. In time, Coffey would open his own aeronautical college that would become part of the government's Civilian Pilot Training Program, CPTP, later the War Training Service Program (WTSP), which trained students to become Tuskegee Airmen. In addition, Robinson's old Gulfport friend, Harry Tartt, a future officer of the U.S. Army in World War II, also taught at his school.[54]

Meanwhile, Robinson's legacy and inspirational example continued to manifest itself far from America's shores in 1937. Dozens of zealous, young African Americans continued to serve with distinction in integrated units during the Spanish Civil War. Robinson's solo effort in Ethiopia served as an inspiring moral example to an entire generation of African Americans. Indeed, Robinson's Italo-Ethiopian War service reminded African Americans of how black America had failed Ethiopia in her hour of need. Now, as if to compensate, a good many black military volunteers continued to flock to Spain to serve in military roles to fight against fascism.[55]

After his close brushes with death in Ethiopia, Robinson wanted no part in another war in a far-away land, especially now that he had opened his aviation college. During the summer of 1937, Robinson again took to the skies in his "gull-wing Stinson" to spread aviation's positive message and to recruit students for his school.[56]

Flying with pilots Joe Muldrow—who was one of Robinson's students in the first black class at Curtiss-Wright Aeronautical School and also a Challenger Air Pilots' Association member, Frank Browning, and Malone, now a close friend, Robinson landed to much fanfare at the Glenview airport in Kansas City, Missouri, on the Fourth of July 1937.[57]

A July 9 newspaper story about Robinson's arrival in Kansas City was most revealing:

Ambitious to make American Negro youth air-minded, Col. John C. Robinson, chief of Haile Selassie's air forces during the Italo-Ethiopian war, landed his five-passenger monoplane in Kansas City municipal [airport] Sunday morning, July 4, to spend a few hours before continuing to Topeka where he spoke Sunday and Monday nights. The grey and blue 1937 Stinson monoplane—NC 16161—hit the runway of the airport at exactly 11:50 Sunday morning. Flying with the colonel were his two copilots, Frank Browning and Joe Muldrew [*sic*], both of Chicago; Mrs. Annie E. Malone, head of the Poro College of Chicago; and Miss Yutha Tolson, Kansas City, who has been in Chicago several weeks taking a special course at the Poro College. Colonel Robinson, Browning and Muldrew, after a few hours rest [then] continued to Topeka [Kansas]. . . . The flyer made the trip from Chicago to St. Louis in an hour and 40 minutes (the wind was against him, slowing his speed). The trip from Kansas City to Topeka was a 30-minute jaunt. Robinson and his copilots are making a tour in the interest of Colonel Robinson's school of aviation in Chicago in which 50 students already are enrolled, 40 white and 10 Negro. Colonel Robinson believes that aviation is a field with a great future for young Negroes who are well trained in aeronautics. At his school on the Poro College grounds in Chicago, established in September 1936, half a dozen instructors are busy teaching youths flying from the bottom up. . . . The Brown Condor will be in Mound Bayou, Miss., for the fiftieth anniversary celebration July 11–17. After that he plans to tour the Southwest in the interest of his flying school.[58]

Ironically, on the same day, this same African American newspaper, the *Kansas City Call*, printed an ugly reminder of what Robinson had left behind long ago: "Mississippi leads the lynch toll, with two persons lynched since January."[59]

During the last week of July, Robinson flew to Mound Bayou, Mississippi, just north of Greenwood, Mississippi, and just east of the Mississippi River. Amid the flat delta lands, Mound Bayou was celebrating its "50th anniversary as a self-governing 100% Negro community," in the words of a July 26, 1937, *Time* magazine article. On a "Jesse Owens Day," which one African American called "the most colorful of all days," the central attraction "was an Aviator, Colonel John C. Robinson, 'the Brown Condor of Ethiopia,' who landed with Mrs. Annie M. Turnbo Malone, president of Chicago Negro Poro College."[60]

Meanwhile, Robinson's school continued to flourish. During the summer of 1937, around fifty students, both black and white, took classes. One eager African American student, Bill Bertha, described the enlightening experience under Robinson's instruction as "very exciting, to be part of this new institution of learning."[61]

By this time, Robinson promoted himself through an "Official State Representative of Colonel John C. Robinson," Anselm J. Finch. He was Robinson's former roommate at Tuskegee Institute, and they had renewed their friendship after Robinson's return from Ethiopia. On July 27, 1937, Finch, at Robinson's urging, wrote a remarkable letter to a white state official at the Mississippi capital:

> We are trying to make the good-will flight of Colonel John C. Robinson [during] the greatest day of understanding in this state for many years. Colonel Robinson is the Negro's greatest aviator. He is proud of Mississippi and we are equally proud of him. He never fails to speak of his many friendly white friends in Mississippi, whether he is in Chicago, Illinois, or Gulfport, Mississippi. He is the same Robinson now [as] he was when he left Gulfport to work his way through school in the auto department. A group of leading colored citizens in and around Jackson mentioned you in our assembly a few hours ago, and suggested that inasmuch as you are interested in our future and the progress of Mississippi, that you will be glad to assist us by way of a contribution to our program of good-will. We have given Colonel Robinson a guarantee and naturally did so because of our faith in our friends. Our white friends in Mississippi have never failed us, and we have faith to believe that in any worthy cause they are still with us and glad to help us in our efforts. The co-operation we receive from our white friends will play the major part in determining the complete carrying out of our goodwill undertaking. With Robinson's saneness, good manners, politness [sic] and his thorough understanding of race relations in the South, his trip will mean much to us all. He is a graduate of Tuskegee and believes profoundly in Booker Washington's philosophy of life.[62]

After attempting to accomplish all that he could to assist the Ethiopian people from 1935–1936, Robinson was now orchestrating a bold initiative to improve racial relations in his native state, where racial conditions were at their worst. In his five-passenger Stinson, Robinson conducted his Mississippi goodwill flight on August 5.[63]

On August 7 Robinson landed in the state capital of Jackson. Here, he gave an interview to a *Clarion Ledger* reporter. The words of this white Mississippi journalist revealed a surprising degree of admiration and respect that he held for the young African American aviator, who must have astounded him, during this dark period in Mississippi history: "Col. John C. Robinson, the Mississippi negro who served as commander of the Ethiopian air corps. Nattily dressed in an olive-grey uniform that carries as insignia the royal crown of Ethiopia and boasts the coat of arms of the African ruler, [in fact] Robinson is an unassuming, rather deferential person. He talks in a quiet voice of" his many war experiences in faraway Ethiopia.[64]

After a speaking engagement at Jackson, Robinson then flew to Meridian. Here, he gave a passionate lecture to the disadvantaged black youth of a new senior high school. The newspaper reporter noted that when Robinson's "present tour is over, he will return to his flying school in Chicago."[65]

But while everything in the field of aviation was progressing for Robinson or perhaps because of that fact, problems developed in his personal life. At some point after his return from Ethiopia, Robinson's marriage broke down. Perhaps the lengthy separation of more than a year when he served in Ethiopia was too much to overcome for the young couple. Moreover, because of Earnize's urban background, far different from the generally more conservative lives of the church-going women of south Mississippi, Robinson's older sister Bertha "did not approve [of her] and there were problems."[66]

In addition, Earnize was also strong-willed and smart like her husband. The lengthy separation from May 1935 to the summer of 1936 only widened the gap between the two. She became much more independent, relying upon her own abilities in managing the automobile repair business, and doing a good job. And the war had changed Robinson. For whatever reason, the marriage was soon over. Even though highly disciplined in both his personal and professional life, Robinson also might not have remained faithful to his wife during his lengthy stay in Ethiopia, where the women were known to be "spectacularly beautiful." And Robinson was not only handsome, but also held high status in Ethiopia. Robinson also was a well-known "'ladies man' and evidently had many girlfriends," be it in Gulfport, Chicago, or Addis Ababa.[67]

After his marriage collapsed, Robinson reestablished closer ties with his family. Now teaching in Gulfport, Robinson's older sister, Bertha, and her children visited their famous uncle and his school in Chicago during this period. Bertha's son, John, who had been named in Robinson's honor, never forgot: "I can only remember as a small child visiting him at his airplane school with my younger brother (Andrew) inspecting and playing on his airplanes. My mother spoke highly of her brother and the difficulty he had as a result of segregation."[68]

Despite his personal difficulties, the period after his return from Ethiopia was generally a good one. The John C. Robinson National Air College was doing well, if not prospering despite the lingering effects of the Great Depression. He also taught an aviation course at Poro College. The head of the Department of Mechanical Industries at Tuskegee, George L. Washington, complimented Robinson, writing, "I know that you are well entrenched in Chicago and Illinois in your aviation mechanics work and have built up a great deal of good will in that section."[69]

In October 1937 Robinson was named "Illinois Aviation Consultant," which was widely promoted in the late October issue of the *Chicago Defender*.[70] In addition, Robinson earned extra income from air cargo delivery and commuter service jobs throughout this period. Times were good, and he had reason to be thankful.[71]

He also continued to barnstorm across the South during the fall. In October, Robinson was once again promoting aviation to black youth in Mississippi. Coffey described the strategy that paid dividends: "I was barnstorming all through the South with my partner, Johnny Robinson. He'd fly ahead in his gull-wing Stinson and give talks at [African American] churches and schools about flying and his experiences running Haile Selassie's air force in Ethiopia. Then he'd sell tickets for the rides and I'd fly in the next day and take people up."[72]

However, the on-and-off friendship between Robinson and Coffey was permanently shattered at some point after his return from Ethiopia. And the problem was not only about Coffey not coming to Robinson's assistance in Ethiopia as promised. It was also about the vivacious, beautiful Willa Brown. In early 1935 at a busy Walgreen's Pharmacy on Chicago's South Side, where she worked, Robinson had first recruited her as a member of his Challenger Air Pilots' Association, before he departed for his Ethiopia adventure. Evidently, Robinson had had an affair with her. But when Robinson was serving in Ethiopia in 1935–1936, Brown began seeing Coffey, whom she then married in 1937. Besides matters of love, Willa might had reaped the perfect revenge of a woman scorned, if in fact Robinson had left Willa behind and broken off the relationship to go to Ethiopia.[73]

Coffey and Brown eventually opened the Coffey School of Aeronautics, which was a carbon copy of Robinson's school, except that it lacked automotive training. Coffey had stolen Robinson's idea for establishing a black aviation school in Chicago. Robinson now faced new competition in the Chicago area, and from an only too familiar, if not uncomfortable, source.[74]

REFUSING TO ALLOW THE TUSKEGEE DREAM TO DIE

With the challenges of another world war on the horizon, Robinson had been Tuskegee's biggest supporter and strongest advocate for black pilot training since

1934, before his summer 1936 disagreements with Tuskegee officials. But Robinson, despite his clash of wills with Barnett and Washington (and the success of his own school in Chicago), still hoped that Tuskegee Institute would commit itself to opening up the field of aviation to black youth. Quite simply, he refused to allow the Tuskegee dream to die.

As early as the fall of 1936, Robinson had written a letter—less than six months after his return from Ethiopia—to George L. Washington that confounded school officials. Robinson presented an almost unbelievable offer to pick up and move his own aviation school and all of its equipment from Chicago to Tuskegee, if only Tuskegee Institute would pay the costs of transportation to the Deep South.[75]

And while his primary dream was to bring aviation to black youth, he discovered that his Chicago school was in fact drawing more white students than African Americans, simply because they had more money. With the nation's largest black population located in the South, a far larger number of potential African American students were available.

Washington passed the offer along to President Patterson, but refused to endorse Robinson's plan, however, and Patterson rejected Robinson's offer.[76]

Robinson was far more committed to an aviation program at the institute than were Tuskegee's officials. From May 1934 to nearly the beginning of World War II, Robinson was in fact Tuskegee's greatest aviation advocate.

At a time when almost all whites held serious doubts about the wisdom of training black pilots, Robinson remained true to his vision. As he explained in letter on May 29, 1939: "From my sixteen years [or] more of experience in the mechanical world of which twelve years have been devoted to the specialization of aviation and, from the experience I have gathered from my travels in over eighteen different countries and observing aeronautical schools and training programs that without any doubt, Tuskegee is the most logical place to be designated for Negro [pilot] training."[77]

But Robinson's long-time influence would play another key role in ensuring that one day the Tuskegee Airmen story would become a reality. The core members of the Challenger Air Pilots' Association formed a new organization, the National Airmen's Association of America, the NAAA. The sole purpose of this association was to aggressively advocate for black participation in the all-white Civilian Pilot Training Program, CPTP. The federal government had set up the CPTP to train military reserve pilots who would be activated for military service once America entered World War II. Black participation in this organization would guarantee that African American pilots would soon be flying in military uniforms in wartime.

Coffey, Robinson's old student, was elected the NAAA's president. Some NAAA members included Willa Brown, Janet Harmon Bragg, and Harold Hurd. Both Bragg and Hurd were Robinson's former students at Curtiss-Wright Aeronautical School. All these young aviators had been members of the old Challenger Aero Club, along with Grover Nash and Dale L. White.[78]

In May 1939 with Germany's invasion of Poland less than four months away, two hopeful NAAA flyers, Chauncey E. Spencer and White, both members of Robinson's former aero club, flew to Washington, D.C. They were determined to plead the case for black CPTP participation in person to white government officials in the nation's capital. Sponsored by the NAAA and the influential *Chicago Defender*, Spencer and White's journey to the nation's capital was in itself a historic flight: a three thousand mile round trip.

After landing safety in Washington, D.C., and in company with civil rights leader Edgar G. Brown, who presided over the government employees union, the two NAAA flyers accidentally encountered Senator Harry S. Truman. This chance meeting with the straight-talking Missouri senator allowed a rare opportunity for Spencer and White to expound at length upon their historic flight and to show off their aircraft. More important, they emphasized to the surprisingly receptive Truman that black aviators should be included in the CPTP.

Open-minded despite his family's Confederate heritage and his rural roots, Truman played a vital role in influencing President Franklin D. Roosevelt, his wife Eleanor, and other top government officials, to embrace the revolutionary concept of black military aviators. As NAAA members believed, "through our efforts [by way of Truman] blacks were able to participate in the Civilian Pilot Training Program."[79]

Indeed, Truman "put through legislation insuring that Negroes would be trained along with whites in the Civilian Pilot Training Program." Senator Everett M. Dirksen of Illinois was another supporter influenced by these bold black Illinois flyers and the NAAA's initiative. The combined efforts and influence of Truman and Dirksen, two rising senators who represented neighboring states, and the NAAA, were successful. In 1939, African Americans gained admission into the CPTP. Half a dozen black colleges in the east—including Hampton and Howard

Universities—and two nonacademic flying schools in the Midwest—became part of the federal aviation program in 1939. But significantly, no black university in the Deep South had been selected because of the more delicate racial situation.

The Civilian Pilot Training Act was officially approved in June 1939. This act opened the door to include blacks already trained by the federally funded CPTP to enter the Army Air Corps in large numbers. No longer could black CPTP-trained pilots be legally denied participation in the Air Corps—despite the opposition of elitist General Henry "Hap" Arnold and other anti-black Air Corps leaders, mostly because the government's primary objective was now to quickly create a large cadre of civilian pilots, after concluding that air power would play a vital role in the upcoming world conflict.

For the first time, race became a secondary priority as the Army Air Corps urgently increased its strength, training tens of thousands of pilots beyond the capabilities of the few Air Corps pilot training bases, such as Kelly and Randolph Army Air Fields at San Antonio, Texas. Consequently, black and white civilian schools—both academic institutions and flying schools—would now launch pilot training programs to compensate for this deficiency: an essential step in the creation of a strong army air arm. Robinson could now envision thousands of young African Americans flying as military aviators and fighting against fascism in the future.[80]

After learning that the Federal Government might allow black education institutions and flying schools to become part of the CPTP, Robinson desired to play a prominent role. Robinson was eager to volunteer his services to Tuskegee Institute, even though it had yet to enter the Civil Aeronautics Authority (CAA) pilot training program. While Hampton University's president had successfully initiated early efforts to join the federal pilot training program, Tuskegee president Patterson, had not done so until March 22, 1939, when he offered Tuskegee's facilities to the Federal Government for the "effort to train Negro pilots and mechanics in the field of aviation."

On April 1, 1939, without yet knowing of Patterson's offer, Robinson volunteered to serve as Tuskegee's primary flight instructor—a considerable personal sacrifice—in the hopes that Tuskegee Institute would soon become part of the CPTP, and on the sole condition that Tuskegee would do so. The John C. Robinson National Air College in Chicago was in full swing. Robinson had invested a total of nearly $20,000 in aviation equipment from 1936 to 1938 to modernize his evergrowing aviation school, which was now registered with the CAA. Nevertheless,

Robinson penned his lengthy letter to President Patterson on April 1, 1939, offering his aviation services to Tuskegee as the head flight instructor.[81]

Indeed, Robinson emphasized the considerable "publicity and agitation [that he had] carried on in Chicago" for larger African American participation in the civilian and military pilot training programs, and he hoped that Tuskegee would play a leading role. President Patterson responded quickly and with enthusiasm. Patterson stated that Tuskegee would indeed be "highly interested" in Robinson's services as Tuskegee's chief flight instructor in the future, if Tuskegee Institute definitely became part of the CPTP. Robinson also learned that Patterson had inquired about participation in the CPTP, but nothing had been decided yet.[82]

Robinson felt encouraged by President Patterson's response. He was enthusiastic at the prospect of becoming Tuskegee's head flight instructor and part of the CAA program. If his ambitious aviation plans for Tuskegee developed as he desired, Robinson would then embark upon an exciting, new enterprise that would eventually open the door for equality to all blacks in the future.

Therefore, Robinson wrote a letter to G. L. Washington, head of Tuskegee's Department of Mechanical Industries on May 23, 1939. And he again penned a letter to President Patterson on May 29. Robinson was becoming increasingly concerned, feeling more anxiety about Tuskegee's prospects for gaining entry to the CPTP. From what he considered reliable sources, Robinson had learned that "no Negro [flight] school will be designated in the South."[83]

Robinson worried that Wilberforce University in Ohio, a northern educational institution with solid aviation experience and reputation, located closer to a leading Air Corps base, Wright-Patterson near Dayton, would gain pilot training for African Americans, winning out over Tuskegee's bid. Nevertheless, Robinson was still interested in teaching aviation at Tuskegee, hoping for the best for the future of his old alma mater.[84]

Robinson's May 29, 1939, letter to Patterson included another proposal: if the government decided that no black pilot training school would be established in the South—a real concern because of omnipresent racial tensions—then perhaps Tuskegee could win acceptance into the CPTP if Robinson's Chicago school was utilized by Tuskegee as an extension of its aviation program. He proposed that after completing ground training at Tuskegee, future black pilots could then journey to Chicago to receive their flight training at the John C. Robinson National Air College.[85]

Robinson's plan made good sense for a number of reasons. First and foremost, he aimed at undercutting the distinct advantages enjoyed by Wilberforce University. He realized that the novel concept of black pilot military training had a much greater chance of succeeding outside the South. In contrast, young black pilots in intense and lengthy aviation training would benefit from a more supportive environment in the vibrant African American community on Chicago's South Side. In addition, Robinson's aviation school was already an established aeronautical institution with a solid track record and a prestigious CAA registration.

As Robinson emphasized "Chicago, being the hub of aviation; Chicago, having the busiest airport in the world; Chicago, having unlimited opportunities in all phases of aviation, should be the most logical place for the [aviation] student to have contact so that their ideas and views could be broadened and their imagination could be increased in the aeronautical world. Then too, they would have an opportunity to mingle with many outstanding people in the field of aviation—being able to go into the different factories—being able to meet many of the inspectors and being able to be exposed to every possible opportunity in the field of aviation to help carry them and help inspire them to do the bigger and better things in the aeronautical world."[86]

Unfortunately, Robinson's plan was far too ambitious for Patterson and Washington. As the head of the Department of Mechanical Industries, therefore, Washington emphasized to Robinson that such an enterprising aviation initiative with America's entry into war on the horizon would be possible only if "adequate funds and teaching facilities for this work are available."[87]

But in truth, while Robinson envisioned Tuskegee Institute as playing a key role in the flight training of African Americans in uniform, the conservative Tuskegee Institute leaders had yet to embrace such a futuristic aviation vision at this time. Washington, an unimaginative, stuffy bureaucrat, summarized in a letter to Robinson what would be a missed opportunity, because of Tuskegee officials' lack of faith in the future important role of hundreds of black pilots flying for America in the U.S. Army Air Corps. Indeed, Washington emphasized that he was far "more concerned and interested in training [for African Americans] for serving airplanes [instead of flying them and] I feel that the Negro has better opportunity of immediate employment in that connection."[88] Unfortunately, therefore, Patterson and Washington only contemplated technical and mechanical aviation training for African Americans at Tuskegee Institute to service aircraft instead of training pilots to fly and fight against the fascist enemies of America.[89]

In addition, besides all-important financial considerations, a combination of other factors also conspired to ensure that Robinson's school would not function as an aviation extension program in Chicago for Tuskegee: the War Department's cynical decision to establish black training at army air fields in the South, in part to enhance the possibility of failure; Tuskegee's officials' provincial thinking about the North; the Coffey School of Aeronautics in Chicago and the Chicago School of Aeronautics in Chicago—the only two such schools in the same city, becoming part of the CPTP, resulting perhaps from politics and because of Coffey's advantage of having located his school at Harlem Airport on the South Side and the effective lobbying efforts by the Chicago mayor and Illinois senators, especially Dirksen, on behalf of Coffey's school; the lingering distrust and misunderstanding between Robinson and Tuskegee officials stemming from disagreements that began in 1936; the considerable political influence of Tuskegee trustee Barnett, who was no longer a Robinson ally; the expiration of Robinson's commercial license; the ultra-conservative nature of Tuskegee leaders and their passive, hesitant, and "low-key approach to the whole idea of participating in flight training operations"; and G. L. Washington's probable fear of losing the leadership of Tuskegee's aviation program to Robinson and perhaps his own personal antagonism and envy toward the idol of African American communities across the land.[90]

Now part of the government aviation program, Coffey's aviation school, which ironically had been modeled after Robinson's, was destined to become part of the Tuskegee Airmen story. Not discouraged, Robinson continued to be a strong vocal advocate for equal rights by promoting black military aviation, especially pilots. In a late December 1939 conversation with Harold S. Darr, a good friend of Robinson who operated the Chicago School of Aeronautics, a private flight school that flew planes out of Harlem Airport and the Glenview Flying Field just north of Chicago, Robinson proposed teaching black cadets at Wendell Phillips High School on the South Side and at Ashburn Field in Bronzeville. In fact, Robinson kept one of his own aircraft at Glenview.

Robinson then advocated that African Americans "should be admitted to primary training" as pilots, just like white airmen—yet another typical Robinson call for complete equality. Like so many others, however, Darr thought Robinson's idea was too radical and that the "social contact might be too much to swallow [for the Air Corps] at one time." Indeed, Robinson's concepts challenged segregation and racism. Despite the success of CPTP black students, the ever-elitist Air Corps still balked at such a revolutionary concept (a perceived threat to Jim Crow and the status quo as black pilots would be black officers ranking above white enlisted soldiers) even as late as the fall of 1940, and even after the start of World War II.[91]

While Darr believed that full integration was too much to expect, Robinson did not. He viewed the war as a golden opportunity. He, therefore, proposed a solution. To accommodate the Air Corps' desire not to integrate and to observe Jim Crow realities that were the law of the land, Robinson proposed the novel concept of billeting black airmen in the African American community on the South Side, and then driving them to the Curtiss-Wright Aeronautical School for their flight training.[92]

Eventually, two black CPTP units would be established in the Chicago area. One of these aviation units would be situated on the South Side at the Coffey School of Aeronautics and the other at the Chicago School of Aeronautics. Since Robinson and Darr were close friends, Robinson even played a key role in this story. Indeed, because Darr had "considerable confidence" in Robinson's aviation abilities, the native Mississippian would serve as the chief flight instructor for this black flight training program centered at Ashburn Field on Chicago's South Side.[93]

During the summer of 1940, meanwhile, Washington attempted to secure flight instructors for Tuskegee, now finally part of the CPTP, after at last learning that pilot training would come to Tuskegee. Washington immediately thought of Robinson, but it was too late. Besides his duties and responsibilities at his school in Chicago, Robinson's commercial license—a requirement for flight trainers at Tuskegee—had expired by this time.[94]

Robinson, who was cynical in regard to race relations, and did not fully appreciate Roosevelt's ambitions to court the black Democratic vote, was convinced that the government was not really serious about including black Air Corps flyers. Indeed, Air Corps leadership rejected the idea until eventually ordered by the War Department to relent in the autumn of 1940.

In November 1940, Robinson denounced the government's hesitancy to include African American airmen, especially pilots, in the Air Corps. Despite the war having begun more than a year before and the realization that America's entry into the conflict was inevitable, no blacks had yet received any type of military pilot training—just CPTP, or civilian, training. Robinson, consequently, declared that the government's plans—still unspecified and unclear—to train black pilots for military service in Chicago was merely a facade. An increasingly angry Robinson felt the U.S. government and the War Department had made only token steps, which had been "set up to save the face of the Army and as an excuse not to admit Negroes into the Army Air Corps."[95]

From beginning to end, Robinson remained a strong equal rights advocate for blacks—military or civilian, male or female—in aviation. Despite hoping for the best, Robinson continued to focus on further developing and promoting his own aviation school. He had more than one hundred students, most of them white. At this time, one of Robinson's most promising black students was Pennsylvania-born Charles Alfred Anderson. Only two years younger than his mentor, Anderson became Robinson's most devoted student.

The capable Anderson qualified as a CPTP Instructor and was then certified by the CAA, through the Department of Commerce. Anderson, and not Robinson, would become the main flight instructor at Tuskegee Army Air Field during World War II. During the war, Anderson would evolve into an inspirational leader to hundreds of young Tuskegee Airmen.[96]

THE TUSKEGEE AIRMEN STORY

Robinson's passion to play a key role at Tuskegee Institute, with America gearing up for war, was as appropriate as it was symbolic. After all, Robinson's entire life seemed to have been in preparation for such a dramatic moment in black aviation history.

Contrary to the popular belief, the legacy of the Tuskegee Airmen had in fact not first taken shape when Tuskegee was initially selected as the CPTP location for black pilot training in 1939. That genesis had come more than a half-decade before, with Robinson's flight to Tuskegee in May 1934 and his repeated attempts to establish a program of aviation instruction at the institute.[97]

Robinson's rise in prominence as the "colored Lindy" in the 1930s played a key role in generating more widespread efforts in pressuring the government and the War Department to include African Americans in pilot training. Inspired in no small part by Robinson's leading wartime role, African Americans insisted on admission as pilots into the Army Air Corps by pointing to their most tangible and inspirational example of a black pilot in both a leadership role and in a wartime environment, the legendary Brown Condor.

What had been impossible for black pressure groups, including the NAACP, before 1935–1936, became possible in large part due to the enduring legacy of Robinson's wartime service in Ethiopia. Most of all, Robinson's example paved the way for an entire generation of African American aviators aspiring to serve in uniform. His many achievements in Ethiopia's skies in peace and war made a mockery of America's timeworn racial stereotypes, dismantling the long-standing myth that blacks could not be pilots.[98]

Robinson's well-publicized achievements also helped to convince the U.S. government of the wisdom of employing black aviators in wartime. It was no mere coincidence that not long after Robinson's return to America from Ethiopia in 1936 that the Roosevelt administration had first demonstrated the first initial signs of a "new responsiveness to racial issues [that] might be used to support black aviation," which developed in 1936.[99]

Less than two years after Robinson had proved to black America what an African American military aviator could accomplish as the commander of the Imperial Ethiopian Air Force, black advocates began to aggressively promote the concept of African American pilots serving in the U.S. Army Air Corps in 1938, after President Roosevelt announced support for a ten-thousand-airplane air force with America's entry into World War II drawing near.[100]

One disgusted journalist from the Associated Negro Press in early December 1938 emphasized not only the inequality, but also the discriminatory situation of barring black pilots from the Air Corps by pointing specifically to Colonel Robinson's shining performance in Ethiopia, ironically at a time when he could not use a white restroom or eat at a white restaurant in the South.[101]

Indeed, employing the popular example of Robinson, the black Lindbergh, and his undeniable accomplishments to expose the folly of the government's exclusion of African Americans from the Air Corps was a brilliant stroke. Support from black leaders and civil and equal rights organizations to promote the participation of African Americans in the Air Corps coincided with the emergence of a new generation of young African Americans, who now knew that military service as pilots in wartime was possible. Robinson had played a decisive role in inspiring and opening "the eyes of a new generation of black youth to the possibilities in the air," the future Tuskegee Airmen.[102]

One such individual was Lawrence E. Roberts, who was born in Vauxhall, New Jersey, in 1922. As a child, he dreamed of becoming an aviator in part from the wartime exploits of the Brown Condor and by Robinson's arrival in nearby New York City. His gifted daughter, Robin Roberts, who gained a national reputation as a leading journalist and sports broadcaster, explained how, "When I really stop to think in the 1930s he had the nerve to take a broomstick handle, go down to his basement in New Jersey, and dream about flying when blacks in this country had very little, if any, rights . . . and for him to not only dream it, but make it a reality and be a part of the Tuskegee Airmen." Indeed, Roberts became a Tuskegee Airman in 1944, flying for America in the struggle against fascism.[103]

But Robinson was not simply inspirational to a new generation of African Americans. Before World War II, Robinson and other black Chicago aviators, including Coffey, "encouraged the U.S. government to admit African Americans to the Civilian Pilot Training Program (CPTP), which helped to train civilian pilots for emergency duty during wartime. With the support of other groups, such as the NAACP, their efforts were successful, and the CPTP was opened up to African Americans in 1939."[104]

In early 1940 Robinson took another step to help make the dreams of black aviators in uniform come true. Developing his own plans to minimize military expenses—in the hope of helping to convince Air Corps leaders to be more responsive to the revolutionary concept of black military pilots, Robinson created an aviation mechanics training program sponsored by the National Youth Administration (NYA) and operated in conjunction with the Chicago School of Aviation. He wrote:

> I worked out a program between the Civilian Army School at Glenview and the N.Y.A. [National Youth Administration]; where the N.Y.A. Resident boys would work 100 hours per month with the Civilian Army School. All expenses [were] paid by the N.Y.A., without any expense to the Army School. I scheduled these boys so that at least ten would be on duty at all times. Their duty was helping maintain and service ships used by the Civilian Army Training Program. They worked under the supervision of three experienced mechanics. These boys had had a minimum of six months' training in my school here and their work was so satisfactory that they were all hired by the Army Program and are being transferred to Georgia; they leave next month. Incidental[ly,] there were white boys that trained under my supervision.[105]

During this period, Robinson also acted as an aviation consultant to the NYA. He supervised the NYA's mechanical school locations in Illinois. All the while, Robinson also continued to operate his own school and train more aviators.[106]

In overall terms, thanks to Robinson's influence, inspirational example, and tireless efforts, Tuskegee Institute would be well placed to become part of the government's CPTP by the time America entered World War II with the Japanese attack on Pearl Harbor, Hawaii, on December 7, 1941.

Ironically, G. L. Washington was named the Director of Aviation Training at Tuskegee—a development that would not have happened had Robinson not first brought aviation to Tuskegee in May 1934, or if he had moved his own Chicago aviation school to Tuskegee as he had proposed.

Brig. Gen. Walter R. Weaver, commanding the Southeastern Air Corps Training Center at Maxwell, Alabama, placed Tuskegee's upcoming important role into perspective: "The negro population deserved a successful experiment in flying training; the success of negro youth in the Air Corps hinged upon the fate of the Tuskegee project."[107]

At last, despite having missed an opportunity to have played a larger role in the Tuskegee Airmen story, Robinson was overjoyed by the news that military aviation and pilot training had finally come to Tuskegee. Government funding was now no longer a serious concern for a recently isolationist nation now attempting to play catch-up in preparing for World War II.[108]

Once again, therefore, Robinson's long-time dream of playing a significant role at Tuskegee was rekindled in February 1941. The War Department established the date of August 23, 1941, as the beginning of the so-called Tuskegee flight program. Now, for the first time in American history, African American cadets would receive military training as pilots. Tuskegee, and specifically Washington, needed highly experienced instructors for the hundreds of young men who wanted to become pilots. Even though Tuskegee already had two flight instructors—Charles Alfred Anderson, known as "Chief," and Lewis Jackson—Robinson still remained an ideal choice.[109]

But before the final decision to allow black pilots into the Air Corps, Robinson had explained the success of his own NYA-sponsored program for training aviation mechanics in connection with the Chicago School of Aviation and proposed a new plan to enhance the changes for pilot training at Tuskegee to Washington in a February 20, 1941, letter:

I am sure the same set up can be worked out in connection with your program there. I have fifteen of our boys who have had at least 12 or more months of [aviation mechanics] training, all high school graduates and would like to come down [to Tuskegee] under any condition[s] and work. I also have two good mechanics who are supervisors here [in Chicago] in Aviation and who would like to come down and work. These two men are graduates of Curtiss Wright and have good, very good mechanical background and experience. [With] these two men [with me] I could very easily take care of all the Mechanical School instructions on the defense program [as well as] service and maintain all of the flight equipment that will be put there. In other words with these two mechanics and the N.Y.A. boys I could maintain and service a minimum of 25 planes [as well as provide] mechanical instructions."[110]

Robinson suggested that President Patterson work through a leading NYA advisor, Mary McLeod Bethune, with the goal of having the NYA director of Illinois officially designate Robinson's aviation equipment at the John C. Robinson National Air College as surplus. This development would create a favorable situation by which the NYA of Alabama could then request that this "surplus" was required to provide Tuskegee with a ready-made aviation mechanical school.[111]

Robinson was optimistic. As he described in his letter on February 20, he emphasized to Washington that his ambitious aviation vision for Tuskegee could be realized based upon "if this deal can be turned, this would give us a complete Mechanical School [at Tuskegee] at once. There is plenty of Aviation Equipment laying [sic] around in Illinois, that is not being used at all, and I sincerely believe through Mrs. Bethune you can get the equipment I am using" in Chicago.[112]

Throughout the late winter and early spring of 1941, Robinson continued to implore Tuskegee's top officials and Bethune to unite on a workable plan of getting his NYA Chicago aviation mechanics training program transferred to Tuskegee. By May 1941 and barely six months after the United States entered the war, Robinson's vision was finally becoming a reality. Indeed, the NYA officials in Alabama "agreed to the plan in principal."[113]

Robinson was so enthusiastic that he flew from Chicago to Tuskegee in early May 1941. Here, he discussed future possibilities with Washington, who was within only days of obtaining official approval to hire several new aviation instructors for Tuskegee. It now seemed as if Robinson's longtime ambition of playing a leading role in military aviation training at Tuskegee was about to happen after all.[114]

A strange fate intervened at the last minute, however. The conference with Washington was cut short when Robinson was surprised to receive a telegram indicating either personal, professional, or financial problems awaited him back in Chicago. He was forced to immediately depart Tuskegee to clear up what, in Robinson's words, was an ill-timed "difficulty."[115]

From Chicago on May 20, 1941, Robinson wrote a long letter to Washington to explain the situation—now also complicated because he had just accepted a new, well-paying position with the Chicago Board of Education and because of his personal commitment to his students and employees of his Chicago flying school—that forced him to turn down Washington's mid-May job offer as flight instructor at Tuskegee at the last minute:

> I am sorry that we could not get together on something definite when I was at Tuskegee, because I definitely set my mind on trying to work out something in connection with Tuskegee if I didn't have to sacrifice too much of the experience and standing that I have in the aeronautical world. Its seems as though it just isn't in the books for me to be connected with Tuskegee in a technical way because every time I am approached to make direct negotiations I cannot get together with [you] or something seems to step in up here in Chicago. I regret this situation very much, but under the present conditions that I am working I would be definitely working against myself financially to come down now. Keep in mind that I want to do everything in my power to assist you in any way that I can from this end up here.[116]

Despite his repeated aviation initiatives to Tuskegee for nearly seven years beginning in 1934, Robinson would never teach young black military pilots at his alma mater. Instead, his student Charles Alfred Anderson, the first black in the United States to earn a commercial pilot's license in the early 1930s, served as the head of the new army flying school at Tuskegee. Born in 1906, "Chief" Anderson would train hundreds of aviation cadets, including the first class, during the primary phase of flight training at Tuskegee Army Air Field.[117]

What other factors could possibly explain Robinson's sudden change of mind, after he had lobbied for years for the coveted position? First and foremost, Washington and Robinson had been at odds for some time. Some upset Tuskegee graduates had even written Washington to complain that, in Washington's words, "we have not been sincere in seeking [Robinson's] services" at Tuskegee.[118]

Another explanation was that Robinson entertained the possibility of becoming the commander of the 99th Pursuit Squadron, the first all-black aviation unit in the army's history. At that time, Robinson had stated to Washington that he was interested in "becoming the 99th [Pursuit and later Fighter] Squadron Commander."[119]

Contrary to his desire, however, Robinson would never wear the uniform of a U.S. officer. Robinson was in fact eager to become a Tuskegee Airman, and serve the United States as he had served Ethiopia in 1935–1936. Harry Tartt, who became a World War II officer, stated that Robinson "wanted to be a colonel but the army only offered him the rank of second lieutenant." Rejecting the offer, after having served with a colonel's rank in commanding the Imperial Ethiopian Air Force and with more military aviation wartime experience than most officers in the Air Corps, Robinson merely responded to the offer by declaring quite correctly, "Second Lieutenants are a dime a dozen."[120]

In the prime of life and still basking in the lofty reputation as the premier military aviator and wartime hero of black America at only age thirty-five, Robinson was not without justification for this seemingly egotistical view. A young African American fresh out of college and without prior military or flying experience could now become a fighter pilot and obtain a second lieutenant's rank in the Air Corps, after successfully completing pilot training at Tuskegee Army Air Field. Robinson, consequently, felt underappreciated by the offer, because he was now in fact the most famous aviator in black America. Robinson already possessed far more flying time and combat experience than any of the men, officers or enlisted, who would become Tuskegee Airmen. Robinson subsequently felt that he was fully qualified to lead the 99th Pursuit Squadron in the war against Germany and, appropriately, Italy. In addition, such a highly visible role would allow Robinson to garner more wartime support and volunteers from black America.

Robinson, however, possessed no prior experience in the U.S. military. He, therefore, was without those vital military, and especially political, connections that were essential to taking command of the Tuskegee Airmen of the 99th Pursuit Squadron. He had seen a good deal of modern warfare in Ethiopia—especially Italy's ruthless brand of blitzkrieg warfare—unlike the Tuskegee Airmen's new, young leader, Colonel Benjamin Oliver Davis Jr., who possessed neither combat experience, nor military aviation experience.

Davis, however, had powerful connections. He enjoyed considerable military and political clout. He was a West Point graduate and the son of America's first black general, and was the highest-ranking African American military officer in the United States. Moreover, the Ethiopian war was too foreign and too far away to influence Robinson's chances at command. Consequently, Davis, and not Robinson, would hold a colonel's rank and command the Tuskegee Airmen.

Robinson's situation was especially ironic because he was in so many ways the father of the Tuskegee Airmen. The reality of pilot training at Tuskegee was very much the fruits of Robinson's early initiatives, influence, and repeated efforts to transform a largely agricultural school into the premier center of black aviation as early as 1934.

Whereas Robinson had seen with clarity how civilian aviation—and later military aviation—was the key to Tuskegee's future and for the social, economic, and political advancement of African Americans, his grand aviation vision had been premature in the 1930s because of the Great Depression and Tuskegee's conservative institutional culture. Robinson had grasped early the importance of black pilot training, both civilian and military at Tuskegee long before the institute's officials or anyone else for that matter. It had taken the crisis of the greatest war in human history, however, to finally turn Robinson's vision into reality. Indeed, combined with his wartime example in Ethiopia, Robinson's early aviation initiatives and repeated efforts at Tuskegee Institute had planted the seed and laid the foundation that was essential for the eventual emergence of the Tuskegee Airmen pilots and their unforgettable role in World War II.

Ironically, beyond a higher level of aviation and wartime experience and demonstrated leadership ability, Robinson also might have been even more qualified than the unproven Colonel Davis to lead the Tuskegee Airmen, because he possessed a widespread popularity among the black community. Robinson's national reputation as the Brown Condor of Ethiopia, and the fact that he was a pioneer and long-time advocate of black aviation, would have served as a catalyst for larger numbers of African American recruits to join the service. Robinson was, in fact, the most inspirational wartime model for the Tuskegee Airmen generation.[121]

Tuskegee Airman Lewis J. Lynch was one young man who was inspired by Robinson's leadership role in Ethiopia. He had learned about the Brown Condor from the many stories printed about Robinson in the *Pittsburgh Courier*.[122]

Like so many other young black men of his generation, Lynch emphasized how Robinson's inspiring influence and example was all-important in demonstrating to him and his generation of young African Americans, both in the North and South, "that a black man could fly."[123]

During the Golden Age of Aviation, Robinson—the second African American to engage in aerial combat in history and first ever to command an air force was the most important military aviation inspirational influence for black Americans. A young African American inspired by Robinson's wartime example explained in the late 1930s of the significant emotional and psychological impact of Colonel Robinson's influential legacy: "I intend to fly some day at any cost. I'd like to . . . study [aviation] under that fellow who flew for Haile Selassie. That's the kind of life I [would] like" for myself.[124] Indeed, by this time Robinson was widely acclaimed as "the greatest Race flyer the world knows today."[125]

Most significant, Robinson's role in Ethiopia provided the future Tuskegee Airmen with an unprecedented moral example of battling against fascism at a time before white America realized it was the world's most serious threat. Robinson's lengthy list of achievements in Ethiopia demonstrated to the Tuskegee Airmen generation how African Americans, whose patriotism and loyalty were questioned by the U.S. government, must take a stand by fighting against fascism and totalitarianism, as well as racism. Robinson had demonstrated that this was a crusade of good versus evil and right versus wrong. Symbolically, one primary military theater of operations for the Tuskegee Airmen would be Italy.

Because he had demonstrated the spirit of Pan-Africanism, black solidarity, and militant activism during wartime in Ethiopia, Robinson also proved that it was important to turn away momentarily from the issues of racism at home in order to confront it abroad, thus illustrating the importance of fighting racism everywhere in what was essentially a universal conflict for human rights. Robinson had also shown black America that Ethiopia's dismal fate, the extinction of a proud, independent East African nation, could befall other countries if fascism and racism were allowed to run unchecked.[126]

Thus, Robinson himself was not really needed at Tuskegee during the war years, because he had already made his most lasting contributions as an inspirational example of the limitless possibilities that existed for black aviators. Robinson's accomplishments, widespread influence, and moral example had already affected the Tuskegee Airmen story in two vital ways: 1) inspiring the Tuskegee Airmen generation by personal example, and 2) repeatedly nurturing the aviation dream, especially flight training, at Tuskegee Institute to fulfill its destiny.

Indeed, in the end, Robinson laid the vital foundation for the eventual rise of the Tuskegee Airmen. He opened the door for black pilots, and the dawning of a new day for all African Americans, as he had long envisioned.

10

THE WINDS OF WORLD WAR

IRONICALLY, "BLACK AMERICA'S best-known aviator" would not play a leading role at Tuskegee Army Air Field throughout the World War II years. Not having Robinson's leadership at Tuskegee was a blow to the program, especially in
the beginning. Indeed, Robinson's absence "from a public relations standpoint . . .
was regrettable" for not only Tuskegee but also black America.[1] After all, Tuskegee trustee Barnett, as he had emphasized to the school president Patterson in late
February 1941, understood the "tremendous . . . publicity value in Colonel Robinson."[2] And now Tuskegee would miss an opportunity to reap the considerable
"publicity value" of Robinson's fame at the beginning of the program when it was
under close scrutiny and criticism, and when so many opponents, including top
anti-black Air Corps leaders, hoped for its failure.

Indignation among blacks rose when it became known that training for the
first Tuskegee Airmen unit, the 99th Pursuit Squadron, would be segregated. Because neither the U.S. Army nor the Air Corps would integrate, the black press,
including the *Chicago Defender* and organizations such as the National Airmen's
Association, increasingly criticized the institutionalized racism of the American
military. This mounting tide "damaged Tuskegee Institute's prestige and Robinson's active involvement [at Tuskegee] would have helped restore the school's
status."[3]

Even Judge William Hastie, an African American leader who had been appointed by President Roosevelt as a civilian aide to assist the Secretary of War on
black-related issues, condemned Tuskegee because he believed that blacks should
train with the same advantages—long advocated by Robinson—as whites. An angry

Hastie denounced Tuskegee for "working hand in glove with the Army Air Command to establish, entrench, and extend a Jim Crow air training program at Tuskegee. Such conduct should be exposed and condemned."[4]

In addition to Robinson, black America had also become disillusioned with Tuskegee by the start of World War II. Tuskegee seemed to have betrayed its own most cherished principles because of "selfish and shortsighted scheming for immediate personal advantage with cynical disregard for the larger interests of the Negro and of the nation," charged Judge Hastie, whose views echoed Robinson's.[5]

Even though the dream of Tuskegee was behind him, Robinson was still eager to serve his nation in World War II, despite his new position with the Chicago Board of Education and the success of the John C. Robinson National Air College. Because he had been denied what he had deemed an appropriate colonel's rank in the Army Air Corps, he now served in a civilian role. Robinson became an aviation instructor at the Biloxi Army Air Corps Technical School at Keesler Field, Biloxi, Mississippi, situated just east of his hometown of Gulfport.[6]

For the thousands of new recruits who needed technical training to maintain the nation's growing armada of airplanes that poured out of America's factories, experts like Robinson were in great need. Robinson was also reconnecting with his roots. His mother, Celeste, still lived in Gulfport at the old family home, and his older sister, Bertha, was teaching school in Gulfport.

Keesler Field was situated along a narrow, low-lying peninsula nestled between the Gulf of Mexico to the south and the Back Bay of Biloxi to the north. Established in the summer of 1941 six months before America's entry into World War II to create "a City within [a] city in Biloxi," Keesler Field was an ideal technical training base for young airmen. Here, the mild winters, warm and fair weather, and seemingly endless sunshine provided an excellent environment for flying over the Gulf of Mexico and the pine-covered coastal plain.[7]

Keesler Field, like other army airfields around America, had been hurriedly quickly created by the War Department. American political and military leaders had realized that rapid military expansion was necessary after the war's outbreak in Europe. Keesler Field, named after a young Mississippi aviator killed in World War I, was established to transfer some of the heavy technical training load off busy Chanute Field, in Illinois. During the interwar period, Chanute Field had served as the sole aviation technical training facility for the Air Corps. As one of the few African Americans instructors at the technical training base, Robinson taught both black and white students, who served in segregated units but trained together, in aviation mechanics at Keesler Field. This position was comparable to his teaching days at the Curtiss-Wright Aeronautical School in Chicago. As on other army bases around the country, black soldiers were segregated. Young African Americans training at Keesler Field were slated for pilot school at Tuskegee Field, if they first successfully qualified for flight training. Later in the war, other blacks who trained at Keesler became aviation technicians and mechanics of the 477th Bombardment Group (Medium)—the first all black bomber unit in American history.[8]

In early 1942, Robinson flew to Tuskegee Army Air Field for the first time. Here, he met with the airfield's Director of Training for Primary Flying, Major Noel Francis Parrish. The diminutive son of a Kentucky preacher, Parrish was open-minded, fair, and strongly anti-segregationist, which was rare for a white from the Upper South.[9]

At Tuskegee, Robinson met with Major Parrish, an experienced Air Corps pilot and future general who would command Tuskegee Army Air Field, and they immediately established a bond. Both men were experienced flyers and instructors. Later, Parrish recalled meeting Robinson for the first time, leaving a lifelong impression: "John Robinson conveyed to me how proud he was to see the new program at Tuskegee. I was very favorably impressed by his quiet, sincere manner. He offered to help in any way we might need him."[10]

Even more, with limited experience around African Americans by early 1942, the Southern-born Major Parrish was yet a bit apprehensive and somewhat unsure of himself and his new role. But, as Parrish explained, "when I looked at that man and saw his skill in the way he handled himself and his bearing, I knew I wasn't going to have any trouble and settled down and trained these men," the Tuskegee Airmen.[11]

And Major Parrish, who would be promoted to colonel in 1943, took comfort in the fact that an experienced black war veteran had offered: "I will do anything to help you" at Tuskegee. Therefore, a reinvigorated Parrish "took inspiration from" Robinson's reassuring words and commitment. Indeed, from 1943 to 1946 as commander at Tuskegee Army Air Field, Colonel Parrish in turn became an inspirational leader for the Tuskegee Airmen. A deep mutual respect developed between the tall, personable Southern colonel and his young black fliers, who relished the opportunity to thrive under Parrish's leadership and fair-minded, sympathetic ways.[12]

Robinson had also traveled from Keesler to Tuskegee Army Air Field as part of a larger assignment. At the request of the War Department, beginning in 1940 Robinson visited airfields to impart his knowledge of aerial and blitzkrieg warfare. He possessed considerable insight into the doctrine of strategic bombing, especially the Italian "strategic formation bombing" he had witnessed in the Italo-Ethiopian War. By this time, the Army Air Corps had embraced its own doctrine of strategic bombardment, thanks to the emergence of its new long-range bomber: the B-17, the Flying Fortress. Robinson was a good choice for the mission. He had witnessed the terrible destructiveness and deadly effects of strategic bombardment more than a half decade before.[13]

Robinson's service as an aviation instructor at Keesler Field was relatively brief, however. An influential white lawyer from Gulfport wrote an angry February 1943 letter to his Mississippi Congressman complaining about the presence of black instructors, including Robinson, at Keesler Field and other Southern bases. Feeling that such a blatant breach of the status quo might upset the caste system in the Deep South, he complained in outrage how white army soldiers were required "to address these Negro instructors Mr. and Mrs. and to pay all deference to them as they would white women and gentlemen occupying the same position."[14]

In February 1943 and equally incensed, the powerful Mississippi governor complained directly to President Roosevelt. He condemned the "bunch of bull-headed Negro instructors," like Robinson, who were educated, competent, spoke their minds, and thought intelligently for themselves.[15]

Thus, with the white backlash, the black civilian instructors on duty at Southern army bases were transferred to the North. Robinson was then assigned to Chanute Army Air Field just south of Chicago, and probably had no idea that an attorney from his own hometown of Gulfport had helped to ensure that he would never live or work in the Deep South again.[16]

Despite having to say good-bye to his Gulfport family, Robinson was very likely delighted to depart the Gulf Coast. One especially egregious example of Keesler Field's particular brand of racism occurred during the summer of 1943, not long after Robinson left for Chanute Field. Incredibly, more than two hundred young African American soldiers, many from Los Angeles, California, Washington, D.C., and New York City, some with college degrees, were put to work on local farms under the hot Mississippi sun. Like slaves before the Civil War, they harvested crops, perhaps including cotton, from the sun-baked fields of the Magnolia State.[17]

Robinson had discovered that though he himself had changed, south Mississippi, like the rest of the Deep South, had remained stuck in its tragic past. Robinson continued to serve as an instructor for the Air Corps, and later the Army Air
Forces, during World War II. Here, in Rantoul, Illinois, he worked month after
month as a civilian aviation instructor to aircraft technicians at Chanute Field.[18]

Chanute Field had been the principal technical training base for both the
Army Air Service, beginning in 1921, and its successor—the Army Air Corps—beginning in 1926, and then *its* successor, the Army Air Forces in 1942. Robinson
was fortunate to have been relocated to an army airfield so close to his home on
Chicago's South Side.[19]

For the same reasons that Robinson had been coveted by the military to teach
aviation, so were the members of the Challenger Air Pilots' Association and Robinson's former students at Curtiss-Wright Aeronautical School. Alumnus Grover
Nash also taught aviation courses at Chanute Field. Former Robinson student and
ex-friend Coffey trained future Tuskegee Airmen at the Coffey School of Aeronautics on Chicago's South Side before they were sent for advanced flight, or pilot, training at Tuskegee. Harold Hurd, another former Robinson student, served
in the training program at Tuskegee Army Air Field. And Charles Alfred Anderson, whose Pan-American Goodwill Flight would not have been possible without
the influence of Robinson's earlier efforts to include African American aviation at
Tuskegee, trained hundreds of cadets at Tuskegee.[20] Clearly, Robinson's own personal aviation legacy continued to live on in the Tuskegee Airmen story in many
ways.

When U.S. Army officials laid belated plans for the creation of the first black
flying unit, they did not want to build entirely new training facilities. They planned
that the relatively small number of aviation instructors would be reassigned from
existing positions. Therefore, Chanute Field had been designated as the army training facility where African American airmen received their technical training, while
Tuskegee Field became the center for pilot training.[21]

The first black military aviation unit in U.S. history, the 99th Pursuit Squadron, had been activated at Chanute Field in March 1941, under the command
of Benjamin O. Davis Jr. While pilots learned to fly at Tuskegee Field, Robinson
helped to train aviation cadets at Chanute. Compared to the famous African American fighter pilots, these nonpilot blacks were the forgotten Tuskegee Airmen, the
nonflyers.

Newly graduated mechanics and aviation technicians of the 99th Pursuit Squadron, later the 99th Fighter Squadron, were then sent to Tuskegee Field to service aircraft, while pilots were trained. Ironically, the War Department had originally planned for the 99th Fighter Squadron to serve in Liberia—a repeat of Robinson's earlier role in Ethiopia—to place the unit on the remote sidelines of North Africa instead of allowing black airmen to serve in the main theater of war in Europe.[22]

Meanwhile, Lieutenant Colonel Davis, a victim of racism as a cadet at West Point who had been appointed to command by Colonel Parrish, and his 99th Fighter Squadron were transferred to the North African theater in April 1943. In early June, the 99th Fighter Squadron flew its first combat mission, with black pilots striking at hostile positions on an island near Sicily. It was symbolic that these African American pilots first went to war against Italians—and Germans only later— in North Africa and Sicily: the same adversary Robinson had faced more than seven years before in Ethiopia.[23]

Even more symbolic, the newly formed first all-black fighter group—the 332nd Fighter Group, which included the 99th Fighter Squadron—would establish its air field at Ramitelli, Italy, and launch repeated air strikes on Italian soil in sleek, new P-51 Mustang fighters by the summer of 1944. As Robinson had envisioned so long ago in his fondest dreams, hundreds of Tuskegee Airmen now aggressively took the war to the Italian homeland. Such belated retribution unleashed on Italian soil for the rape of Ethiopia must have made Robinson proud. By this time a united West had joined the fight against the curse of fascism.[24]

Robinson was now part of a groundbreaking military aviation program that involved integrated training for both black and white mechanics and technicians at Chanute Field. Here, in hastily constructed wooden buildings, both black and white instructors taught aviation to young African American students. Of course, such integration of aviation training personnel was nothing new for Robinson, who had broken the color barrier at Curtiss-Wright Aeronautical School more than a decade before.[25]

By the end of 1943, Robinson was still stationed at Chanute Field, while serving as an instructor with the Army Air Forces Technical Training Command and doing the kind of work that he loved, while continuing to do his part in battling against fascism.[26]

Meanwhile, Ethiopia and her oppressed people saw the end of their darkest period of their history. After having rallied resistance from Ethiopian guerrilla bands that were armed by Great Britain, whose army had repeatedly beaten the Italian forces and Germany's famed Afrika Korps under the "Desert Fox"—Erwin Rommel—in North Africa, Emperor Selassie was restored to power when the resurgent British drove out the Italians and recaptured Addis Ababa in early April 1944. Ethiopia's recapture was the "first territorial victory of the Democracies over the Axis" since the war's beginning.[27]

Now a new opportunity in Ethiopia presented itself to Robinson, who was jubilant with the East African nation's liberation. Through his longtime connections with leading expatriate Ethiopians living in the United States and their influential supporters, Robinson asked the Ethiopian government to officially request military aviation instructors and technicians from the U.S. Armed Air Forces as part of the Lend-Lease program. And Robinson just happened to be a member of the Army Air Forces Technical Training Command from which aviation instructors could be drawn for service in Ethiopia. [28]

FINAL RETURN TO ETHIOPIA

Robinson's life would change forever, when he was released from assigned duty as an instructor of the U.S. Air Force Technical Training Command to serve with the Ethiopian government as part of the Lend-Lease program.[29] Selassie and Ethiopia, after a lengthy Italian occupation, needed Robinson's services once again, this time not as a civilian volunteer, but as an instructor of the U.S. Army Air Forces.

As in the past, Emperor Selassie viewed aviation as a key to Ethiopia's modernization and future. After requesting loans from the United States to help rebuild his battered nation in need of resurrection, one of the emperor's first requests was for two airplanes and other military equipment. The United States now allowed war material and American technicians to come to Ethiopia's assistance through the Lend-Lease Program.[30]

Having served as the Imperial Ethiopian Air Force's commander, as the emperor's personal pilot, and then with his triumphant return to America, Robinson was at an apex of his military career. Therefore, Ethiopia possessed special meaning and significance for Robinson. Ancient Abyssinia was his adopted homeland. Besides its people, Robinson could not forget Ethiopia's natural beauty; the rugged Semien mountains that touched the clouds; the majesty of the Blue Nile River spilling out of Ethiopia's largest lake, Lake Tzana in the Gondar region; the goat-like Walia ibex walking gracefully along the steep mountainsides; the groves of coffee trees thriving in the misty, coolness of the central highlands; the beautiful East African and Moorish architecture of ancient structures, including even stone castles built before Christ's birth; the common, but surprisingly comfortable, tukuls of the village people; pleasant mountain breezes sweeping through the flowering virgin trees of the most picturesque country he had ever seen; the many ancient Christian places of worship—including the Church of Saint Mary of Zion in the ancient holy city of Axum, of which ancient proverb said contained the Ark of the Covenant, brought back to Ethiopia by the Queen of Sheba from King Solomon in Israel; the stately Jewish synagogues and Moslem Mosques erected centuries before; the festive Mercato marketplace of Addis Ababa—the largest in all of Africa—filled with so many exotic sights and sounds; the natural ease and simple dignity of the nomadic and village peoples of Ethiopia, the Galla, Tigrean, Sankilla, and Amhara; the Ethiopians' noble bearing, and pride in their ancient heritage and culture; the throngs of smiling children who flocked around him whenever he walked Addis Ababa's dusty streets; the colorful, light clothes—the lengthy shammas that flowed gracefully over women's thin bodies; and the warm greetings and embraces of these remarkable people of firm faith, courage, and resilience who viewed him as a national hero.

Moreover, with his marriage to Earnize over (he never remarried), he now had no permanent personal ties binding him to Chicago. In Ethiopia he would have a chance to start over, embracing new dreams, opportunities, and ambitions.

In fact, Robinson was only a small part of Emperor Selassie's new vision of the future. Selassie had embarked upon the task of rebuilding his nation and needed a good many skilled Westerners with technical expertise in order to bring Ethiopia into the modern world. One of the key links with that world was aviation.[31] Robinson, now in his late thirties, realized that some of his highest ambitions could not be realized in the United States. Jim Crow restrictions and racial limitations were still set firmly in place, despite the success of the Tuskegee air program. Robinson had repeatedly beaten the odds in overcoming a host of racial stereotypes and institutionalized restrictions, yet his many achievements were still not enough for either political equality or social acceptance. Robinson had become less tolerant of prejudice and discrimination by now. Because these limitations were so deeply woven in the fabric of American society, Robinson realized that once again he would have to go beyond U.S. borders.

Since the first time he had journeyed to Ethiopia in May 1935, Robinson had grown not only older, but also wiser. He was no longer that same naive young man who was overflowing with idealism, romanticism, and Pan-African sentiment.

Robinson could not know that he would never again see the United States, his hometown of Gulfport, or his family and friends. On a cold January 2, 1944, he led a group of aviation technicians on the first part of the journey to Ethiopia, when they steamed down the Mississippi River, heading for New Orleans. Robinson's team of experts included James William Cheeks from Ohio; Edward Eugene Jones of Chicago; Andrew Howard Hester of Illinois; and Joseph Muldrow of South Carolina. On this mission, Joe Muldrow would become Robinson's right-hand man. In fact, he had been a member of Robinson's first black class at Curtiss-Wright Aeronautical School in Chicago. And Robinson and Muldrow were both native Southerners, unlike the other black Americans now journeying to Ethiopia. The U.S. government had released Muldrow from his job at a Detroit defense plant for duty with Robinson.

After landing in Cape Town, South Africa, Robinson and his team began an arduous overland journey by rail and truck from Africa's southern tip north into the heart of the continent. During the lengthy trip, which severely taxed their endurance, they encountered considerable British racism—in the European colonial tradition—in both southern Africa and in Kenya. A tired Robinson and his weary team finally reached Addis Ababa on April 19.[32]

The capital and the East African country had both changed dramatically from when he had first visited nearly a decade before. Ironically, the five terrible years of Italian occupation, despite its oppression and the death of so many defiant Ethiopians, had actually brought an unexpected measure of progress and prosperity both to Addis Ababa and Ethiopia. Like the conquering ancient Romans who left their most enduring legacies in stone, especially magnificent aqueducts, throughout much of the ancient world, the Italians excelled at infrastructure improvements and grandiose construction projects that included lengthy stone bridges, paved roads, and stately buildings. In an attempt to create a new Rome, Italian military and civilian engineers and construction crews had ironically "laid the foundations for Haile Selassie's modern state."[33]

Robinson would no longer be the lone African American to serve the emperor. The emperor's special mission for Robinson was once again to rebuild the Imperial Ethiopian Air Force, but there were no planes in Ethiopia at this time. Therefore, Robinson and his team went to work at an industrial complex in Addis Ababa, while awaiting the arrival of two Cessna aircraft from the United States, a gift of the Lend-Lease program.

Like Robinson, Cheeks, Hester, and Jones had been "leased" from the U.S. Army Air Forces Technical Training Command to work in Ethiopia at the Selassie government's request. The efforts of Prince Yilma Deressa, of the Ethiopian Ministry of Finance, had led to the choice of these five capable African American pilots and airplane mechanics, whom Robinson had first recommended to the Ethiopian government. Significantly, Robinson had taught both Muldrow and Jones in Chicago. Therefore, Robinson now possessed an excellent cadre of skilled aviation experts. With money from the Ethiopian government, Robinson began to purchase additional aircraft. As in 1935–1936, Robinson once again labored to create a new modern air force for the rejuvenated Ethiopian nation.[34]

As it was in 1935, Robinson's mission was no small task. Just as in the Italo-Ethiopian War, the Imperial Ethiopian Air Force existed only on paper, having been destroyed by the war.

Robinson created a comprehensive training program, placing the capable Muldrow in charge of engine rebuilding. Robinson organized and conducted aviation classes for a good many young Ethiopians at the complex, laying a foundation for the future Imperial Ethiopian Air Force. By November 2, 1944, the two aircraft requested by Emperor Selassie under the Lend-Lease Program arrived safely in Addis Ababa. With these two Cessnas now in his possession, Robinson transferred his aviation training to the Addis Ababa airport.[35]

Robinson's aviation efforts in 1944 were successful in part because he now possessed a highly efficient, dedicated group—known affectionately as "the Brood"—of skilled African Americans. Meanwhile, Robinson continued to instruct Ethiopian students in the two twin-engine Cessnas. These aircraft had been flown to Addis Ababa by Capt. Ernest Hulme and Technical Sergeant Oberhelman of the U.S. Army Air Forces. Black and white Americans now worked closely together as a team, far away from the oppression of Jim Crow America. Among his hardworking "Brood," only Robinson possessed an aviation license. Robinson reaped an unexpected dividend when the two American military men remained behind in the capital to help him with aviation training. At this time, Mischa Babitchev, the half-Russian, half-Ethiopian director of air transport for the Ethiopian government, who had served in Robinson's air force during the Italo-Ethiopian War, was appointed ambassador to the Ethiopian Embassy in Moscow. With Emperor Selassie's appointment and blessings, Robinson replaced his old friend as the head of the Imperial Ethiopian Air Force. He even regained his former position and rank of colonel.

This time, however, Robinson wore no resplendent uniform. A rare 1944 photo shows Robinson simply wearing an old U.S. airmen's uniform with a non-regulation buckle. The only insignia on his uniform is above his right pocket, a large embroidered gold wing that indicated the Imperial Ethiopian Air Force. And in the style of American military airmen of the period, he had his dark tie tucked inside his shirt.[36]

After Hulme and Oberhelman departed to return to their unit, "the Brood" became even more indispensable to Robinson. Indeed, "It was this particular group, which included several well-trained [black] aviationists, that was instrumental along with Colonel Robinson in both reinstating the air force training, which had been arrested by the war, and laying the groundwork for the establishment of a modern Ethiopian air corps."[37]

This development was possible because Robinson established a pilot training school, sponsored by his friend Prince Makonnen Haile Selassie, the Duke of Harar and Emperor Selassie's son, for the sole purpose of training larger numbers of Ethiopian students in December 1944. From late 1944 to the end of 1946, by way of his comprehensive training program (known as the Ethiopian Air Force Training Program), Robinson and his team trained more than eighty Ethiopian aviation cadets. In the process, they laid the foundation not only for the Imperial Ethiopian Air Force but also for a commercial airline. Several of these young men were destined to become rising stars in the future of Ethiopian aviation and would eventually gain the rank of colonel in the modern Imperial Ethiopian Air Force. One young man, Abera Wolde Mariam, was one of his original 1944 recruits; he later became a major general, and then the chief of the modern Imperial Ethiopian Air Force of more than two hundred aircraft.[38]

By 1946, after the end of World War II, all the members of the Brood, except for David Talbot of British Guyana, returned to the United States. Robinson remained behind.[39]

Yet another longtime aviation dream came true for Robinson in February 1947 when Ethiopia, as the emperor desired, gained its first airline under Robinson, who created the Sultan Airways, Ltd., or the East African Airlines. Robinson was the airline's organizer, having trained and supervised its pilots, and then served as its manager. He operated a fleet of aircraft that consisted of American-made DC-3s. The new airline's pilots were former flyers of the Royal Air Force and Ethiopians who had been trained by Robinson.[40]

Robinson's historic accomplishment, something that he never could have achieved in the United States at the time, was heralded as far away as Chicago. The *Chicago Defender* boasted of Robinson's remarkable achievement: "Col. Robinson Launches East African Airlines."[41]

In time, Robinson's airlines would rise higher in stature. Many were fully convinced that the "Ethiopians would one day operate one of the world's most efficient airlines."[42] Robinson's contributions to Ethiopia's first airlines have since been forgotten. The government-owned East African Airlines was later named the Ethiopian Airlines. By way of an agreement between the American company and the Ethiopian government, Trans-World Airlines provided aircrews and technical personnel to service a fleet of a dozen DC-3 aircraft. Eventually, the airline would be operated and managed by Trans-World Airlines, providing intercontinental flights as far north as Germany. But in the beginning, Robinson had been the founding father of this enterprise that linked Ethiopia with the rest of the world, fulfilling yet another one of Emperor Selassie's—and Robinson's—longtime ambitions.[43]

By 1947, life in Ethiopia for Robinson was good. He had established the American Institute, an elementary and secondary school in the heart of Addis Ababa in 1946, and it thrived. Overlooking the Addis Ababa airport, at the high elevation of eight thousand feet, where he worked with a newfound sense of peace, Robinson now lived amid the cool highlands in a nice whitewashed Italian-style villa, constructed by Mussolini's Italians.[44]

Meanwhile, some seven thousand miles away from Ethiopia, Robinson's own personal aviation legacy continued to live on in the United States in yet another distinct and historic way. President Truman signed Executive Order 9981 on July 26, 1948. This groundbreaking act officially ended the American military's policy of racial segregation, ensuring full equal treatment and opportunity for African Americans serving their nation.[45] Ironically, in following his own dreams in Ethiopia, Robinson was not aware of this historic event.[46]

In 1948, however, Robinson's fortunes suddenly took a turn for the worse. His undoing resulted from political intrigue and professional jealousy initiated by a former comrade-in-arms, the aristocratic Count von Rosen. The Swede had flown the Fokker ambulance plane in Colonel Robinson's Imperial Ethiopian Air Force during the Italian invasion. An ugly blend of elitism, European arrogance, and racism lay at the root of the difficulty. Robinson's elevated status as an Ethiopian national war hero would not be enough to save him; the emperor now needed Sweden as an ally since neither the United States nor Great Britain was willing to provide greater support. Indeed, von Rosen had already won the emperor's favor because he had purchased additional aircraft for Ethiopia from Sweden. Appointed by the emperor, von Rosen gained a major's rank in Colonel Robinson's Imperial Ethiopian Air Force. However, von Rosen was upset that his rank was below Robinson's. But most irritating of all to the aristocratic Count von Rosen was that he now would have to take orders from an African American. In no uncertain terms and taking advantage of his powerful connections, von Rosen freely voiced his displeasure to the entire Swedish diplomatic community of Addis Ababa. Influential Swedish diplomats then pressured Emperor Selassie to address the situation.

The inevitable clash finally erupted when they picked up a surplus Douglas C-47 cargo plane that Robinson had secured for the air force. Colonel Robinson directed Major von Rosen to fly beside him in the right seat as copilot for the trip to Addis Ababa. However, the proud Swede refused to accept this subordinate role, because he would not fly with a "n—." Robinson then completed the mission on his own, flying the huge transport to the capital without a copilot. Meanwhile, von Rosen flew back to Addis Ababa in another aircraft. After both pilots landed, they exchanged hot words. A fistfight resulted between the Swede and the Mississippian. Like Joe Louis in the fight ring, Robinson broke the count's jaw with one blow. With bruises to his face and an outsized ego, Count von Rosen took the matter directly to the emperor. Robinson never explained his side of the story, since he felt that it had only been a personal matter between two men, and a relatively minor incident. Robinson earned the emperor's disfavor in large part because Selassie was most of all concerned about Ethiopia's vital economic, military, and political ties to Sweden. To Robinson's chagrin, he was promptly arrested, while von Rosen lay in a hospital bed to verify his charges. While damage had been done to Von Rosen's jaw, far more had been inflicted on Robinson's good name.[47]

The prestigious *African Affairs: The Journal of the Royal African Society* reported how "the only news of Ethiopia is of foreigners [and a] fight took place between the coloured American aviator, Colonel John C. Robinson, and the Swedish [von

Rosen] who had apparently accused him of 'being nothing better than a Chicago gangster'; it led to the removal of the former to prison and the latter to hospital."[48]

Despite his arrest by the government that he had so often risked his life to preserve in the past, Robinson still possessed influential allies in Addis Ababa, where the legacy of the Brown Condor had not been forgotten. The Ethiopian Supreme Court came to Robinson's rescue, securing his release. The story even made the pages of the *New York Times* on September 19, 1947, under the headline "Brown Condor Wins Stay [and] Ethiopian Air Force Officer Freed from Prison Pending Review." The journalist described from Addis Ababa on September 18 how "the Ethiopian Supreme Court ordered John C. Robinson, American colonel in the Ethiopian Air Force, known as the 'Brown Condor,' released from prison immediately today, pending review of his conviction of assault. Colonel Robinson was convicted of assault and battery against Count Gustov Von Rosen . . . and was sentenced to three months' imprisonment. Colonel Robinson left the Acaki prison smiling and with a red rose plunked from the prison flower beds in his mouth."[49]

Clearly, Robinson had lost none of his flair for the dramatic, or even his cockiness, during his brief prison stay. Emperor Selassie had little choice but to side with Count von Rosen, who had threatened that Sweden's badly needed aid, including weaponry, would be cut off. When Emperor Selassie's aide explained this delicate political situation, Robinson simply resigned as the head of the Imperial Ethiopian Air Force rather than harm his majesty's vital relations with Sweden.[50]

Only under house arrest for two days after his release from prison, "Robinson [yet] remained the most popular African American, if not American, in Ethiopia. He had a reputation of being the spokesman for African Americans in the country, which was reinforced when he announced that thirty additional technicians would arrive. Rumor also linked him to a supposed plan to bring in some twenty black American women with experience in aircraft factory work."[51]

Robinson had already been at the vortex of yet another complex international dispute, which had nothing to do with the Swedes. After the British had liberated Ethiopia in 1944, they had established a carefully crafted agreement with Emperor Selassie in which only British officials would hold key positions in the ministries of the Ethiopian government. The British government viewed Robinson and his "Brood" as a symbolic threat to the colonial and racial status quo.

Robinson and his team had already experienced British racism on their overland journey from South Africa to Ethiopia. This British hostility toward Robinson and his "Brood" had only continued in Addis Ababa. Ethiopians were worried that the British were bent on gaining permanent control of Ethiopia to turn it into yet another colony. British concerns about race relations had already led to a diplomatic complication, which resulted in the State Department expressing to the Ethiopian ambassador in Washington, D.C., "that Ethiopia had not informed the British in advance concerning the group of African Americans about to begin working for the government." More than anyone else, Robinson had become the focal point of this mounting international and racial tension with the British.[52]

As if white British and Swedish racism was not enough, Robinson also continued to feel the sting of Ethiopian racism because he was a descendent of slaves. Xenophobic Ethiopians, due in part to a backlash because of Italian and then British occupation, regarded Robinson and the African Americans as too "European in habits and outlook." Also some Ethiopians were jealous of Robinson's technical expertise and lofty reputation. Many Ethiopians were further envious that Robinson had been held in high imperial esteem for so long. Relations between the Ethiopians and the "Brood" had become so strained that Robinson went personally to Emperor Selassie to attempt to calm the situation and to ensure better relations between these two peoples of color.[53]

Robinson was now a private citizen of Ethiopia and no longer the air force commander. But his connections with other royal family members remained good. This was especially the case with Emperor Selassie's well-liked middle son, Prince Makonnen Haile Selassie. Robinson had first become friends with the prince back in 1935, and this friendship had remained strong over the years. Robinson opened up an import business with the prince. He repaid the prince's confidence by serving as the chief instructor of his flying school at Addis Ababa, by royal appointment. Robinson also flew as the prince's personal pilot.[54]

Additionally, "Robinson served off and on as an advisor to the Ministry of War." This appointment indicated the extent that Emperor Selassie continued to value Robinson and his advice in aviation and military matters.[55]

By the early 1950s, Robinson's old restlessness returned. After more than half a dozen years of living in Ethiopia, he no doubt missed the fast pace and excitement of American life, the vibrant African American community, and his old friends and acquaintances in both Chicago and Gulfport. He also missed his close-knit family. But most of all, Robinson had become disenchanted with life in Ethiopia. Perhaps the turning point had been the incident with Count von Rosen. Robinson was disillusioned by the incident, especially his personal disappointment that the Swede and the emperor had taken sides against him.[56]

After Selassie's return from exile, Swedish assistants, technicians, and advisors had been the first foreigners to pour into Ethiopia. Then, Sweden assisted in Ethiopia's postwar development. The Swedes, consequently, had gained considerable influence over the emperor, as Robinson had learned the hard way.[57]

By May 1951, Robinson informed an *Ebony* reporter that he was "Disillusioned by these political maneuvering [and therefore] Robinson is thinking of returning to the States."[58] At this time, in the reporter's words, Robinson was faced with the seemingly permanent situation of "Selassie's apparent indifference to him."[59]

However, the *Ebony* correspondent marveled in May 1951 how Robinson to this day "remains something of a national hero to the Ethiopian people." By this time, the famed "Brown Condor" was in fact the most popular and "the best-known Negro American in Ethiopia," the reporter concluded.[60] Generations of Ethiopians had embraced the heroic memory of this popular outsider and "national hero," who had risked all in Ethiopia's defense, while serving at great risk thousands of miles from home.[61]

Robinson decided to return to Gulfport, with his eventful life coming full circle. At long last, he planned to close the final Ethiopian chapter of his life after nearly a quarter century of accomplishments, sacrifices, and unforgettable memories of good times and bad.[62]

A TRAGIC ENDING IN ETHIOPIA

By 1954, forty-eight-year-old John Robinson continued to cherish the essence of flight, the feeling of freedom in the air. For Robinson, flying was almost a spiritual experience, an expression of release from the monotony of life, personal troubles, and man's seemingly endless inhumanity to his fellow man.

At Addis Ababa, meanwhile, Robinson continued to teach young people at the flying school. For two decades, Robinson found special meaning and pleasure as an instructor to youth of all colors. Through these receptive young people, he was once more able to relive the beginning of his own magical love affair—his life's greatest passion—with aviation. He gained the same personal fulfillment as his own former teachers at Gulfport, at Tuskegee Institute and the Curtiss-Wright Aeronautical School. Robinson was able to accomplish in Ethiopia exactly what meant most to him throughout his life: bestowing the gift of aviation on young people.

A new day dawned bright and clear over Addis Ababa in mid-March, seemingly promising nothing eventful or exciting. On March 13, 1954, however, Robinson suddenly learned that a young Ethiopian boy had been seriously injured by a rotating aircraft propeller at an airstrip in a nearby town. A blood transfusion was urgently needed, but the only blood supply available was in Addis Ababa.

Robinson unhesitatingly volunteered for this mercy mission, despite no time to spare. At the main Addis Ababa airport he hurriedly prepared to take off in an available training plane. With Robinson as copilot was a trusty engineer, Bianchi Bruno, whom he had taught how to fly. The Italian would have been Robinson's enemy less than twenty years before, but now Robinson saw Bruno as a close friend and trusted fellow aviator.

Ever since his first solo flight outside Chicago in February 1920, Robinson's luck had been nothing short of miraculous, especially in wartime. He had numerous near-fatal accidents. But he had always escaped serious injury, despite so many close calls, including aerial combat with his Italian opponents. Robinson had somehow always survived the odds decade after decade.

Orchestrating a smooth take-off from the runway as so often in the past, he lifted off into the thin, fresh air of the central highlands. Not long after becoming airborne, however, something went wrong with his aircraft's engine. The little training plane suddenly tumbled from the sky over Addis Ababa. Before he lost complete control, however, Robinson somehow managed to maneuver the falling aircraft away from a residence for nurses. Robinson's light aircraft smashed into the ground. A broken engine valve had accomplished what no Italian fighter pilot or machine gunner could do month after month in the blue skies over Ethiopia: end Robinson's stroke of luck.

The fiery crash instantly killed Bruno, but Robinson somehow survived the impact. He either managed to crawl out of or was pulled from the twisted, burning wreckage just in the nick of time, after spilled airplane fuel ignited to turn his aircraft into a wall of flames.[63]

Robinson was in critical condition, however, with serious third-degree burns and injuries. He was rushed to the main Addis Ababa hospital, which was largely staffed by European physicians. Ironically, this modern hospital was better than where an injured Robinson could have been transported to in his segregated homeland of Mississippi, or even in Chicago, because of his color.

Here, Robinson lay in intensive care and in severe pain day after day. At some point, Emperor Selassie paid him a visit. Whatever words, if any, were exchanged between the emperor and the former head of his air force were not recorded.

Robinson struggled for life through the middle of March and into the month's third week. Nevertheless, the end was near. No one could survive the number of injuries or the amount of third-degree burns that he had received. He was slowly dying.

Robinson now must have wondered if he would ever get home again as he had planned. He might have reflected on the irony of after having achieved so much in life, he was unlikely to achieve his last goal of just going home once again. Because he had defied the odds many times in the past, however, Robinson no doubt yet believed that he would recover, and return to Gulfport and his family once again.

Unfortunately, Robinson's condition worsened. As his chances for survival diminished, perhaps he found solace and hope from reading the small Bible that his mother, Celeste, had given him when, as a young man, he set out from home for the first time to journey alone to Tuskegee. He placed himself in God's hands, feeling a comforting sense of serenity, despite the pain.

Almost exactly twenty years since he first proffered the dream of an aviation school to Tuskegee Institute, March 22 marked the tenth day of Robinson's hospitalization. Emperor Selassie made sure Robinson received the best possible care. Perhaps a source of comfort to him at this time, Robinson's vision for a new generation of black aviators had reached maturation at Tuskegee, resulting in more than one thousand black pilots, along with thousands of African American support airmen, who fought in World War II.

In turn, the Tuskegee Airmen's wartime accomplishments had opened the door for the full integration of the U.S. military shortly following the war's conclusion. In the end, these groundbreaking developments had ensured greater social, political, and economic advantages for African Americans. The youthful visions of a young Mississippian had finally come full circle thanks to Robinson's tenacity, skill, and bravery during the 1920s and 1930s.

In the end, the historic developments that helped transform the American military and society might not have been possible had it not been for Robinson, who refused to accept the oppressive status quo of Jim Crow and who believed anything was possible for all young black men and women. The remarkable life of this aviation prophet and visionary ended when John Charles Robinson, passed on March 27, 1954, at the age of forty-eight. In his final moments, perhaps Robinson thought back briefly on that warm south Mississippi day so long ago when he had seen his first airplane in flight. But most important, he knew that even after he died, his aviation legacy would live on without him. Just before passing away, Robinson might have once again felt that he was yet soaring high in the clouds and blue skies over his hometown of Gulfport, the Gulf of Mexico, Chicago, and any other place that he loved, but would never see again.

Ethiopians, including Emperor Selassie, mourned Robinson's death. In solemn recognition of his role in defending Ethiopia in 1935–1936, and his faithfulness and fidelity on behalf of this ancient African nation and her people for much of his life, Robinson's body was laid to rest with full military honors by the Ethiopian armed forces at Addis Ababa. During the funeral, large numbers of grief-stricken "Ethiopians lined the streets for miles" to pay their final respects to their hero. In the end, it was appropriate that Robinson died in a land where he was loved, and was widely known as "the Brown Condor of Ethiopia" and with a people who he cherished and had defended with his life.

In a fitting tribute, a military salute was fired by the resplendently uniformed detail of members of the Emperor's Imperial Guard. Here, under the bright Ethiopian sunshine beside towering palms and eucalyptus, Robinson was buried under the shadow of Mount Entoto in Gulele Cemetery, with the full honors of a national hero.[64]

The *New York Times* ran an article about Robinson's life on March 28, 1954, under the headline "Air Veteran Dead of Ethiopia Crash."[65] The reporter merely explained how, "Col. John C. Robinson, a veteran American Negro aviator who flew for Ethiopia . . . died [March 27, 1954] of injuries from a plane crash two weeks ago. The training plane he was flying crashed and burned March 13 at the Addis Ababa Airport, after narrowly missing a nurses' home."[66]

Perhaps the most symbolic tribute to Robinson's life came not in Ethiopia during his funeral but in Chicago and, ironically, not from his fellow African Americans. Most appropriately, Emperor Selassie bestowed this final tribute in Bronzeville. On June 8, 1954, barely two months after Robinson's tragic death and just after returning from a tour of Washington, D.C., Emperor Selassie visited the bustling city where the former commander of his Imperial Ethiopian Air Force had prospered and broke racial barriers. The emperor's itinerary in Chicago was tight. Here, he was planning to meet with the leading black and white politicians, civic leaders, and businessmen.

Suddenly, while on his way to a key meeting, Emperor Selassie barked a sharp order to his chauffeur-aide, "Take me to the South Park Baptist Church!" Knowing the emperor's hectic schedule and the importance of not missing the upcoming meeting, his concerned advisor responded, "But your majesty, it is not on our itinerary." Nevertheless, Selassie again ordered to be taken to this little church in the heart of Bronzeville near Lake Michigan. The revered spiritual leader of the Ethiopian Orthodox faith, Selassie was now driven to the small wooden church where Robinson had faithfully worshiped and found a spiritual haven from life's storms. Selassie understood that he had a debt to pay to the self-sacrificing African American aviator.

With his large entourage, and in his characteristic soft voice, the Ethiopian emperor addressed the congregation with emotion and sincerity. He spoke words of dignity and respect: "I want to thank the people who prayed for Ethiopia [in 1935–1936], who supported Ethiopia with their prayers and their money, who shipped a field hospital to the war front, and most of all, who sent Ethiopia their beloved son; Col. John C. Robinson, who passed and ascended to heaven just a few months ago."[67]

Indeed, for the first time in American history, an African American who had descended from lowly slaves was honored by a royal emperor who was idolized throughout the world for the courage he displayed in attempting to save his ancient nation. The famed "Lion of Judah" praised Robinson at length. Selassie never forgot how the native Mississippian had been entrusted with the all but impossible task of creating a viable Imperial Ethiopian Air Force almost from scratch during the chaos of wartime. Even more significant and at great risk, Robinson had accomplished more in attempting to save the life of the most enduring symbol of African sovereignty, independence, and anti-European colonialism than any other American during the Italo-Ethiopian War.

At the South Park Baptist Church, Emperor Selassie also paid Robinson a stirring personal tribute in part because he realized how the Brown Condor of Ethiopia's commitment to the cause of Ethiopian independence had been even greater than so many of his own Ethiopian people during the Italo-Ethiopian War. Despite leaving behind his friends, wife, family, and a successful career, he had unselfishly cast his destiny against the surging fascist tide, risking all for a land and people he had never seen before. Perhaps more than anyone else, Emperor Selassie would have fully understood the grim sincerity of Robinson's words when the native Mississippian found himself in the midst of an unwinnable conflict as he wrote in a letter from Addis Ababa on November 28, 1935: "If we all have to die, I think we should all die like men and have it over with."[68]

Significantly, Emperor Selassie bestowed his final tribute at a time when both white and black America had forgotten about Robinson's many accomplishments, not only as the Imperial Ethiopian Air Force's commander, but also for breaking down racial barriers for African Americans in aviation and in promoting aviation to black America during the period between the wars.

Ironically, Robinson, the inspirational father of the Tuskegee Airmen, the black Lindbergh of the Golden Age of Aviation, and the first head of the Imperial Ethiopian Air Force, now lay thousands of miles from his native homeland in a lonely grave in Addis Ababa. Yet, the legacy of the Brown Condor lived on in Ethiopia. In the summer of 1979, a quarter century after his death, one young Ethiopian aviation student in the United States met Robinson's old friend, Cornelius R. Coffey in Chicago. Coffey was shocked when this Ethiopian student proudly boasted of the man who had become one of Ethiopia's national heroes: "He told me that his father had told him about an American who had to leave [Ethiopia] in 1936 but returned in 1944 and had an accident, died, and was buried in Addis Ababa, the capital. He was shocked to find out that the man was my dear friend John C. Robinson."[69]

Indeed, the enduring legend of the Brown Condor survived in the hearts and minds of the Ethiopian people more than a quarter century after his tragic demise. Robinson was still "a national hero" in the country he helped defend.[70]

Indeed, it was rare in the annals of Ethiopia's lengthy history "that a black *ferengi* (foreigner) of slave origins could gain statue and respect in the highly caste-oriented and allegedly anti-Negro kingdom of Ethiopia."[71]

From mid-August 1992 to late March 1994, the United States undertook a humanitarian mission for the relief of the starving people of Somalia, after years of civil war and famine. One of the primary bases for America's relief effort in the Horn of Africa was located at Addis Ababa. Ironically, and like their white comrades, hundreds of young African American men and women, now proud members of the U.S. Air Force, were unaware that they took off from the city where a young man named John Charles Robinson had once commanded an entire air force, and where he had died selflessly in an attempt to help others while flying their own humanitarian missions over the grave of this long-forgotten African American aviator, who died so far from home.[72]

EPILOGUE

THE GOLDEN AGE OF AVIATION and its legendary aviation heroes left an unforgettable chapter in American history. The single most heralded aviation achievement of that remarkable era was Lindbergh's solo trans-Atlantic flight in May 1927.

However, even though his courage electrified the world, Lindbergh's achievement was hardly a noteworthy milestone in regard to American society's moral progress and enlightenment. In contrast, Robinson's now forgotten accomplishments in the Ethiopian military and in civilian aviation in the United States transformed him into black America's best-known aviator during the 1930s and, more significantly, elevated aviation to a higher moral plane, more than any other American of his day had been able to do.

By serving as the Imperial Ethiopian Air Force's commander and fighting fascism, Robinson reached a moral high ground that Lindbergh's achievements lacked. Robinson provided the world with a symbolic and meaningful example of courage. Most important, Robinson demonstrated to people around the world the responsibility and obligation of confronting fascism early, long before America became involved in another world war. In the skies above Ethiopia, Robinson came to represent democracy and freedom in a clash of right versus wrong that was closely watched by the world, especially black America.[1]

Afro-American studies scholar William R. Scott summarized the importance of Robinson's historic and prominent role in the Italo-Ethiopian War: "Rarely, if ever, is any mention made by historians of John Robinson's role . . . during the Italo-Ethiopian conflict. The colonel has been all but forgotten in Black America. . . . Nonetheless, it is important to remember him [because] Colonel Robinson stands out in Afro-American history as perhaps the first of a minute few of black Americans to take up arms to defend the African homeland against the forces of European colonialism."[2]

In this sense, Robinson was following the egalitarian tradition of Toussaint Louverture, who had led the ex-slaves of Saint Domingue—known today as Haiti—in a struggle for his people's freedom in a fiery revolution that stabbed French imperialism, colonialism, and the institution of slavery in the heart. After all, by the mid-1930s, most of Africa and her people were under the colonial exploitation of European powers.[3]

Additionally, in battling for civil rights, Robinson had a peacetime influence on aviation that was equally significant in moral terms, as it challenged Jim Crow and helped open the doors for future generations of African Americans, including the Tuskegee Airmen. In this regard, he was very much a race pioneer in America. Robinson's aviation contributions, therefore, were important because they represented and exemplified the true meaning of American egalitarian values—both at home and abroad. Lindbergh, conversely, was sympathetic toward the same fascism that Robinson had fought against in 1935–1936.

While Robinson was a shining moral example to black America, Lindbergh was a highly visible, vocal advocate of both appeasement and pro-fascist sentiment—toward Germany rather than Italy in this case—on the eve of America's entry into World War II. Consequently, while Robinson deserved—but never widely received—recognition as the black Lindbergh in white America's eyes, he more profoundly represented the true definition of an authentic American hero for his early stand against racism and oppression overseas and at home, and in fighting for human rights. In fully understanding the awful truth about fascism's evils—still unrecognized by white America, black Americans and the Ethiopian people, who correctly understood that fascism equaled racism—Colonel Robinson was elevated to the status of folk hero both during and after the Italo-Ethiopian War.[4]

Further, in landing his biplane at Tuskegee Institute in May 1934 and lobbying relentlessly for the creation of an aviation curriculum at the school, he personally bestowed upon the institution a bold vision for blacks in aviation that would be fulfilled during the coming world war. With clarity and guided by only a dream, Robinson envisioned how Tuskegee Institute and Africans Americans could reap immense social, political, and economic dividends from the promotion of aviation. Through his own efforts, he introduced his alma mater to the potential possibilities of black aviation, while presenting a more promising future for Tuskegee and black youth across America. Then, in an effort that spanned years, Robinson continued a vigorous campaign to bring his vision to full fruition at Tuskegee, promising a brighter future for African Americans, awakening Tuskegee's leaders, and playing a decisive role in convincing them that aviation should become a permanent part of the institute.

This development was significant, timely, and historic, because without that early foundation, the War Department's decision to transform Tuskegee into the principal center for black pilot training might never have developed. Robinson's forgotten role in promoting, inspiring, and advocating aviation for Tuskegee Institute was a key component in opening the door for hundreds of black pilots during World War II. In this way and combined with his inspirational moral example as the Brown Condor of Ethiopia, Robinson was indeed the father of the Tuskegee Airmen.

For years and on both sides of the Atlantic, Robinson played a leading part in making black American air conscious in the years before World War II. He demonstrated to an entire generation of African Americans that a black aviator could perform heroically in combat and even command an air force in wartime, while battling for black freedom against colonialism, racism, and imperialism, both in America and overseas.[5]

Robinson's vision remained an enduring legacy to the American, African, and the Ethiopian people for generations to come. But while his dream would survive, Robinson's memory among African Americans would not. Today, ironically, John Charles Robinson lies in an obscure grave in Gulele Cemetery in Addis Ababa, and his name has been forgotten in America.

The long-ago fame and adulation of black America, which had welcomed the lone America war hero back to the United States from a faraway foreign war against fascism, quickly faded away. Today, Robinson's memory and legacy have been lost to Americans, both black and white, just as the memory of the Italo-Ethiopian War, which was soon overshadowed by World War II, and its special meaning in terms of race, morality, and colonialism has also faded. Near Robinson's grave in Addis Ababa, hundreds of Ethiopians today walk past his final resting place without noticing or realizing his longtime contributions on behalf of their beloved nation. Unfortunately, the wartime legend of the Brown Condor of Ethiopia and its inspirational moral example have seemingly vanished into thin air.

Unlike Robinson, the Tuskegee Airmen eventually found the national spotlight to rightly earn a distinguished place in the annals of American history. However, without Robinson's efforts and achievements on both sides of the Atlantic, there might well have been no Tuskegee Airmen of World War II fame.

Robinson's almost total obscurity today is especially ironic, because he was so widely viewed as the long-awaited Black Lindbergh for an entire generation of African Americans during the period between the world wars. In the words of historian Robert J. Jakeman, "no black aviator had achieved the right balance of flying expertise and public acclaim to become the nation's 'black Lindy,'" except Robinson.[6]

In commanding the first integrated air force in history in wartime, Robinson fulfilled a history-making role that thrust him upon the world stage, quite unlike any other African American of his day. As explained in an April 4, 1936, *Chicago Defender* article about Robinson, "Race interest in aviation . . . reached its highest point, among race members with the success of John Robinson . . . as the head of the royal air force of Ethiopia [and] known now everywhere as the Brown Condor" of Ethiopia.[7]

During the golden age of aviation, "Colonel Robinson [was] the Negro's greatest aviator."[8] In the end, Robinson's remarkable life represented a triumph of the human spirit against seemingly insurmountable obstacles and odds that a Jim Crow society had so unfairly stacked against him.

Janet Harmon Bragg emphasized the importance of Robinson's inspirational, symbolic, and moral impact on an entire generation of African Americans, including the Tuskegee Airmen, at a critical time in American history: "They do not think of Lindbergh . . . but of Johnny Robinson."[9]

Aviation Cadets Trained by John Robinson's Team

Abraha Kelet

Assefa Gebresilase

Taye Tarea

Gelan Urgessa

Guetacheou Tarekegne

Chanalew Belai

Mengheshia Yilma

Getachew Tarekenny

Ambaye Alemayehu

Mamo Admassu

Asefa Ayele

Elias Abate

Teferi Woldeamak

Berrhe Jakob

Asefa Teklezion

Amanuel Tesfamikel

Membere Woldetensaye

Mengesha Seyfe

Makonin Wondim

Okbit Debessay

Betaye Debassay

Ameha Zionkifle

Chefeke Teketay

Merkorios Haile

Gizaw Gedle Giorgis

Yohanis Haile

Yeheyis Gabre Selasse

Ehdego Andegiorgis

Gugsa Habtemekael

Mulageta Ababe

Menasse Belachou

Zerefu Zerudu

Larkow Markas

Zedeke Begashet

Agzau Gebrehanna

Tedla Desta

Kelilachew Tekle

Hawariat Taye

Metcha Getachew

Kenfere Zegeye

Worku Abraha

Abera Tadesse

Aleme Bekele

Efrem Asafaw

Wolde Mikael

Girma Bedane

Negashe Woldemikael

Alem Ayehu Abebe

Tesfaye Mankere

Lt. Tesfaye Tamarat

Fikeru Samuel

Dachew Admasu

INTRODUCTION

1. *Chicago Defender*, April 4, 1936.
2. *Chicago Defender*, May 9, 1936.
3. Von Hardesty, *Black Wings: Courageous Stories of African Americans in Aviation and Space History* (New York: HarperCollins, 2008), 32–33.
4. "Americans in Ethiopia, Score of U.S. Negroes Helping to Develop Ancient African Land," *Ebony*, May 1951; "Ethiopia Gets New Flyer," *New York Times*, August 23, 1935.
5. Robert J. Jakeman, *The Divided Skies: Establishing Segregated Flight Training at Tuskegee, Alabama, 1934–1942* (Tuscaloosa: University of Alabama Press, 1992), 61, 64, 87, 27–29, 307–10; *Campus Digest: The Voice of the Tuskegee Student*, September 28, 1935.
6. Janet Waterford [Janet Harmon Bragg/Janet Waterford Bragg], "The Real Story of Col. John Robinson, or How a Gulfport, Miss. Boy Grew to Be the No. 1 Flyer of His Race" (series of articles), *Chicago Defender*, April 4–May 16, 1936.
7. Jakeman, *The Divided Skies*, 264.
8. Ibid.

CHAPTER 1. A RARE BEACON OF HOPE, GULFPORT

1. John K. Bettersworth, *Mississippi: The Land and the People* (Austin: Steck-Vaughn Company, 1981), 234–38; Val Husley, *Biloxi, 300 Years* (Virginia Beach: Donning Company, 1998), 38–55; Charles Sullivan, *The Mississippi Gulf Coast: Portrait of a People* (Northridge, CA: Windsor Publications, 1985), 106–31; John Tuepker, *The Effects of World War II on Blacks in Harrison County, Mississippi* (MA thesis, Gulfport, MS: University of Southern Mississippi, 1993): 5–6, 13; Margie Riddle Bearss, *Sherman's Forgotten Campaign: The Meridian Expedition* (Baltimore: Gateway Press, 1987), 164–244.
2. Sullivan, *The Mississippi Gulf Coast*, 112–14; Tuepker, *Effects of World War II on Blacks*, 13.

3. Tuepker, *Effects of World War II on Blacks*, 13; Sidney L. Rushing, in interview with author, Gulfport, MS, August 11, 2001.

4. William R. Scott, "Colonel John C. Robinson: The Condor of Ethiopia," *Pan-African Journal* 5, no. 1 (Spring 1972): 59; Thomas E. Simmons, *The Brown Condor: The True Adventures of John C. Robinson* (Silver Spring, MD: Bartleby Press, 1988), 5; Fourteenth United States Census, 1920, Gulfport, MS, Mississippi Department of Archives and History (MDAH), Jackson, MS; Betty Kaplan Gubert, Miriam Sawyer, and Caroline M. Fannin, *Distinguished African Americans in Aviation and Space Science* (Westport, CT: Oryx Press, 2002), 252; Jack Diamond, "Haile Selassie's Ace Airman Back in New York, Glad War Days Ended," *Enterprise* (Riverside, CA), May 21, 1936.

5. Fourteenth U.S. Census, 1920, Gulfport, MS; Rushing, in interview with author, July 19 and August 11, 2001; Scott, "Colonel John C. Robinson," 59; Simmons, *The Brown Condor*, 5–7; Sullivan, *The Mississippi Gulf Coast*, 115; "Col. Robinson Starts Own Aviation College," *Amsterdam News* (New York), April 3, 1954; Tuepker, *Effects of World War II on Blacks*, 13; Melissa M. Scallan, "Group Seeks to Honor Aviator Brown Condor," *Sun Herald*, March 16, 2002; Thomas E. Simmons address, "Memory and Heritage: The Brown Condor and the Coast in the Depression and World War II Symposium," University of Southern Mississippi, Gulf Park Campus, Gulfport, MS, March 15, 2002 (hereafter cited as the Brown Condor Symposium); John C. Stokes, in interview with author, St. Albans, NY, March 9 and April 24, 2003; Richard G. Henning, Staff Meteorologist, 46th Weather Squadron, "A History of Hurricanes in the Western Florida Panhandle, 1599–1999," History Office, Eglin AFB, FL; Gubert, Sawyer, and Fannin, *Distinguished African Americans in Aviation*, 252.

6. William S. Osborn, "Curtains for Jim Crow: Law, Race, and the Texas Railroads," *Southwestern Historical Quarterly* 150, no. 3 (January 2002): 402; David Brion Davis, *The Problem of Slavery in the Age of Revolution, 1770–1823* (New York: Oxford University Press, 1999), 564; Simmons, *The Brown Condor*, 6.

7. On May 22, 1907, Gulfport's founder, Captain Jones, deeded lots 11 and 12 in block 90 in Gulfport. When John Robinson was only age two, Jones presented these lots to the church trustees, including Cobb, for the erection of Gulfport's newest church. T. J. Jones, Deed to Church Trustees, May 22, 1907, City of Gulfport, County of Harrison, State of Mississippi, Harrison County Court Records, Harrison County Courthouse, Gulfport, MS.

8. Gubert, Sawyer, and Fannin, *Distinguished African Americans in Aviation*, 252.

9. Ron Dick, *Reach and Power: The Heritage of the United States Air Force in Pictures and Artifacts* (Washington, DC: Air Force History and Museum Programs, 1997), 3–5.

10. Kat Bergeron, "Brown Condor—Gulfport Aviation Pioneer Broke Color Barriers," *Sun Herald*, March 15, 2002; Simmons Address, Brown Condor Symposium, March 15, 2002; Gubert, Sawyer, and Fannin, *Distinguished African Americans in Aviation*, 252; Simmons, *The Brown Condor*, 4–5.

11. Doris L. Rich, *The Magnificent Moisants: Champions of Early Flight* (Washington, DC: Smithsonian Institution Press, 1998), 1–34.
12. Ibid., 36–37.
13. Ibid., 72–77.
14. Ibid., 78–85.
15. Ibid., 85–86; Simmons, *The Brown Condor*, 4–5; Charles A. Lindbergh, *We: The Famous Flier's Own Story of His Life and His Transatlantic Flight, Together with his Views on the Future of Aviation* (Cutchogue, NY: Buccaneer Books, n.d.), 94–95.
16. Bergeron, "Brown Condor"; Simmons, *The Brown Condor*, 4–5; Rich, *The Magnificent Moisants*, 89; Simmons Address, Brown Condor Symposium, March 15, 2002.
17. Bergeron, "Brown Condor," *Sun Herald*; Simmons, *The Brown Condor*, 4–5.
18. Bergeron, "Brown Condor," *Sun Herald*; Simmons, *The Brown Condor*, 4–5.
19. Katie Booth's quotation from Bergeron, "Brown Condor," *Sun Herald*; Simmons, *The Brown Condor*, 4–5; Katie Booth Biographical Sketch, History Makers Archives, Chicago, IL; Gubert, Sawyer, and Fannin, *Distinguished African Americans in Aviation*, 252.
20. Bergeron, "Brown Condor," *Sun Herald*; Simmons, *The Brown Condor*, 4–5; Rich, *The Magnificent Moisants*, 99; Simmons Address, Brown Condor Symposium, March 15, 2002.
21. Bergeron, "Brown Condor," *Sun Herald*; Simmons, *The Brown Condor*, 4–5; Simmons Address, Brown Condor Symposium, March 15, 2002; Gubert, Sawyer, and Fannin, *Distinguished African Americans in Aviation*, 252.
22. Rich, *The Magnificent Moisants*, 87–96; Bergeron, "Brown Condor," *Sun Herald*; Simmons Address, Brown Condor Symposium, March 15, 2002; Gubert, Sawyer, and Fannin, *Distinguished African Americans in Aviation*, 252.
23. Simmons, *The Brown Condor*, 6; Simmons Address, Brown Condor Symposium, March 15, 2002.
24. Fourteenth U.S. Census, 1920, Gulfport, MS; Simmons, *The Brown Condor*, 5; Jerry Kinser, "'Condor' Soars," *Sun Herald*, February 28, 1988; Rushing, in interview with author, August 11 and 16, 2001; Simmons Address, Brown Condor Symposium, March 15, 2002.
25. Rushing, in interview with author, August 11, 2001; Fourteenth U.S. Census, 1920, Gulfport, MS.
26. Rushing, in interview with author, August 11, 2001.
27. Photograph, Sidney L. Rushing Collection, Gulfport, MS; Simmons Address, Brown Condor Symposium, March 15, 2002; Simmons, *The Brown Condor*, 5.
28. Simmons Address, Brown Condor Symposium, March 15, 2002; Rushing, in interview with author, July 19 and August 11, 2001; Kinser, "'Condor' Soars"; Katie Booth, in interview with author, August 11, 2001.
29. Simmons Address, Brown Condor Symposium, March 15, 2002; Rushing, in interview with author, July 19, 2001; Fourteenth U.S. Census, 1920, Gulfport, MS; Gubert, Sawyer, and Fannin, *Distinguished African Americans in Aviation*, 252.

30. Janet Harmon Bragg and Marjorie M. Kriz, *Soaring Above Setbacks: The Autobiography of Janet Harmon Bragg* (Washington, DC: Smithsonian Institution Press, 1996), 27; Harry Charles Tartt, in interview with author, Gulfport, Mississippi, October 25, 2001; Reverend Harry Charles Tartt Biographical Sketch, History Makers Archives.

31. *Chicago Defender*, April 4, 1936.

32. Rushing, in interview with author, August 11, 2001.

33. Ibid.; Simmons Address, Brown Condor Symposium, March 15, 2002; Mark Ribowsky, *Don't Look Back: Satchel Paige in the Shadows of Baseball* (New York: Simon & Schuster , 1994), 9, 23, 39; Kyle McNary, *Ted "Double Duty" Radcliffe* (Minneapolis: McNary Publishing, 1994), 12; Waterford, "The Real Story of Col. John Robinson."

34. Rushing, in interview with author, August 11, 2001; Booth, in interview with author, August 11, 2001; Fourteenth U.S. Census, 1920, Gulfport, MS.

35. Rushing, in interview with author, August 11, 2001; Booth, in interview with author, August 11, 2001; Fourteenth U.S. Census, 1920, Gulfport, MS.

36. Waterford, "The Real Story of Col. John Robinson"; Tartt, in interview with author, October 25, 2001.

37. Jones, Deed to Church Trustees; Rushing, in interview with author, August 11, 2001; Tartt, in interview with author, October 25, 2001; Waterford, "The Real Story of Col. John Robinson"; Fourteenth U.S. Census, 1920, Gulfport, MS; Roger Wilkins, *Jefferson's Pillow: The Founding Fathers and the Dilemma of Black Patriotism* (Boston: Beacon Press, 2001), 109–11; Simmons Address, Brown Condor Symposium, March 15, 2002; Rev. Tartt, Brown Condor Symposium, March 15, 2002; Stokes, in interview with author, March 9, 2003; Kat Bergeron, "A Religious Restoration, Group Fights to Save Church," *Sun Herald*, March 10, 2006; Simmons, *The Brown Condor*, 12.

38. Simmons, *The Brown Condor*, 12; John Hope Franklin, *From Slavery to Freedom: A History of Negro Americans* (New York: Alfred A. Knopf, 1974), 246–47.

39. Simmons, *The Brown Condor*, 12–13.

40. Godine quoted in Jules Loh, "Stalking the 'Brown Condor,'" *Sun Herald*, August 7, 1988.

41. Tartt, in interview with author, October 25, 2001; Rev. Tartt, Brown Condor Symposium, March 15, 2002; Rev. Tartt Biographical Sketch, History Makers Archives.

42. Simmons Address, Brown Condor Symposium, March 15, 2002.

43. Henning, "History of Hurricanes in Western Florida Panhandle "

44. Rev. Tartt, Brown Condor Symposium, March 15, 2002.

45. Tartt, in interview with author, October 25, 2001; Waterford, "The Real Story of Col. John Robinson."

46. Waterford, "The Real Story of Col. John Robinson"; Bragg and Kriz, *Soaring Above Setbacks*, xiv–5.

47. Waterford, "The Real Story of Col. John Robinson"; Tartt, in interview with author, October 25, 2001.

48. Ibid.; Rev. Tartt, Brown Condor Symposium, March 15, 2002.
49. Simmons, *The Brown Condor*, 10.
50. Ibid., 11.
51. Tartt, in interview with author, October 25, 2001; Husley, *Biloxi*, 70; Bragg and Kriz, *Soaring Above Setbacks*, 27; Rev. Tartt, Brown Condor Symposium, March 15, 2002; "Air Veteran Dead of Ethiopia Crash," *New York Times*, March 28, 1954; Gubert, Sawyer, and Fannin, *Distinguished African Americans in Aviation*, 252.
52. Annie Mae Gaston, Brown Condor Symposium, March 15, 2002.
53. Rev. Tartt, Brown Condor Symposium, March 15, 2002; Simmons, *The Brown Condor*, 14; Katie Booth, Brown Condor Symposium, March 15, 2002; Gubert, Sawyer, and Fannin, *Distinguished African Americans in Aviation*, 252; Booth, in interview with author, November 15, 2001.
54. Tartt, in interview with author, October 25, 2001.
55. Waterford, "The Real Story of Col. John Robinson."
56. Ibid.
57. Charles Dubra, Brown Condor Symposium, March 15, 2002; Simmons, *The Brown Condor*, 15.
58. "'Brown Condor' Takes a Swim," *Sun Herald*, May 12, 2002.
59. Fourteenth U.S. Census, 1920, Gulfport, MS.
60. Ibid.; Stokes, in interview with author, March 9, 2003; Diamond, "Haile Selassie's Ace Airman Back in New York."
61. Rushing, in interview with author, August 11, 2001; Fourteenth U.S. Census, 1920, Gulfport, MS.
62. Simmons, *The Brown Condor*, 13.
63. Ibid.; Simmons Address, and Rev. Tartt and Booth interviews, Brown Condor Symposium, March 15, 2001.

CHAPTER 2. TURNING POINT:
TUSKEGEE INSTITUTE AND GOING NORTH

1. Waterford, "The Real Story of Col. John Robinson"; Simmons Address, Brown Condor Symposium, March 15, 2002.
2. Ibid.; Simmons, *The Brown Condor*, 15.
3. Simmons, *The Brown Condor*, 13–15; Simmons Address, Brown Condor Symposium, March 15, 2002.
4. Bergeron, "Brown Condor—," *Sun Herald*.
5. Booker T. Washington, *Up From Slavery* (Garden City, NY: Doubleday, Page & Co., 1901), iii–5; Booker T. Washington, ed., *Tuskegee & Its People: Their Ideals and Achievements* (New York: Negro Universities Press, 1969), v; Frederick Douglass, *Narrative of the Life of Frederick Douglass* (Garden City, NY: Doubleday and Company, Inc., 1963), 1–2.
6. Washington, *Up From Slavery*, 17–50.
7. Ibid., 51–52; Franklin, *From Slavery to Freedom*, 284.
8. Washington, *Up From Slavery*, 51–53, 57.
9. Ibid., 57.

10. J. Alfred Phelps, *Chappie: America's First Black Four-Star General, The Life and Times of Daniel James, Jr.* (Novato, CA: Presidio, 1991), 16.

11. Earl Schenck Miers, ed., *The American Story: The Age of Exploration to the Age of the Atom* (Great Neck, NY: Channel Press, 1956), 248–51; Phelps, *Chappie*, 16.

12. Washington, *Up From Slavery*, 70.

13. Miers, *American Story*, 249–51.

14. Washington, *Tuskegee & Its People*, v–vi; Franklin, *From Slavery to Freedom*, 285.

15. *The Appeal* (St. Paul, MN), July 3, 1897.

16. Washington, *Tuskegee & Its People*, 6.

17. Ibid., 21.

18. Ibid.

19. Washington, *Tuskegee & Its People*, v–vi.

20. A. E. White, "Harlem in Wild Acclaim over Return of 'Brown Condor,'" Claude A. Barnett Papers, Chicago Historical Society, Chicago.

21. Washington, *Tuskegee & Its People*, 23–24.

22. Waterford, "The Real Story of Col. John Robinson"; Simmons, *The Brown Condor*, 15; Gubert, Sawyer, and Fannin, *Distinguished African Americans in Aviation*, 252.

23. Waterford, "The Real Story of Col. John Robinson"; Simmons, *The Brown Condor*, 15; Simmons Address, Brown Condor Symposium, March 15, 2002; *Clarion Ledger* (Jackson, MS), August 8, 1937.

24. Franklin, *From Slavery to Freedom*, 286, 290.

25. Scott, "Colonel John C. Robinson," 59; Simmons Address, Brown Condor Symposium, March 15, 2002.

26. Benjamin O. Davis, Jr., *Benjamin O. Davis, Jr., American: An Autobiography* (Washington, DC: Smithsonian Institution Press, 1991), 17–18; Fred Jerome and Rodger Taylor, *Einstein on Race and Racism* (New Brunswick, NJ: Rutgers University Press, 2005), 33.

27. Simmons Address, Brown Condor Symposium, March 15, 2002; "The Lynching Calendar: African Americans Who Died of Racial Violence in the United States during 1865–1965," online (accessed June 11, 2005); Simmons, *The Brown Condor*, 16.

28. Simmons, Brown Condor Symposium, March 15, 2002; Wayne Biddle, *Barons of the Sky: From Early Flight to Strategic Warfare: The Story of the American Aerospace Industry* (New York: Simon & Schuster, 1991), 168; Simmons, *The Brown Condor*, 17.

29. Allan H. Spear, *Black Chicago: The Making of a Negro Ghetto, 1890–1920* (Chicago: University of Chicago Press, 1967), 134–35.

30. Ibid., 81, 135.

31. Ibid., 135–140

32. Simmons, *The Brown Condor*, 17–18.

33. Ibid.

34. Ibid., 19; Doris L. Rich, *Queen Bess: Daredevil Aviator* (Washington, DC: Smithsonian Institution Press, 1993), 107–11; Von Hardesty and Dominick Pisano,

Black Wings: The American Black in Aviation (Washington, DC: Smithsonian Institution Press, 1983), 6; Hardesty, *Black Wings: Courageous Stories*, 6–10, 16–17.

35. Simmons, *The Brown Condor*, 19–33.

36. Charles E. Francis, *The Tuskegee Airmen: The Men Who Changed a Nation* (Boston: Branden Publishing Company, 1993), 17.

37. Simmons, *The Brown Condor*, 33; Simmons Address, Brown Condor Symposium, March 15, 2002.

38. Waterford, "The Real Story of Col. John Robinson."

39. Ibid.; Scott, "Colonel John C. Robinson," 59; Rich, *Queen Bess*, 24–25; Simmons, *The Brown Condor*, 35; John C. Stokes, Jamaica, New York, in interview with author, March 9, 2003.

40. Rich, *Queen Bess*, 14, 29–30; Spear, *Black Chicago*, 137.

41. Rich, *Queen Bess*, 1–34; Hardesty, *Black Wings: Courageous Stories*, 6–10.

42. Waterford, "The Real Story of Col. John Robinson"; Scott, "Colonel John C. Robinson," 59; Spear, *Black Chicago*, 137, 156–57; Simmons, *The Brown Condor*, 13.

43. Spear, *Black Chicago*, 1–12, 129–46, 156, 163, 222.

44. Rich, *Queen Bess*, 17–18, 20; Bragg and Kriz, *Soaring Above Setbacks*, 17; Katie Booth, in interview with author, Gulfport, MS, August 11, 2001; Spear, *Black Chicago*, 23–27, 51–89, 91, 104, 109, 112–13, 126; A'Lelia Bundles, *On Her Own Ground: The Life and Times of Madam C. J. Walker* (New York: Scribner, 2001), 1–365; John C. Stokes, in interview with author, St. Albans, NY, March 9, 2003; Waterford, "The Real Story of Col. John Robinson"; Cornelius Robinson Coffey biographical information, Octave Chanute Aerospace Museum, Rantoul, IL; "Air Veteran Dead of Ethiopia Crash," *New York Times*.

45. "Ethiopia Honors Dead U.S. Flyer," *Amsterdam News*, April 3, 1954; Rev. Tartt, in interview with author, October 25, 2001; Waterford, "The Real Story of Col. John Robinson"; "Air Veteran Dead of Ethiopia Crash," *New York Times*; Gubert, Sawyer, and Fannin, *Distinguished African Americans in Aviation*, 253; Stokes, in interview with author, March 9, 2003.

46. "Ethiopia Honors Dead U.S. Flyer," *Amsterdam News*; Bragg and Kriz, *Soaring Above Setbacks*, 108; "Extend Fete for 'Brown Condor,'" *Daily Times* (Chicago), May 25, 1936; Waterford, "The Real Story of Col. John Robinson"; "Air Veteran Dead of Ethiopia Crash," *New York Times*; Simmons, *The Brown Condor*, 35.

47. Waterford, "The Real Story of Col. John Robinson."

48. "Ethiopia Honors Dead U.S. Flyer," *Amsterdam News*; Waterford, "The Real Story of Col. John Robinson"; "Air Veteran Dead of Ethiopia Crash," *New York Times*.

49. "Ethiopia Honors Dead U.S. Flyer," *Amsterdam News*; *Chicago Defender*, April 4, 1936; "Air Veteran Dead of Ethiopia Crash," *New York Times*.

50. Loh, "Stalking the 'Brown Condor'"; "Extend Fete for 'Brown Condor,'" *Daily Times*; Simmons, *The Brown Condor*, 118–19; Cornelius Robinson Coffey biographical information, Octave Chanute Aerospace Museum, Rantoul, IL; Lawrence

P. Scott and William M. Womack, *Double V: The Civil Rights Struggle of the Tuskegee Airmen* (East Lansing: Michigan State University Press, 1994), 44–45; Gubert, Sawyer, and Fannin, *Distinguished African Americans in Aviation*, 253; Giles Lambertson, "The Other Harlem," *Air & Space*, March 2010, http://www .airspacemag.com/history-of-flight/The-Other-Harlem-Airport.html (accessed January 9, 2012).

51. Scott and Womack, *Double V*, 44–45; Cornelius Robinson Coffey biographical information, Octave Chanute Aerospace Museum, Rantoul, IL; Bragg and Kriz, *Soaring Above Setbacks*, 29.

52. "Aviatrices Welcome Col. John Robinson," *Chicago Defender*, May 30, 1936.

53. Cyril Gordon Burge, *Encyclopedia of Aviation* (London: Sir Isaac Pitman & Sons, 1935), 421.

54. Waterford, "The Real Story of Col. John Robinson."

55. Ibid.; Hardesty, *Black Wings: Courageous Stories*, 32–33; "Air Veteran Dead of Ethiopia Crash," *New York Times*.

56. Waterford, "The Real Story of Col. John Robinson."

57. A Zion Psalm commemorating His Imperial Majesty visit to Chicago, June 8, 1954, Ites-Zine Archive 6, Current News from June 2003, online (accessed June 11, 2005); Waterford, "The Real Story of Col. John Robinson."

58. Waterford, "The Real Story of Col. John Robinson"; Simmons, *The Brown Condor*, 36.

59. Waterford, "The Real Story of Col. John Robinson"; Simmons, *The Brown Condor*, 37.

60. Gubert, Sawyer, and Fannin, *Distinguished African Americans in Aviation*, 253.

61. Waterford, "The Real Story of Col. John Robinson."

62. Ibid.; Hardesty, *Black Wings: Courageous Stories*, 9.

63. Waterford, "The Real Story of Col. John Robinson"; Simmons, *The Brown Condor*, 118–19; "Air Veteran Dead of Ethiopia Crash," *New York Times*.

64. Waterford, "The Real Story of Col. John Robinson"; Bragg and Kriz, *Soaring Above Setbacks*, 29; Scott and Womack, *Double V*, 45; "Air Veteran Dead of Ethiopia Crash," *New York Times*.

65. Waterford, "The Real Story of Col. John Robinson"; Scott and Womack, *Double V*, 44.

66. Waterford, "The Real Story of Col. John Robinson."

67. Bragg and Kriz, *Soaring Above Setbacks*, 27; Waterford, "The Real Story of Col. John Robinson"; Scott and Womack, *Double V*, 44.

68. Francis, *The Tuskegee Airmen*, 17; Simmons, *The Brown Condor*, 36; Gubert, Sawyer, and Fannin, *Distinguished African Americans in Aviation*, 253.

69. Scott and Womack, *Double V*, 44; Bragg and Kriz, *Soaring Above Setbacks*, 27; Simmons, *The Brown Condor*, 36.

70. "Air Veteran Dead of Ethiopia Crash," *New York Times*; *Amsterdam News*, April 3, 1954; Simmons Address, Brown Condor Symposium, March 15, 2002; Waterford, "The Real Story of Col. John Robinson"; Simmons, *The Brown Condor*, 36.

71. Washington, *Up From Slavery*, 24–25.
72. Ibid., 25–26.

CHAPTER 3. BREAKING DOWN MORE RACIAL BARRIERS

1. C. R. Roseberry, *Glenn Curtiss: Pioneer of Flight* (Garden City, NY: Doubleday, 1972), 448–49; Robert Scharff and Walter S. Taylor, *Over Land and Sea: A Biography of Glenn Hammond Curtiss* (New York: David McKay Company, 1968), 296–97.

2. Roseberry, *Glenn Curtiss*, 362; Scott, "Colonel John C. Robinson," 60; Bergeron, "Brown Condor," *Sun Herald*; Loh, "Stalking the 'Brown Condor'"; Simmons, *The Brown Condor*, 36.

3. Bergeron, "Brown Condor," *Sun Herald*; Loh, "Stalking the 'Brown Condor'"; Simmons Address, Brown Condor Symposium, March 15, 2002; Simmons, *The Brown Condor*, 36; Gubert, Sawyer, and Fannin, *Distinguished African Americans in Aviation*, 253; "Air Veteran Dead of Ethiopia Crash," *New York Times*.

4. Bergeron, "Brown Condor," *Sun Herald*; Scott, "Colonel John C. Robinson," 60–61.

5. Janet Waterford [Janet Harmon Bragg/Janet Waterford Bragg], "Robinson Organizes Brown Eagle Aero Club in Effort to Interest Race in Flying" (series of articles), *Chicago Defender*, April 11–May 23, 1936.

6. Scott, "Colonel John C. Robinson," 60–61; Simmons Address, Brown Condor Symposium, March 15, 2002; Gubert, Sawyer, and Fannin, *Distinguished African Americans in Aviation*, 253.

7. Scott and Womack, *Double V*, 44; Waterford, "Robinson Organizes Brown Eagle Aero Club."

8. Waterford, "Robinson Organizes Brown Eagle Aero Club."

9. Bragg and Kriz, *Soaring Above Setbacks*, 27; Bergeron, "Brown Condor—," *Sun Herald*; Simmons Address, Brown Condor, Symposium, March 15, 2002; Simmons, *The Brown Condor*, 46.

10. Scott and Womack, *Double V*, 44; Simmons, *The Brown Condor*, 46; Lambertson, "The Other Harlem."

11. Waterford, "The Real Story of Col. John Robinson."

12. Ibid.

13. Waterford, "Robinson Organizes Brown Eagle Aero Club"; Waterford, "The Race and Aviation," Chicago Defender, May 30, 1936; Scott, "Colonel John C. Robinson," 60–61; Scott and Womack, *Double V*, 44.

14. "Col. John C. Robinson Lands at Local Airport," *Kansas City Call*, July 9, 1937; Scott and Womack, *Double V*, 44

15. Bragg and Kriz, *Soaring Above Setbacks*, 27; Scott and Womack, *Double V*, 44.

16. Bragg and Kriz, *Soaring Above Setbacks*, 27; Scott and Womack, *Double V*, 44; Simmons, *The Brown Condor*, 13.

17. Gubert, Sawyer, and Fannin, *Distinguished African Americans in Aviation*, 253.

18. Scott and Womack, *Double V*, 44.

19. Waterford, "Robinson Organizes Brown Eagle Aero Club."

20. *Chicago Defender*, May 2, 1936.
21. Waterford, "Robinson Organizes Brown Eagle Aero Club"; Bragg and Kriz, *Soaring Above Setbacks*, 27, 109; Jakeman, *The Divided Skies*, 63; Joseph E. Harris, *African-American Reactions to War in Ethiopia, 1936–1941* (Baton Rouge: Louisiana State University Press, 1994), 56.
22. Bragg and Kriz, *Soaring Above Setbacks*, 45; Waterford, "Robinson Organizes Brown Eagle Aero Club."
23. Waterford, "Robinson Organizes Brown Eagle Aero Club"; Bragg and Kriz, *Soaring Above Setbacks*, 27.
24. Waterford, "Robinson Organizes Brown Eagle Aero Club."
25. Bragg and Kriz, *Soaring Above Setbacks*, 27.
26. Waterford, "Robinson Organizes Brown Eagle Aero Club."
27. Ibid.; Scott and Womack, *Double V*, 45.
28. "Air Veteran Dead of Ethiopia Crash," *New York Times*; Simmons Address, Brown Condor Symposium, March 15, 2002; Simmons, *The Brown Condor*, 37
29. Waterford, "Robinson Organizes Brown Eagle Aero Club."
30. Ibid.; Scott and Womack, *Double V*, 45.
31. Waterford, "Robinson Organizes Brown Eagle Aero Club."
32. *Chicago Defender*, April 18, 1936; Scott and Womack, *Double V*, 45.
33. *Chicago Defender*, April 18, 1936; Hardesty and Pisano, *Black Wings: The American Black.*
34. "Air Veteran Dead of Ethiopia Crash," *New York Times*; Hardesty and Pisano, *Black Wings: The American Black*, 12; Bragg and Kriz, *Soaring Above Setbacks*, 26–29; *Chicago Defender*, April 18, 1936; Scott and Womack, *Double V*, 45; Hardesty, *Black Wings: Courageous Stories*, 35, 38–39.
35. Bragg and Kriz, *Soaring Above Setbacks*, vii–viii, 27–28; *Chicago Defender*, April 18, 1936; Simmons, *The Brown Condor*, 118–19; Hardesty, *Black Wings: Courageous Stories*, 32, 35.
36. Bragg and Kriz, *Soaring Above Setbacks*, 12–24, 26.
37. Hardesty and Pisano, *Black Wings: The American Black*, 15; Bragg and Kriz, *Soaring Above Setbacks*, 107–8; Simmons, *The Brown Condor*, 60.
38. Simmons, *The Brown Condor*, 118–19.
39. Bragg and Kriz, *Soaring Above Setbacks*, 28.
40. Ibid., 27.
41. Hardesty and Pisano, *Black Wings: The American Black*, 12; Bragg and Kriz, *Soaring Above Setbacks*, 27, 107; Jack Salzman, David Lionel Smith, and Cornel West, eds., *Encyclopedia of African-American Culture and History*, vol. 1 (New York: Simon & Schuster, Macmillan, 1996), 29; Waterford, "The Real Story of Col. John Robinson."
42. Hardesty and Pisano, *Black Wings: The American Black*, 21.
43. Jakeman, *The Divided Skies*, 66.
44. *Chicago Defender*, April 18, 1936; Bragg and Kriz, *Soaring Above Setbacks*, 26–28; Janet Waterford [Janet Harmon Bragg/Janet Waterford Bragg], "Robinson Excelled as an Instructor in Aviation Because of His Keen Insistence on Real Dis-

cipline," *Chicago Defender*, April 25, 1936; White, "Harlem in Wild Acclaim," Barnett Papers.

45. Bragg and Kriz, *Soaring Above Setbacks*, 28.
46. Salzman, Smith, and West, *Encyclopedia of African-American Culture and History*, 29; Simmons Address, Brown Condor Symposium, March 15, 2002.
47. *Chicago Defender*, April 18, 1936.
48. Scott and Womack, *Double V*, 45.
49. Waterford, "Robinson Organizes Brown Eagle Aero Club."
50. Bragg and Kriz, *Soaring Above Setbacks*, 29, 31–32; Simmons, *The Brown Condor*, 118–19; Salzman, Smith, and West, *Encyclopedia of African-American Culture and History*, 29; Simmons Address, Brown Condor Association, March 15, 2002; Jakeman, *The Divided Skies,* 63–64; Hardesty and Pisano, *Black Wings: The American Black*, 5.
51. *New York Times*, March 28, 1954; Bragg and Kriz, *Soaring Above Setbacks*, 108; "Extend Fete for 'Brown Condor,'" *Daily Times*; Simmons Address, Brown Condor Symposium, March 15, 2002; Jakeman, *The Divided Skies*, 63–64; Gubert, Sawyer, and Fannin, *Distinguished African Americans in Aviation*, 253.
52. Waterford, "The Real Story of Col. John Robinson"; Simmons Address, Brown Condor Symposium, March 15, 2002; William J. Powell, intro. by Von Hardesty, *Black Aviator: The Story of William J. Powell* (Washington, DC: Smithsonian Institution Press, 1994), 149; Gubert, Sawyer, and Fannin, *Distinguished African Americans in Aviation*, 251.
53. Waterford, "The Real Story of Col. John Robinson"; Scott and Womack, *Double V*, 46.
54. Waterford, "The Real Story of Col. John Robinson."
55. Ibid.; Waterford, "Robinson Organizes Brown Eagle Aero Club"; Gubert, Sawyer, and Fannin, *Distinguished African Americans in Aviation*, 253.
56. Waterford, "The Real Story of Col. John Robinson."
57. Bragg and Kriz, *Soaring Above Setbacks*, 29, 32; Hardesty and Pisano, *Black Wings: The American Black*, 12; Scott, "Colonel John C. Robinson," 61; Janet Waterford, "The Race and Aviation," *Chicago Defender*, May 30, 1936; Jakeman, *The Divided Skies*, 63–64; Scott and Womack, *Double V*, 45.
58. Bragg and Kriz, *Soaring Above Setbacks*, 29–30; Thomas J. Keller, "History of the Village of Robbins, Illinois," William Leonard Public Library, Robbins, IL; Scott and Womack, *Double V*, 45–46; Waterford, "Robinson Organizes Brown Eagle Aero Club."
59. Waterford, "Robinson Organizes Brown Eagle Aero Club."
60. "Air Veteran Dead of Ethiopia Crash," *New York Times*; Bragg and Kriz, *Soaring Above Setbacks*, 30; Hardesty and Pisano, *Black Wings: The American Black*, 12; Simmons, *The Brown Condor*, 118–19; Jakeman, *The Divided Skies*, 66; Waterford, "Robinson Organizes Brown Eagle Aero Club"; Gubert, Sawyer, and Fannin, *Distinguished African Americans in Aviation*, 253.
61. Bragg and Kriz, *Soaring Above Setbacks*, 30.
62. Waterford, "Robinson Excelled as an Instructor in Aviation."

63. Ibid.
64. Bragg and Kriz, *Soaring Above Setbacks*, 30–31.
65. Ibid., 31–32.
66. Ibid., 34; Bragg and Kriz, *Soaring Above Setbacks*, 108.
67. Janet Waterford [Janet Harmon Bragg/Janet Waterford Bragg], "Robinson Arouses Race Interest in Aviation," *Chicago Defender*, May 2, 1936.
68. Waterford, "Robinson Organizes Brown Eagle Aero Club"; Scott and Womack, *Double V*, 45.
69. Hardesty and Pisano, *Black Wings: The American Black*, 8–9; Hardesty, *Black Wings: Courageous Stories*, 41–51.
70. Hardesty and Pisano, *Black Wings: The American Black*, 8–9.
71. Scott and Womack, *Double V*, 45–46; Waterford, "Robinson Organizes Brown Eagle Aero Club."
72. Bragg and Kriz, *Soaring Above Setbacks*, 32; Hardesty and Pisano, *Black Wings: The American Black*, 13.
73. Janet Waterford, "Robinson Arouses Race Interest in Aviation."
74. Harold Hurd biographical sketch, Chicago Department of Aviation, Chicago, IL; Lambertson, "The Other Harlem."
75. Jakeman, *The Divided Skies*, 1–7.
76. Janet Waterford, "Robinson Arouses Race Interest in Aviation."
77. Scott and Womack, *Double V*, 46.
78. Ibid., 46–47.
79. Jakeman, *The Divided Skies*, 1–7; Scott and Womack, *Double V*, 46.
80. Janet Waterford, "Robinson Arouses Race Interest in Aviation"; Scott and Womack, *Double V*, 47.
81. Scott and Womack, *Double V*, 46.
82. Janet Waterford [Janet Harmon Bragg/Janet Waterford Bragg], "John Robinson Wings His Way Down to Tuskegee," *Chicago Defender*, May 9, 1936.
83. Ibid.; Bragg and Kriz, *Soaring Above Setbacks*, 32; Scott and Womack, *Double V*, 47.
84. Bragg and Kriz, *Soaring Above Setbacks*, 32; Simmons, *The Brown Condor*, 62, 65; Jakeman, *The Divided Skies*, 1–2; Hardesty, *Black Wings: Courageous Stories*, 31.
85. Waterford, "John Robinson Wings His Way Down to Tuskegee."

CHAPTER 4. TWIN DREAMS—TUSKEGEE AND ETHIOPIA

1. Jakeman, *The Divided Skies*, 1–2, 6–7; Jerry Kinser, "Gulfport Neighborhood Honors Native Son 'Brown Condor,'" *Sun Herald*, February 26, 1989; Simmons, *The Brown Condor*, 62, 65; Bragg and Kriz, *Soaring Above Setbacks*, 32; Scot French, *The Rebellious Slave: Nat Turner in American Memory* (Boston: Houghton Mifflin, 2004), 174.
2. Hardesty and Pisano, *Black Wings: The American Black*, 19–55; Franklin, *From Slavery to Freedom*, 286, 289–90.
3. Jakeman, *The Divided Skies*, 1–2.
4. Lindbergh, *We*, 45.

5. Jakeman, *The Divided Skies*, 1–2; Waterford, "John Robinson Wings His Way Down to Tuskegee."
6. Jakeman, *The Divided Skies*, 1–2, 6–7.
7. Ibid., 1–2, 67.
8. Scott and Womack, *Double V,* 48.
9. Ibid.
10. Jakeman, *The Divided Skies*, 1–2, 67; Bragg and Kriz, *Soaring Above Setbacks*, 32; Scott and Womack, *Double V*, 42.
11. Ibid.
12. Ibid., 1–2, 6–7, 9.
13. Loh, "Stalking the 'Brown Condor.'"
14. Jakeman, *The Divided Skies*, 1–2, 6–7.
15. Ibid., 7.
16. Ibid., 7–8; Francis, *The Tuskegee Airmen*, 19–21; Hardesty and Pisano, *Black Wings: The American Black*, 16–17.
17. Jakeman, *The Divided Skies*, 1–2, 6–7, 9–10; Hardesty and Pisano, *Black Wings: The American Black*, 16–17.
18. Jakeman, *The Divided Skies*, 10.
19. Ibid., 7, 13; Marvin E. Fletcher, *America's First Black General: Benjamin O. Davis, Sr., 1880–1970* (Lawrence: University Press of Kansas, 1989), 13–76.
20. Fletcher, *America's First Black General*, 86–147.
21. Jakeman, *The Divided Skies*, 1–2, 6–7, 9–11.
22. Ibid., 17–20.
23. Ibid., 23.
24. Waterford, "John Robinson Wings His Way Down to Tuskegee"; Scott and Womack, *Double V*, 49.
25. Rev. Tartt, Brown Condor Symposium, March 15, 2002.
26. Ibid.; *Chicago Defender*, May 2, 1936.
27. Bragg and Kriz, *Soaring Above Setbacks*, 42, photograph caption; Rich, *Queen Bess*, 119; A Zion Psalm commemorating His Imperial Majesty visit to Chicago; Hardesty, *Black Wings: Courageous Stories*, 21, 23.
28. Powell, *Black Aviator*, xviii; Scott and Womack, *Double V*, 61.
29. Scott and Womack, *Double V*, 49; Hardesty, *Black Wings: Courageous Stories*, 41.
30. Scott and Womack, *Double V*, 49.
31. Ibid.
32. Ibid.
33. Ibid., 49–50, 61, 63.
34. Raynal C. Bolling Files, History Office, 11th Wing, Bolling AFB, Washington, DC; Charles Joseph Gross, *The Air National Guard and the American Military Tradition* (Washington, DC: National Guard Bureau, U.S. Government Printing Office, 1995), 1–30.
35. Davis, *Benjamin O. Davis, Jr.*, 17.
36. Spear, *Black Chicago*, 199–200.

37. Neil A. Wynn, *The Afro-American and the Second World War* (New York: Holmes and Meier Publishers, 1993), 41.

38. Davis, *Benjamin O. Davis, Jr.*, 23; Jakeman, *The Divided Skies*, 68.

39. *The Florida Historical Quarterly* 81, no. 2 (Fall 2002), dust jacket, 1.

40. Jakeman, *The Divided Skies*, 23.

41. Harold G. Marcus, *Haile Sellassie I: The Formative Years, 1892–1936* (Lawrenceville, NJ: Red Sea Press, 1995), ix–41, 78–123; Mohamed Amin, Duncan Willetts, and Alastair Matheson, *Journey Through Ethiopia* (Nairobi: Camerapix Publishers International, 1997), 13, 17.

42. Marcus, *Haile Sellassie I*, 50; Von Hardesty, *Black Wings: Courageous Stories*, 31.

43. Marcus, *Haile Sellassie I*, 94–95, 107.

44. Haile Selassie, *The Emperor Haile Sellassie I, King of Kings of All Ethiopia and the Lord of All Lords* (Chicago: Research Associates School Times Publications, 1999), vol. 1, *My Life and Ethiopia's Progress, 1892–1937*, 72.

45. Marcus, *Haile Sellassie I*, 138; Harris, *African-American Reactions to War*, 30–33, 55; Simmons, *The Brown Condor*, 73.

46. Marcus, *Haile Sellassie I*, 98, 138; Harris, *African-American Reactions to War*, 30–31, 55; Simmons, *The Brown Condor*, 73.

47. Hardesty and Pisano, *Black Wings: The American Black*, 8; John Peer Nugent, *The Black Eagle* (New York: Stein and Day Publishers, 1971), 17–19.

48. Hardesty and Pisano, *Black Wings: The American Black*, 8; Salzman, Smith, and West, *Encyclopedia of African-American Culture and History*, 28; Nugent, *The Black Eagle*, 35, 39–47; Jakeman, *The Divided Skies*, 59; Harris, *African-American Reactions to War*, 55.

49. Nugent, *The Black Eagle*, 46–47.

50. Jakeman, *The Divided Skies*, 59.

51. Nugent, *The Black Eagle*, 53–56, 63, 67; Jakeman, *The Divided Skies*, 59.

52. Nugent, *The Black Eagle*, 74–75; Harris, *African-American Reactions to War*, 54–55.

53. Nugent, *The Black Eagle*, 76–78; Salzman, Smith, and West, *Encyclopedia of African-American Culture and History*, 28; Jakeman, *The Divided Skies*, 21, 59.

54. Nugent, *The Black Eagle*, 77–78; Jakeman, *The Divided Skies*, 21, 59; Harris, *African-American Reactions*, 55.

55. Nugent, *The Black Eagle*, 78.

56. Ibid., 39–47, 77–78.

57. Jakeman, *The Divided Skies*, 59–61.

58. Ibid., 60.

59. Ibid., 59–61; Simmons, *The Brown Condor*, 73–75.

60. Thomas M. Coffey, *Lion by the Tail: The Story of the Italian-Ethiopian War* (New York: Viking Press, 1974), 3–13; Anthony Mockler, *Haile Sellassie's War* (New York: Olive Branch Press, 2003), 37–39.

61. Coffey, *Lion by the Tail*, 14–19.

62. Ibid., 17–18; Mockler, *Selassie's War*, 39–41.

63. Marcus, *Haile Sellassie I*, 55.

64. Ibid., 127–33.

65. Ibid., 100–101; Harris, *African-American Reaction to War*, 46–47, 55.

66. Coffey, *Lion by the Tail*, 75; White, "Harlem in Wild Acclaim," Barnett Papers; Jakeman, *The Divided Skies*, 1–2, 6–7, 22; Simmons, *The Brown Condor*, 75; Harris, *African-American Reaction to War*, 55–56.

67. White, "Harlem in Wild Acclaim," Barnett Papers; Simmons, *The Brown Condor*, 75; Richard B. Moore, "Africa Conscious Harlem," *Freedomways* 3, no. 3 (Summer 1963): 328; Harris, *African-American Reactions to War*, 8–9, 22–23.

68. *Chicago Defender*, June 20, 1936.

69. Harris, *African-American Reactions to War*, 46–47.

70. White, "Harlem in Wild Acclaim," Barnett Papers; Simmons, *The Brown Condor*, 75; Malaku E. Bayen to Claude A. Barnett, January 3, 1935, Barnett Papers, Box 170, Folder 9, Chicago Historical Society, Chicago, IL; Simmons Address, BCS, March 15, 2002; Scott, "Colonel John C. Robinson," 61; *Chicago Defender*, May 23, 1936.

71. White, "Harlem in Wild Acclaim," Barnett Papers; Simmons, *The Brown Condor*, 75; Jakeman, *The Divided Skies*, 22; Scott, "Colonel John C. Robinson," 61; Scott and Womack, *Double V*, 51.

72. Waterford, "John Robinson Wings His Way Down to Tuskegee."

73. Scott and Womack, *Double V*, 51.

74. Mockler, *Selassie's War*, 14–15, 47; Marcus, *Haile Sellassie I*, 100–1.

75. Charles Norman, "'Brown Condor,' Pilot of Selassie, Feted as Harlem's Newest Hero," *Daily Progress* (Jacksonville, TX), May 25, 1936.

76. A. J. Barker, *The Civilizing Mission: A History of the Italo-Ethiopian War of 1935–1936* (New York: Dial Press, 1968), 11; Mockler, *Selassie's War*, 42–44; Marcus, *Haile Sellassie I*, 143–45.

77. "Air Veteran Dead of Ethiopia Crash," *New York Times*; Simmons, *The Brown Condor*, 76.

78. Moore, "Africa Conscious Harlem," 318.

79. Robert G. Weisbord, "Black America and the Italian-Ethiopian Crisis: An Episode in Pan-Negroism," *The Historian* 34, no. 2 (February 1977): 230; Harris, *African-American Reactions to War*, 19–20.

80. William L. Andrews, ed., *Sisters of the Spirit: Three Black Women's Autobiographies of the Nineteenth Century* (Bloomington: Indiana University Press, 1986), 57–160; Harris, *African-American Reactions to War*, 19–20.

81. Andrews, ed., *Three Black Women's Autobiographies of the Nineteenth Century*, 117–18.

82. Moore, "Africa Conscious Harlem," 319; "Come Sunday Morning: The Amazing Story of Abyssinian Baptist Church," *Essence*, June 2001, 74.

83. Weisbord, "Black America and the Italian-Ethiopian Crisis," 230; Harris, *African-American Reactions to War in Ethiopia, 1936–1941*, 20.

84. Bahru Zewde, *A History of Modern Ethiopia, 1855–1991* (Athens: Ohio University Press, 2001), 81–82.

85. Ibid., 231; Moore, "Africa Conscious Harlem," 320–27; Franklin, *From Slavery to Freedom*, 364–65; Spear, *Black Chicago*, 193.

86. Weisbord, "Black America and the Italian-Ethiopian Crisis," 230–31; Ribowsky, *Don't Look Back*, 64.

87. Spear, *Black Chicago*, 193.

88. Ibid.

89. Weisbord, "Black America and Italian-Ethiopian Crisis," 232.

90. Ibid.; Spear, *Black Chicago*, 195–96.

91. Weisbord, "Black Americans and Italian-Ethiopian Crisis," 232–33.

92. Ibid., 231–32.

93. Rev. Tartt Interview, Brown Condor Symposium, March 15, 2002; Wynn, *Afro-American and the Second World War*, 11.

94. Spear, *Black Chicago*, 137–38, 146.

95. Weisbord, "Black America and Italian-Ethiopian Crisis," 240–41.

96. Spear, *Black Chicago*, 91, 130, 146, 156–57, 191–92.

97. Scott, "Colonel John C. Robinson," 59.

98. Waterford, "Robinson Arouses Race Interest in Aviation"; Cleveland G. Allen, "Col. Robinson Exhibits His Leadership," *Chicago Defender*, May 30, 1936; Janet Waterford, "The Race and Aviation," *Chicago Defender*, May 30, 1936.

99. Hardesty and Pisano, *Black Wings: The American Black*, 5–6; Alan L. Gropman, *The Air Force Integrates, 1945–1964* (Washington, DC: Office of Air Force History, 1978), 4; Rich, *Queen Bess*, 29–39; Jakeman, *The Divided Skies*, 68–87.

100. Gropman, *The Air Force Integrates*, 2–3; Alan L. Gropman, "The Air Force, 1941–1951: From Segregation to Integration," *Air Power History*, 40, no. 2 (Summer 1993): 25; Alan M. Osur, *Blacks in the Army Air Forces During World War II* (Washington, DC: Office of Air Force History, 1986), 1–3.

101. Osur, *Blacks in the Army Air Forces*, 2.

102. Davis, *Benjamin O. Davis, Jr.*, 25.

103. Phillip Tucker, *From Auction Block to Glory: The African American Experience* (New York: MetroBooks, 1998), 1–122; Frank N. Schubert, *Black Valor: Buffalo Soldiers and the Medal of Honor, 1870–1898* (Wilmington, DE: Scholarly Resources Books, 1997), 1–144; Gropman, *The Air Force Integrates*, 3–4.

104. Gropman, *The Air Force Integrates*, 4.

105. W. Jeffrey Bolster, *Black Jacks: African American Seaman in the Age of Sail* (Cambridge, MA: Harvard University Press, 1997), 1–189.

106. Davis, *Benjamin O. Davis, Jr.*, 18.

107. Robert A. Rosenstone, *Crusade of the Left: The Lincoln Battalion in the Spanish Civil War* (New York: Pegasus, 1969), 110.

108. William Loren Katz, "Fighting Another Civil War," *American Legacy: Celebrating African-American History and Culture* 7, no. 4 (Winter 2002): 73–82; Rosenstone, *Crusade of the Left*, 109–10; John Carver Edwards, *Airmen Without*

Portfolio: U S. Mercenaries in Civil War Spain (Westport, CT: Praeger, 1997), 1–125; Harris, *African-American Reactions to War*, 60–61.

109. Ellen Gibson Wilson, *The Loyal Blacks* (New York: G. P. Putnam's Sons, 1976), 24–27; Sylvia R. Frey, *Water From the Rock: Black Resistance in the Revolutionary Age* (Princeton, NJ: Princeton University Press, 1991), 63, 67; Charles Johnson, Patricia Smith, and WGBH Series Research Team, *Africans in America America's Journey Through Slavery* (New York: Harcourt Brace, 1998), 163–68; Harris, *African-American Reactions to War*, 60–61.

110. Zeev Sternhell with Mario Sznajder and Maia Asheri, *The Birth of Fascist Ideology* (Princeton: Princeton University Press, 1994), 3–4, 6–7, 10, 222–26.

111. Ibid., 6.

112. Ibid., 31–35, 222–23.

113. John Gunther, *Inside Europe* (New York: Harper & Brothers, 1938), 187–90.

114. Sternhell, Sznajder, and Asheri, *The Birth of Fascist Ideology*, 190–92, 197–98, 202–3; Coffey, *Lion by the Tail*, 20–21; James Dugan and Laurence Lafore, *Days of Emperor and Clown: The Italo-Ethiopian War, 1935–1936* (Garden City, NY: Doubleday, 1973), 73.

115. Sternhell, Sznajder, and Asheri, *The Birth of Fascist Ideology*, 202–4, 218.

116. Ivone Kirkpatrick, *Mussolini: A Study in Power* (New York: Hawthorn Books, 1964), 276–78; Gunther, *Inside Europe*, 215–16, 221; Barker, *The Civilizing Mission*, 15–27; Kirkpatrick, *Mussolini*, 320; Eric Sevareid, *Between the Wars* (New York: Berkley Publishing, 1978), 129; A. J. P. Taylor, *The Origins of the Second World War* (New York: Atheneum, 1962), 88.

117. Kirkpatrick, *Mussolini*, 286; Gunther, *Inside Europe*, 216–17; Zewde, *History of Modern Ethiopia*, 153.

118. Kirkpatrick, *Mussolini*, 305; Lawrence Rees, *War of the Century: When Hitler Fought Stalin*, (London: BBC Worldwide Ltd., 1999), 14, 20, 33; Zewde, *History of Modern Ethiopia*, 153; Coffey, *Lion by the Tail*, 21, 112; Dugan and Lafore, *Days of Emperor and Clown*, 96.

119. Ernest R. May, ed., *Knowing One's Enemies: Intelligence Assessment Before the Two World Wars* (Princeton, NJ: Princeton University Press, 1984), 363–64.

120. Gunther, *Inside Europe*, 216; Kirkpatrick, *Mussolini*, 305, 308.

121. Barker, *The Civilizing Mission*, 16–24; Kirkpatrick, *Mussolini*, 304–5, 320; Zewde, *History of Modern Ethiopia, 1855–1991*, 56, 72–73; Coffey, *Lion by the Tail*, 20; Dugan and Lafore, *Days of Emperor and Clown*, 26.

122. Ian Knight, "Humiliation at Adwa," *Military Illustrated* 163 (April 2002): 16–23; Greg Blake, "Ethiopia's Decisive Victory at Adowa," *Military History*, October 1997, 62–68; Marion Gartler, Frederick H. Bair, and George L. Hall, *Understanding Ethiopia* (River Forest, IL: Laidlaw Brothers, 1965), 20; Barker, *The Civilizing Mission*, 23–25; Zewde, *History of Modern Ethiopia*, 76–79; Mockler, *Haile Selassie's War*, xxxix–xxxxi.

123. Jakeman, *The Divided Skies*, 21; Blake, "Ethiopia's Decisive Victory," 68; Barker, *The Civilizing Mission*, 24–25; Zewde, *History of Modern Ethiopia*, 81.

124. William R. Scott, *A Study of Afro-American and Ethiopian Relations, 1896–1941* (PhD diss., Princeton University, 1971), 29–30; Spear, *Black Chicago*, 194–95.

125. Gunther, *Inside Europe*, 218; Harris, *African-American Reactions to War*, 21.

126. Gunther, *Inside Europe*, 217.

127. Ibid.; Harris, *African-American Reactions to War*, 21–22.

128. Gunther, *Inside Europe*, 218–19.

129. Ibid., 226–27; Mockler, *Selassie's War*, 44–45.

130. Barker, *The Civilizing Mission*, 25–26.

131. Ibid., 26–27; Zewde, *History of Modern Ethiopia*, 111–13.

132. Barker, *The Civilizing Mission*, 314, 319–21; Ludwig F. Schaefer, *The Ethiopian Crisis: Touchstone of Appeasement?* (Boston: D. C. Heath and Company, 1961), vii–98; Coffey, *Lion by the Tail*, 112; Dugan and Lafore, *Days of Emperor and Clown*, 76–77; Mockler, *Selassie's War*, 44–45.

133. Selassie, *Autobiography of Emperor Sellassie I*, vol. 1, 210–13.

134. John C. Robinson to Claude A. Barnett, November 21, 1935, Box 170, Folder 9, Claude A. Barnett Papers, Chicago Historical Society, Chicago, IL.

135. Barker, *The Civilizing Mission*, 319; Mockler, *Selassie's War*, 44–45.

136. Dugan and Lafore, *Days of Emperor and Clown*, 63.

137. Jakeman, *The Divided Skies*, 23.

138. Herman C. Morris and Harry B. Henderson, eds., *World War II in Pictures* (New York: The Journal of Living Publishing Corporation, 1945), 27.

CHAPTER 5. COMMANDING EMPEROR
SELASSIE'S IMPERIAL ETHIOPIAN AIR FORCE

1. Coffey, *Lion by the Tail*, xi; Simmons, *The Brown Condor*, 76.

2. Hardesty and Pisano, *Black Wings: The American Black*, 14; John C. Robinson to Claude A. Barnett, November 21, 1935, Box 170, Folder 9, Chicago Historical Society, Chicago, IL; Scott and Womack, *Double V*, 50.

3. Robinson to Barnett, November 21, 1935.

4. Phillip Knightley, *The First Casualty: From the Crimea to Vietnam: The War Correspondent as Hero, Propagandist and Myth Maker* (New York: Harcourt Brace Jovanovich, 1975), 173.

5. "Extend Fete for 'Brown Condor,'" *Daily Times*; *Daily Herald* (Gulfport, MS), June 26, 1936; "Air Veteran Dead of Ethiopia Crash," *New York Times*; "Col. Robinson, Haile's Flier, Welcomed Here," *Daily News* (Chicago), May 25, 1936.

6. Waterford, "John Robinson Wings His Way Down to Tuskegee."

7. Ibid.

8. *Pittsburgh Courier*, October 12, 1935; Rich, *Queen Bess*, 30–39; Jakeman, *The Divided Skies*, 22.

9. Jakeman, *The Divided Skies*, 21.

10. White, "Harlem in Wild Acclaim," Barnett Papers.

11. Ibid.

12. Ibid.; Knightley, *The First Casualty*, 174.

13. Harris, *African-American Reactions to War*, 6; Selassie, *Autobiography of Emperor Sellassie I*, 65; Amin, Willetts, and Matheson, *Journey Through Ethiopia*, 30, 99–100.

14. Mockler, *Selassie's War*, 3–10; Selassie, *Autobiography of Emperor Sellassie I*, 13–48; Amin, Willetts, and Matheson, *Journey Through Ethiopia*, 178–83.

15. Selassie, *Autobiography of Emperor Sellassie I*, 48–49.

16. Ibid., 3, 118–19; Morris and Henderson, *World War II In Pictures*, 26; Amin, Willetts, and Matheson, *Journey Through Ethiopia*, 13, 17.

17. Selassie, *Autobiography of Emperor Sellassie*, 118–22, 168; Franklin, *From Slavery to Freedom*, 13; Gartler, Bair, and Hall, *Understanding Ethiopia*, 47; Lila Perl, *Ethiopia, Land of the Lion* (New York: William Morrow, 1972), 9–10, 28–31, 34–35; Zewde, *History of Modern Ethiopia*, 1, 7; Coffey, *Lion by the Tail*, ix–x, 6–7; Dugan and Lafore, *Days of Emperor and Clown*, 11–15, 39; Joel A. Rogers, *Sex and Race* (St. Petersburg, FL: Helga M. Rogers, 1967), vol. 1, 2–3; Mockler, *Selassie's War*, xiii; Ernle Bradford, *Thermopylae: The Battle for the West* (New York: Da Capo Press, 1993), 21; John Maxwell O'Brien, *Alexander the Great: The Invisible Enemy* (New York: Routledge, 1992), 217; Amin, Willetts, and Matheson, *Journey Through Ethiopia*, 17–18, 22.

18. Jakeman, *The Divided Skies*, 22; Gartler, Bair, and Hall, *Understanding Ethiopia*, 8–11, 16, 28–29; Perl, *Ethiopia*, 10–11; Zewde, *History of Modern Ethiopia*, 1–2, 68; Coffey, *Lion by the Tail*, 45–46, 48; Dugan and Lafore, *Days of Emperor and Clown*, 14–15, 28, 51; Mockler, *Selassie's War*, 13; Joel A. Rogers, *The Real Facts About Ethiopia* (pamphlet, publisher unknown, 1936), 9—10; Knightley, *The First Casualty*, 173; Amin, Willetts, and Matheson, *Journey Through Ethiopia*, 96–115.

19. Jared Diamond, *Guns, Germs, and Steel: The Fates of Human Societies* (New York: W. W. Norton, 1999), 100–101; Amin, Willetts, and Matheson, *Journey Through Ethiopia*, 132–35.

20. John C. Robinson to Claude A. Barnett, June 3, 1935, Claude Barnett Papers, Box 170, Folder 9, Chicago Historical Society, Chicago, IL.

21. Kirkpatrick, *Mussolini*, 309–10; Coffey, *Lion by the Tail*, 42; Mockler, *Haile Selassie's War*, 46; David Nicolle, *The Italian Invasion of Abyssinia, 1935–1936* (London:Osprey Publishing, 2000), 12, 23, 34–41.

22. Robinson to Barnett, June 3, 1935, Barnett Papers; Simmons, *The Brown Condor*, 87; Robinson to Barnett, November 21, 1935; Knightley, *The First Casualty*, 173–74.

23. Zewde, *History of Modern Ethiopia*, 147–48; Weisbord, "Black America and the Italian-Ethiopian Crisis," 240; Coffey, *Lion by the Tail*, 107–8; Dugan and Lafore, *Days of Emperor and Clown*, 55; Mockler, *Selassie's War*, 12, 14, 44, 49–51; Simmons, *The Brown Condor*, 87; Robinson to Barnett, November 21, 1935; Harris, *African-American Reaction to War*, 30–32.

24. White, "Harlem in Wild Acclaim," Barnett Papers; Coffey, *Lion by the Tail*, 9.

25. *The Clarion Ledger*, August 8, 1937.

26. Scott and Womack, *Double V*, 51; Harris, *African-American Reaction to War*, 56.

27. Bragg and Kriz, *Soaring Above Setbacks*, 75; Scott and Womack, *Double V*, 51.

28. Harris, *African-American Reaction to War*, 57.

29. Robinson to Barnett, June 3, 1935.

30. Ibid.

31. Nugent, *The Black Eagle*, 96–99; Norman, "'Brown Condor' Feted as Harlem's Newest Hero"; Weisbord, "Black America and the Italian-Ethiopian Crisis," 235; Simmons, *The Brown Condor*, 87, 89; Robinson to Barnett, November 21, 1935; Scott and Womack, *Double V*, 51–52; Harris, *African-American Reaction to War* 56; Knightley, *The First Casualty*, 173–74.

32. Robinson to Barnett, November 21, 1935; White, "Harlem in Wild Acclaim," Barnett Papers.

33. "Ethiopia Gets New Flier," *New York Times*, August 23, 1935.

34. Ibid.; Joel Williamson, *New People: Miscegenation and Mulattoes in the United States* (New York: Free Press, 1980), 3.

35. Scott, "Colonel John C. Robinson," 62–63; Robinson to Barnett, November 21, 1935; White, "Harlem in Wild Acclaim," Barnett Papers; Jakeman, *The Divided Skies*, 22; Coffey, *Lion by the Tail*, 147; Scott and Womack, *Double V*, 352.

36. Jakeman, *The Divided Skies*, 22; Nugent, *The Black Eagle*, 102–3; Harris, *African-American Reaction to War*, 54.

37. Harris, *African-American Reaction to War*, 56.

38. Editor, "Ethiops' Rabble Army Won All Frays–Flyer," *Afro-American* (Baltimore, MD), June 13, 1936; Nugent, *The Black Eagle*, 57, 74–75; Bragg and Kriz, *Soaring Above Setbacks*, 32; Robinson to Barnett, November 21, 1935; Scott, "Colonel John C. Robinson," 62–63; Coffey, *Lion by the Tail*, 50, 147; Mockler, *Selassie's War*, 46; Nicolle, *The Italian Invasion of Abyssinia, 1935–36*, 21, 24.

39. "Ethiops' Rabble Army Won " June 13, 1936; Nugent, *The Black Eagle*, 57; Bragg and Kriz, *Soaring Above Setbacks*, 32; Robinson to Barnett, November 21, 1935; Coffey, *Lion by the Tail*, 50.

40. Hans Wilhelm Lockot, *The Mission: The Life, Reign and Character of Haile Selassie I* (London: C. Hurst and Company, 1993), 29–30; Coffey, *Lion by the Tail*, 147; Dugan and Lafore, *Days of Emperor and Clown*, 49.

41. Dugan and Lafore, *Days of Emperor and Clown*, 49; Mockler, *Selassie's War*, 11.

42. Mockler, *Selassie's War*, xxxxi.

43. Zewde, *History of Modern Ethiopia, 1855–1991*, 159; Coffey, *Lion by the Tail*, 50; Mockler, *Selassie's War*, 11–13, 47; Simmons, *The Brown Condor*, 97; *Pittsburgh Courier*, October 12, 1935; Nicolle, *The Italian Invasion of Abyssinia, 1935–36*, 24, 33.

44. Nicolle, *The Italian Invasion of Abyssinia, 1935–36*, 24.

45. Ibid.

46. "Selassie's Air Aide Back from Africa," *New York Times*, May 19, 1936.

47. Ibid.

48. Enzo Angelucci and Paolo Matricardi, *World Aircraft, 1918–1935* (Chicago: Rand McNally, 1977), 26–27.

49. William H. McDaniel, *The History of Beech* (Wichita, KS: McCormick-Armstrong Co., 1971), 1–17; Simmons Address, March 15, 2002; Scott, "Colonel John C. Robinson," 6; Roger E. Bilstein, *The American Aerospace Industry: From Workshop to Global Enterprise* (New York: Twayne Publishers, 1996), 53–54; Simmons, *The Brown Condor*, 112, 134–35.

50. Coffey, *Lion by the Tail*, 308; Simmons Address, March 15, 2002; Bilstein, *The American Aerospace Industry*, 53.

51. Coffey, *Lion by the Tail*, 147; Lockot, *The Mission*, 29–30; Biddle, *Barons of the Sky*, 201; Simmons, *The Brown Condor*, 97.

52. Ethiopundit, *The Rise and Fall of the Ethiopian Air Force*, online (accessed June 11, 2005).

53. Robinson to Barnett, November 21, 1935, Barnett Papers.

54. Coffey, *Lion by the Tail*, 131, 147.

55. Mockler, *Selassie's War*, 51.

56. Lockot, *The Mission*, xii; Nicolle, *The Italian Invasion of Abyssinia, 1935–36*, 23; Marcus, *Haile Sellassie I*, 154–55.

57. Mockler, *Haile Selassie's War*, 51; Marcus, *Haile Sellassie I*, 154–55.

58. Lockot, *The Mission*, 41–42; Mockler, *Selassie's War*, 51; Nicolle, *The Italian Invasion of Abyssinia 1935–36*, 21, 23; Edward W. Bennett, *German Rearmament and the West, 1932–1933* (Princeton, NJ: Princeton University Press, 1979), 368; Angelucci and Matricardi, *World Aircraft*, 136–37; Ethiopian Air Force, Wikipedia (accessed June 21, 2005).

59. Nugent, *The Black Eagle*, 57; David Irving, *The Rise and Fall of the Luftwaffe: The Life of Field Marshall Erhard Milch* (Boston: Little, Brown, 1973), 25–27; Scott, "Colonel John C. Robinson," 62; Alfred Goldberg, *A History of the United States Air Force, 1907–1957* (Princeton, NJ: Van Nostrand, 1957), 38; Angelucci and Matricardi, *World Aircraft*, 136–37.

60. Mockler, *Selassie's War*, 51, 140; Scott, "Colonel John C. Robinson," 63; Nicolle, *The Italian Invasion of Abyssinia 1935–36*, 20–21, 24, 33; Ethiopian Air Force, Wikipedia; Simmons, *The Brown Condor*, 90–91, 131–32.

61. Nicolle, *Italian Invasion of Abyssinia 1935–36*, 24, 34.

62. Maurer Maurer, ed., *The United States Air Service in World War I: The Final Report and a Tactical History*, vol. 1 (Washington, DC: U.S. Government Printing Office, 1978), 172, 186

63. Ibid., 206.

64. Ibid., 179–80.

65. White, "Harlem in Acclaim," Barnett Papers.

66. Coffey, *Lion by the Tail*, 307; Mockler, *Selassie's War*, 12, 72; Nicolle, *The Italian Invasion of Abyssinia, 1935–36*, 20, 31.

67. Mockler, *Selassie's War*, 29; Robinson to Barnett, June 3, 1935, Barnett Papers.

68. Diamond, "Haile Selassie's Ace Airman Back in New York"; Coffey, *Lion by the Tail*, 147; Professor Negussay Ayele, "African Americans and Ethiopia on the Eve of the Fascist Invasion," 2003, Tadias, http://www.tadias.com/v1n7/AE_2_2003 -3.html.

69. Biddle, *Barrons of the Sky*, 201–6.

70. "Ethops' Rabble Army," *Afro-American*; Scott, "Colonel John C. Robinson," 62–63; Robinson to Barnett, November 21, 1935, Barnett Papers; Marcus, *Haile Sellassie I*, 154–55, 158; Nicolle, *The Italian Invasion of Abyssinia, 1935–36*, 33; "Ethiopia Prepares to Take to the Skies," *Chicago Defender*, November 2, 1935.

71. Ibid.; Robinson to Barnett, November 21, 1935, Barnett Papers; Scott, "Colonel John C. Robinson," 62–63; Scott and Womack, *Double V*, 54.

72. Coffey, *Lion by the Tail*, 110.

73. Marcus, *Haile Sellassie I*, 158.

74. Ibid., 164.

75. Robinson to Barnett, June 3, 1935, Barnett Papers.

76. "Ethiops' Rabble Army," *Afro-American*.

77. Diamond, "Haile Selassie's Ace Airman Back in New York"; Gartler, Bair, and Hall, *Understanding Ethiopia*, 38, 44–46.

78. Perl, *Ethiopia*, 12–14, 18, 56; Dugan and Lafore, *Days of Emperor and Clown*, 15.

79. Perl, *Ethiopia*, 14, 17–18; Amin, Willetts, and Matheson, *Journey Through Ethiopia*, 22–31.

80. Perl, *Ethiopia*, 14, 17–18.

81. Ibid., 76–78.

82. Bragg and Kriz, *Soaring Above Setbacks*, 79; Franklin, *From Slavery to Freedom*, 184–85.

83. Diamond, "Haile Selassie's Ace Airman Back in New York"; White, "Harlem in Wild Acclaim," Barnett Papers; Perl, *Ethiopia*, 141–42.

84. Kirkpatrick, *Mussolini*, 316–17; Christopher Hibbert, *Il Duce: The Life of Benito Mussolini* (Boston: Little, Brown, 1962), 71.

85. Coffey, *Lion by the Tail*, 103.

86. Zewde, *History of Modern Ethiopia*, 155; Major Ralph Stearley, "The Conflict of Ethiopia and the Use of Aircraft in the Operation," Air Corps Tactical School Lecture, February 2, 1939, United States Air Force Historical Research Agency, Maxwell Air Force Base, Montgomery, AL.

87. Nicolle, *The Italian Invasion of Abyssinia, 1935–36*, 37.

88. Kirkpatrick, *Mussolini*, 319.

89. Coffey, *Lion by the Tail*, 45.

90. Ibid., 254.

91. Mockler, *Selassie's War*, 47.

92. Knightley, *The First Casualty*, 178.

93. Dugan and Lafore, *Days of Emperor and Clown*, 103.

94. Barker, *The Civilizing Mission*, 9, 314, 320–23; Kirkpatrick, *Mussolini*, 298–303; Henry Adams and eds. of Time-Life Books, *Italy at War* (Alexandria: Time-Life Books, 1982), 32; Schaefer, *The Ethiopian Crisis*, 25; Dugan and Lafore, *Days of Emperor and Clown*, 112–36; Sevareid, *Between the Wars*, 125, 128.

95. Kirkpatrick, *Mussolini*, 321.

96. "Ethiopia Prepares to Take to the Skies," *Chicago Defender*.

97. "Interviewed in London by Defender Man," *Chicago Defender*, October 12, 1935.

98. Jakeman, *Divided Skies*, 29, 64; Weisbord, "Black America and Italian-Ethiopian Crisis," 236–39; Coffey, *Lion by the Tail*, 128; Sevareid, *Between the Wars*, 131–32; *Chicago Defender*, April 25, 1936 and May 9, 23, and 30, 1936.

99. William D. Feeny, *In Their Honor: True Stories of Fliers for whom United States Air Force Bases Are Named* (New York: Duell, Sloan and Pearce, 1963), 125–28; Gene Gurney, *Five Down and Glory: A History of the American Air Ace*, ed. Mark P. Friedlander, Jr. (New York: Putnam, 1958), 29–41; James J. Hudson, *Hostile Skies: A Combat History of American Air Service in World War I* (Syracuse, NY Syracuse University Press, 1968), 233–36; Herbert Molloy Mason, *The United States Air Force: A Turbulent History* (New York: Mason/Charter, 1976), 68–73; Sydney P. Chivers, *Flying Tigers: Pictorial History of the American Volunteer Group* (Conoga Park, CA: Challenge Publications, n.d.), 1–50.

100. Gurney, *Five Down and Glory*, 78–85.

CHAPTER 6. THE FASCIST INVASION OF ETHIOPIA

1. "King Loses Hope; League Is Too Slow," *Chicago Defender*, October 26, 1935.

2. Nugent, *The Black Eagle*, 98.

3. *Afro-American*, September 28, 1935.

4. Coffey, *Lion by the Tail*, 62; "King Loses Hope; League Is Too Slow," *Chicago Defender*.

5. Coffey, *Lion by the Tail*, 68.

6. Dugan and Lafore, *Days of Emperor and Clown*, 117–18.

7. *Chicago Defender*, January 4, 1936.

8. Coffey, *Lion by the Tail*, 70.

9. Selassie, *Autobiography of Emperor Sellassie I*, 226–27; Robert T. Elson, *Prelude to War*; Adams, *Italy at War*, 148–49.

10. Knight, "Humiliation at Adwa," *Military Illustrated*, 19; Coffey, *Lion by the Tail*, 46; Dugan and Lafore, *Days of Emperor and Clown*, 175; Mockler, *Selassie's War*, xxxx; Nicolle, *The Italian Invasion of Abyssinia, 1935–36*, 4; Amin, Willetts, and Matheson, *Journey Through Ethiopia*, 14–15, 90, 102.

11. Mockler, *Selassie's War*, 60, 71.

12. Norman, "'Brown Condor' Feted as Harlem's Newest Hero"; Coffey, *Lion by the Tail*, 197; Mockler, *Selassie's War*, 59; Selassie, *Autobiography of Emperor Sellassie I*, 210, 214.

13. Coffey, *Lion by the Tail*, 45; Selassie, *Autobiography of Emperor Sellassie I*, 226–27.

14. *Journal and Guide* (Norfolk, VA), October 5, 1935.

15. "Robinson Tells All in the Bombing of Adowa," *Chicago Defender*, October 12, 1935.

16. Ibid.

17. Coffey, *Lion by the Tail*, 123–24, 153, 157, 162–63; John Carey, ed., *Eyewitness to History* (Cambridge, MA: Harvard University Press, 1988), 513–14; Dugan and Lafore, *Days of Emperor and Clown*, 174; Mockler, *Selassie's War*, 55, 61–62; Ray Moseley, *Mussolini's Shadow: The Double Life of Count Galeazzo Ciano*

(New Haven, CT: Yale University Press, 1999), 17; Nicolle, *The Italian Invasion of Abyssinia, 1935–36*, 36; Elson, *Prelude to War*, 150–51; "Solemn Hours," *Time*, October 14, 1935.

18.   Selassie, *Autobiography of Emperor Sellassie I*, 228.
19.   "Solemn Hours," *Time*.
20.   Large, "Mussolini's 'Civilizing Mission,'" *Quarterly Journal of Military History* 5, no. 2 (Winter 1993): 48.
21.   Coffey, *Lion by the Tail*, 162–63; Dugan and Lafore, *Days of Emperor and Clown*, 174; Large, "Mussolini's 'Civilizing Mission,'" 48; Mockler, *Selassie's War*, 55, 61–62; Moseley, *Mussolini's Shadow*, 18; *Chicago Defender*, November 2, 1935; Angelucci and Matricardi, *World Aircraft*, 16–17.
22.   "Robinson Tells All in the Bombing of Adowa," *Chicago Defender*.
23.   Ibid.
24.   "Solemn Hours," *Time*.
25.   Robinson to Barnett, November 21, 1935, Barnett Papers; Mockler, *Selassie's War*, 61; Scott and Womack, *Double V*, 52.
26.   "Robinson Tells All in the Bombing of Adowa," *Chicago Defender*.
27.   Scott and Womack, *Double V*, 52.
28.   "Robinson Tells All in the Bombing of Adowa," *Chicago Defender*.
29.   Coffey, *Lion by the Tail*, 162–63; Mockler, *Haile Selassie's War*, 61–62; "Robinson Tells All in the Bombing of Adowa," *Chicago Defender*.
30.   "Robinson Tells All in the Bombing of Adowa," *Chicago Defender*.
31.   Ibid.
32.   Coffey, *Lion by the Tail*, 162–63; Mockler, *Selassie's War*, 55; Simmons, *The Brown Condor*, 110; Scott and Womack, *Double V*, 52.
33.   "Robinson Tells All in the Bombing of Adowa," *Chicago Defender*.
34.   Moseley, *Mussolini's Shadow*, 1–17; Robert Payne, *The Life and Death of Adolf Hitler* (New York: Barnes and Noble Books, 1995), 443–44.
35.   Moseley, *Mussolini's Shadow*, 17, 21.
36.   Coffey, *Lion by the Tail*, 162–63, 191; Gunther, *Inside Europe*, 194, 207–9; Large, "Mussolini's 'Civilizing Mission'"; Dugan and Lafore, *Days of Emperor and Clown*, 70; Mockler, *Selassie's War*, 24–25, 55; "Solemn Hours," *Time*.
37.   Adams, *Italy At War*, 37; Mockler, *Selassie's War*, 25, 55.
38.   Marcus, *Haile Sellassie I*, 167.
39.   *Chicago Defender*, November 30, 1935.
40.   "Robinson Tells All in the Bombing of Adowa," *Chicago Defender*.
41.   Giulio Douhet, *The Command of the Air*, trans. Dino Ferrari (Washington, DC: Office of Air Force History, 1983), vii–147.
42.   *Journal and Guide* (Norfolk, VA), October 5, 1935.
43.   *Journal and Guide*, October 5, 1935; Bernard C. Nalty, John F. Shiner, and George M. Watson, *With Courage: The U.S. Army in World War II*, ed. Alfred M. Beck (Washington, DC: Air Force History & Museums Program, 1994), 26; Adams, *Italy at War*, 25–27, 72; Mockler, *Selassie's War*, 24–25; May, *Knowing One's Enemies*, 357, 365; Hibbert, *Il Duce*, 58–59.

44. *Journal and Guide*, October 5, 1935; Gartler, Bair, and Hall, *Understanding Ethiopia*, 9–10; Perl, *Ethiopia*, 12; Coffey, *Lion by the Tail*, 307; Amin, Willetts, and Matheson, *Journey Through Ethiopia*, 75–79.
45. *Journal and Guide*, October 5, 1935.
46. Burge, *Encyclopedia of Aviation*, 171.
47. Wesley Frank Craven and James Lea Cate, eds., *The Army Air Forces in World War II* (Washington, DC: Office of Air Force History, 1983), 66.
48. Douhet, *The Command of the Air*, 20.
49. Stearley, "The Conflict of Ethiopia and the Use of Aircraft in the Operation."
50. Thomas H. Greer, *The Development of Air Doctrine in the Army Air Arm, 1917–1941* (Washington, DC: Office of Air Force History, 1985), 102.
51. Douhet, *The Command of the Air*, 96.
52. William Mitchell, *Winged Defense* (New York: G. P. Putnam's Sons, 1925), 19.
53. Greer, *The Development of Air Doctrine*, 102.
54. Zewde, *History of Modern Ethiopia*, 159.
55. *Chicago Defender*, December 11, 1935.
56. Robinson to Barnett, November 21, 1935, Barnett Papers.
57. Ibid.
58. Ibid.; Coffey, *Lion by the Tail*, 147; Mockler, *Selassie's War*, 72; Scott and Womack, *Double V*, 52–53.
59. Robinson to Barnett, November 21, 1935, Barnett Papers.
60. *Clarion Ledger*, August 8, 1937.
61. Scott and Womack, *Double V*, 52–53.
62. Robinson to Barnett, November 21, Barnett Papers.
63. Ibid.
64. White, "Harlem in Wild Acclaim," Barnett Papers.
65. Gunther, *Inside Europe*, 209.
66. Moseley, *Mussolini's Shadow*, 18.
67. Marcus, *Haile Sellassie I*, 99.
68. Robinson to Barnett, November 21, 1935, Barnett Papers.
69. Dugan and Lafore, *Days of Emperor and Clown*, 171–72; Simmons, *The Brown Condor*, 111; Selassie, *Autobiography of Emperor Sellassie I*, 230.
70. Selassie, *The Autobiography of Emperor Sellassie I*, 230–31; "Solemn Hours," *Time*.
71. "King Loses Hope; League Is Too Slow," *Chicago Defender*, October 26, 1935; *Chicago Defender*, December 11, 1935; Marcus, *Haile Sellassie I*, 170.
72. *Chicago Defender*, December 7, 1935.
73. Weisbord, "Black America and the Italian-Ethiopian Crisis," 230–41.
74. *Afro-American*, October 19, 1935.
75. "Organize Ethiopia 'Friends' In Ala.," *Chicago Defender*, December 21, 1935.
76. A. N. Fields, "Looking Backward Over 1935," *Chicago Defender*, January 4, 1936.
77. Selassie, *Autobiography of Emperor Sellassie I*, 236.
78. *Pittsburgh Courier*, October 12, 1935.

79. Bragg and Kriz, *Soaring Above Setbacks*, 111.
80. Ibid.
81. Robinson to Barnett, November 21 and 28, 1935, Barnett Papers
82. Greer, *The Development of Air Doctrine*, 102; Scott, "Colonel John C. Robinson," 63.
83. "Child Reported Killed by a Bomb," *New York Times*, October 20, 1935.
84. Norman, "'Brown Condor,' Pilot of Selassie"; White, "Harlem in Wild Acclaim," Barnett Papers; Foreign Dispatches, Random Remarks on Current Affairs, "The Ethiopian-Italian War: The African American Connection," September 26, 2004, online (accessed June 11, 2005).
85. Mockler, *Selassie's War*, 71.
86. Ibid., 72; Norman, "'Brown Condor' Feted as Harlem's Newest Hero."
87. "Air Veteran Dead of Ethiopia Crash," *New York Times*.
88. Selassie, *Autobiography of Emperor Sellassie*, 239; Foreign Dispatches, "The Ethiopian-Italian War."
89. Harris, *African-American Reaction to War*, 57; Foreign Dispatches, "The Ethiopian-Italian War."
90. Harris, *African American Reaction to War*, 57; White, "Harlem," Barnett Papers; Coffey, *Lion by the Tail*, 147; Mockler, *Selassie's War*, 72; Simmons, *The Brown Condor*, 115–16, 126–27; Scott, "Colonel John C. Robinson," 63; Foreign Dispatches, "The Ethiopian-Italian War," September 26, 2004.
91. Mockler, *Selassie's War*, 72.
92. Scott, "Colonel John C. Robinson," 63.
93. Ibid., 64.
94. "Americans in Ethiopia," *Ebony*, May 1951, 80.
95. Simmons, *The Brown Condor*, 98.
96. *Pittsburgh Courier*, October 12, 1935; Foreign Dispatches, "The Ethiopian-Italian War."
97. Norman, "'Brown Condor' Feted as Harlem's Newest Hero."
98. Diamond, "Haile Selassie's Ace Airman Back in New York."
99. Ibid.
100. *Evening News* (London), October 17, 1935; Coffey, *Lion by the Tail*, 195–96; Marcus, *Haile Sellassie I*, 168.
101. *Evening News*, October 17, 1935; Correlli Barnett, ed., *Hitler's Generals* (New York: Quill/William Morrow, 1989), 279.
102. Kirkpatrick, *Mussolini*, 328; Coffey, *Lion by the Tail*, 173–76, 179; Dugan and Lafore, *Days of Emperor and Clown*, 175; Mockler, *Selassie's War*, 61–65; "Solemn Hours," *Time*.
103. Coffey, *Lion by the Tail*, 209.
104. Ibid., 209–10; Elson, *Prelude to War*, 151; Mockler, *Selassie's War*, 67; Harris, *African-American Reactions to the War*, 34–35.
105. Dugan and Lafore, *Days of Emperor and Clown*, 152; Elson, *Prelude to War*, 151; Sevareid, *Between the Wars*, 128, 132–33; Harris, *African-American Reactions to the War*, 34.

106. Gunther, *Inside Europe*, 211; Coffey, *Lion by the Tail*, 194–95, 212–13; Mockler, *Selassie's War*, 62–63, 68; Taylor, *The Origins of the Second World War*, 88, 95.

107. Gunther, *Inside Europe*, 211; Kirkpatrick, *Mussolini*, 330–31.

108. Zewde, *History of Modern Ethiopia*, 154.

109. Dugan and Lafore, *Days of Emperor and Clown*, 177.

110. Mockler, *Selassie's War*, 69–70.

111. Coffey, *Lion by the Tail*, 195–96; Elson, *Prelude to War*, 155; Mockler, *Selassie's War*, 70.

112. Robert A. Pape, *Bombing to Win: Air Power and Coercion in War* (Ithaca, NY: Cornell University Press, 1996), 334–35.

113. Robinson to Barnett, November 21, 1935, Barnett Papers.

114. Ibid.

115. Dugan and Lafore, *Days of Emperor and Clown*, 184; Diamond, "Haile Selassie's Ace Airman Back in New York"; Morris and Henderson, *World War II in Pictures*, 28–29.

116. Robinson to Barnett, November 21, 1935, Barnett Papers.

117. Nugent, *The Black Eagle*, 100–101.

118. Ibid., 100–102.

119. Robinson to Barnett, November 21, 1935, Barnett Papers; Bragg and Kriz, *Soaring Above Setbacks*, 111.

120. Robinson to Barnett, November 21, 1935, Barnett Papers.

121. Moore, "Africa Conscious Harlem," 328; Harris, *African-American Reactions to War*, 38–39.

122. Harris, *African-American Reactions to War*, 40–42.

123. "Ethiops' Rabble Army," *Afro-American*; Weisbord, "Black America and the Italian-Ethiopian Crisis," 237.

124. *Afro-American*, October 12, 1935.

125. Robinson and Barnett, November 21, 1935, Barnett Papers.

126. Ibid.

127. Robinson to Barnett, June 3, 1935, Barnett Papers; Harris, *African-American Reactions to War*, 8, 14–15, 30–31.

128. *Chicago Defender*, January 4, 1936.

129. Robinson to Barnett, November 28, 1935, Barnett Papers; Weisbord, "Black America and the Italian-Ethiopian Crisis," 239–40; Dugan and Lafore, *Days of Emperor and Clown*, 57; Sevareid, *Between the Wars*, 131.

130. Robinson to Barnett, November 21, 1935, Barnett Papers; Harris, *African-American Reactions to War*, 52–54.

131. Bragg and Kriz, *Soaring Above Setbacks*, 61, 111.

132. Womack and Scott, *Double V*, 63, 85.

133. Robinson to Barnett, November 21, 1935, Barnett Papers.

134. Ibid.

135. Scott, "Colonel John C. Robinson," 64.

136. Robinson to Barnett, November 21, 1935, Barnett Papers.

137. Rogers, *Sex and Race*, vol. 1, in foreword, n.p.

138. Coffey, *Lion by the Tail*, 254; Knightley, *The First Casualty*, 183–84.
139. Coffey, *Lion by the Tail*, 254, 291.
140. "Duce's Men Lag Behind as Cowards," *Chicago Defender*, June 6, 1936.
141. Selassie, *Autobiography of Emperor Sellassie I*, 243.
142. John C. Robinson to Claude A. Barnett, November 28, 1935, Barnett Papers.
143. Mockler, *Selassie's War*, 23–24.
144. Dugan and Lafore, *Days of Emperor and Clown*, 210–11.
145. "Rejects Peace Plan of Laval and Hoare," *Chicago Defender*, December 14, 1935.
146. *Chicago Defender*, June 20, 1936.
147. "Toronto Paper in Bomb Protest," *Chicago Defender*, December 28, 1935.
148. Dugan and Lafore, *Days of Emperor and Clown*, 210–11; Coffey, *Lion by the Tail*, 219–20; Simmons, *The Brown Condor*, 129; *Chicago Defender*, June 20, 1936; Selassie, *Autobiography of Emperor Sellassie I*, 243; Knightley, *The First Casualty*, 181.
149. Coffey, *Lion by the Tail*, 274, 307–8; Mockler, *Haile Selassie's War*, 15, 74; Selassie, *The Autobiography of Emperor Sellassie I*, 245, 251.
150. John C. Robinson to Claude A. Barnett, November 28, 1935, Barnett Papers; Gartler, Bair, and Hall, *Understanding Ethiopia*, 8–12; Perl, *Ethiopia*, 11; Coffey, *Lion by the Tail*, 219, 241; Amin, Willets, and Matheson, *Journey Through Ethiopia*, 78–79.
151. Harris, *African-American Reaction to War*, 30–32.
152. Robinson to Barnett, November 28, 1935, Barnett Papers.
153. Ibid.; Scott, "Colonel John C. Robinson," 66–67; Coffey, *Lion by the Tail*, 49, 53, 58; Harris, *African-American Reactions to War*, 1–4.
154. Mockler, *Selassie's War*, 59.
155. Diamond, "Haile Selassie's Ace Airman Back in New York"; Harris, *African-American Reactions to War*, 18.
156. Selassie, *Autobiography of Emperor Sellassie I*, 80.
157. Zewde, *History of Modern Ethiopia*, 93–94; Coffey, *Lion by the Tail*, 12, 39, 49–50.

CHAPTER 7. THE GODS OF WAR TURN AGAINST ETHIOPIA

1. Robinson to Barnett, November 28, 1935, Barnett Papers.
2. Ibid.
3. Ibid.
4. Katz, "Fighting Another Civil War," *American Legacy*, 74; Jakeman, *The Divided Skies*, 21; Moore, "Africa Conscious Harlem," 328.
5. Coffey, *Lion by the Tail*, 248; Sevareid, *Between the Wars*, 132–33.
6. Coffey, *Lion by the Tail*, 302.
7. Dugan and Lafore, *Days of Emperor and Clown*, 125–26, 187–89, 201; Sevareid, *Between the Wars*, 132–33; Mockler, *Selassie's War*, 53.
8. Dugan and Lafore, *Days of Emperor and Clown*, 126.
9. Robinson to Barnett, November 28, 1935, Barnett Papers.
10. Ibid.

11. Ibid.
12. Ibid.
13. Ibid.
14. Diamond, "Haile Selassie's Ace Airman Back in New York."
15. Ibid.
16. Ibid.
17. Bragg and Kriz, *Soaring Above Setbacks*, 72.
18. Diamond, "Haile Selassie's Ace Airman Back in New York"; Perl, *Ethiopia*, 12–13.
19. Gartler, Bair, and Hall, *Understanding Ethiopia*, 37; Amin, Willetts, Matheson, *Journey Through Ethiopia*, 108, 113.
20. Simmons, *The Brown Condor*, 133.
21. Selassie, *Autobiography of Emperor Sellassie I*, 259; Ethiopian Air Force, Wikipedia.
22. Joel A. Robers, "Col. Robinson Stages Air Duel in Clouds with Enemy Planes," *Pittsburgh Courier*, December 14, 1935.
23. Zewde, *History of Modern Ethiopia*, 159; "Ethiops' Rabble Army Won," *Afro-American*; Simmons, *The Brown Condor*, 133; Ethiopian Air Force, Wikipedia.
24. Diamond, "Haile Selassie's Ace Airman Back in New York"; Kirkpatrick, *Mussolini*, 331; Mockler, *Selassie's War*, 23.
25. Diamond, "Haile Selassie's Ace Airman Back in New York."
26. Selassie, *Autobiography of Emperor Sellassie I*, 263.
27. Diamond, "Haile Selassie's Ace Airman Back in New York"; Simmons, *The Brown Condor*, 135.
28. White, "Harlem in Wild Acclaim," Barnett Papers.
29. "Explains Why Defense of Realm Failed," *Chicago Defender*, June 20, 1936.
30. White, "Harlem in Wild Acclaim," Barnett Papers.
31. Simmons, *The Brown Condor*, 121–24.
32. Ibid., 124; White, "Harlem in Wild Acclaim," Barnett Papers.
33. Ibid.
34. Ibid.
35. "American Negro Pilot Bests Two Italian Planes," *New York Times*, October 5, 1935.
36. Ibid.
37. Dugan and Lafore, *Days of Emperor and Clown*, 146; Knightley, *The First Casualty*, 182.
38. White, "Harlem in Wild Acclaim," Barnett Papers; Moore, "Africa Conscious Harlem," 328; Rogers, *Sex and Race*, vol. 1, 303–4.
39. Rogers, *Sex and Race*, vol. 1, in foreword; Scott and Womack, *Double V*, 53.
40. Simmons, *The Brown Condor*, 133.
41. Scott, "Colonel John C. Robinson," 63.
42. Ibid.; *Pittsburgh Courier*, February 1, 1936.
43. Hardesty and Pisano, *Black Wings: The American Black*, 14; Diamond, "Haile Selassie's Ace Airman Back in New York."
44. Gunther, *Inside Europe*, 228; Knightley, *The First Casualty*, 184.
45. *Campus Digest*, September 28, 1935.
46. Ibid., October 12 and 26, 1935.

47. Ibid., September 28, 1935.

48. Ibid.

49. Ibid.

50. *Campus Digest*, October 26, 1935.

51. Rogers, *The Real Facts About Ethiopia*, 30.

52. "Robinson Tells All in the Bombing of Adowa," *Chicago Defender*; "Ethiopia Gets New Flyer," *New York Times*.

53. Barnett to E. G. Roberts, July 17, 1935, Barnett Papers.

54. *The Digest*, September 28, 1935.

55. Hardesty and Pisano, *Black Wings: The American Black*, 13; Bragg and Kriz, *Soaring Above Setbacks*, 28; Hardesty, *Black Wings: Courageous Stories*, 38–39.

56. Robinson to Barnett, November 21, 1935, Barnett Papers; "'Brown Condor' Steals 'Black Eagles' Stuff," *Philadelphia Tribune*, October 10, 1935.

57. A Zion Psalm commemorating His Imperial Majesty visit to Chicago.

58. Adams, *Italy at War*, 74–75; Angelucci and Matricardi, *World Aircraft*, 176–77.

59. Dugan and Lafore, *Days of Emperor and Clown*, 116; Knightley, *The First Casualty*, 184.

60. Dugan and Lafore, *Days of Emperor and Clown*, 200–201, 233.

61. Mockler, *Selassie's War*, 76–77.

62. Ibid., 77–78.

63. Ibid., 76–78; Simmons, *The Brown Condor*, 129.

64. "Defender Man First to Greet Col. Robinson," *Chicago Defender*, May 23, 1936.

65. Mockler, *Selassie's War*, 78–81.

66. Stearley, "The Conquest of Ethiopia and the Use of Aircraft in the Operation."

67. Ibid.; Mockler, *Selassie's War*, 81; Zewde, *History of Modern Ethiopia*, 154; Marcus, *Haile Sellassie I*, 172.

68. Marcus, *Haile Sellassie I*, 173.

69. Ibid., 175.

70. "Ethiops' Rabble Army Won," *Afro-American*.

71. Ibid., 78, 81; Diamond, "Haile Selassie's Ace Airman Back in New York"; White, "Harlem in Wild Acclaim," Barnett Papers.

72. Mockler, *Selassie's War*, 78–82.

73. Marcus, *Haile Sellassie I*, 175.

74. Simmons, *The Brown Condor*, 133; *Pittsburgh Courier*, February 1, 1936.

75. Simmons, *The Brown Condor*, 133.

76. Scott and Womack, *Double V*, 49, 54.

77. Mockler, *Selassie's War*, 82–83, 94–95, 104.

78. Ibid., 76–77, 83–85; Dugan and Lafore, *Days of Emperor and Clown*, 243–45; Zewde, *History of Modern Ethiopia*, 154.

79. Dugan and Lafore, *Days of Emperor and Clown*, 251–53, 293.

80. Ibid., 253–54; Zewde, *History of Modern Ethiopia*, 154–55; Mockler, *Selassie's War*, 97–102; Stearley, "The Conquest of Ethiopia and the Use of Aircraft in the Operation."

81. Dugan and Lafore, *Days of Emperor and Clown*, 254.

82. Mockler, *Selassie's War*, 102.
83. Ibid., 258–59; Mockler, *Selassie's War*, 104–5; Nicolle, *The Italian Invasion of Abyssinia*, 34, 37
84. Selassie, *Autobiography of Emperor Sellassie I*, 270.
85. Mockler, *Selassie's War*, 106.
86. Dugan and Lafore, *Days of Emperor and Clown*, 259–62, 266; Mockler, *Selassie's War*, 106–10.
87. Marcus, *Haile Sellassie I*, 175.
88. Coffey, *Lion by the Tail*, 147, 307–8; Diamond, "Haile Selassie's Ace Airman Back in New York"; Mockler, *Selassie's War*, 106, 111; Simmons, *The Brown Condor*, 120.
89. Coffey, *Lion by the Tail*, 308–9.
90. Ibid., 308–10; White, "Harlem in Wild Acclaim," Barnett Papers.
91. "Ethiopians Keeping Silent on Statecraft," *Chicago Defender*, April 11, 1936.
92. Mockler, *Selassie's War*, 113.
93. Ibid., 114.
94. "Selassie Leads 300,000 Men on Ethiopian Front," *Chicago Defender*, April 4, 1936.
95. Marcus, *Haile Sellassie I*, 176–77.
96. Dugan and Lafore, *Days of Emperor and Clown*, 263–66.
97. Mockler, *Selassie's War*, 115–16.
98. Dugan and Lafore, *Days of Emperor and Clown*, 265–68, 296; Elson, *Prelude to War*, 162; Mockler, *Selassie's War*, 47–48, 116–19.
99. Sevareid, *Between the Wars*, 134.
100. Nicolle, *The Italian Invasion of Abyssinia*, 21.
101. "Defender Man First to Greet Col. Robinson," *Chicago Defender*.
102. Ibid.; Morris and Henderson, *World War II in Pictures*, 33.
103. "Time of Awake," *Chicago Defender*, May 9, 1936.
104. "Ethiopia Prepares to Take to the Skies," *Chicago Defender*; "Haile Ready to Unite Forces in Addis Ababa," *Chicago Defender*, May 2, 1936.
105. Mockler, *Selassie's War*, 120–21.
106. Stearley, "The Conquest of Ethiopia and the Use of Aircraft in the Operation."
107. Nicolle, *The Italian Invasion of Abyssinia*, 42.
108. Selassie, *Autobiography of Emperor Sellassie I*, 262–64.
109. "Leading Mountain Attack," *Chicago Defender*, April 25, 1936; Knightley, *The First Casualty*, 181.
110. "Leading Mountain Attack," *Chicago Defender*.
111. "Selassie's Strategy Is Big Surprise," *Chicago Defender*, April 25, 1936.
112. "Leading Mountain Attack," *Chicago Defender*; "Selassie's Strategy Is Big Surprise," *Chicago Defender*.
113. Dugan and Lafore, *Days of Emperor and Clown*, 278–79; Mockler, *Selassie's War*, 120–22, 130.
114. Ibid., 131; "Leading Mountain Attack," *Chicago Defender*.
115. Moseley, *Mussolini's Shadow*, 19.
116. Ibid., 19.

117. "Italy Loses 8,000 Men in Bloody Fight," *Chicago Defender*, May 2, 1936.

118. "Ethiopia Dynamites Roads," *Washington Post*, April 23, 1936.

119. Ibid.

120. "Defender Man First to Greet Col. Robinson," *Chicago Defender*.

121. Norman, "'Brown Condor' Feted as Harlem's Newest Hero"; Diamond, "Haile Selassie's Ace Airman Back in New York"; Mockler, *Selassie's War*, 132.

122. "Ethiopia Dynamites Roads," *Washington Post*.

123. Mockler, *Selassie's War*, 137; "Selassie's Air Aide Back from Africa," *New York Times*.

124. Mockler, *Selassie's War*, 140; Lockot, *The Mission*, 41; Nicolle, *The Italian Invasion of Abyssinia*, 21.

125. "Selassie's Air Aide Back from Africa," *New York Times*.

126. "French Flying Ace Heads for Addis Ababa," *Chicago Defender*, May 2, 1936.

127. Selassie, *The Autobiography of Sellassie I*, 290.

128. Knightley, *The First Casualty*, 187–88.

129. Coffey, *Lion by the Tail*, 336; "Emperor in Statement on Defeat," *Chicago Defender*, May 8, 1936.

130. "Actor Discusses Effects of Italo-Ethiopian War," *Chicago Defender*, January 4, 1936.

131. Nicolle, *The Italian Invasion of Abyssinia*, 43; "Selassie's Air Aide Back from Africa," *New York Times*.

132. Robinson to Barnett, Barnett Papers, November 21 and 28, 1935; Large, "Mussolini's 'Civilizing Mission.'"

133. Norman, "'Brown Condor,' Feted as Harlem's Newest Hero."

134. Mockler, *Selassie's War*, 124; "Defender Man First to Greet Col. Robinson," *Chicago Defender*.

135. Nicolle, *The Italian Invasion of Abyssinia*, 21.

136. "Italians Shoot Five Ethiopian Chieftains," *Chicago Defender*, May 23, 1936.

137. Coffey, *Lion by the Tail*, 336.

138. Ibid., May 23, 1936.

139. "Reveal Six Attempts to Kill 'Condor,'" *Chicago Defender*, May 30, 1936.

140. Bragg and Kriz, *Soaring Above Setbacks*, 32–33; Simmons, *The Brown Condor*, 144; Nick Nesbitt, *Universal Emancipation: The Haitian Revolution and the Radical Enlightenment* (Charlottesville: University of Virginia Press, 2008), 199.

141. "Reveal Six Attempts to Kill 'Condor,'" *Chicago Defender*.

142. "Defender Man First to Greet Col. Robinson," *Chicago Defender*.

143. Schaefer, *The Ethiopian Crisis*, xv–98; Coffey, *Lion by the Tail*, xi.

144. Rogers, *Sex and Race*, vol. 1, in foreword.

145. "Reveal Six Attempts to Kill 'Condor,'" *Chicago Defender*.

146. Hurley Green III, "Family Remembers Legacy of Famous Relative," *Chicago Independent Bulletin*, August 19, 2004; Gubert, Sawyer, and Fannin, *Distinguished African Americans in Aviation*, 254.

CHAPTER 8. RETURNING A WAR HERO

1. Scott, "Colonel John C. Robinson," 64–65.

2. Scott and Womack, *Double V*, 71.
3. Scott, "Colonel John C. Robinson," 64–65; "War Ace is Welcomed by Harlemites," *Chicago Defender*, May 23, 1936; Jakeman, *The Divided Skies*, 26–27; Simmons, *The Brown Condor*, 151.
4. *Chicago Defender*, May 30, 1936.
5. "Defender Man First to Greet Col. Robinson," *Chicago Defender*; Jakeman, *The Divided Skies*, 26–27; Scott and Womack, *Double V*, 65–66.
6. "Defender Man First to Greet Col. Robinson," *Chicago Defender*.
7. Waterford, "The Real Story of Col. John Robinson"; Jakeman, *The Divided Skies*, 27–29, 61, 64.
8. Jakeman, *The Divided Skies*, 25–26.
9. Scott, "Colonel John C. Robinson," 64.
10. Ibid.
11. Scott, "Colonel John C. Robinson," 64; Jakeman, *The Divided Skies*, 27; Scott and Womack, *Double V*, 66.
12. Norman, "'Brown Condor,' Feted as Harlem's Newest Hero."
13. Ibid.; newspaper photo in Barnett Papers, CHS.
14. Norman, "'Brown Condor,' Pilot of Selassie."
15. Simmons, *The Brown Condor*, 156.
16. *New York Times*, May 18, 1936.
17. White, "Harlem in Wild Acclaim," Barnett Papers; Jakeman, *The Divided Skies*, 27.
18. "We'll Sing Ethiopia," Barnett Papers; Jakeman, *The Divided Skies*, 27.
19. White, "Harlem in Wild Acclaim," Barnett Papers.
20. "We'll Sing Ethiopia," Barnett Papers.
21. Ibid.
22. Ibid.
23. White, "Harlem in Wild Acclaim," Barnett Papers.
24. Ibid.
25. Ibid.
26. Ibid.
27. Ibid.
28. Ibid.; Jakeman, *The Divided Skies*, 27.
29. White, "Harlem in Wild Acclaim," Barnett Papers,.
30. Ibid.
31. *Afro-American*, June 6, 1936.
32. "Colored U.S. Mechanic Hailed as Hero of Selassie's Pilots," *Star* (Washington, DC), May 25, 1936.
33. Ibid.
34. Diamond, "Haile Selassie's Ace Airman Back in New York."
35. Simmons, *The Brown Condor*, 157.
36. "Defender Man First to Greet Col. Robinson," *Chicago Defender*.
37. Ibid.
38. Ibid.; Diamond, "Haile Selassie's Ace Airman Back in New York."
39. "Defender Man First to Greet Col. Robinson," *Chicago Defender*.

40. Ibid.
41. "Col. John C. Robinson Lands at Local Airport," *Kansas City Call*.
42. *Chicago Defender*, May 30, 1936.
43. Ibid.; Jakeman, *The Divided Skies*, 27–29.
44. Scott, "Colonel John C. Robinson," 65; Simmons, *The Brown Condor*, 157; Jakeman, *The Divided Skies*, 27–29; Goldie M. Walden, "Socialites Greet Hero at Airport," *Chicago Defender*, May 30, 1936.
45. Vera B. Slaughter, "Twenty Thousand Greet 'Brown Condor' at Airport," *Chicago Defender*, May 30, 1936.
46. Ibid.
47. Ibid.
48. Scott and Womack, *Double V*, 71.
49. Ibid.
50. "Ethiops' Rabble Army Won," *Afro-American*; *Chicago Defender*, May 23, 1936; Jakeman, *The Divided Skies*, 29, 61, 64.
51. Jakeman, *The Divided Skies*, 27–29, 61, 64, 87, 264, 307–8; Simmons Address, March 15, 2002.
52. Jakeman, *The Divided Skies*, 64.
53. Leonard Mosley, *Lindbergh: A Biography* (Garden City, NY: Doubleday, 1976), 209–10; Jakeman, *The Divided Skies*, 27–29, 61, 64.
54. Mosley, *Lindbergh*, 12–37.
55. Ibid., xix.
56. Jakeman, *The Divided Skies*, 27, 29, 61.
57. Jakeman, *The Divided Skies*, 59–61.
58. Ibid., 60–61; Lindbergh, *We*, 48–60.
59. Harris, *African-American Reaction to War*, 120–21.
60. Ibid., 122–23.
61. Ibid., 127–28.
62. Ibid., 132–41.

CHAPTER 9. AVIATION VISIONS BURN BRIGHTLY

1. Scott, "Colonel John C. Robinson," 65.
2. "Col. Robinson, Haile's Flier, Welcomed Here," *Daily News*; Norman, "'Brown Condor,' Pilot of Selassie"; *New York Times*, May 18, 1936; "Air Veteran Dead of Ethiopia Crash," *New York Times*.
3. "Selassie's Air Aide Back from Africa," *New York Times*.
4. Diamond, "Haile Selassie's Ace Airman Back in New York"; White, "Harlem in Wild Acclaim," Barnett Papers.
5. Diamond, "Haile Selassie's Ace Airman Back in New York."
6. White, "Harlem in Wild Acclaim," Barnett Papers; Simmons, *The Brown Condor*, 135.
7. Jakeman, *The Divided Skies*, 23–25.
8. Ibid., 25.
9. Jakeman, *The Divided Skies*, 25–29.

10. "Col. Robinson Is Feted at Poro College," *Chicago Defender*, June 6, 1936.
11. "Rally to Buy Col. Robinson a New Plane," *Chicago Defender*, June 13, 1936.
12. Ibid.
13. James G. Fleming, "Col. Robinson Acclaimed as Ethiopia Hero," *Amsterdam News*, New York, May 23, 1936.
14. Jakeman, *The Divided Skies*, 29.
15. Ibid.; Simmons, *The Brown Condor*, 161.
16. Simmons, *The Brown Condor*, 163.
17. Ibid., 165–66; Jakeman, *The Divided Skies*, 23, 29.
18. Jakeman, *The Divided Skies*, 29–30.
19. Lindbergh, *We*, 45–47; Simmons, *The Brown Condor*, 171–72.
20. Scallar, "Group Seeks to Honor Aviator Brown Condor"; Rushing in interview with author, July 12, 2001; Simmons Address, Brown Condor Symposium, March 15, 2002, Gulfport, MS; Simmons in interview with author, January 13, 2003; "Defender Man First to Greet Col. Robinson," *Chicago Defender*; Simmons, *The Brown Condor*, 15.
21. "Gulfport Negro Who Piloted Emperor Haile Selassie Visits Home; Relates His Experiences in Wartime Flying," *Daily Herald* (Gulfport, MS), June 26, 1936; Rushing in interview with author, July 12, 2001; Simmons, *The Brown Condor*, 173–75.
22. "Gulfport Negro Who Piloted Emperor Haile Selassie Visits Home," *Daily Herald*; Simmons, *The Brown Condor*, 175–76.
23. Simmons, *The Brown Condor*, 179.
24. Katie Booth, in interview with author, Gulfport, MS, August 8, 2001; French, *The Rebellious Slave*, 184–85.
25. "Gulfport Negro Who Piloted Emperor Haile Selassie Visits Home," *Daily Herald*.
26. Annie Mae Johnson [Gaston], Brown Condor Symposium, March 15, 2002; Simmons Address, March 15, 2002; Simmons, *The Brown Condor*, 182–85.
27. Albert Gaston, Brown Condor Symposium, March 15, 2002.
28. Annie Mae Gaston, Brown Condor Symposium, March 15, 2002.
29. "Defender Man First to Greet Col. Robinson," *Chicago Defender*.
30. Jakeman, *The Divided Skies*, 30.
31. Robinson to Barnett, July 1, 1936, Barnett Papers, Chicago Historical Society.
32. Ibid.
33. Jakeman, *The Divided Skies*, 29–30; Washington to Robinson, July 7, 1936, Patterson Papers, Tuskegee University Archives (TUA hereafter).
34. Washington to Robinson, July 7, Patterson Papers, TUA; Jakeman, *The Divided Skies*, 30.
35. Washington to Robinson, July 7, 1936, Patterson Papers, TUA.
36. Jakeman, *The Divided Skies*, 31; Washington to Robinson, July 7, 1936, Patterson Papers, TUA.
37. Jakeman, *The Divided Skies*, 24–32; Washington to Robinson, July 7, 1936, Patterson Papers, TUA.

38. George L. Washington to Robinson, July 7, 1936, Patterson Papers, TUA; Jakeman, *The Divided Skies*, 1–2, 23–30.

39. Washington to Robinson, July 7, 1936, Patterson Papers, TUA; Jakeman, *The Divided Skies*, 30, 32; Hardesty and Pisano, *Black Wings: The American Black*, 21.

40. Washington to Robinson, July 7, 1936, Patterson Papers, TUA; Jakeman, *The Divided Skies*, 30.

41. Washington to Robinson, July 7, 1936, Patterson Papers, TUA; Jakeman, *The Divided Skies*, 30–32.

42. Jakeman, *The Divided Skies*, 31–32.

43. Spear, *Black Chicago*, 82–83; "Col. Robinson, Haile's Flier, Welcomed Here," *Daily News*; Diamond, "Haile Selassie's Ace Airman Back in New York"; "Air Veteran Dead of Ethiopia Crash," *New York Times*.

44. Spear, *Black Chicago*, 82–83.

45. "Col. Robinson Starts Own Aviation College," *Amsterdam News*, October 3, 1936; Simmons, *The Brown Condor*, photo between pages 118–19; Green, "Family Remembers Famous Relative."

46. Robinson to Barnett, July 1, 1936, Barnett Papers; Jakeman, *The Divided Skies*, 29–30; Simmons Address, March 15, 2002; "Col. Robinson, Haile's Flier, Welcomed Here," *Daily News*.

47. Bragg and Kriz, *Soaring Above Setbacks*, 33; Simmons, *The Brown Condor*, 161; "Col. John C. Robinson Lands at Local Airport," *Kansas City Call*.

48. Bragg and Kriz, *Soaring Above Setbacks*, 33.

49. Katz, "Fighting Another Civil War," *American Legacy*, 73–75; Jerome and Taylor, *Einstein on Race and Racism*, 61.

50. "Col. Robinson Starts Own Aviation College," *Amsterdam News*; Womack and Scott, *Double V*, 65, 70.

51. "Col. Robinson Starts Own Aviation College," *Amsterdam News*; Gubert, Sawyer, and Fannin, *Distinguished African Americans in Aviation*, 254.

52. "Col. Robinson's National Air College Stages Gala Opening," *Chicago Defender*, October 3, 1936.

53. Bragg and Kriz, *Soaring Above Setbacks*, 33.

54. Ibid.; e-mail, from Dr. Patrick Smith, University of Southern Mississippi, Gulfport, MS, to author, September 26, 2002; Hardesty and Pisano, *Black Wings: The American Black*, 21; Simmons, *The Brown Condor*, 186; "Col. John C. Robinson Lands at Local Airport," *Kansas City Call*.

55. Harris, *African-American Reactions to War*, 60–62.

56. Bragg and Kriz, *Soaring Above Setbacks*, 33; Simmons, *The Brown Condor*, 186.

57. "Col. John C. Robinson Lands at Local Airport," *Kansas City Call*.

58. Ibid.

59. Ibid.

60. "Mound Bayou," *Time*, July 26, 1937.

61. Green, "Family Remembers Famous Relative."

62. John C. Robinson File, Anselm J. Finch letter to Friend, July 27, 1937, Mississippi Department of Archives and History, Jackson, MS; *Clarion Ledger* (Jackson, MS), August 8, 1937.

63. Robinson File, Finch letter to friend, July 27, 1937; *Clarion Ledger*, August 8, 1937.
64. *Clarion Ledger*, August 8, 1937.
65. Ibid.
66. Thomas E. Simmons, in interview with author, Gulfport, MS, January 13, 2003; "Col. Robinson, Haile's Flier, Welcomed Here," *Daily News*; *New York Times*, March 28, 1954.
67. Simmons to author, January 13, 2003; Coffey, *Lion by the Tail*, 48–49; Simmons, Brown Condor Symposium, Gulfport, MS, question-and-answer session, March 15, 2002; "Col. Robinson, Haile's Flier, Welcomed Here," *Daily News*; "Air Veteran Dead of Ethiopia Crash," *New York Times*; Simmons, *The Brown Condor*, 15.
68. Stokes in interview with author, March 9, 2003.
69. George L. Washington to John C. Robinson, May 22, 1941, Frederick Douglass Patterson Papers, TUA; Scott and Womack, *Double V*, 85.
70. "Colonel Robinson Is Named Ill. Aviation Consultant," *Chicago Defender*, October 28, 1937.
71. Scott and Womack, *Double V*, 68–69.
72. Henry Allen, "To Fly, to Brave the Wind," *Washington Post*, Style Section, September 26, 1979.
73. Scott and Womack, *Double V*, 63, 85.
74. Ibid.
75. John C. Robinson to George L. Washington, November 4, 1936, Patterson Papers, TUA.
76. Jakeman, *The Divided Skies*, 30–32.
77. Ibid., 115.
78. Hardesty and Pisano, *Black Wings: The American Black*, 21; Bragg and Kriz, *Soaring Above Setbacks*, 32, 35–36; Simmons, *The Brown Condor*, 118–19; Salzman, Smith, and West, *Encyclopedia of African-American Culture and History*, 29.
79. Bragg and Kriz, *Soaring Above Setbacks*, 36–39; Simmons, *The Brown Condor*, 118–19; Hardesty and Pisano, *Black Wings: The American Black*, 20; Phillip Thomas Tucker, *The South's Finest: The First Missouri Confederate Brigade from Pea Ridge to Vicksburg* (Shippensburg, PA: White Mane Publishing, 1993), 1–25.
80. Jakeman, *The Divided Skies*, 88–111; Hardesty and Pisano, *Black Wings: The American Black*, 19, 21.
81. Jakeman, *The Divided Skies*, 112–14; John C. Robinson to Frederick Douglass Patterson, April 1, 1939, Civil Aeronautics Authority Folder, Frederick Douglass Patterson Papers, TUA.
82. Patterson to Robinson, April 8, 1939, Patterson Papers, Civil Aeronautics Authority Folder, TUA; Jakeman, *The Divided Skies*, 113–14.
83. John C. Robinson to Frederick Douglass Patterson, May 29, 1939, Ro-Ry Folder, GC 1939, Patterson Papers, TUA; John C. Robinson to George L. Washington, May 23, 1939, Ro-Ry Folder, GC 1939, Patterson Papers, TUA.
84. Ibid.
85. Robinson to Patterson, May 29, 1939, Patterson Papers, Ro-Ry Folder, GC 1939, TUA; Jakeman, *The Divided Skies*, 112–13, 116.

86. Robinson to Patterson, May 29, 1939, Patterson Papers, Ro-Ry Folder, GC 1939, TUA.

87. George L. Washington to John C. Robinson, June 7, 1939, Patterson Papers, George L. Washington Folder, LC 1939, TUA.

88. Ibid.

89. Washington to Robinson, June 7, 1939, Patterson Papers, Washington Folder, LC 1939, TUA; Jakeman, *The Divided Skies*, 116–17.

90. Washington to Robinson, June 7, 1939, Washington Folder, LC 1939, TUA; Hardesty and Pisano, *Black Wings: The American Black*, 21, 27; Jakeman, *The Divided Skies*, 30–31, 113–19, 145, 163; Patterson to Robinson, June 7, 1939, George L. Washington Folder, LC 1939, TUA; Scott and Womack, *Double V*, 88.

91. Jakeman, *The Divided Skies*, 110–14, 142, 160–61.

92. Ibid., 161.

93. Ibid., 163.

94. Jakeman, *The Divided Skies*, 144–45.

95. John C. Robinson's statements summarized in memorandum, November 30, 1940, Folder 1, Box 171, Claude A. Barnett Papers, CHS; Jakeman, *The Divided Skies*, 110–14.

96. Simmons, Brown Condor Symposium, question-and-answer session, March 15, 2002; Hardesty and Pisano, *Black Wings: The American Black*, 27.

97. Jakeman, *The Divided Skies*, 1–17.

98. Ibid., 27–29, 61, 64–79, 158–59; Simmons to author, March 10, 2003.

99. Jakeman, *The Divided Skies*, 79.

100. Ibid., 86–87.

101. *Atlanta Daily World*, December 8, 1938.

102. Jakeman, *The Divided Skies*, 87.

103. Kimberly C. Roberts, "ABC's Robin Roberts Recalls the Relationship That Shaped Her Life," *Philadelphia Tribune* online (accessed June 11, 2005); Col. Lawrence Roberts, U.S. Air Force Biographies, Keesler Air Force Base, MS.

104. Gubert, Sawyer, and Fannin, *Distinguished African Americans in Aviation*, 254.

105. John C. Robinson to George L. Washington, February 20, 1941, George L. Washington Folder, Frederick Douglass Patterson Papers, TUA.

106. Green, "Family Remembers Famous Relative"; Gubert, Sawyer, and Fannin, *Distinguished African Americans in Aviation*, 254.

107. Osur, *Blacks in the Army Air Forces During World War II*, 24; Hardesty and Pisano, *Black Wings: The American Black*, 21; Jakeman, *The Divided Skies*, 86–87, 158–59.

108. Jakeman, *The Divided Skies*, 240–60; Simmons, *The Brown Condor*, 192.

109. Jakeman, *The Divided Skies*, 240–61; Von Hardesty and Pisano, *Black Wings*, 27.

110. Robinson to Washington, February 20, 1941, Patterson Papers, TUA.

111. Ibid.

112. Ibid.

113. Jakeman, *The Divided Skies*, 262.

114. Ibid., 262.

115. Ibid.

116. John C. Robinson to George L. Washington, May 20, 1941, Ro-Ry Folder, GC 1941, Frederick Douglass Patterson Papers, TUA; Jakeman, *The Divided Skies*, 262; Simmons, *The Brown Condor,* 191.

117. Hardesty and Pisano, *Black Wings: The American Black*, 27; Hardesty, *Black Wings: Courageous Stories*, 70; Simmons, *The Brown Condor*, 191.

118. Robinson to Washington, May 20, 1941, Frederick Douglass Patterson Papers, TUA; Jakeman, *The Divided Skies*, 30–31, 262–63.

119. George L. Washington to John C. Robinson, May 22, 1941, George L. Washington Folder, Frederick Douglass Patterson Papers, T U A.

120. Rev. Tartt in interview with author, October 25, 2001.

121. Jakeman, *The Divided Skies*, 22–23, 87, 158–59, 262–64, 303–8; E. Franklin Frazier, *Negro Youth at the Crossways: Their Personality Development in the Middle States* (Washington, DC: American Council on Education, 1940), 165–66; Washington in interview with Robinson, May 22, 1941, Washington Folder, Patterson Papers, TUA; Diamond, "Haile Selassie's Ace Airman Back in New York."

122. *Pittsburgh Courier*, October 13, 1935; January 4, 1936; and February 1, 1936; Lewis J. Lynch, in interview with author, Tuskegee Airmen Annual Convention, Atlanta, GA, August 14, 2002; Jakeman, *The Divided Skies*, 87; Hardesty and Pisano, *Black Wings: The American Black*, 14.

123. Lynch in interview with author, August 14, 2002; Jakeman, *The Divided Skies*, 87; Hardesty and Pisano, *Black Wings: The American Black*, 14.

124. Frazier, *Negro Youth at the Crossways*, 165–66; Jakeman, *The Divided Skies*, 87, 158–59, 264, 303–8.

125. "Defender Man First to Greet Col. Robinson," *Chicago Defender*.

126. Jakeman, *The Divided Skies*, 87, 264, 303–8; Thomas Simmons to author, March 10, 2003; Hardesty and Pisano, *Black Wings: The American Black*, 14–66; "Defender Man First to Greet Col. Robinson," *Chicago Defender*.

CHAPTER 10. THE WINDS OF WORLD WAR

1. Jakeman, *The Divided Skies*, 264.

2. Claude A. Barnett to Frederick Douglass Patterson, February 27, 1941, Claude A. Barnett Correspondence, Frederick Douglass Patterson Papers, TUA.

3. Jakeman, *The Divided Skies*, 193–95, 264; William H. Hastie, *On Clipped Wings, The Story of Jim Crow in the Army Air Corps* (New York, NAACP, 1943), 10–20.

4. Hastie, *On Clipped Wings*, 10; Hardesty, *Black Wings: Courageous Stories*, 65.

5. Hastie, *On Clipped Wings*, 10.

6. Thomas E. Simmons conversation with author, July 11, 2001; Jimmie Bell, "Famed Black Gulfport Pilot Flew Haile Selassie," *Sun Herald*, August 29, 1975; History of Keesler Air Force Base Files, 81st Training Wing History Office, Keesler Air Force Base, Biloxi, MS.

7. History of Keesler Air Force Base Files, Keesler AFB, Biloxi, MS; *Daily Herald* (Biloxi, MS), June 21 and 23, 1941; F. Val Hulsey, "A History of the Site and Its

Environs to 1941," 81st Training Wing History Office, Keesler Air Force Base, Biloxi, MS; "Defender Man First to Greet Col. Robinson," *Chicago Defender*.

8.   History of Keesler Air Force Base Files, Keesler AFB, Biloxi, MS.

9.   Hardesty and Pisano, *Black Wings: The American Black*, 29; Hardesty, *Black Wings: Courageous Stories*, 69.

10.   Hardesty, *Black Wings: Courageous Stories*, 69; Simmons, *The Brown Condor*, 192.

11.   Hardesty, *Black Wings: Courageous Stories*, 69; Simmons, Brown Condor Symposium, question-and-answer session, March 15, 2002.

12.   Ibid.; Hardesty and Pisano, *Black Wings: The American Black*, 29; Hardesty, *Black Wings: Courageous Stories*, 69.

13.   Bell, "Black Pilot Flew Selassie"; Simmons, *The Brown Condor*, 195; Scott and Womack, *Double V*, 85; Green, "Family Remembers Famous Relative."

14.   Osur, *Blacks in the Army Air Forces During World War II*, 34–35.

15.   Ibid., 34–35 and 159, note 61.

16.   Ibid.; Scott, "Colonel John C. Robinson," 66; Rev. Tartt, Brown Condor Symposium, March 15, 2002.

17.   History of Keesler Field, 8 July 1943 to 31 December 1943, KF-U313-KF-U-318, vol. 5, Keesler Air Force Base, Biloxi, MS.

18.   Talbot, David Abner, *Contemporary Ethiopia* (New York: Philosophical Library, 1952), 208; Hardesty and Pisano, *Black Wings: The American Black*, 30; Scott, "Colonel John C. Robinson," 66; Rev. Tartt, Brown Condor Symposium, March 15, 2002.

19.   Donald O. Weckhorst, *75 Year Pictorial History of Chanute Air Force Base, Rantoul, Illinois* (Nappanee, IN: Evangel Press, 1992), 62–147.

20.   Hardesty and Pisano, *Black Wings: The American Black*, 15, 21–22, 27; Bragg and Kriz, *Soaring Above Setbacks*, 39, 53; Jakeman, *The Divided Skies*, 6–9.

21.   Osur, *Blacks in the Army Air Forces During World War II*, 24; Scott, "Colonel John C. Robinson," 66; Rev. Tartt, Brown Condor Symposium, March 15, 2002; Jakeman, *The Divided Skies*, 27–29, 61, 64–79, 158–59.

22.   Weckhorst, *History of Chanute Air Force Base*, 148–52; Rev. Tartt, Brown Condor Symposium, March 15, 2002; Hardesty, *Black Wings: Courageous Stories*, 74, 77–78.

23.   Hardesty and Pisano, *Black Wings: The American Black*, 36–39; Hardesty, *Black Wings: Courageous Stories*, 77–78.

24.   Hardesty and Pisano, *Black Wings: The American Black*, 40–41.

25.   Osur, *Blacks in the Army Air Forces During World War II*, 70–71.

26.   Scott, "Colonel John C. Robinson," 66.

27.   Morris and Henderson, *World War II in Pictures*, 212–13.

28.   Harris, *African-American Reaction to War in Ethiopia*, 143–47; Scott and Womack, *Double V*, 85; Scott, "Colonel John C. Robinson," 66.

29.   Harris, *African-American Reaction to War*, 147.

30.   Harris, *African-American Reactions to War*, 142–44, 147; Simmons, *The Brown Condor*, 194–95; Harris, *African-American Reactions to War*, 147; Green, "Family Remembers Famous Relative."

31. Harris, *African-American Reactions to War*, 142–43, 147; Green, "Family Remembers Famous Relative"; Amin, Willetts, and Matheson, *Journey Through Ethiopia*, 10–19; Simmons, *The Brown Condor*, 194–95; "Air Veteran Dead of Ethiopia Crash," *New York Times*.

32. Harris, *African-American Reactions to War*, 144–47, 149.

33. Barker, *The Civilizing Mission*, 323–24.

34. Simmons to author, January 13, 2003; Simmons Address, March 15, 2002; Simmons, *The Brown Condor*, 195; Scott, "Colonel John C. Robinson," 66; Harris, *African-American Reactions to War*, 143–47.

35. Harris, *African-American Reactions to War*, 146–47.

36. Ibid.; Scott, "Colonel John C. Robinson," 66; Ethiopian Air Force, Wikipedia.

37. Harris, *African-American Reactions*, 146–47; Scott, "Colonel John C. Robinson," 66.

38. Harris, *African-American Reactions to War*, 147–48, 167–68; Scott, "Colonel John C. Robinson," 66; Hardesty, *Black Wings: Courageous Stories*, 33.

39. Harris, *African-American Reactions to War*, 144, 150.

40. Ibid., 148; Chatwood Hall, "Col. Robinson Launches East African Airlines," *Chicago Defender*, February 21, 1948; Green, "Family Remembers Famous Relative," *Chicago Independent Bulletin*; Gubert, Sawyer, and Fannin, *Distinguished African Americans in Aviation*, 252.

41. Hall, "Robinson Launches Airlines," *Chicago Defender*.

42. Dugan and Lafore, *Days of Emperor and Clown*, 123.

43. Gartler, Bair, and Hall, *Understanding Ethiopia*, 25; Simmons, *The Brown Condor*, 195; Harris, *African-American Reactions*, 148.

44. Harris, *African-American Reactions to War*, 150; Simmons, *The Brown Condor*, 196.

45. Hardesty and Pisano, *Black Wings: The American Black*, 57, 60.

46. Ibid., 20, 57, 60; Bragg and Kriz, *Soaring Above Setbacks*, 36–39.

47. Mockler, *Selassie's War*, 72–150; Harris, *African-American Reactions to War*, 148; Thomas E. Simmons, Gulfport, MS, September 3, 2002, e-mail; Ethiopian Air Force, Wikipedia; Simmons, *The Brown Condor*, 196–97.

48. Henry Swanzy, "Quarterly Notes," *African Affairs: The Journal of the Royal African Society* 47, no. 187 (April 1948): 79.

49. *New York Times*, September 19, 1947.

50. Thomas Simmons, *The Brown Condor*, September 3, 2002, e-mail.

51. Harris, *African-American Reactions to War*, 148.

52. Ibid., 149–50.

53. Ibid., 150–51.

54. Scott, "Colonel John C. Robinson," 66; Bragg and Kriz, *Soaring Above Setbacks*, 75; Mockler, *Selassie's War*, 399.

55. Harris, *African-American Reactions to War*, 150.

56. "Americans in Ethiopia, Score of U.S. Negroes Helping to Develop Ancient African Land," *Ebony*, May 1951, 80; Gwendolyn Midlo Hall, *Africans in Colonial Louisiana: The Development of Afro-Creole Culture in the Eighteenth Century* (Baton Rouge: Louisiana State University Press, 1992), 188.

57. Lockot, *The Mission*, 40–41, 108; Simmons, *The Brown Condor*, 197.
58. "Americans in Ethiopia," *Ebony*, 80.
59. Ibid.
60. Ibid.; Lockot, *The Mission*, 37.
61. "Americans in Ethiopia," *Ebony*, 80.
62. Ibid.
63. "Air Veteran Dead of Ethiopia Crash," *New York Times*; Robinson to Barnett, November 21, 1935, Barnett Papers; Simmons Address, March 15, 2002; Simmons, *The Brown Condor*, 12, 197–98; "Famed 'Brown Condor' Injured in Ethiopian Crash," ANP Release, March 15, 1954.
64. "Ethiopia Honors Dead U.S. Flyer," *Amsterdam News*; Robinson to Barnett, November 21, 1935, Barnett Papers; Simmons Address, March 15, 2002; Simmons, *The Brown Condor*, 13, 198; Jakeman, *The Divided Skies*, 1–32; "Air Veteran Dead of Ethiopia Crash," *New York Times*; "Famed 'Brown Condor' Injured in Ethiopian Crash," ANP Release.
65. "Air Veteran Dead of Ethiopia Crash," *New York Times*.
66. Ibid.
67. A Zion Psalm commemorating His Imperial Majesty visit to Chicago; *Washington Post*, May 16, 1954; *New York Times*, May 16, 1954.
68. A Zion Palm commemorating His Imperial Majesty visit to Chicago; Robinson to Barnett, November 28, 1935, Barnett Papers, November 28, 1935.
69. Bragg and Kriz, *Soaring Above Setbacks*, 111; Jakeman, *The Divided Skies*, 1–32, 87; "Air Veteran Dead of Ethiopia Crash," *New York Times*; Hardesty and Pisano, *Black Wings: The American Black*, 23–59.
70. "Americans in Ethiopia," *Ebony*, 80.
71. Ibid.; Scott, "Colonel John C. Robinson," 67.
72. Daniel L. Haulman, "Crisis in Somalia: Operations Provide Relief and Restore Hope," in *Short of War, Major USAF Contingency Operations 1947–1997*, A. Timothy Warnock, ed., (Washington, DC: Air University Press, in association with Air Force History and Museums Program, 2000), 209–12.

EPILOGUE

1. Jakeman, *The Divided Skies*, 264.
2. Scott, "Colonel John C. Robinson," 66.
3. Nick Nesbitt, *Universal Emancipation: The Haitian Revolution and the Radical Enlightenment* (Charlottesville: University of Virginia Press, 2008), 1–197; Nick Nesbitt, ed., *Toussaint L'Ouverture: The Haitian Revolution* (Brooklyn: Verso, 2008), vii–116.
4. Jakeman, *The Divided Skies*, 27–29, 63–64, 158–59, 263–64.
5. Jakeman, *The Divided Skies*, 1–29, 63–64, 87, 115, 264, 307–8; Simmons Address, March 15, 2002.
6. Jakeman, *The Divided Skies*, 29.
7. Waterford, "The Real Story of Col. John Robinson."
8. Finch to friend, July 27, 1937, Robinson File, Mississippi Department of Archives and History, Jackson, MS.
9. Waterford, "John Robinson Wings His Way Down to Tuskegee."

BIBLIOGRAPHY

MANUSCRIPTS AND PRIMARY SOURCE MATERIAL

Barnett, Claude A., Papers, Chicago Historical Society, Chicago, IL.

Barnett, Claude A., to E. G. Roberts, July 17, 1935, box 170, folder 9, Claude A. Barnett Papers, Chicago Historical Society, Chicago, IL.

Barnett, Claude A., to Frederick Douglass Patterson, February 27, 1941, Claude A. Barrett Correspondence 1936–1942, Frederick Douglass Patterson Papers, Tuskegee University Archives, Tuskegee, AL.

Bayen, Malaku E., to Claude A. Barnett, January 3, 1935, Claude A. Barnett Papers, box 170, folder 9, Chicago Historical Society, Chicago, IL.

Bolling, Raynal C., files, History Office, 11th Wing, Bolling Air Force Base, Washington, DC.

Booth, Katie, biographical sketch, History Makers Archives, Chicago, IL.

Coffey, Cornelius Robinson, biographical sketch, Octave Aerospace Museum, Rantoul, IL.

Finch, Anselm J., letter to friend, July 27, 1937, John C. Robinson File, Mississippi Department of Archives and History, Jackson, MS.

Fourteenth U.S. Census, 1920, Gulfport, MS, at Mississippi Department of Archives and History, Jackson, MS.

"Harlem in Wild Acclaim over Return of 'Brown Condor.'" Claude A. Barnett Papers, Chicago Historical Society, Chicago, IL.

Henning, Richard G., staff meteorologist, 46th Weather Squadron, "A History of Hurricanes in the Western Florida Panhandle, 1559–1999," History Office, Eglin Air Force Base, Panama City, Florida.

History of Keesler Field, 8 July 1943 to 31 December 1943, vol. 5, History Office, 81st Training Wing, Keesler Air Force Base, Biloxi, MS.

Hulsey, F. Val, Kessler Air Force Base, "A History of the Site and Its Environs to 1941," History Office, 81st Training Wing, Keesler Air Force Base, Biloxi, MS.

Hurd, Harold, biographical sketch, Chicago Department of Aviation, Chicago, IL.

Jones, T. J., May 22, 1907, Deed to Church Trustees, City of Gulfport, County of Harrison, State of Mississippi, Harrison County Court Records, Harrison County Courthouse, Gulfport, MS.

Keller, Thomas J. "History of the Village of Robbins, Illinois," William Leonard Public Library, Robbins, IL.

Robinson, John C., file, Mississippi Department of Archives and History, Jackson, MS.

Robinson, John C., statements summarized in memorandum, November 30, 1940, box 171, folder 1, Claude A. Barnett Papers, Chicago Historical Society, Chicago, IL.

Robinson, John C., to Claude A. Barnett, June 3, 1935, box 170, folder 9, Claude A. Barnett Papers, Chicago Historical Society, Chicago, IL.

Robinson, John C., to Claude A. Barnett, November 21, 1935, box 170, folder 9, Claude A. Barnett Papers, Chicago Historical Society, IL.

Robinson, John C., to Claude A. Barnett, November 28, 1935, box 170, folder 9, Claude A. Barnett Papers, Chicago Historical Society, Chicago, Illinois.

Robinson, John C., to Claude A. Barnett, July 1, 1936, box 171, folder 1, Claude A. Barnett Papers, Chicago Historical Society, Chicago, IL.

Robinson, John C., to George L. Washington, November 4, 1936, Frederick Douglass Patterson Papers, Tuskegee University Archives, Tuskegee, AL.

Robinson, John C., to Frederick Douglass Patterson, May 29, 1939, Ro-Ry folder, GC 1939, Frederick Douglass Patterson Papers, Tuskegee University Archives, Tuskegee, AL.

Robinson, John C., to George L. Washington, February 20, 1941, George L. Washington folder, box 1, series 2, Frederick Douglass Patterson Papers, Tuskegee University Archives, Tuskegee, AL.

Robinson, John C., to George L. Washington, May 20, 1941, Ro-Ry folder, GC 1941, Frederick Douglass Patterson Papers, Tuskegee University Archives, Tuskegee, AL.

Rushing, Sidney L., Collection, Gulfport, MS.

Stearley, Maj. Ralph, "The Conflict of Ethiopia and the Use of Aircraft in the Operation," Air Corps Tactical School Lecture, February 2, 1939, U.S. Air Force Historical Research Agency, Maxwell Air Force Base, Montgomery, AL.

Tartt, Harry Charles, biographical sketch, History Makers Archives, Chicago, IL.

Washington, George L., to John C. Robinson, July 7, 1936, George L. Washington Folder, Frederick Douglass Patterson Papers, Tuskegee University Archives, Tuskegee, AL.

Washington, George L., to John C. Robinson, June 7, 1939, Frederick Douglass Patterson Papers, Tuskegee University Archives, Tuskegee, AL.

Washington, George L., to John C. Robinson, May 22, 1941, George L. Washington Folder, box 1, series 2, Frederick Douglass Patterson Papers, Tuskegee University Archives, Tuskegee, AL.

"'We'll Sing Ethiopia,' Song Dedicated to Col. John C. Robinson, Honors Returning War Hero," Claude A. Barnett Papers, Chicago Historical Society, Chicago, IL.

White, A. E. "Harlem in Acclaim over Return of 'Brown Condor.'" Claude A. Barnett Papers, Chicago Historical Society, Chicago, IL.

BOOKS AND PERIODICALS

Adams, Henry, and eds. of Time-Life Books. *Italy at War*. Alexandria: Time-Life Books, 1982.

Aldridge, James F. *Wright From the Start: The Contributions of Dayton's Science and Engineering Community to American Air Power in the Twentieth Century*. Dayton: History Office, Aeronautical Systems Center, Wright-Patterson Air Force Base, OH.

"Americans in Ethiopia, Score of U.S. Negroes Helping to Develop Ancient African Land." *Ebony*, May 1951.

Amin, Mohamed, Duncan Willetts, and Alastair Matheson. *Journey Through Ethiopia*. Nairobi: Camerapix Publishers International, 1997.

Andrews, William L., ed., *Sisters of the Spirit: Three Black Women's Autobiographies of the Nineteenth Century*. Bloomington: Indiana University Press, 1986.

Angelucci, Enzo, and Paolo Matricardi. *World Aircraft, 1918–1935*. Chicago: Rand, McNally, 1977.

Barker, A. J. *The Civilizing Mission: A History of the Italo-Ethiopian War of 1935–1936*. New York: Dial Press, 1968.

Barnett, Correlli, ed. *Hitler's Generals*. New York: Quill/William Morrow, 1989.

Bearss, Margie Riddle. *Sherman's Forgotten Campaign: The Meridian Expedition*. Baltimore: Gateway Press, 1987.

Bennett, Edward W. *German Rearmament and the West, 1932–1933*. Princeton, NJ: Princeton University Press, 1979.

Bettersworth, John K. *Mississippi: The Land and the People*. Austin: Steck-Vaughn Company, 1981.

Biddle, Wayne. *Barons of the Sky: From Early Flight to Strategic Warfare; The Story of the American Aerospace Industry*. New York: Simon & Schuster, 1991.

Bilstein, Roger E. *The American Aerospace Industry: From Workshop to Global Enterprise*. New York: Twayne Publishers, 1996.

Blainey, Geoffrey. *The Causes of War*. New York: Free Press, 1973.

Blake, Greg. "Ethiopia's Decisive Victory at Adowa," *Military History* (October 1997): 62–68.

Bolster, W. Jeffrey. *Black Jacks: African American Seamen in the Age of Sail*. Cambridge, MA: Harvard University Press, 1997.

Bradford, Ernle. *Thermopylae: The Battle for the West*. New York: Da Capo Press, 1993.

Bragg, Janet Harmon, and Marjorie M. Kriz. *Soaring Above Setbacks: The Autobiography of Janet Harmon Bragg, African American Aviator*. Washington, DC: Smithsonian Institution Press, 1996.

Bundles, A'Lelia. *On Her Own Ground: The Life and Times of Madam C. J. Walker*. New York: Scribner, 2001.

Burge, Cyril Gordon. *Encyclopedia of Aviation*. London: Sir Isaac Pitman & Sons, 1935.

Campus Digest: The Voice of the Tuskegee Student (various 1935 and 1936 issues).

Carey, John, ed. *Eyewitness to History*. Cambridge, MA: Harvard University Press, 1988.

Chivers, Sydney P. *Flying Tigers: Pictorial History of the American Volunteer Group*. Conoga Park: Challenge Publications, n.d.

Coffey, Thomas M. *Lion by the Tail: The Story of the Italian-Ethiopian War*. New York: Viking Press, 1974.

"Come Sunday Morning: The Amazing Story of Abyssinian Baptist Church." *Essence*, June 2001.

Craven, Wesley Frank, and James Lea Cate, eds. *The Army Air Forces in World War II*. Washington, DC: Office of Air Force History, 1983.

Davis, Benjamin O., Jr. *Benjamin O. Davis, Jr., American: An Autobiography*. Washington, DC: Smithsonian Institution Press, 1991.

Davis, David Brion. *The Problem of Slavery in the Age of Revolution, 1770–1823*. New York: Oxford University Press, 1999.

Diamond, Jared. *Guns, Germs, and Steel: The Fates of Human Societies*. New York: W. W. Norton, 1999.

Dick, Ron. *Reach and Power: The Heritage of the United States Air Force in Pictures and Artifacts*. Washington, DC: Air Force History and Museum Programs, 1997.

Donald, David. "The Scalawag in Mississippi Reconstruction." In Kenneth M. Stampp and Leon F. Litwack, eds., *Reconstruction: An Anthology of Revisionist Writings*. Baton Rouge: Louisiana State University Press, 1969.

Douglass, Frederick. *Narrative of the Life of Frederick Douglass*. Garden City, NY: Doubleday, 1963.

Douhet, Giulio. *The Command of the Air*. Translated by Dino Ferrari. Washington, DC: Office of Air Force History, 1983.

Dugan, James, and Laurence Lafore. *Days of Emperor and Clown: The Italo-Ethiopian War 1935–1936*. Garden City, NY: Doubleday, 1973.

Edwards, John Carver. *Airmen Without Portfolio: United States Mercenaries in Civil War Spain*. Westport, CT: Praeger, 1997.

Elson, Robert T., ed., and eds. of Time-Life Books. *Prelude to War*. Alexandria: Time-Life Books, 1976.

Fenny, William D. *In Their Honor: True Stories of Fliers for Whom United States Air Force Bases Are Named*. New York: Duell, Sloan and Pearce, 1963.

Fletcher, Marvin E. *America's First Black General, Benjamin O. Davis, Sr., 1880–1970*. Lawrence: University of Kansas Press, 1989.

Florida Historical Quarterly 81, no. 2 (Fall 2002), dust jacket, 1.

Francis, Charles E. *The Tuskegee Airmen: The Men Who Changed a Nation*. Boston: Branden Publishing Company, 1993.

Franklin, John Hope. *From Slavery to Freedom: A History of Negro Americans*. New York: Alfred A. Knopf, 1974.

Frazier, E. Franklin. *Negro Youth at the Crossways: Their Personality Development in the Middle States*. Washington, DC: American Council on Education, 1940.

French, Scott. *The Rebellious Slave: Nat Turner in American Memory*. New York: Houghton Mifflin, 2004.

Frey, Sylvia R. *Water From the Rock: Black Resistance in the Revolutionary Age*. Princeton, NJ: Princeton University Press, 1991.

Gartler, Marion, Frederick Bair, and George L. Hall. *Understanding Ethiopia*. Summit: Laidlaw Brothers Publishers, 1965.

Goldberg, Alfred. *A History of the United States Air Force, 1907–1957*. Princeton, NJ: Van Nostrand, 1957.

Greer, Thomas H. *The Development of Air Doctrine in the Army Air Arm, 1917–1941*. Washington, DC: Office of Air Force History, 1985.

Gropman, Alan L. "The Air Force, 1941–1951: From Segregation to Integration," *Air Power History*, 40, no. 2 (Summer 1993).

———. *The Air Force Integrates, 1945–1964*. Washington, DC: Office of Air Force History, 1978.

———. "General Benjamin O. Davis, Jr., American Hero," *Air Power History* 46, no. 2 (Summer 1999).

Gross, Charles Joseph. *The Air National Guard and the American Military Tradition*. Washington, DC: National Guard Bureau, U.S. Government Printing Office, 1995.

Gunther, John. *Inside Europe*. New York: Harper & Brothers, 1938.

Gurney, Gene. *Five Down and Glory: A History of the American Air Ace*. Edited by Mark P. Friedlander, Jr. New York: Putnam, 1958.

Hall, Gwendolyn Midlo. *Africans in Colonial Louisiana: The Development of Afro-Creole Culture in the Eighteenth Century*. Baton Rouge: Louisiana State University Press, 1992.

Hardesty, Von. *Black Wings: Courageous Stories of African Americans in Aviation and Space History*. New York: HarperCollins, 2008.

——— and Dominick Pisano. *Black Wings: The American Black in Aviation*. Washington, DC: Smithsonian Institution Press, 1983.

Harris, Joseph E. *African-American Reactions to War in Ethiopia 1936–1941*. Baton Rouge: Louisiana State University Press, 1994.

Hastie, William H. *On Clipped Wings, The Story of Jim Crow in the Army Air Corps* (pamphlet). New York: NAACP, 1943.

Haulman, Daniel L. "Crisis in Somalia: Operation Provide Relief and Restore Hope," in *Short of War, Major USAF Contingency Operations 1947—1997*, edited by A. Timothy Warnock. Washington, DC: Air University Press, in association with Air Force History and Museums Program, 2000.

Herodotus. *The Histories*. New York: Penguin, 1966.

Hibbert, Christopher. *Il Duce: The Life of Benito Mussolini*. Boston: Little, Brown, 1962.

Hudson, James J. *Hostile Skies: A Combat History of American Air Service in World War I*. Syracuse, NY: Syracuse University Press, 1968.

Husley, Val. *Biloxi, 300 Years*. Virginia Beach: Donning Company, 1998.

Irving, David. *The Rise and Fall of the Luftwaffe: The Life of Field Marshall Erhard Milch*. Boston: Little, Brown, 1973.

Jakeman, Robert J. *The Divided Skies: Establishing Segregated Flight Training at Tuskegee, Alabama, 1934–1942*. Tuscaloosa: University of Alabama Press, 1992.

Johnson, Charles, Patricia Smith, and WGBH Series Research Team. *Africans in America: America's Journey Through Slavery.* Harcourt Brace, 1998.

Katz, William Loren. "Fighting Another Civil War." *American Legacy* 7, no. 4 (Winter 2002).

Kirkpatrick, Ivone. *Mussolini: A Study in Power.* New York: Hawthorn Books, 1964.

Knight, Ian. "Humiliation at Adwa." *Military Illustrated*, no. 163 (April 2002).

Knightley, Phillip. *The First Casualty: From the Crimea to Vietnam: The War Correspondent as Hero, Propagandist and Myth Maker.* New York: Harcourt Brace, 1975.

Lambertson, Giles. "The Other Harlem." *Air & Space*, March 2010.

Lanning, Michael Lee. *The African American Soldier: From Crispus Attucks to Colin Powell.* Yucca Valley: Citadel, 1997.

Large, David Clay. "Mussolini's 'Civilizing Mission.'" *Quarterly Journal of Military History*, 5, no. 2. (Winter 1993).

Limerick, Patricia Nelson. *The Legacy of Conquest: The Unbroken Past of the American West.* New York: W. W. Norton, 1987.

Lindbergh, Charles A. *We: The Famous Flier's Own Story of His Life and His Transatlantic Flight, Together with His Views on the Future of Aviation.* Cutchogue, NY: Buccaneer Books, n.d.

Lockot, Hans Wilhelm. *The Mission: The Life, Reign and Character of Haile Selassie I.* London: C. Hurst, 1993.

Marcus, Harold G. *Haile Sellassie I: The Formative Years, 1892–1936.* Lawrenceville, NJ: Red Sea Press, 1995.

Mason, Herbert Molloy. *The United States Air Force: A Turbulent History.* New York: Mason/Charter, 1976.

Maurer, Maurer, ed. *The United States Air Service in World War I: The Final Report and a Tactical History*, vol. 1. Washington, DC: U.S. Government Printing Office, 1978.

May, Ernest R., ed. *Knowing One's Enemies: Intelligence Assessment Before the Two World Wars.* Princeton, NJ: Princeton University Press, 1984.

McDaniel, William H. *The History of Beech.* Wichita, KS: McCormick-Armstrong Co., 1971.

McNary, Kyle. *Ted "Double Duty" Radcliffe.* Minneapolis: McNary Publishing, 1994.

"Memory and Heritage: The Brown Condor and the Coast in the Depression and World War II," symposium, University of Southern Mississippi, Gulf Park Campus, Gulfport, Mississippi, March 15, 2002.

Miers, Earl Schenck. *America's First Black Four-Star General: The Life and Times of Daniel James, Jr.* Novato: Presidio Press, 1991.

Mitchell, William. *Winged Defense.* New York: Putnam, 1925.

Mockler, Anthony. *Haile Selassie's War.* New York: Olive Branch Press, 2003.

Moore, Richard B. "Africa Conscious Harlem." *Freedomways* 3, no. 3 (Summer 1963).

Morris, Herman Charles, and Harry B. Henderson, , eds. *World War II in Pictures.* New York: The Journal of Living Publishing Corporation, 1945.

Moseley, Ray. *Mussolini's Shadow: The Double Life of Count Galeazzo Ciano.* New Haven, CT: Yale University Press, 1999.

Mosley, Leonard. *Lindbergh: A Biography*. Garden City, NJ: Doubleday, 1976.

Nalty, Bernard C., John F. Shiner, and George M. Watson. *With Courage: The U.S. Army in World War II*. Washington, DC: Air Force History & Museums Program, 1994.

Nesbitt, Nick, ed. *Toussaint L'Ouverture: The Haitian Revolution*. Brooklyn, NY: Verso, 2008.

Nesbitt, Nick. *Universal Emancipation: The Haitian Revolution and the Radical Enlightenment*. Charlottesville: University of Virginia Press, 2008.

Nicolle, David. *The Italian Invasion of Abyssinia, 1935–36*. London: Osprey Publishing, 2000.

Nugent, John Peer. *The Black Eagle*. New York: Stein and Day, 1971.

O'Brien, John Maxwell. *Alexander the Great: The Invisible Enemy*. New York: Routledge, 1992.

Osborn, William S. "Curtains for Jim Crow: Law, Race, and the Texas Railroads." *Southwestern Historical Quarterly* 150, no. 3 (January 2002).

Osur, Alan M. *Blacks in the Army Air Forces During World War II*. Washington, DC: Office of Air Force History, 1986.

Pape, Robert A. *Bombing to Win: Air Power and Coercion in War*. Ithaca: Cornell University Press, 1996.

Payne, Robert. *The Life and Death of Adolf Hitler*. New York: Barnes and Noble Books, 1995.

Perl, Lila. *Ethiopia, Land of the Lion*. New York: William Morrow, 1972.

Phelps, J. Alfred. *Chappie: America's First Black Four-Star General: The Life and Times of Daniel James, Jr*. Novato, CA: Presidio Press, 1991.

Powell, William J. Intro. by Von Hardesty. *Black Aviator: The Story of William J. Powell*. Washington, DC: Smithsonian Institution Press, 1994.

Rees, Lawrence. *War of the Century: When Hitler Fought Stalin*. New York: New Press, 1999.

Ribowsky, Mark. *Don't Look Back: Satchel Paige in the Shadows of Baseball*. New York: Da Capo Books, 1994.

Rich, Doris L. *The Magnificent Moisants, Champions of Early Flight*. Washington, DC: Smithsonian Institution Press, 1998.

———. *Queen Bess: Daredevil Aviator*. Washington, DC: Smithsonian Institution Press, 1993.

Rogers, Joel A. *The Real Facts about Ethiopia*. New York: Joel A. Rogers, 1936.

———. *Sex and Race*, vol. 1. St. Petersburg, FL: Helga M. Rogers, 1967.

Rosenstone, Robert A. *Crusade of the Left: The Lincoln Battalion in the Spanish Civil War*. New York: Pegasus, 1969.

Salzman, Jack, David Lionel Smith, and Cornel West, eds. *Encyclopedia of African-American Culture and History*. New York: Simon & Schuster, Macmillan, 1996.

Schaefer, Ludwig F. *The Ethiopian Crisis: Touchstone of Appeasement?* Boston: D. C. Heath and Company, 1961.

Scharff, Robert, and Walter S. Taylor. *Over Land and Sea: A Biography of Glenn Hammond Curtiss*. New York: David McKay, 1968.

Schubert, Frank N. *Black Valor: Buffalo Soldiers and the Medal of Honor, 1870–1898*. Wilmington, DE: Scholarly Resources Books, 1997.

Scott, Lawrence P., and William M. Womack. *Double V: The Civil Rights Struggle of the Tuskegee Airmen*. East Lansing: Michigan State University Press, 1994.

Scott, William R. "Colonel John C. Robinson: The Condor of Ethiopia." *Pan-African Journal* 5, no. 1 (Spring 1972).

Selassie, Haile. *The Autobiography of Emperor Haile Sellassie I, King of Kings of All Ethiopia and the Lord of All Lords, My Life, The Emperor's Progress, 1892–1937*. 2 vols. Chicago: Research Associates School Times Publications, 1999.

Sevareid, Eric. *Between the Wars*. New York: Berkley Publishing Company, 1978.

Simmons, Thomas E. *The Brown Condor: The True Adventures of John C. Robinson*. Silver Spring, MD: Bartleby Press, 1988.

"Solemn Hours," *Time*, October 14, 1935.

Spear, Allan H. *Black Chicago: The Making of a Negro Ghetto*, 1890–1920. Chicago: University of Chicago Press, 1967.

Sternhell, Zeev, with Mario Sznajder and Maia Asheri. *The Birth of Fascist Ideology*. Princeton: Princeton University Press, 1994.

Sullivan, Charles. *The Mississippi Gulf Coast: Portrait of a People*. Northbridge: Windsor Publications, 1985.

Swanzy, Henry. "Quarterly Notes," *African Affairs: The Journal of the Royal African Society* 47, no. 187 (April 1948).

Talbot, David A. *Contemporary Ethiopia*. New York: Philosophical Library, 1952.

Taylor, A. J. P. *The Origins of the Second World War*. New York: Atheneum, 1962.

Tucker, Phillip Thomas. *Cathy Williams: From Slave to Female Buffalo Soldier*. Mechanicsburg, PA: Stackpole Books, 2002.

———. *From Auction Block to Glory: The African American Experience*. New York: MetroBooks, 1998.

———. *The South's Finest: History of the First Missouri Confederate Brigade*. Shippensburg, PA: White Mane Publishing, 1992.

Washington, Booker T., ed. *Tuskegee & Its People: Their Ideals and Achievements*. New York: Negro Universities Press, 1969.

Washington, Booker T. *Up From Slavery*. Garden City, NY: Doubleday, Page & Co., 1901.

Weckhorst, Donald O. *75 Year Pictorial History of Chanute Air Force Base, Rantoul, Illinois*. Nappanee, IN: Evangel Press, 1992.

Weisbord, Robert G. "Black America and the Italian-Ethiopian Crisis: An Episode in Pan-Negroism." *The Historian* 34, no. 2 (February 1977).

Wilkens, Roger. *Jefferson's Pillow: The Founding Fathers and the Dilemma of Black Patriotism*. Boston: Beacon Press, 2001.

Wilson, Ellen Gibson. *The Loyal Blacks*. New York: Capricorn Books, 1976.

Wynn, Neil A. *The Afro-American and the Second World War.* New York: Holmes and Meier Publishers, 1993.

Zewde, Bahru. *A History of Modern Ethiopia, 1855–1991.* Athens: Ohio University Press, 2001.

NEWSPAPER ARTICLES

"Actor Discusses Effects of Italo-Ethiopian War." *Chicago Defender,* January 4, 1936.

Afro-American (Baltimore), September 28 and October 19, 1935; June 6, 1936.

"Air Veteran Dead of Ethiopia Crash." *New York Times,* November 28, 1954.

Allen, Henry. "To Fly, to Brave the Wind." *Washington Post,* September 26, 1979.

Amsterdam News (New York), May 23 and October 3, 1936; April 3, 1954.

Appeal (St. Paul, MN), July 3, 1897.

Atlanta Daily World, December 8, 1938.

"Aviatrices Welcome Col. John Robinson." *Chicago Defender,* May 30, 1936.

Bell, Jimmie. "Famed Black Gulfport Pilot Flew Haile Selassie." *Sun Herald,* August 29, 1975.

Bergeron, Kate. "Brown Condor—Gulfport Aviation Pioneer Broke Color Barriers." *Sun Herald,* March 15, 2002.

"'Brown Condor' Takes a Swim." *Sun Herald,* May 12, 2002.

Chicago Defender, October 12, October 26, November 2, November 30, December 7, December 11, and December 14, 1935; January 4, April 4, April 11, April 18, April 25, May 2, May 9, May 16, May 23, May 30, June 6, and June 20, 1936; October 28, 1937.

Clarion Ledger (Jackson, MS), August 8, 1937, and miscellaneous clippings.

"Col. John C. Robinson Lands at Local Airport," *Kansas City Call,* July 9, 1937.

"Col. Robinson, Haile's Flier, Welcomed Here." *Daily News* (Chicago), May 25, 1936.

"Col. Robinson Is Feted at Poro College." *Chicago Defender,* June 6, 1936.

"Colonel Robinson Is Named Ill. Aviation Consultant." *Chicago Defender,* October 28, 1937.

"Colonel Robinson Starts Aviation College." *Amersterdam News,* October 3, 1936.

Daily Herald (Gulfport, MS_, June 26, 1936; June 21 and 23, 1941.

Daily Progress (Jacksonville, TX), May 35, 1936.

Daily Times (Chicago), May 25, 1936, and miscellaneous clippings.

"Defender Man First to Greet Col. Robinson." *Chicago Defender,* May 23, 1936.

Diamond, Jack. "Haile Selassie's Ace Airman Back in New York, Glad War Days Ended." *Enterprise,* May 21, 1936.

"Emperor in Statement on Defeat." *Chicago Defender,* May 8, 1936.

"Ethiopians Keeping Silent on Statecraft." *Chicago Defender,* April 11, 1936.

"Ethiopia Prepares to Take to the Skies." *Chicago Defender,* November 2, 1935.

"Ethiops' Rabble Army Won All Frays—Flyer." *Afro-American* (Baltimore), June 13, 1936.

Evening News (London), October 17, 1935.

"Explains Why Defense of Realm Failed." *Chicago Defender*, June 20, 1936.

"Extend Fete for 'Brown Condor.'" *Daily Times* (Chicago), May 25, 1936.

Fleming, James G. "Col. Robinson Acclaimed as Ethiopia Hero." *Amsterdam News*, New York, May 23, 1936.

"French Flying Ace Heads for Addis Ababa." *Chicago Defender*, May 2, 1936.

Gondo, Nancy. "Rickenbacker, the Ace of Aces." *Investor's Business Daily*, November 5, 2004.

Green, Hurley, III. "Family Remembers Legacy of Former Relation." *Chicago Independent Bulletin*, April 9, 2004.

"Gulfport Negro Who Piloted Emperor Haile Selassie Visits Home; Relates His Experiences in Wartime Flying." *Daily Herald* (Gulfport, MS), June 26, 1936.

"Haile Ready to Unite Forces in Addis Ababa." *Chicago Defender*, May 2, 1936.

Hall, Chatwood. "Col. Robinson Launches East African Airlines." *Chicago Defender*, February 21, 1948.

"Interviewed in London by Defender Man." *Chicago Defender*, October 12, 1935.

"Italians Shoot Five Ethiopian Chieftains." *Chicago Defender*, May 23, 1936.

"Italy Loses 8,000 Men in Bloody Fight." *Chicago Defender*, May 2, 1936.

Journal and Guide, Norfolk, Virginia, October 5, 1935.

"King Loses Hope; League Is Too Slow." *Chicago Defender*, October 26, 1935.

Kinser, Jerry. "Condor Soars." *Sun Herald*, February 28, 1988.

———. "Gulfport Neighborhood Honors Native Son 'Brown Condor.'" *Sun Herald*, February 26, 1989.

"Leading Mountain Attack." *Chicago Defender*, April 25, 1936.

Loh, Jules. "Stalking the 'Brown Condor.'" *Sun Herald*, August 7, 1988.

New York Times, August 23 and October 5, 1935; May 18, 1936, September 19, 1947; May 16, 1954; March 28, 1964.

Norman, Charles. "'Brown Condor,' Pilot of Selassie, Feted as Harlem's Newest Hero." *Daily Progress* (Jacksonville, TX), May 25, 1936.

"Organize Ethiopia 'Friends' In Ala." *Chicago Defender*, December 21, 1935.

Philadelphia Tribune, October 10, 1935.

Pittsburgh Courier, October 12, October 13, and December 14, 1935; January 4 and February 1, 1936; and miscellaneous clippings.

"Rally to Buy Col. Robinson a New Plane." *Chicago Defender*, June 13, 1936.

"Reveal Six Attempts to Kill 'Condor.'" *Chicago Defender*, May 30, 1936.

Roberts, Kimberly C. "ABC's Robin Roberts Recalls the Relationship That Shaped Her Life." *Philadelphia Tribune* online (accessed June 11, 2005).

Scallan, Melissa M. "Group Seeks to Honor Aviator Brown Condor." *Sun Herald*, March 16, 2002.

"Selassie Leads 300,000 Men on Ethiopian Front." *Chicago Defender*, April 4, 1936.

"Selassie's Strategy Is Big Surprise." *Chicago Defender*, April 25, 1936.

Slaughter, Vera B. "Twenty Thousand Greet 'Brown Condor' at Airport." *Chicago Defender*, May 30, 1936.

Star (Washington, DC), May 25, 1936.

Sun Herald (Gulfport, MS), miscellaneous clippings.

"Time of Awake." *Chicago Defender*, May 9, 1936.

Washington Post, May 15 and16, 1954

Waterford, Janet [Janet Harmon Bragg/Janet Waterford Bragg]. "John Robinson Wings His Way Down to Tuskegee," *Chicago Defender*, May 9, 1936.

———. "The Real Story of Col. John Robinson, or How a Gulfport, Miss. Boy Grew to Be the No. 1 Flyer of His Race" (series of articles). *Chicago Defender*, April 4–May 16, 1936.

———. "Robinson Arouses Race Interest in Aviation." *Chicago Defender*, May 2, 1936.

———. "Robinson Excelled as an Instructor in Aviation Because of His Keen Insistence on Real Discipline." *Chicago Defender*, April 25, 1936.

———. "Robinson Organizes Brown Eagle Aero Club in Effort to Interest Race in Flying" (series of articles). *Chicago Defender*, April 11–May 23, 1936.

THESES AND DISSERTATIONS

Scott, William R. *A Study of Afro-American and Ethiopian Relations, 1896–1941*. PhD dissertation, 1971. Princeton University, Princeton, NJ.

Tuepker, John. *The Effects of World War II on Blacks in Harrison County, Mississippi*. MA thesis, 1993. University of Southern Mississippi, Gulfport, MS.

INTERVIEWS WITH AUTHOR

Booth, Katie, Gulfport, MS, August 11, 2001.

O'Neil, John "Buck," Kansas City, MO, August 17, 2001.

Rushing, Sidney L., Gulfport, MS, July 19 and August 11 and 16, 2001.

Simmons, Thomas E., Gulfport, MS, by phone, July 11, 2001.

Tartt, Rev. Harry, Gulfport, MS, October 25, 2001.

CORRESPONDENCE TO AUTHOR

Booth, Katie, Gulfport, MS, August 8, 2001.

Lynch, Lewis J., Tuskegee Airmen Annual Convention, Atlanta, GA, August 14, 2002.

Rushing, Sidney L., Gulfport, MS, July 12, 2001.

Simmons, Thomas E., Gulfport, MS, September 3, 2002 (e-mail); January 13, 2003; March 10, 2003.

Smith, Dr. Patrick, University of Southern Mississippi, Gulfport, MS, September 26, 2002, by e-mail.

Stokes, John C., St. Albans and Jamaica, NY, March 9, 2003; April 24, 2003.

Tartt, Harry Charles, Gulfport, MS, October 25, 2001.

INTERNET SOURCES

Ayele, Negussay. "African Americans and Ethiopia on the Eve of the Fascist Invasion." 2003, Tadias Online.

A Zion Psalm commemorating His Imperial Majesty visit to Chicago, June 8, 1954, Ites-Zine Archive 6, Current News from June 2003.

"Ethiopian Air Force," Wikipedia.

"The Ethiopian-Italian War: The African American Connection," Foreign Dispatches, Random Remarks on Current Affairs, September 26, 2004.

"The Lynching Calendar: African Americans Who Died of Racial Violence in the United States during 1865–1965."

"The Rise and Fall of the Ethiopian Air Force," Ethiopundit.

.

INDEX

ABOUT THE AUTHOR

PHILLIP THOMAS TUCKER has a doctorate in American history from St. Louis University in St. Louis, Missouri. Tucker is the author or editor of more than twenty books, including award winners and History and Military Book Club selections, devoted to various groundbreaking aspects of African American, Civil War, Revolutionary War, women's, and Irish history. For more than twenty years, he has worked as a U.S. Air Force historian, mostly in Washington, D.C. He lives in Maryland.